A SEMANTIC
AND STRUCTURAL ANALYSIS
OF 1 THESSALONIANS

Summer Institute of Linguistics

SEMANTIC AND STRUCTURAL ANALYSIS SERIES

JOHN BANKER, GENERAL EDITOR

A SEMANTIC AND STRUCTURAL ANALYSIS OF 1 THESSALONIANS

Robert H. Sterner

Summer Institute of Linguistics

The Greek text used in this SSA is from the fourth revised edition
of the United Bible Societies' *Greek New Testament*.

© 1998 by the Summer Institute of Linguistics, Inc.
ISBN: 1-55671-071-2
Library of Congress Catalog Card Number: 98-61045
Printed in the United States of America

**Summer Institute of Linguistics
7500 W. Camp Wisdom Road
Dallas, TX 75236, U.S.A.**

CONTENTS

Acknowledgments vii

Abbreviations and Explanation viii

General Introduction 1
    Paragraph Pattern Chart 3
    Communication Relations Chart 4

Introduction to the Semantic Structure of 1 Thessalonians 5
    The Constituent Organization of 1 Thessalonians 7
    Overview: Thematic Units and Their Theme Statements 8

The Presentation and Discussion of the Semantic Units of 1 Thessalonians 11
1 Thessalonians 1:1–5:28 (Epistle) 11
    Epistle Constituent 1:1 (Opening of the Epistle) 12
    Epistle Constituent 1:2–5:24 (Part: Body of the Epistle) 14
        Part Constituent 1:2–3:13 (Division: Rapport Basis of 1:2–5:24) 16
            Division Constituent 1:2–2:16 (Complex Section: Rapport Basis$_1$ of 1:2–3:13) 18
                Section Constituent 1:2–10 (Rapport Basis$_1$ of 1:2–2:16) 20
                Section Constituent 2:1–12 (Rapport Basis$_2$ of 1:2–2:16) 32
                Section Constituent 2:13–16 (Rapport Basis$_3$ of 1:2–2:16) 46
            Division Constituent 2:17–3:13 (Expressive Section: Rapport Basis$_2$ of 1:2–3:13) 54
                Section Constituent 2:17–20 (Emotive Problem of 2:17–3:13) 56
                Section Constituent 3:1–5 (Seeking of 2:17–3:13) 62
                Section Constituent 3:6–10 (Solution of 2:17–3:13) 68
                Section Constituent 3:11–13 (Reaction/transition of 2:17–3:13) 76
        Part Constituent 4:1–5:24 (Division: Appeal of 1:2–5:24) 81
            Division Constituent 4:1–2 (Hortatory Paragraph: Introduction of 4:1–5:24) 83
            Division Constituent 4:3–5:11 (Complex Section: Focal Appeal of 4:1–5:24) 86
                Section Constituent 4:3–12 (Hortatory Subsection: Focal Appeal$_1$ of 4:3–5:11) 88
                    Subsection Constituent 4:3–8 (Appeal$_1$ of 4:3–12) 89
                    Subsection Constituent 4:9–12 (Appeal$_2$ of 4:3–12) 96
                Section Constituent 4:13–5:11 (Complex Subsection: Focal Appeal$_2$ of 4:3–5:11) 101
                    Subsection Constituent 4:13–18 (Nucleus$_1$ of 4:13–5:11) 102
                    Subsection Constituent 5:1–8 (Nucleus$_2$ of 4:13–5:11) 114
                    Subsection Constituent 5:9–11 (Nucleus$_3$ of 4:13–5:11) 125
            Division Constituent 5:12–22 (Hortatory Section: General Appeal of 4:1–5:24) 129
                Section Constituent 5:12–15 (Hortatory Subsection: General Appeal$_1$ of 5:12–22) 130
                    Subsection Constituent 5:12–13 (Appeal$_1$ of 5:12–15) 131
                    Subsection Constituent 5:14–15 (Appeal$_2$ of 5:12–15) 135
                Section Constituent 5:16–22 (Hortatory Subsection: General Appeal$_2$ of 5:12–22) 138
                    Subsection Constituent 5:16–18 (Appeal$_1$ of 5:16–22) 138
                    Subsection Constituent 5:19–22 (Appeal$_2$ of 5:16–22) 140
            Division Constituent 5:23–24 (Expressive Paragraph: Closing of 4:1–5:24) 143
    Epistle Constituent 5:25–28 (Closing of the Epistle) 146

Bibliography 148

ACKNOWLEDGMENTS

For almost three decades a number of colleagues in the Summer Institute of Linguistics have been developing the theory for analyzing Greek discourse that I have applied to 1 Thessalonians. For the work of John Beekman, John and Kathleen Callow, John Tuggy, John Banker, and Ellis Deibler I am especially indebted.

Fifteen years ago when I first studied the boundaries and coherence of constituent units in this epistle, I referred to the preliminary work of Robert and Carolyn Lee, "An Analysis of the Larger Semantic Units of 1 Thessalonians," and of Jim Park, "Discourse Analysis of 1 Thessalonians." I appreciated the help of Marilyn Turnbow at that time, who typed my first draft.

More recently I have been grateful for the invaluable advice of Ellis Deibler, who reviewed the early stages of my exegesis and analysis and gave suggestions especially from a semantic perspective; John Tuggy, who gave insights on paragraph patterns and the discourse structure of the epistle; and John Banker, who, in addition to giving excellent advice on many points, helped me to unravel Paul's syllogistic-type logic and to apply the theory correctly in "Intent and Paragraph Pattern" write-ups.

James E. Mignard reviewed the SSA from a Greek perspective and advised of places where the modern German version *Die Gute Nachrict* supports various positions. Copy editor Betty Eastman read through the SSA on two occasions and deserves special praise for her careful attention to all details. Dick Blight helped upgrade computer files. For the many hours all of these people have invested in this work, I am grateful.

I am also thankful for the loving support of my wife, Joyce, and children, Daniel, Timothy, and Julie. They have encouraged me in many ways in my work on the team of SSA researchers.

Finally, I am grateful for the wisdom given by God's Spirit, not only to me as I studied this epistle but to the commentators and translators of the many books and versions that I consulted. I deeply value the knowledge and insights gained. I trust that the same Spirit will help you who use this SSA to better understand and communicate the foundational truths in the epistle.

ABBREVIATIONS AND SYMBOLS IN THE DISPLAYS

com	comment	I(&S&T)*		[PLP]	paralipsis
cpr	comparison	I(&S)*		[PRS]	personification
[DOU]	doublet	[IDM]	idiom	pur	purpose
[ELP]	ellipsis	(inc)	inclusive	[RHQ]	rhetorical question
eqv	equivalent	[IRO]	irony	sim	simultaneous
[EUP]	euphemism	[LIT]	litotes	[SIM]	simile
(exc)	exclusive	[MET]	metaphor	spf	specific
grd	grounds	[MTY]	metonymy	[SYN]	synecdoche
[HEN]	hendiadys	NEG	negative		
[HYP]	hyperbole	NUC	nucleus		

* *I(&S&T)* and *I(&S)* are representations of first person plural pronouns (which are almost the only first person pronoun forms found in 1 Thessalonians). These abbreviations are intended to remind the SSA user that the pronoun 'we' principally expresses the sentiments of Paul (I), the author of the letter, but can refer as well to Silas (S) and Timothy (T). (See the general introduction for a more detailed explanation of this convention.)

ABBREVIATIONS IN THE TEXT

BAGD	Bauer, Arndt, Gingrich, and Danker, *Greek-English Lexicon of the New Testament and Other Early Literature*	NCV	New Century Version
		NEB	New English Bible
		NIV	New International Version
BDF	Blass, Debrunner, and Funk, *A Greek Grammar of the New Testament*	NJB	New Jerusalem Bible
		NKJV	New King James Version
CBW	C. B. Williams, *New Testament in the Language of the People*	NLT	New Living Translation
		NRSV	New Revised Standard Version
CEV	Contemporary English Version	NT	New Testament
DGN	*Die Gute Nachricht*	OT	Old Testament
EHP	E. H. Peterson, *The Message: The New Testament in Contemporary Language*	REB	Revised English Bible
		RSV	Revised Standard Version
GW	*God's Word*	SSWC	Beekman, Callow, and Kopesec, *Semantic Structure of Written Communication* (or the theory that it presents)
GHL	Gleason H. Ledyard, *The New Life Testament*		
JB	Jerusalem Bible		
JBP	J. B. Phillips, *The New Testament in Modern English*	TEV	*Good News Bible: The Bible in Today's English Version*
KJV	King James Version	TNT	*Translator's New Testament*
LXX	Septuagint	UBS	United Bible Societies
MJTGNT	Hodges and Farstad, *The Greek New Testament according to the Majority Text*	UBSGNT	United Bible Societies' *Greek New Testament* (fourth revised edition, except where otherwise noted)
mss.	manuscripts		
NAB	New American Bible	WFB	W. F. Beck, *New Testament in the Language of Today*
NASB	New American Standard Bible		
NBV	New Berkeley Version		

References to Greek words and their glosses in BAGD are made in the text by the following formula: page number, period, and entry citation (e.g., BAGD, p. 405.I2bβ).

EXPLANATION OF THE *BASES* LABELS USED IN THE DISPLAYS

Authoritative Basis: Appeals to an authority. *Examples:* 'Since God commanded', 'Since you know what we apostles said'.
Axiomatic Basis: Appeals to a self-evident truth. *Example:* 'Since God is love'.
Emotive Basis: Appeals to the emotions. *Example*: 'Since I love you deeply'.
Motivational Basis: Appeals to a positive value or goal that should motivate the readers. *Example*: 'Since believers will be rewarded when Christ returns'.
Rapport Basis: States positive emotive feelings that build a relationship with the readers. *Examples*: 'I am proud of you', 'I thank God for you'.
Trust Basis: Appeals to an assurance the writer has about the readers. *Example*: 'Since you desire to please the Lord'.
Warning Basis: Appeals to a negative characteristic or action that should warn the readers. *Example*: 'Since the Lord will punish evildoers'.

GENERAL INTRODUCTION

The theory on which a Semantic and Structural Analysis is based

This analytical commentary on Paul's first letter to the Thessalonian church is based on a theory of semantic structure set forth in *The Semantic Structure of Written Communication* (Beekman, Callow, and Kopesec 1981). More recently K. Callow's *Man and Message* (forthcoming) presents a broader basis for this theory.

This Semantic and Structural Analysis (SSA), like the others in the series, has been prepared with the needs of the Bible translator in view, though it should be useful to all serious students of God's Word. It aims to arrive at the meaning the original writer intended to communicate to the original recipients, but it differs from most other commentaries in that it is based on a particular theory of the structure of meaning. Consequently, a consistent and comprehensive approach to the analysis of the meaning is applied to the total document, whether that meaning is conveyed by the smallest segments of the written communication, such as words and their component parts, or whether it is conveyed by the largest segments, such as paragraphs and various combinations of paragraphs.

This SSA of 1 Thessalonians does not include a detailed section on the theory and presentation of semantic and structural analyses as some of the earlier SSAs do (Colossians, 2 Thessalonians). Readers with their own collections of SSAs do not need this section in every SSA. So, for economy's sake, it has been omitted here. Readers may refer to the Colossians or 2 Thessalonians SSA for this information. The 1 Thessalonians SSA, however, does include a chart of communication relations and a chart of paragraph patterns, providing easy access to these important tools. (A separate manual explaining the theory, presentation, and use of SSAs is being prepared for future publication.)

Format and conventions

Each semantic unit of 1 Thessalonians will be presented in a display, with the discourse structure and relational structure shown at the left of the display and the referential contents at the right. The reader should note the following conventions:

1. Italics in the content propositions of the display designate implicit material that has been supplied. In some cases, however, it has been difficult to decide what is implicit material and what is actually a component of the meaning of the Greek word or words being translated.
2. Parentheses are used to enclose alternative renderings, for example, 'my God (*or*, God whom I worship)'. They are also used to enclose specifications for pronouns, for example, 'we(exc)' and 'we(inc)'.
3. All but three of the first person pronominal references in 1 Thessalonians are plural. Whenever the first person plural is taken as including the readers, the pronoun is marked in the display as inclusive, for example, 'our(inc) Lord Jesus Christ' in 1:1a. However, most of the first person references are used in the exclusive sense, referring either to Paul himself (an epistolary or editorial 'we') or to Paul, Silas, and, in all but a couple of cases, also Timothy (see the discussion on p. 5). Because it is difficult to determine Paul's intent, these pronouns may be represented in the displays either by 'I(&S&T)', for example, 'I(&S&T) always thank God for you all' in 1:2a, or by 'we(exc)', for example, 'when we(exc) pray for you' in 1:2b. Both are intended to communicate the same meaning; 'we(exc)' is used when repetition of 'I(&S&T)' would make reading the successive propositions awkward. 'I(&S)' and 'me(&S)' are used in paragraphs 3:1–5 and 3:6–10, which refer to Timothy's being sent back to Thessalonica by Paul (and possibly Silas).
4. Square brackets indicate the clarification of an antecedent, for example, 'More than that [1:5b]' in proposition 1:5c. They also enclose abbreviations for figures of speech used in the Greek text: '[MET]' for metaphor.
5. In an orienter-content relationship where the content consists of more than one proposition, the content label is not used in most cases, but a dotted line alerts the reader that an orienter-content relationship is intended. The content consists of everything on the vertical line to which the dotted line connects, that is, each proposition of the multipropositional unit immediately below the orienter (see the display of 2:11a—12c for an example).

In this SSA a distinction is made between communication relations on the lower propositional levels and paragraph-pattern relationships on the highest level within the paragraph. The paragraph-pattern type in any paragraph will be based on the author's intent for that paragraph. For example, when the author comes to a point in the discourse where he wants to directly affect the audience's behavior, he will use a hortatory paragraph pattern. Because of this change of perspective from earlier SSAs, the reader will find that a supportive subparagraph unit in a hortatory paragraph that would have been labeled grounds in earlier SSAs is now labeled *basis*, and the corresponding supported unit will be called APPEAL rather than HEAD or EXHORTATION. Similar changes have been made in other types of paragraph patterns. For more information on paragraph patterns see Tuggy's 1992 article, "Semantic Paragraph Patterns," and also the chart of paragraph pattern subtypes here on page 3.

Another change in this SSA is that the label NUCLEUS is used instead of HEAD for nuclear units. Also, whenever a nuclear unit has a different relationship to two or more nonnuclear units on the same vertical line, each of the relationships is labeled separately (e.g., see the display of 5:10a), rather than as HEAD or NUCLEUS as used to be done by the earlier SSA authors.

The use of a Semantic and Structural Analysis

For the translator, who must not only determine the meaning of a passage but also resolve a myriad of translation problems, it may seem like sheer drudgery to wade through the detailed reasoning backing up the exegetical decisions in an SSA. On the other hand, the detailed reasoning is necessary to determine the best analysis. Any interpretation should be backed up with solid reasoning, and there is no way this can be done without detailed analysis, including reference to the Greek text. Thus, to determine whether or not the reasoning is solid, the translator must study the analysis that follows each display, including the notes, which explain such things as the reason why any implicit item was supplied.

But does the user of an SSA have any other appropriate option than reading every part of the SSA? Some translators first read the propositions in a display along with other commentaries, versions, and helps; then where there is obvious agreement, they may move ahead with confidence; but where there is a difference between the display's renderings and those of others, the notes in the SSA on that particular verse or portion of a verse should be consulted to see what factors led to the decision represented in the display. (*An Exegetical Summary of 1 & 2 Thessalonians* by Richard Blight lists additional commentaries that support the various interpretations given in this SSA.) Translators should then be better able to make their own factually based judgment as to the best interpretation. In some cases a note provides an alternative propositionalization, and this may occasionally appear to the translator to be the better solution. Also, since the SSA is prepared with the needs of translators in mind, the notes may supply relevant information difficult to find elsewhere. Translators who are searching for such information in the course of working on a particular verse should consult the SSA notes for that verse to see if the problem is dealt with.

To obtain the greatest benefit from an SSA, the notes should be consulted as consistently as possible. Just as a part of any book or discourse is best understood in its complete context, so discussion of a single point in the SSA in many cases will be best understood if the user is familiar with the SSA as a whole. Moreover, the renderings in the display work together with the notes to provide the information translators need. Since the propositions are limited in the information they can provide, the notes contribute to a fuller understanding of what they are seeking to communicate.

A caution

It must be understood that the SSA propositions are not a translation in the common sense. Rather they express the analysis of the meaning of the Greek text in propositional English surface-structure form and with various restrictions. For instance, abstract nouns are avoided as much as possible by changing them into propositional verb form. Finite forms of the verb are normally used rather than participles. Words are used only in their primary senses. For live metaphors, the full meaning of the figure intended by the original author is given. As a result, the propositions do not always sound natural, "flowing," as a good translation should. The inclusion of implicit material often makes them sound too overloaded with information and too interpretive. Their primary purpose, remember, is to be a source of information, not a model for word-for-word translation into any real language.

In some of its patterns, the propositionalization more closely approximates patterns of non-

Indo-European languages than of English or Greek. For example, if a language naturally uses abstract nouns in more or less the same way English or Greek does, it would be expected that using abstract nouns in a translation would in many cases be more natural and effective than following the display's propositional form. But if the receptor language does not normally use abstract nouns, the propositional form may indeed be helpful since its patterns and obligatory elements are those of verbal constructions rather than those associated with abstract nouns. But even in these languages the propositional form ought not be followed word for word; instead, a natural translation will follow the patterns of the receptor language.

Likewise, the implicit material is not intended to be translated in its entirety. Only that which is valid or necessary in the receptor language should be used in translating.

		SOLUTIONALITY	CAUSALITY	VOLITIONALITY
IDEAS	EXPOSITORY −sequence	+problem (expo)+SOLUTION ±evidence$_n$ ±(complication+SOLUTION)	+cause$_n$+EFFECT; +major premise+minor premise+INFERENCE; +evidence$_n$+INFERENCE; +PRINCIPLE+application$_n$	+justification$_n$+CLAIM
	NARRATIVE +sequence	+problem+RESOLUTION ±resolving incident$_n$ ±(complication+RESOLUTION)	+occasion+OUTCOME	+step$_n$+GOAL
EMOTIONS	EXPRESSIVE −sequence	+problem (emo)+SOLUTION ±seeking/belief ±(complication+SOLUTION)	+situation$_n$+REACTION ±belief	+belief$_n$+CONTROL
	DESCRIPTIVE +sequence	+problem (desc)+SOLUTION ±experience$_n$ ±(complication+SOLUTION)	+situation$_n$+REACTION	+description$_n$+DECLARATION
BEHAVIOR	HORTATORY −sequence	+problem (hort)+APPEAL ±basis$_n$ ±(complication+SOLUTION)	+basis$_n$+APPEAL; +APPEAL+application$_n$; +basis$_n$+COMMISSIVE	+motivation+ENABLEMENT$_n$; +motivation$_n$+APPEAL
	PROCEDURAL +sequence	+problem (proc)+SOLUTION ±step$_n$ ±(complication+SOLUTION)	+APPEAL+outcome$_n$	+STEP$_n$+accomplishment

Paragraph Pattern Subtypes in Various Discourse Genres

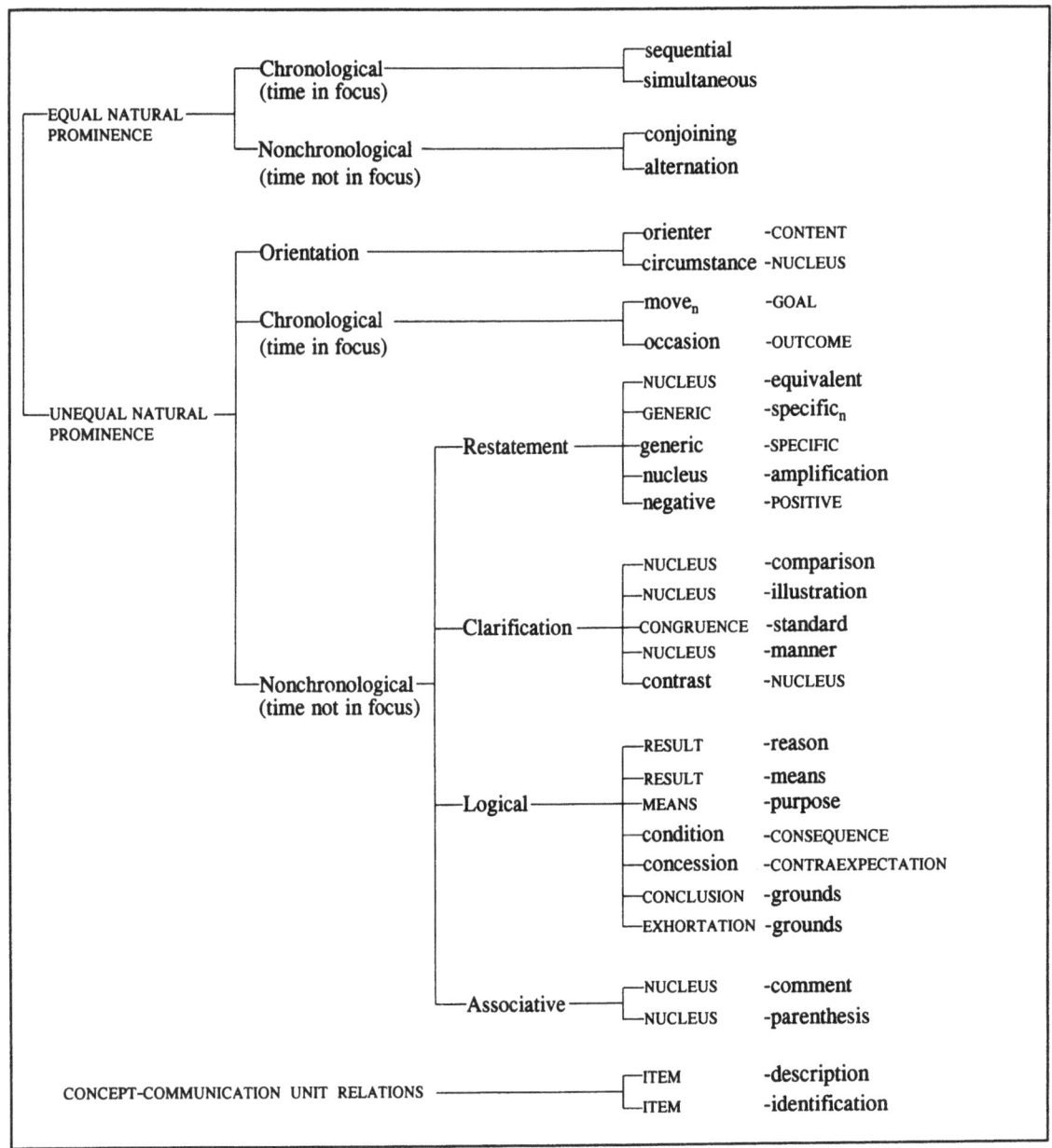

Communication Relations

Notes:
1. Since 1 Thessalonians is nonnarrative, not all the narrative relations are included in this chart.
2. The relations are given in the order in which they are most commonly found in the Greek NT; thus, a result is usually followed by the reason for it, as signaled by ὅτι, γάρ, διά + accusative, etc.
3. The naturally prominent member of a paired relation is shown in capitals. In one or two cases, one does not seem to be more naturally prominent than the other, e.g., nucleus-amplification.
4. It should be noted that marked-prominence devices can be used to make the less prominent member of a pair as prominent as the one that is naturally prominent. And thematic prominence can reverse the natural prominence, so that, for example, a purpose will be of greater prominence than its means. This does not happen often, however.
5. Communication relation charts in the early SSAs also included macrostructure relations such as those of the epistle level (*opening-BODY-closing*) and those of the body level (*introduction-NUCLEUS-closure/summary*). In the present theory these are classified separately.

INTRODUCTION TO THE SEMANTIC STRUCTURE OF 1 THESSALONIANS

Participants in the communication situation

The letter of 1 Thessalonians is addressed to the believers in the city of Thessalonica (1 Thess. 1:1). The founding of the church there is recorded in Acts 17:1-9. When on Paul's second missionary journey the Holy Spirit led him and his companions to travel from Asia Minor to Macedonia, they ministered first in Philippi; then, after suffering persecution there (Acts 16:12-40; 1 Thess. 2:2), they traveled to Thessalonica.

Following his usual practice, Paul's ministry in Thessalonica was in the synagogue first, and some of the Jews and many Gentile proselytes and influential women were convinced of the truth of Paul's message about Jesus the Messiah. Other Jews, however, became jealous and stirred up a mob to seek out Paul and his companion Silas. Though Paul and Silas were not found, the believers in Thessalonica thought it best that they leave the city quickly, and they sent them away under the cover of darkness.

It cannot be stated with certainty how long Paul and his companions ministered in Thessalonica. The Acts account mentions that Paul argued in the synagogue for three Sabbaths. Then immediately it describes the riot and the spiriting away of Paul by the believers. Some commentators (including Frame, Morris) say that such a short period, about a month, was sufficient time to establish this group of believers. Others (Best, Hiebert, Marshall, Wanamaker) feel that Acts is a condensed account and that more time was necessary for Paul to establish himself in a trade (1 Thess. 2:9), provide a model for the believers (1:5; 2:10), evangelize idol-worshiping Gentiles (1:9), and receive a gift or gifts from the believers in Philippi (Phil. 4:16), which was 150 kilometers away.

Thessalonica, the chief port city for Macedonia, was located on the great Egnatian Way, which was the main land route for commerce and military movements between the Adriatic Sea and Asia Minor. With about 200,000 inhabitants it was the largest city in Macedonia. News about the new and persevering faith of the Thessalonian believers would have spread quickly in all directions from this bustling center (1 Thess. 1:8).

Paul, Silvanus (a variant of Silas), and Timothy are the designated senders of this letter (1:1).

In Acts Silas is explicitly mentioned as accompanying Paul on his first visit to Thessalonica (Acts 17:4, 5, 10). Timothy had joined Paul and Silas in Lystra of Asia Minor (Acts 16:1-3). He is next mentioned as staying with Silas in Berea (Acts 17:14); and since Berea was the city to which Paul and Silas fled from Thessalonica, most commentators assume that Timothy was with Paul and Silas in Thessalonica also.

Silas was probably Paul's equal in status as a messenger of the gospel and thus worthy of mention in the opening. While Timothy was clearly their subordinate, he was the emissary sent back to encourage the Thessalonians (1 Thess. 3:1-6), and he, too, would want to communicate his deep feelings for these believers.

With only three exceptions, the first person pronominal references in the letter are plural. In a few of these Paul surely means to include his readers in the reference, as for example when he writes 'our God' and 'our Lord Jesus Christ' in 1:3. In some passages, namely the descriptive units in which Paul praises his readers, he may intend them to understand that the sentiments are those of Silas and Timothy as well. Silas and Timothy may even have participated in the composition of the letter (Bruce, Frame, Marshall). However, it seems best to understand Paul to be the primary author (Best, Bruce, Frame, Marshall, Morris, Wanamaker). This assumption is supported by the exceptions (2:18, 3:5, 5:27) in which he uses 'I' (Wanamaker, pp. 67-68). Therefore the majority of the first person plural pronouns in the letter may be considered epistolary or editorial, referring to Paul himself. (See point 3 on p. 1 for an explanation of the abbreviations used to render first person plural pronouns in the displays.)

Wanamaker (p. 17) is confident of the letter's Pauline authorship:

> Although Pauline authorship of 1 Thessalonians was occasionally questioned in the nineteenth century, . . . no contemporary scholars of repute seem to doubt the authentic Pauline character of the letter.

The occasion and purpose of the epistle

Paul and his co-workers were concerned about the new believers they had so abruptly left in

Thessalonica. It appears that someone, perhaps Timothy or another believer who had recently passed through Thessalonica, had brought word that the Thessalonians were now experiencing persecution (1 Thess. 1:6, 2:14). Would they become unsettled by their trials and waver in their faith (1 Thess. 3:3, 5)?

At least twice Paul attempted to return to Thessalonica but was unable to do so (1 Thess. 2:18). Finally, when he could bear the suspense no longer, he sent Timothy from Athens (1 Thess. 3:1-2). Timothy was to find out how the believers were faring and encourage them in the faith (1 Thess. 3:2-3, 5). (Wanamaker [pp. 37-45] and a few other scholars suggest that the letter we know as 2 Thessalonians was written before 1 Thessalonians and that Timothy carried the former to Thessalonica. The majority of commentators, however, prefer the traditional ordering of the epistles.)

It is unclear whether Timothy returned while Paul was still in Athens or whether his coming with Silas from Macedonia to Corinth (Acts 18:5) was the occasion on which he first reported back to Paul. In either case, Paul was delighted with Timothy's news. Timothy reported that the Thessalonian believers were continuing strong in their faith (1 Thess. 3:6-8).

Paul writes this letter to express his joy and thanksgiving at receiving Timothy's news, his sincere love for the Thessalonians, and his great desire to visit them. Many commentators (Bruce, Frame, Marshall, Morris included) suppose that in 2:1-12 Paul is defending his motives and the conduct of his ministry against critics in Thessalonica. Others, however, feel that he "offers his own conduct as a moral example of how a Christian should behave" and secondarily demonstrates to his readers his continuing concern for them (Wanamaker, p. 61).

Because Paul's intended visit had been thwarted, he ministers through the letter. It seems that one intent he has is to clarify issues raised by the Thessalonians with Timothy and address problems Timothy may have discerned. He instructs the Thessalonians about personal holiness and responsibility (4:1-12), the Lord Jesus' return (4:13-5:11), and ministry within the fellowship of believers (5:12-22). There seem to be no major crises or ethical deviations that Paul felt compelled to correct, as he did in some of his other epistles.

If Paul did write 1 Thessalonians in Corinth at the time recorded in Acts 18:1-18, we can date the epistle about A.D. 50-51. There is a secular inscription that dates Gallio's proconsulship at about that time (Bruce, p. xxxv).

The genre of the epistle

The thanksgiving portions of 1 (and 2) Thessalonians do not fit the epistolary pattern of Paul's other letters. Normally Paul expresses his thanksgiving in a section immediately after the letter opening. In 1 Thessalonians, however, there are three distinct thanksgivings scattered throughout the first division of the book: 1:2-10, 2:13-14, and 3:8-9. Wanamaker (pp. 45-50) explains this aberration by considering the Thessalonian letters from the perspective of Greco-Roman letter-writing theory, which closely followed rhetorical theory. First Thessalonians clearly fits the genre of *epideictic,* or demonstrative, rhetoric that sought to lead people into appropriate behavior through praise or blame. By filling the first division of his letter with praise for his readers Paul affirms their exemplary behavior and aims to encourage them to continue in their faith and practice in spite of persecution.

Wanamaker says that the main themes of the letter are introduced in 1:2-10, which is the first unit of the body of the letter: praise (1:2-3, 6-9; cf. 2:13-14, 19-20; 3:6-10; 4:1, 9-10; 5:11); Paul's ministry to the Thessalonians and his character (1:5; cf. 2:1-12, 2:17-3:10); persecution (1:6; cf. 2:13-16; 3:3-4); and Christian behavior and eschatological expectation (1:9-10; cf. chaps. 4 and 5).

When the letter is analyzed as demonstrative rhetoric, as Wanamaker recommends and as done in this SSA, the structure is understood in the light of Paul's purpose, method of argumentation, and use of emotion. The unity of the letter is thereby demonstrated in a way that analysis merely by theme or epistolary components may miss.

INTRODUCTION TO THE SEMANTIC STRUCTURE OF 1 THESSALONIANS 7

THE CONSTITUENT ORGANIZATION OF 1 THESSALONIANS

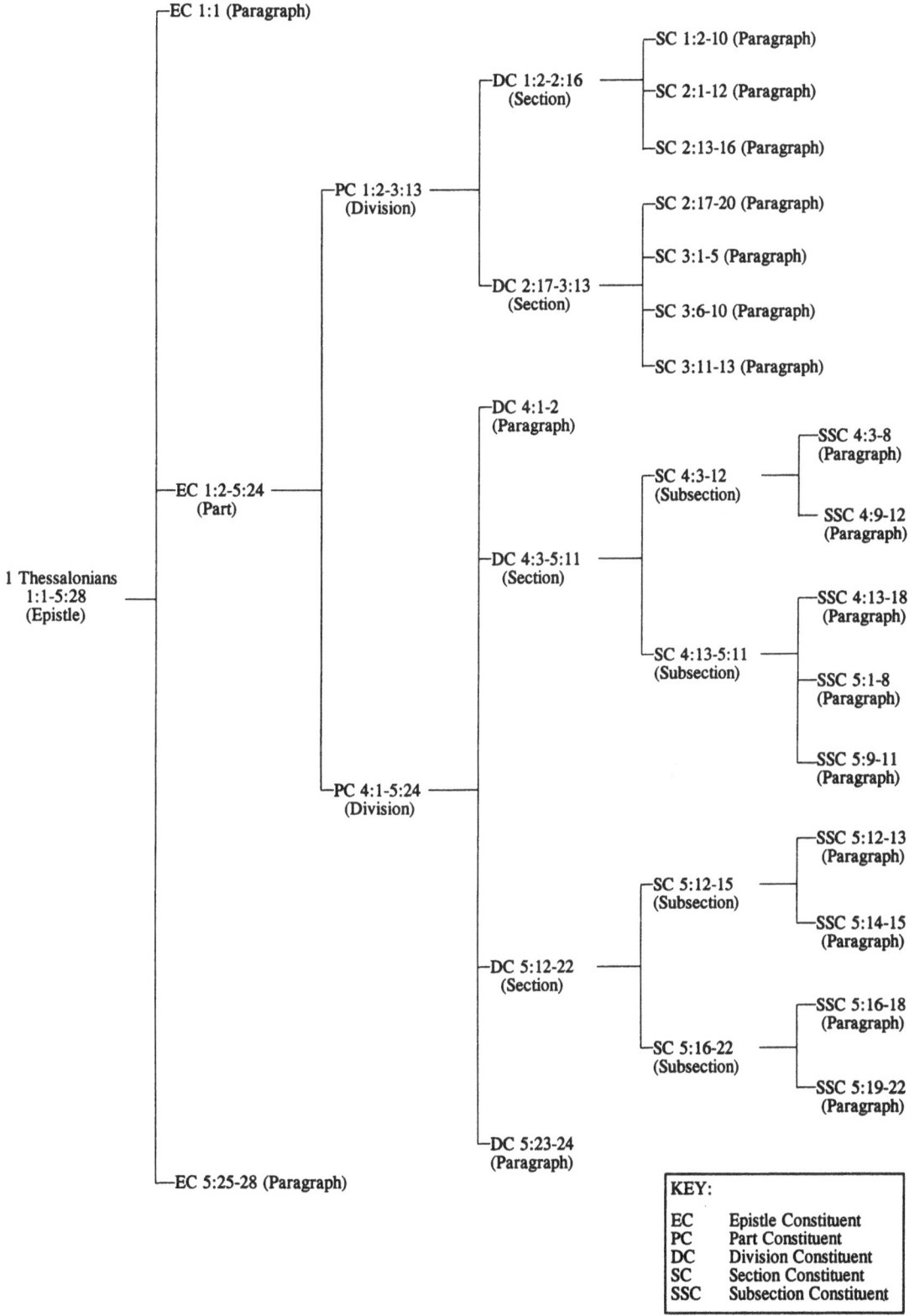

OVERVIEW: THEMATIC UNITS AND THEIR THEME STATEMENTS

1 THESSALONIANS 1:1–5:28 (Epistle)
Theme: I, Paul, am sending this letter to you people in Thessalonica who worship God. I always thank God for you all because I know that God chose you and because you accepted as true the message from God. Timothy has told me the good news that you still trust in God. As a result I cannot adequately thank God. God wants you to be distinct people who behave right in every way. Be sexually pure. Love each other. Be vigilant and self-controlled as you wait for the Lord Jesus to return. Do good deeds to each other and to all people. Always rejoice and thank God. Affectionately greet each other for Silas, Timothy, and me. May the Lord bless you.

EPISTLE CONSTITUENT 1:1 (Complex Paragraph: Opening of the Epistle)
Theme: I, Paul, am sending this letter to you people in Thessalonica who worship God our Father and our Lord Jesus Christ. May they continue to bless you.

EPISTLE CONSTITUENT 1:2–5:24 (Part: Body of the Epistle)
Theme: I always thank God for you all because I know that God chose you and because you accepted as true the message from God. When I was with you, you know that we behaved irreproachably toward you. You cause us to be proud and joyful. Timothy has told me the good news that you still trust in God. As a result I have been cheered up and I cannot adequately thank God for what he has done for you. God wants you to be distinct people who behave right in every way. Be sexually pure. Love each other. Be vigilant and self-controlled as you wait for the Lord Jesus to return. Esteem and love your leaders and do good deeds to each other and to all people. Always rejoice and thank God.

PART CONSTITUENT 1:2–3:13 (Expressive Division: Rapport Basis of 1:2–5:24)
Theme: I always thank God for you all because I know that God chose you and because you accepted as true the message from God. When I was with you, you know that we behaved irreproachably toward you. When people forced me, Silas, and Timothy to be separated from you, I strongly desired to be with you because it is you who cause us to be proud and joyful. When I could no longer endure, I sent Timothy to you. Now Timothy has just returned and has told me the good news that you still trust in God. As a result I have been cheered up and I cannot adequately thank God for what he has done for you. Very frequently I ask God that I will be able to visit you.

DIVISION CONSTITUENT 1:2–2:16 (Complex Section: Rapport Basis₁ of 1:2–3:13)
Theme: I always thank God for you all because I know that God chose you and because you accepted as true the message from God. Those things are evidenced by the fact that you imitated us and the Lord Jesus. That is, although people greatly persecuted you, you were joyful. As a result, you became an example to all the believers in Macedonia and Achaia. Also, you imitated the believers in Judea in that you suffered when your own countrymen mistreated you. When I was with you, you know that I behaved irreproachably toward you and that I continually urged that you behave in the way that God's people should.

####### SECTION CONSTITUENT 1:2–10 (Expressive Paragraph: Rapport Basis₁ of 1:2–2:16)
Theme: I always thank God for you all because, when I pray, I continually remember the way you live as believers and because I know that God chose you. That is evidenced by the fact that the Holy Spirit enabled us to powerfully tell you the gospel and you reacted in the same way that you know we did and the Lord Jesus did; that is, although people persecuted you greatly you were joyful. As a result you inspired all the believers in Macedonia and Achaia to trust in God firmly as you do.

####### SECTION CONSTITUENT 2:1–12 (Descriptive Paragraph: Rapport Basis₂ of 1:2–2:16)
Theme: You and God know it is true that I behaved in a very virtuous, upright, and irreproachable manner toward you. You know also that I continually exhorted, encouraged, and urged that you behave in the way that God's people should.

####### SECTION CONSTITUENT 2:13–16 (Expressive Paragraph: Rapport Basis₃ of 1:2–2:16)
Theme: I continually thank God also because when you heard the message which we told you, you accepted as true not a message that originates from human beings. Rather, you accepted as true the message that originates from God as evidenced by the fact that you suffered when your own countrymen mistreated you in the same way that Jewish people in Judea who are united to Jesus suffered when Jewish people who are not united to him mistreated them.

DIVISION CONSTITUENT 2:17–3:13 (Expressive Section: Rapport Basis₂ of 1:2–3:13)
Theme: When people forced me, Silas, and Timothy to be separated from you for a short time, I strongly desired to be with you because it is you who cause us to be proud and joyful. When I could no longer endure, I sent Timothy to find out whether or not you were still trusting in God. Now Timothy has just returned and has told me the good news that you still trust in God. As a result I have been cheered up and I cannot adequately thank God for what he has done for you. Very frequently I ask God that I will be able to visit you.

SECTION CONSTITUENT 2:17–20 (Expressive Paragraph: Emotive Problem of 2:17–3:13)
Theme: When people forced me, Silas, and Timothy to be separated from you for a short time, I strongly desired to be with you because it is because of you that we are proud and are joyful.

SECTION CONSTITUENT 3:1–5 (Expressive Paragraph: Seeking of 2:17–3:13)
Theme: When I could no longer endure, I sent Timothy to you in order to find out whether or not you were still trusting in God.

SECTION CONSTITUENT 3:6–10 (Expressive Paragraph: Emotive Solution of 2:17–3:13)
Theme: Now Timothy has just returned to me from you and has told me the good news that you still trust in God. As a result I have been cheered up and I cannot thank God adequately for what he has done for you and because of my greatly rejoicing because of you. Very frequently I ask God that I will be able to visit you and help you trust him more strongly.

SECTION CONSTITUENT 3:11–13 (Expressive Paragraph: Reaction/Transition of 2:17–3:13) *Theme: I pray that God will help us return to you and that the Lord Jesus will help you to love each other and other people more and more, just as we love you.*

PART CONSTITUENT 4:1–5:24 (Hortatory Division: Appeal of 1:2–5:24)
Theme: God wants you to be distinct people who behave right in every way. Be sexually pure. Love each other. Be vigilant and self-controlled as you wait for the Lord Jesus to return. Esteem and love your leaders and do good deeds to each other and to all people. Always rejoice and thank God.

DIVISION CONSTITUENT 4:1–2 (Hortatory Paragraph: Introduction of 4:1–5:24)
Theme: Just as we told you previously, I strongly urge you to increasingly behave in a way that will please God.

DIVISION CONSTITUENT 4:3–5:11 (Complex Section: Focal Appeal of 4:1–5:24)
Theme: God wants you to be distinct people who live in a sexually pure way. Also, I urge you to increasingly love each other, to strive to live unobtrusively, and to work at your own occupations. God will raise to live again those believers who died and will bring them to the sky with Jesus. We believers should not be unprepared for the time when Jesus returns as unbelievers will be unprepared. On the contrary, we must be vigilant and self-controlled. Since all this is true, encourage each other.

SECTION CONSTITUENT 4:3–12 (Hortatory Subsection: Focal Appeal₁ of 4:3–5:11)
Theme: God wants you to be distinct people by your behaving in a sexually pure way. Also, I urge you to increasingly love each other, to strive to live unobtrusively, and to work at your own occupations.

SUBSECTION CONSTITUENT 4:3–8 (Hortatory Paragraph: Appeal₁ of 4:3–12)
Theme: God wants you to be distinct people by your behaving in a sexually pure way.

SUBSECTION CONSTITUENT 4:9–12 (Hortatory Paragraph: Appeal₂ of 4:3–12)
Theme: I urge you to increasingly love each other, to strive to live unobtrusively, and to work at your own occupations.

SECTION CONSTITUENT 4:13–5:11 (Complex Subsection: Focal Appeal₂ of 4:3–5:11)
Theme: God will raise to live again those believers who died and will bring them to the sky with Jesus. We believers should not be unprepared for the time when Jesus returns as unbelievers will be unprepared. On the contrary, we must be vigilant and self-controlled. God has destined us believers to be saved from being punished in the future and to be able to live together with our Lord Jesus after he returns. Since all this is true, encourage each other.

SUBSECTION CONSTITUENT 4:13–18 (Expressive Paragraph: Nucleus₁ of 4:13–5:11)
Theme: God will raise to live again those believers who died and will bring them to the sky with Jesus. Encourage each other by telling this message.

SUBSECTION CONSTITUENT 5:1–8 (Hortatory Paragraph: Nucleus₂ of 4:13–5:11)
Theme: We believers should not be unprepared for the time the Lord Jesus returns as unbelievers will be unprepared. On the contrary, we must be vigilant and self-controlled.
SUBSECTION CONSTITUENT 5:9–11 (Expressive Paragraph: Nucleus₃ of 4:13–5:11)
Theme: God has destined us believers to be saved from being punished in the future and to be able to live together with our Lord Jesus after he returns. Since this is true, encourage each other.

DIVISION CONSTITUENT 5:12–22 (Hortatory Section: General Appeal of 4:1–5:24)
Theme: Highly esteem and love the leaders who care for and instruct you. Warn believers who will not work, and encourage and help those who need it. Be patient with all people and do good deeds to them all. Always rejoice, pray, and thank God. Evaluate all messages that people claim the Holy Spirit gave them. Accept authentic messages and obey them.

SECTION CONSTITUENT 5:12–15 (Hortatory Subsection: General Appeal₁ of 5:12–22)
Theme: Highly esteem and love the leaders who care for and instruct you. Warn believers who will not work, and encourage and help those who need it. Be patient with all people and do good deeds to them all.

SUBSECTION CONSTITUENT 5:12–13 (Hortatory Paragraph: Appeal₁ of 5:12–15)
Theme: Recognize as leaders those people who care for and instruct you; highly esteem and love them. Live peacefully with each other.

SUBSECTION CONSTITUENT 5:14–15 (Hortatory Paragraph: Appeal₂ of 5:12–15)
Theme: Warn believers who will not work, and encourage and help those who need it. Be patient with all people. Do good deeds to them all, including those who do evil deeds to you.

SECTION CONSTITUENT 5:16–22 (Hortatory Subsection: General Appeal₂ of 5:12–22)
Theme: Always rejoice, pray, and thank God. Evaluate all messages that people claim the Holy Spirit gave them. Accept authentic messages and obey them.

SUBSECTION CONSTITUENT 5:16–18 (Hortatory Paragraph: Appeal₁ of 5:16–22)
Theme: Always rejoice, pray, and thank God.

SUBSECTION CONSTITUENT 5:19–22 (Hortatory Paragraph: Appeal₂ of 5:16–22)
Theme: Evaluate all messages that people claim the Holy Spirit gave them. Accept authentic messages and obey them.

DIVISION CONSTITUENT 5:23–24 (Expressive Paragraph: Closing of 4:1–5:24)
Theme: I pray that God will cause you to be distinct people who behave right in every way, and I am sure that he will do this.

EPISTLE CONSTITUENT 5:25–28 (Complex Paragraph: Closing of the Epistle)
Theme: Pray for us. Affectionately greet all the fellow believers for us, and make certain that someone reads this letter aloud to all of them. May the Lord bless you.

THE PRESENTATION AND DISCUSSION OF THE SEMANTIC UNITS OF 1 THESSALONIANS

1 THESSALONIANS 1:1–5:28 (Epistle)

THEME: I, Paul, am sending this letter to you people in Thessalonica who worship God. I always thank God for you all because I know that God chose you and because you accepted as true the message from God. Timothy has told me the good news that you still trust in God. As a result I cannot adequately thank God. God wants you to be distinct people who behave right in every way. Be sexually pure. Love each other. Be vigilant and self-controlled as you wait for the Lord Jesus to return. Do good deeds to each other and to all people. Always rejoice and thank God. Affectionately greet each other for Silas, Timothy, and me. May the Lord bless you.

MACROSTRUCTURE	CONTENTS
opening	1:1 I, Paul, am sending this letter to you people in Thessalonica who worship God our Father and our Lord Jesus Christ. May they continue to bless you.
BODY	1:2–5:24 I always thank God for you all because I know that God chose you and because you accepted as true the message from God. When I was with you, you know that we behaved irreproachably toward you. You cause us to be proud and joyful. Timothy has told me the good news that you still trust in God. As a result I have been cheered up and I cannot adequately thank God for what he has done for you. God wants you to be distinct people who behave right in every way. Be sexually pure. Love each other. Be vigilant and self-controlled as you wait for the Lord Jesus to return. Esteem and love your leaders and do good deeds to each other and to all people. Always rejoice and thank God.
closing	5:25–28 Pray for us. Affectionately greet all the fellow believers for us, and make certain that someone reads this letter aloud to all of them. May the Lord bless you.

INTENT AND MACROSTRUCTURE

One of Paul's intents in his letter to the Thessalonians is to affect the behavior of these believers. This is signaled overtly by the many exhortations in the 4:1–5:24 division of the body of the letter. It may also be signaled in references to the past and present faith and witness of the Thessalonians (e.g., 1:3–10; 2:13–14; 3:2–3, 6), to Paul's own behavior when he ministered in Thessalonica (2:1–12), and in his first wish-prayer (3:11–13). By these references Paul may be implicitly encouraging his readers to continue strong in faith and practice and in imitation of him.

In addition, Paul intends to affect the emotions of the Thessalonian believers and thus establish rapport with them after an enforced absence. In the first division (1:2–3:13) of the body of the letter he does this by telling how thankful he is for their strong faith and steadfastness in persecution (1:2–10; 2:13–14; 3:9) and how much they mean to him and his companions (2:7–12, 2:17–3:13). In the second division (4:1–5:24) Paul seeks to encourage them with truths about the return of the Lord Jesus (4:13–5:11), especially concerning what will happen to those believers who have died.

Paul also intends to affect the Thessalonians' ideas, particularly in 4:14–17 and 5:4–5, which tell about the time when the Lord Jesus will return to earth and their part in it.

COHERENCE

The epistle has the characteristic parts of a letter of Paul's time period: an *opening* address and greeting, BODY (the basic message Paul wants to communicate), and *closing* comments and farewell.

PROMINENCE AND THEME

The BODY is the naturally prominent part of the letter. However, the *opening* and *closing* are thematic because of their functions of identifying the writer and recipients and of establishing rapport by giving blessings and final greetings. Therefore the theme for the whole letter includes not only the theme of the BODY (most of it) but also parts of the themes of the *opening* and *closing*.

EPISTLE CONSTITUENT 1:1
(Complex Paragraph: Opening of the Epistle)

THEME: I, Paul, am sending this letter to you people in Thessalonica who worship God our Father and our Lord Jesus Christ. May they continue to bless you.

STRUCTURE	CONTENTS
ADDRESS	1:1a *I, Paul, being together* with Silas and Timothy, *am sending this letter* to *you who are* the group of people in Thessalonica *city* who *worship* (*or, trust in*) God *our(inc)* Father [MET] and *our(inc)* Lord Jesus Christ.
BLESSING	1:1b *We(exc)* desire that God *our(inc)* Father and Jesus Christ *our(inc)* Lord *will continue to* act graciously toward you and *will continue to* cause you to live well/peacefully.

INTENT AND PARAGRAPH PATTERN

In 1:1 we see the typical structure of a Greek letter opening of the time. The address generally consisted of the author (and those with him, if any) and the addressee(s). The greeting was often simply a form of the word χαίρειν 'greetings'.

The author's intent in writing such an opening was twofold: to identify himself and establish rapport with the recipients of the letter. It is for the purpose of rapport that Paul expands his description of the Thessalonians with 'in God the Father and the Lord Jesus Christ' and transforms the usual greeting into a distinctly Christian blessing.

The 1:1 paragraph comprises two conjoined constituents, ADDRESS and BLESSING, and thus has more than one distinct function, clearly recognizable in the surface structure. Because of this it is semantically different from all other paragraphs in the letter except the 5:25–28 closing, which is likewise multifunctional. (This is true of the openings and closings of other Pauline letters as well.) It is therefore labeled a complex paragraph.

NOTES

1:1a *I*, Paul, *being together* with Silas and Timothy, *am sending this letter* In the Greek the second name, Σιλουανός 'Silvanus', is transliterated from Latin. It most likely refers to the person Luke calls by the Greek form Σιλᾶς 'Silas' (see Acts 17:4, 5, 10). It is suggested that 'Silas' be used in translation; the longer form can be mentioned in a footnote or glossary, if desired.

As he does here, Paul mentions one or more associates in the openings of some of his other letters, but 1 and 2 Thessalonians differ from them in that Paul uses first person plural forms almost exclusively in these two letters. In contrast, in 1 Corinthians, for example, where Sosthenes is mentioned in the opening, Paul uses singular forms in the body of that letter to indicate that he is the author. The body of 1 Thessalonians begins with the plural 'we thank' (1:2), and the first person plural is used throughout the rest of the letter with only three exceptions. The nominative form of the names 'Paul, Silvanus, and Timothy' in the opening and the use of the first person plural throughout the letter could imply that all three are authors. However, it is generally assumed that Paul is the primary author (see "Participants in the Communication Situation" on p. 5). Therefore, in the display Silas and Timothy are said to be together with Paul.

It is probable that Paul dictated the letter as he composed it. If in the receptor language 'writing' connotes no more than actually penning the letter, then 'sending' may be more accurate.

to *you who are* the group of people in Thessalonica *city* who *worship* (*or, trust in*) God *our(inc)* Father and *our(inc)* Lord Jesus Christ Paul addresses the recipients with τῇ ἐκκλησίᾳ Θεσσαλονικέων ἐν θεῷ πατρὶ καὶ κυρίῳ Ἰησοῦ Χριστῷ 'to the church of Thessalonians in God (the) father and (the) Lord Jesus Christ'. Best says that originally the term ἐκκλησία denoted an assembly of people, but the Septuagint used the term for the people of God, whether actually in assembly or not. Therefore in the NT the term had a definite religious content and was used for the Christian community as a whole, for the Christian community in a town, or even in a house.

An exegetical problem is presented by ἐν 'in' in the phrase 'to the church of Thessalonians *in* God the Father and the Lord Jesus Christ'. The generally preferred view is that ἐν here refers to being spiritually joined to, or in union with, God and Jesus Christ. This corresponds to the way many commentators understand Paul's use of 'in

Christ'. But, as J. Callow notes (1982:23–24), Paul in other contexts does not use 'in God' with the same sense as 'in Christ': "It is probably the case, as suggested by several commentators and grammarians, that the 'in' expression is added to distinguish the Christian church from a Gentile assembly and from Jewish congregations or synagogues." The rendering in the display 'group of people . . . who worship (or, trust in) God . . . and our Lord Jesus Christ' reflects this understanding of the 'in' phrase as well as the meaning of 'community' suggested by Best.

Paul uses the term 'Father' here in a metaphorical sense. The ground of comparison is the close relationship a family head has with his children. God has such a relationship with those who worship and trust in him.

In the opening verse of 2 Thessalonians (1:1) Paul adds the pronoun ἡμῶν 'our' to the corresponding phrase: 'in God *our* Father and (our) Lord Jesus Christ'. That is appropriate as the meaning of 1 Thess. 1:1 as well and is so rendered in the display. The alternative would be 'in God (the) Father (of Christ and of us)', which seems unwarranted by the context.

in Thessalonica *city* The Greek has a genitive, Θεσσαλονικέων 'of Thessalonians'. In his letters Paul usually refers to the location rather than the people. No semantic distinction appears to be intended by the use of the genitive, so the more usual Pauline form is given in the display. Thessalonica, with as many as 200,000 inhabitants, is classified as a city.

1:1b *We(exc) desire that God our(inc) Father and Jesus Christ our(inc) Lord will continue to act graciously toward you and will continue to cause you to live well/peacefully* The phrase χάρις ὑμῖν καὶ εἰρήνη 'grace to you and peace' is understood as Paul's and his companions' desire for the Thessalonians. The MJTGNT in 1 Thess. 1:1 has the words ἀπὸ θεοῦ πατρὸς ἡμῶν καὶ κυρίου Ἰησοῦ Χριστοῦ 'from God our Father and (our) Lord Jesus Christ' (as does 2 Thess. 1:1 in both MJTGNT and UBSGNT). Whether or not we accept the variant reading in 1 Thess. 1:1, the meaning is the same: God the Father and the Lord Jesus are the agents that grant grace and peace.

This verse is a formal greeting and should be rendered in a way that is appropriate to a greeting. The noun χάρις 'grace' "represents an event, an action on the part of God (and the Lord Jesus) towards sinful mankind, but there is no English verb to represent such an event" (J. Callow 1983:28). In the display the event is represented by 'will continue to act graciously toward you'.

The noun εἰρήνη 'peace' represents the state enjoyed by the recipients of God's grace. Wanamaker says, "While there is always a danger of reading too much into isolated occurrences of words, Paul undoubtedly intended 'grace and peace' to evoke in his readers a sense of divine blessing upon their lives characterized by God's freely given favor and the sense of completeness or wholeness (the root idea of the Hebrew word *shalom*) that results from reconciliation with God through Christ's death." Thus 'peace' expresses more than a lack of strife and more than inner peacefulness. It is the state of those who are experiencing God's grace, God's blessing. "Hence, in translation some general word should be used that is appropriate for *spiritual* blessedness rather than material prosperity, which is not a NT emphasis" (J. Callow, 1982:24–25).

BOUNDARIES AND COHERENCE

The initial boundary of 1a–b coincides with the beginning of the epistle discourse. The final boundary is marked by the formalized blessing, which typically ends such letter openings.

Verse 1 follows the structure of the openings of Greek letters of the time, which in their most basic form consisted of only three expressions: the name of the writer in the nominative case, the name of the addressee in the dative case, and the greeting. As in the typical Greek letter opening and the opening units of Paul's other letters, there is no verb in this verse. The first verb in the epistle, εὐχαριστοῦμεν 'we thank', at the very beginning of v. 2, marks the beginning of the next unit, the BODY of the epistle.

PROMINENCE AND THEME

The ADDRESS and BLESSING each have a distinct function in the *opening* of the epistle, and thus they are related in a conjoining relationship rather than a subordinating one. This means that the theme must be drawn from both of them. As far as the ADDRESS is concerned, only Paul's name is mentioned in the theme, since, as mentioned in the introduction and in the note on 1:1a, Paul is the primary author of the epistle. In the BLESSING part of the theme, *they* refers to 'God our Father and Jesus Christ our Lord'; *bless* refers to the granting of both grace and peace; and *May* is substituted for 'we desire that'.

EPISTLE CONSTITUENT 1:2–5:24
(Part: Body of the Epistle)

THEME: I always thank God for you all because I know that God chose you and because you accepted as true the message from God. When I was with you, you know that we behaved irreproachably toward you. You cause us to be proud and joyful. Timothy has told me the good news that you still trust in God. As a result I have been cheered up and I cannot adequately thank God for what he has done for you. God wants you to be distinct people who behave right in every way. Be sexually pure. Love each other. Be vigilant and self-controlled as you wait for the Lord Jesus to return. Esteem and love your leaders and do good deeds to each other and to all people. Always rejoice and thank God.

MACROSTRUCTURE	CONTENTS
rapport basis	1:2–3:13 I always thank God for you all because I know that God chose you and because you accepted as true the message from God. When I was with you, you know that we behaved irreproachably toward you. When people forced me, Silas, and Timothy to be separated from you, I strongly desired to be with you because it is you who cause us to be proud and joyful. When I could no longer endure, I sent Timothy to you. Now Timothy has just returned and has told me the good news that you still trust in God. As a result I have been cheered up and I cannot adequately thank God for what he has done for you. Very frequently I ask God that I will be able to visit you.
APPEAL	4:1–5:24 God wants you to be distinct people who behave right in every way. Be sexually pure. Love each other. Be vigilant and self-controlled as you wait for the Lord Jesus to return. Esteem and love your leaders and do good deeds to each other and to all people. Always rejoice and thank God.

INTENT AND MACROSTRUCTURE

In 1 Thessalonians Paul is continuing by correspondence the ministry that he, Silas, and Timothy started when they were in Thessalonica. His intent is to affect the emotions, ideas, and, most importantly, the behavior of the Thessalonians so that they do more and more the things that please God (4:1). In wish-prayers (3:11–13, 5:23–24) at the end of each of the constituent units of 1:2–5:24 Paul says that he wants the Thessalonians to be blameless when the Lord Jesus returns to earth.

The BODY of the letter is composed of two divisions. In the first (1:2–3:13) Paul expresses heartfelt appreciation. He tells how thankful he is for the Thessalonians and their faithfulness to God and how much they mean to him and his companions. This division functions as a *rapport basis* for the second division, an APPEAL (4:1–5:24). The transition to the APPEAL is indicated in part by λοιπὸν οὖν ἀδελφοί 'for the rest, then, brothers' in 4:1.

BOUNDARIES AND COHERENCE

The initial boundary of 1:2–5:24 was discussed under 1:1 (see "Boundaries"). The closing boundary seems to occur between 5:24 and 5:25. Verses 5:23–24 are a wish-prayer in which the main verbs are in the optative mood. At 5:25 Paul opens a new unit with the vocative 'brothers'. In it he reverts to imperatives. The content of these commands, however, contrasts with previous exhortations. Imperatives in 5:11–22 give general exhortations regarding relationships with others in the Christian community and regarding religious disciplines and attitudes, while the exhortations of 5:25–27 relate specifically to the communication situation of the letter: pray for us (5:25), greet each other (5:26), read this letter to all (5:27). (See "Boundaries" under 4:1–5:24 for probable reasons why the closing boundary of the BODY does not occur between 5:22 and 5:23.)

One aspect of referential coherence between the constituent divisions of 1:2–5:24 is based on Paul's personal ministry among the Thessalonians. He reminds them of what they should know because of his teaching when he was with them: 'you know' (1:5; 2:1, 2, 5, 11; 3:3, 4; 4:2; 5:2); 'you remember' (2:9); 'you are witnesses' (2:10); 'we told you before' (3:4; 4:6); 'you received from us' (4:1); and 'you have no need that we write you' (4:9; 5:1).

Referential coherence is also established by references to:

1. The second coming of the Lord. This topic is developed in detail in the second division in 4:13–5:11. It is also mentioned in 1:10, 2:19, 3:13, and 5:23.

2. Sanctified behavior. Exhortation to live sanctified lives (ἁγιασμός 'sanctification') is found in 4:3-8, specifically in 4:3, 4, and 7. Cognate words are found in the wish-prayers at the close of the divisions: ἁγιωσύνη 'holiness' in 3:13 and ἁγιάζω 'to sanctify' in 5:23. Other expressions within the same semantic domain are ἀμέμπτως 'blamelessly' (2:10, 5:23) and ἄμεμπτος 'blameless' (3:13); ἅγιος 'holy' (1:5, 6; 3:13; 4:8; 5:26, and 27 [in MJTGNT]) and ὁσίως 'in a holy way' (2:10); δικαίως 'righteously' (2:10); and ἀξίως 'worthily' (2:12).

3. Christian virtues. Forms of the stem πιστ- meaning 'faith', 'to believe', 'to be entrusted', or 'faithful' are used fourteen times (1:3, 7, 8; 2:4, 10, 13; 3:2, 5, 6, 7, 10; 4:14; 5:8, 24), making this a prominent concept of the epistle. Other virtues are ἀγαπ- 'love', 'to love', 'beloved' (1:3, 4; 2:8; 3:6, 12; 4:9; 5:8, 13) and φιλαδελφία 'brotherly love' (4:9); ἐλπίς 'hope' (1:3, 2:19, 4:13, 5:8); and εὐχαριστ- 'to thank', 'thankfulness' (1:2, 2:13, 3:9, 5:18). Words in the domain of work are ἐργ- 'work', 'to work' (1:3, 2:9, 4:11, 5:13), κοπ- 'labor', 'to labor' (1:3, 2:9, 3:5, 5:12), and μόχθος 'toil' (2:9).

4. The gospel and the word. Words with the stem εὐαγγελ- 'gospel', 'to declare good news' are found in 1:5; 2:2, 4, 8, 9; 3:2, 6. Occurrences of λόγος 'word', are in 1:6, 8; 2:5, 13; 4:15, 18.

Relational coherence is established by λοιπὸν οὖν 'now then/therefore' at the beginning of 4:1-5:24, the second division. These words may signal that the *rapport basis* (1:2-3:13) is the foundation of the APPEAL (4:1-5:24).

PROMINENCE AND THEME

Although the APPEAL (4:1-5:24) has natural prominence in the 1:2-5:24 BODY of the letter, the *rapport basis* (1:2-3:13) plays an important role in accomplishing Paul's intent. Therefore, while the BODY's theme is basically the same as the theme for the APPEAL, it also includes elements of the theme for the *rapport basis*.

PART CONSTITUENT 1:2–3:13
(Emotive Division: Rapport Basis of 1:2–5:24)

THEME: I always thank God for you all because I know that God chose you and because you accepted as true the message from God. When I was with you, you know that we behaved irreproachably toward you. When people forced me, Silas, and Timothy to be separated from you, I strongly desired to be with you because it is you who cause us to be proud and joyful. When I could no longer endure, I sent Timothy to you. Now Timothy has just returned and has told me the good news that you still trust in God. As a result I have been cheered up and I cannot adequately thank God for what he has done for you. Very frequently I ask God that I will be able to visit you.

MACROSTRUCTURE	CONTENTS
rapport basis₁	1:2–2:16 I always thank God for you all because I know that God chose you and because you accepted as true the message from God. Those things are evidenced by the fact that you imitated us and the Lord Jesus. That is, although people greatly persecuted you, you were joyful. As a result, you became an example to all the believers in Macedonia and Achaia. Also, you imitated the believers in Judea in that you suffered when your own countrymen mistreated you. When I was with you, you know that I behaved irreproachably toward you and that I continually urged that you behave in the way that God's people should.
RAPPORT BASIS₂ (contains climax unit of 1:2–3:13)	2:17–3:13 When people forced me, Silas, and Timothy to be separated from you for a short time, I strongly desired to be with you because it is you who cause us to be proud and joyful. When I could no longer endure, I sent Timothy to find out whether or not you were still trusting in God. Now Timothy has just returned and has told me the good news that you still trust in God. As a result I have been cheered up and I cannot adequately thank God for what he has done for you. Very frequently I ask God that I will be able to visit you.

INTENT AND MACROSTRUCTURE

In the 1:2–3:13 division Paul's primary intent is to affect the emotions of the Thessalonians, building rapport with them. He does this by telling how thankful he is for their strong faith and steadfastness in persecution (1:2–10, 2:13–14, 3:9) and how much they mean to him and his companions (2:7–12, 2:17–3:13). Such statements signal that the genre is emotive. The type of emotive discourse in all except one of the paragraphs in the 1:2–3:13 division is expressive, and that exception (2:1–12) is descriptive, which is a type of emotive genre just as expressive is.

The division consists of two sections (1:2–2:16 and 2:17–3:13). They function as *rapport bases* for the APPEAL in the 4:1–5:24 division. The second of these sections begins with the conjunction δέ, a developmental marker (see the note on 2:16c) that shows that the second section builds on the first. The second section also contains the climactic paragraph of the division (see "Intent" under 2:17–3:13). For that reason its label in the display is in uppercase letters.

Paul may have had a secondary purpose in writing this division—that is, to encourage the Thessalonians in their faith and practice. The expressions of thanksgiving and affirmation not only touch the emotions but they also are a means of implicitly exhorting the Thessalonians to remain faithful to the Lord despite persecution and to live praiseworthy and blameless lives. Theoretically, discourse genres are ranked according to influence, from those that affect ideas to those that affect emotions and behavior. Here, where Paul's primary intent is to affect emotions, it is to be expected that a secondary intent is to affect the behavior of the readers; this is borne out by Paul's subsequent appeals in chapters 4 and 5.

BOUNDARIES AND COHERENCE

The initial boundary of 1:2–3:13 was discussed under the 1:1 display ("Boundaries"). The terminal boundary, between 3:13 and 4:1, is well established since the wish-prayer of 3:11–13 is in the optative mood and at 4:1 Paul switches to the indicative mood. He uses the orienters 'ask' and 'urge', which indicates a change to overt appeals. The wish-prayer ends with an eschatological reference similar to those at concluding verses (1:10, 2:12, 2:16) of other paragraphs in the 1:2–3:13

division. The terms λοιπὸν οὖν 'in addition then' and the vocative 'brothers' also indicate a major transition at 4:1.

A primary aspect of referential coherence in 1:2–3:13 is the use of verb or noun forms of εὐχαριστ- 'thanksgiving' (1:2, 2:13, and 3:9). The first mention at the beginning of the unit (1:2) is joined with a reference to Paul's prayers for the Thessalonians; the final reference (3:9) is followed by a report of prayer (3:10) and a wish-prayer (3:11–13). These constitute a sandwich arrangement: references to prayer open and close the 1:2–3:13 division.

The abundant use of first and second person plural pronouns throughout the division gives referential coherence and marks this as a very personal unit. Also, the concept of faith (forms of the stem πιστ-) is a key referential concept (1:3, 7, 8; 2:4, 10, 13; 3:2, 5, 6, 7, 10).

PROMINENCE AND THEME

Thanksgiving is prominent in the 1:2–3:13 division, being introduced in 1:2–10 and resumed in 2:13–14. A concluding thanksgiving in the form of a rhetorical question is given in 3:9. Because the first *rapport basis* (1:2–2:16) contains the major thanksgiving sections, it plays a role in Paul's purpose. In the second (2:17–3:13), Paul tells over and over again how much the Thessalonians mean to him and his companions. This, too, contributes prominently to Paul's intent of affecting their emotions.

The theme for the division contains much of the first and last sentences of the theme of 1:2–2:16. These state the naturally prominent reasons for Paul's thanksgiving in that section and his declaration of irreproachable ministry to the Thessalonians. The remainder of the theme of 1:2–3:13 consists of the theme of 2:17–3:13, which is the climactic section of 1:2–3:13 and expresses Paul's longing, pride, joy, and thanksgiving.

DIVISION CONSTITUENT 1:2–2:16
(Complex Section: Rapport Basis₁ of 1:2–3:13)

> *THEME: I always thank God for you all because I know that God chose you and because you accepted as true the message from God. Those things are evidenced by the fact that you imitated us and the Lord Jesus. That is, although people greatly persecuted you, you were joyful. As a result, you became an example to all the believers in Macedonia and Achaia. Also, you imitated the believers in Judea in that you suffered when your own countrymen mistreated you. When I was with you, you know that I behaved irreproachably toward you and that I continually urged that you behave in the way that God's people should.*

MACROSTRUCTURE	CONTENTS
rapport basis₁	1:2–10 I always thank God for you all because, when I pray, I continually remember the way you live as believers and because I know that God chose you. That is evidenced by the fact that the Holy Spirit enabled us to powerfully tell you the gospel and you reacted in the same way that you know we did and the Lord Jesus did; that is, although people persecuted you greatly you were joyful. As a result you inspired all the believers in Macedonia and Achaia to trust in God firmly as you do.
RAPPORT BASIS₂ (peak₁ unit of 1:2–3:13)	2:1–12 You and God know it is true that I behaved in a very virtuous, upright, and irreproachable manner toward you. You know also that I continually exhorted, encouraged, and urged that you behave in the way that God's people should.
RAPPORT BASIS₃ (peak₂ unit of 1:2–3:13)	2:13–16 I continually thank God also because when you heard the message which we told you, you accepted as true not a message that originates from human beings. Rather, you accepted as true the message that originates from God as evidenced by the fact that you suffered when your own countrymen mistreated you in the same way that Jewish people in Judea who are united to Jesus suffered when Jewish people who are not united to him mistreated them.

INTENT AND MACROSTRUCTURE

Paul's intent in the 1:2–2:16 section is to affect the emotions of his readers, thus building rapport with them. He does this by twice expressing his thanksgiving to God for the way the Thessalonians have responded to the gospel (1:2–10 and 2:13–14). Paul also tells in detail how he and his companions ministered among the Thessalonians (2:1–12). He does this because he wants them to recognize his love and concern for them as expressed in selfless and irreproachable ministry. The expressions of thanksgiving and descriptions of loving ministry signal that this is emotive discourse. It is labeled a complex section because the first and third constituent units are expressive, while the second is descriptive (both being types of emotive discourse).

The section is composed of three conjoined paragraphs. The second of these paragraphs begins with γάρ 'for', signaling a return to a previously mentioned topic (see the note on 2:1). The third paragraph begins with καί 'and'.

In the first *rapport basis* (1:2–10) Paul begins with a thanksgiving statement (vv. 2–3) that is similar to the thanksgivings that follow the opening greetings in many of his letters. In vv. 4–10, however, he extensively develops a particular point of gratefulness—how the Thessalonians responded to his ministry with faith and witness. These verses show Paul's intent to build rapport with his readers.

In the second *RAPPORT BASIS* (2:1–12) Paul seems to reach the first discourse peak of 1:2–3:13. In 1:5 and 1:9 he briefly mentioned his prior ministry among the Thessalonians. His return to that topic in 2:1–12 (and resulting shift to speaking about himself rather than the Thessalonians' response) gives the unit prominence. In addition, extensive negative-positive descriptions (2:1–9) and emphatic declarations (2:10–12) give unusual rhetorical prominence to 2:1–12.

The third *RAPPORT BASIS* (2:13–16) may either be a post-peak unit (denouement) or a second peak. The latter view has merit. Paul returns to the reason for thanksgiving first mentioned in 1:4–10 and further develops it. He brings the Thessalonians back on stage and repeats the words ὑμεῖς μιμηταὶ ἐγενήθητε 'you became imitators' (1:6; 2:14). This reviving of a previous theme, repetition of key words, and further development of the concept of persecution all seem to move the discourse along to a new height. It serves Paul's intent by continuing to build rapport with the readers.

The labels for the second and third paragraphs are in uppercase letters in the display because they are considered peak units of 1:2–3:13.

BOUNDARIES AND COHERENCE

The initial boundary of 1:2–2:16 was discussed under 1:1 ("Boundaries"). As to the terminal boundary between 2:16 and 2:17, it is well-defined. At 2:17 Paul indicates a change of subject matter with the forefronting of new agents, 'we' (the messengers). He also uses the vocative, 'brothers'. Paragraph 2:13–16 (which immediately precedes the terminal boundary) concerns the Thessalonians' response to God's message and concerns unbelieving Jews who persecuted his messengers, concluding with an eschatological comment (2:16c) similar to those at the ends (1:10c, 2:12e) of the two preceding paragraphs. (Propositions 1:10c and 2:16c are references to God's coming wrath.). Then at v. 17 Paul begins a discussion of his longing to see the Thessalonians and his attempts to return to them or get word of how they are faring.

Section 1:2–2:16 displays referential coherence through the repetition of parallel expressions: 'we always thank God for you all' (1:2a) and 'we continually thank God' (2:13a); 'you became imitators of us' (1:6a) and 'you became imitators of the churches' (2:14a). In addition, in all three of the constituent paragraphs there are references to the message Paul and his companions preached and the Thessalonians received: 'the gospel' (1:5; 2:2, 4, 8, 9); 'the word of God' (2:13); 'the word of the Lord' (1:8); and 'word' (1:5, 6, and twice in 2:13). Also uniting the section is the prominent idea that the Thessalonians suffered persecution as did Paul, the Lord Jesus, and the churches in Judea (1:6; 2:2, 14–15).

PROMINENCE AND THEME

In the 1:2–2:16 section thanksgiving to God for the Thessalonians is prominent; it appears in the first *rapport basis* (1:2–10) and is developed further in the third (2:13–16). Paul's love and concern for the Thessalonians is prominent in the second RAPPORT BASIS (2:1–12), in which Paul describes his philosophy of ministry. All three paragraphs contribute directly to Paul's intent of building rapport by affecting the emotions of his readers. The theme for the section is derived from the themes of its three constituent paragraphs.

Because of the almost identical structures of paragraphs 1:2–10 and 2:13–16 and the concepts shared by both, their themes are combined and intermingled in the first part of the 1:2–2:16 theme. The overall theme contains Paul's expression of thanksgiving (derived from propositions 1:2a and 2:13a), the main reasons for his thanksgiving (1:4, 2:13d), the major evidence for each reason (1:6b-c, 2:14a-b), and the prominent result (1:7). The theme's last sentence is basically the 2:1–12 theme.

SECTION CONSTITUENT 1:2–10
(Expressive Paragraph: Rapport Basis₁ of 1:2–2:16)

THEME: I always thank God for you all because, when I pray, I continually remember the way you live as believers and because I know that God chose you. That is evidenced by the fact that the Holy Spirit enabled us to powerfully tell you the gospel and you reacted in the same way that you know we did and the Lord Jesus did; that is, although people persecuted you greatly you were joyful. As a result you inspired all the believers in Macedonia and Achaia to trust in God firmly as you do.

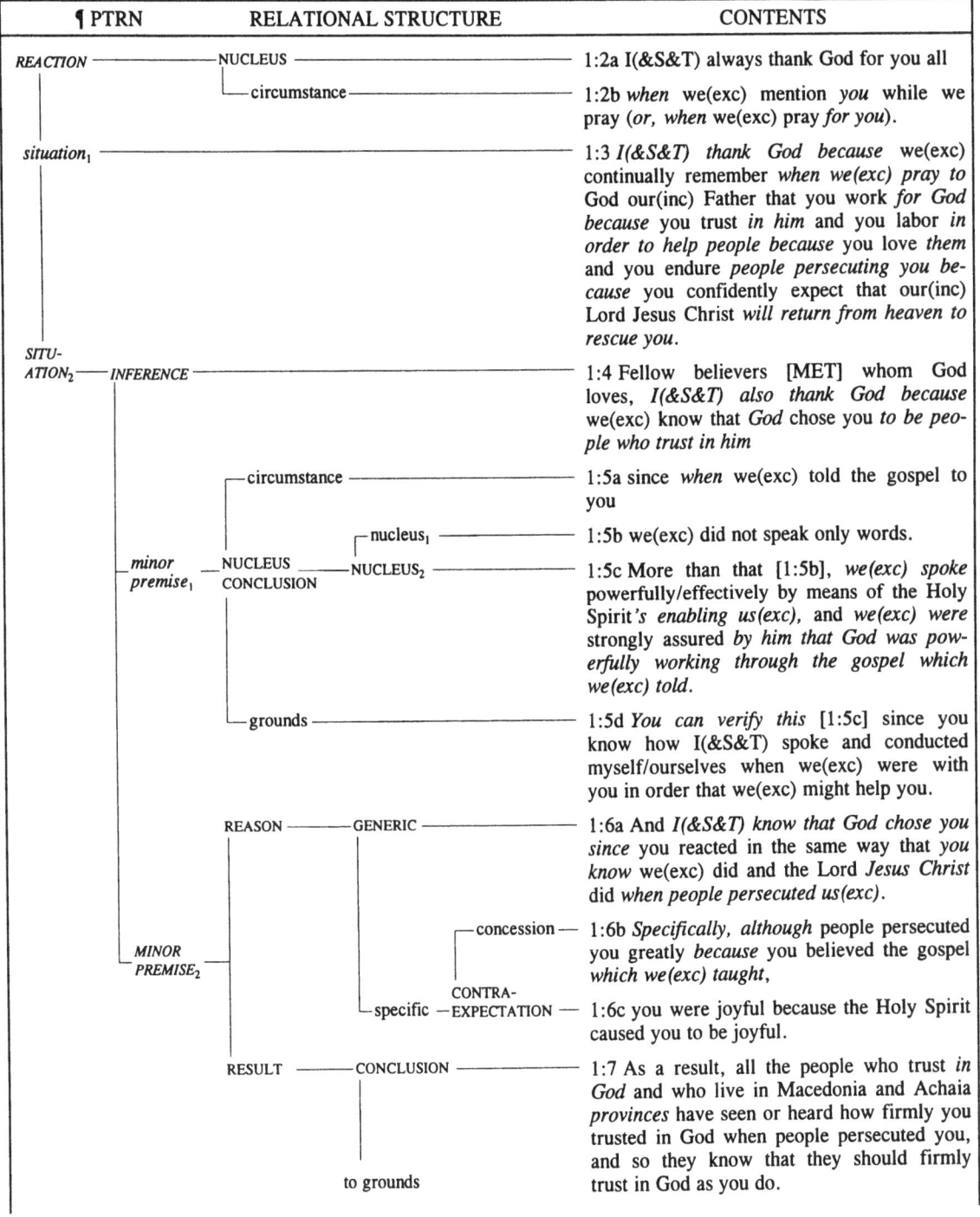

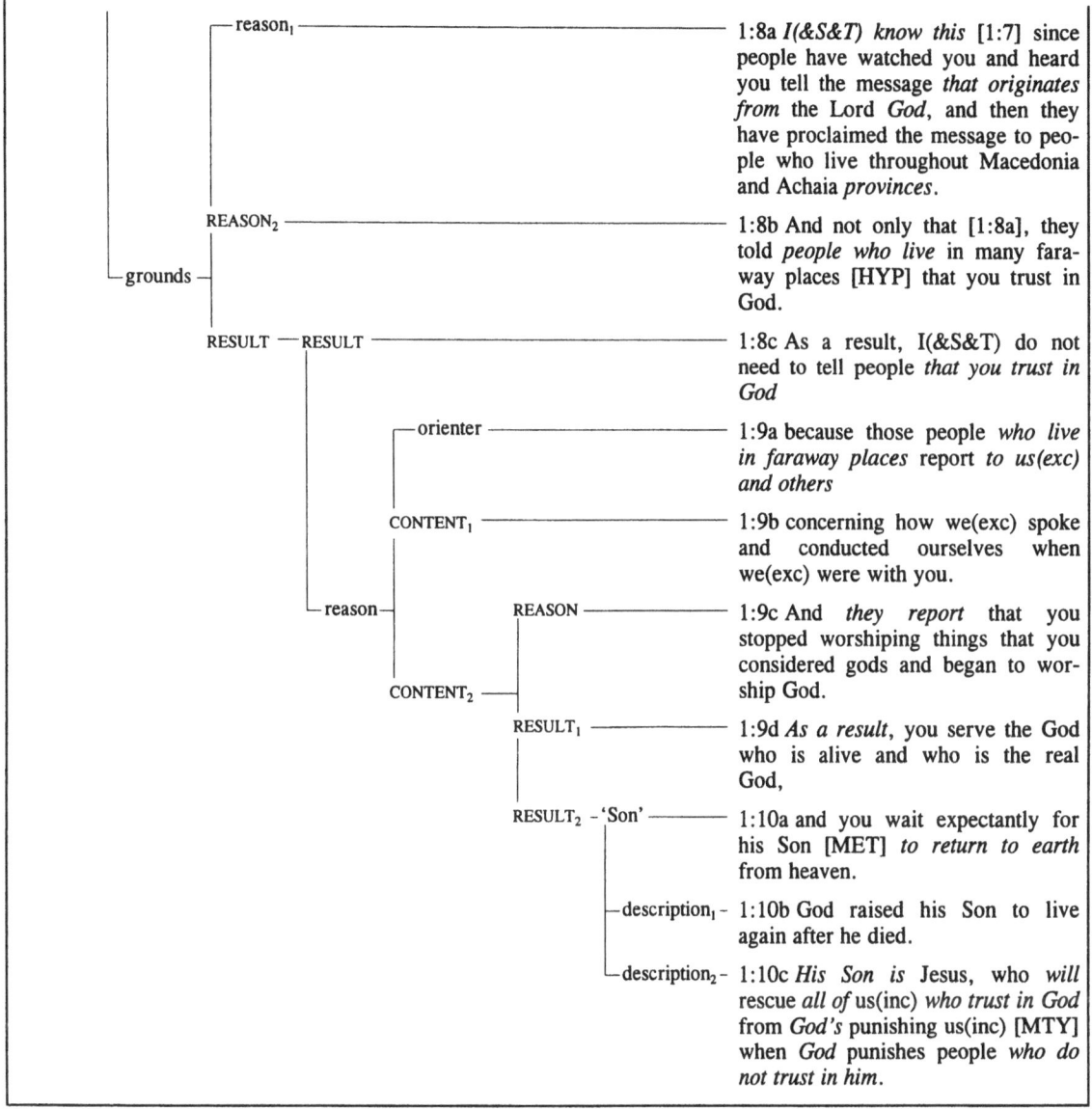

INTENT AND PARAGRAPH PATTERN

Paul's primary intent in the 1:2–10 paragraph is to affect the emotions of his readers. He expresses thankfulness to God for them (v. 2) and praise (implicit) because of the way they have lived as Christians (vv. 3, 9–10) and have endured and furthered the spread of the gospel in spite of persecution (vv. 6–8). The statement of thankfulness indicates that the genre is emotive, and of the expressive type in view of Paul's stating his thankfulness in result-reason relations rather than sequential ones.

The paragraph consists of three propositional groups (2a–b, 3, and 4–10), the second and third of which are introduced by participles and are considered reasons for the first. Here in 1:2–10 Paul is not presenting an emotive problem, so this is not a solutionality subtype. Neither is he listing his beliefs that result in control of his emotions, which would indicate volitionality. Rather there are result-reason relations here, signaling the paragraph pattern subtype of causality, the constituents of which (in an expressive paragraph) are labeled REACTION and *situation*.

The second SITUATION (vv. 4–10) is an embedded paragraph in which Paul tells how he knows that God chose the Thessalonians. It consists of three propositional groups (4, 5a–d, 6a–10c). The second group is introduced by ὅτι 'because' and the third, beginning with καί 'and', is conjoined to the second. The second and third groups are two grounds for Paul's conclusion in v. 4 that God chose the Thessalonians. His primary intent in the 4-10 embedded paragraph is to affect ideas; thus the genre is expository.

In 4-10 Paul uses deductive reasoning, which might be called a categorical syllogism. The unstated major premise is that when God brings people into his kingdom he does so by supernatural means. The *minor premises* are that the messengers ministered with supernatural power and assurance (5a-c) and the Thessalonians responded to persecution with supernatural joy and endurance (6-7). Evidence for the *minor premises* is found in 5d and 8-10. A syllogism signals the paragraph pattern subtype of causality since the conclusion must follow, based on the premises. In an expository paragraph one of the label sets for a conclusion-grounds (causality) relation is *major premise, minor premise, INFERENCE*.

Since Paul mentions and then extensively develops in vv. 4-10 the INFERENCE (conclusion) that the Thessalonians were chosen by God, it seems that a secondary intent is to implicitly encourage the Thessalonian believers to live up to their privileged position by being faithful to the Lord. He reminds them of their past response to the gospel and of their witness as a way of encouraging faithfulness in the present.

According to rhetorical theory, 1:2-10 is the exordium (introduction) of the letter (Wanamaker, p. 73). The exordium was intended to make the reader(s) attentive to the writer and well disposed to his exhortation. The exordium also announced the main themes of the letter. The theme of thanksgiving and the subthemes of gospel proclamation and conversion, persecution, imitation, work, witness, and eschatological expectation are introduced in this paragraph (see "The Genre of the Epistle" on p. 6 for specific references). They are developed further, especially in the rest of the 1:2-3:13 division, but also in the letter as a whole.

NOTES

1:2a I(&S&T) The first person plural bound pronoun 'we' probably refers to Paul, the primary author of the letter (see p. 5, "Participants in the Communication Situation").

always The adverb πάντοτε 'always' is taken by some as hyperbole. However, it seems better to understand it as being qualified by the clause following it (Frame): we always thank God for you *when* we mention you in our prayers.

1:2b when we(exc) mention *you* while we pray (*or*, when we(exc) pray *for* you) The phrase μνείαν ποιούμενοι ἐπὶ τῶν προσευχῶν ἡμῶν 'making mention (of you) in our prayers' is the first of three participial phrases that modify εὐχαριστοῦμεν 'we thank'. The relationship can be rendered as nucleus-circumstance (Bruce, Hiebert; GW, JBP): 'we thank God *when* we mention you in our prayers'. Alternatively, the two events of giving thanks and praying may be rendered as conjoined events that are not sequential but are without reference to temporal ordering (CEV, NRSV, REB, TEV, TNT): 'we thank God *and* mention you in our prayers'. The nonsubordinate verb εὐχαριστοῦμεν 'we thank' is the main verb of the first few verses of the paragraph and indicates that this is a thanksgiving constituent and not a prayer. Thus, it seems preferable to background the mention of prayer in 1:2b by using a circumstance proposition. However, conjoining with the use of 'and' is not an incorrect rendering.

The word μνείαν 'mention' can also mean 'remember'. Because a different word, μνημονεύοντες 'remembering', is used in v. 3, and because μνείαν means 'mention' in extrabiblical sources and elsewhere in Paul, most commentators and versions render it 'mention' here.

In MJTGNT ὑμῶν 'of you' is present, but it is omitted and not mentioned by UBSGNT. Even if the omission is accepted, the pronoun is still implied by the context.

1:3 I(&S&T) thank God because we(exc) continually remember The second subordinate participle, μνημονεύοντες 'remembering', is understood by almost all commentators consulted as introducing the first reason (*situation*) for Paul's thanksgiving. Frame calls this clause the immediate ground of their thanksgiving, and he calls the phrase beginning with εἰδότες 'knowing' in v. 4 the ultimate ground. This assessment is correct as the clause beginning in v. 4 is more fully developed by subordinate clauses.

Commentators and versions disagree as to whether ἀδιαλείπτως 'unceasingly' modifies the participle in 1:2b (which would give 'unceasingly making mention of you') or the participle in 1:3 ('unceasingly remembering'). Greek letter-writing style would allow for either. The second option is perhaps preferable for several reasons: (1) The adverb is adjacent to the participle 'remembering' but removed by a prepositional phrase from 'making mention'. (2) The adverb is marked as prominent by forefronting if it modifies 'remembering', thus emphasizing Paul's emotion. (3) The parallelism seems more appropriate between the

1:2a REACTION (result) proposition and the 1:3 *situation* (reason), which would give 'I(&S&T) always thank God . . . *because* we(exc) continually remember', than between the 1:2a NUCLEUS and its 1:2b temporal circumstance clause, which would give 'I(&S&T) always thank God *when* we(exc) continually mention you'. Hiebert says, "Since the Thessalonians have already been assured that the missionaries are always thanking God for them, it is less significant to add that they are continually praying for them than to assure them that they have continual remembrance of their Christian character and its fruits." Assuming it is used in a parallel way to πάντοτε 'always' (1:2a), ἀδιαλείπτως 'unceasingly' is rendered 'continually' in the display.

when we(exc) pray to God our(inc) Father The phrase ἔμπροσθεν τοῦ θεοῦ καὶ πατρὸς ἡμῶν 'before the God and Father of us' actually occurs at the end of v. 3. However, almost all versions and several commentators (e.g., Best, Marshall, Wanamaker) connect it with the participle 'remembering' at the beginning of the verse. This interpretation fits with the fact that in Greek prepositional phrases tend to occur clause final; here only the object (albeit a complex object) intervenes between the participle and the prepositional phrase. In 3:9 a similar phrase, ἔμπροσθεν τοῦ θεοῦ ἡμῶν 'before the God of us', occurs in a context (3:9–10) that similarly speaks of Paul's thanksgiving to God and prayer. If the phrase in 1:3 is understood as referring to prayer, it parallels Paul's usage in 3:9 and fits the immediate context well.

Because of the phrase's position at the end of the verse, other commentators take different views. One view connects the phrase with the three preceding phrases, 'work of faith', 'labor of love', and 'steadfastness of hope'. It then means that the Thessalonians work, labor, and persevere with the awareness that they are in God's presence and under his care (Bruce, Hiebert, Miller). Another view relates the phrase only to the phrase that immediately precedes, 'steadfastness of hope of our Lord Jesus Christ' (Frame, Morris). This means that Christ will be their hope when they stand before God as judge. This view is supported by the fact that Paul uses the exact same phrase in 3:13 in connection with παρουσία, the 'coming' of the Lord Jesus; and he uses a similar phrase, ἔμπροσθεν τοῦ κυρίου ἡμῶν Ἰησοῦ 'before our Lord Jesus', in 2:19, again in connection with the coming of the Lord. However, 2:19 and 3:13 both make explicit the connection with the coming of Christ whereas 1:3 does not. Therefore, considering the use of almost the same phrase in 3:9 in a context of thanksgiving and prayer and the lack of an explicit reference to the coming of Christ in 1:3, the first of these three interpretations may be slightly preferable. It is rendered in the display 'when we pray to God our Father'.

If Greek had an inclusive/exclusive distinction, it is almost certain Paul would now switch to an inclusive 'our' in the phrase 'God our Father': God was the Father of his readers as well. Nothing in the context indicates that Paul is making a special point by saying τοῦ θεοῦ καὶ πατρὸς ἡμῶν 'the God *and* Father of us' here or in 3:11 and 3:13, so the phrase is rendered without 'and': 'God our(inc) Father'.

that you work *for God because* you trust *in him* The phrase τοῦ ἔργου τῆς πίστεως 'the work of faith' is the first of three parallel constructions each containing a genitive noun. It is preceded by ὑμῶν 'your', which relates not only with this phrase but with the two parallel phrases that follow. The genitive nouns in the three phrases are most often interpreted as subjective genitives or genitives of source. The work the Thessalonians do proceeds from their faith (Best, Frame, Morris, Wanamaker; NCV, NIV, TEV). Other interpretations are that their work *shows* that they have faith (Bruce; JB, REB) or that their work is *characteristic* of people who have faith (Eadie). Each of these interpretations of the genitive seems acceptable. However, the first seems more basic. A person's work for God is the outworking of his faith; that this work shows he has faith is secondary. The first interpretation is therefore followed here. (REB and Eadie apply the other two interpretations to 'labor of love' and 'steadfastness of hope' as well, but this will not be mentioned again in the notes.)

The object of the Thessalonians' faith or trust is not expressed. Commentators have understood it to be God, Christ, both God and Christ, or the gospel. Any one of these is possible. In 1:8 Paul says 'your faith in God has become known everywhere'; and in 1:9 he says 'you turned to God from idols'. Based on these references in the context, the pronoun 'him', referring to God, is supplied in the display as the object of their faith. The noun 'faith', rendered 'trust' in the display, is a key term of Scripture and means to entrust one's life and destiny to God because of who he is and what he has done for the individual.

The word ἔργον 'work' does not specify what type of work they did. Most commentators understand it as spiritual activities, either generally serving God and Christ or specifically helping others, spreading the gospel, etc. Wanamaker says it was "the totality of their new Christian life-style that distinguished them from the pagans around them and from their own past." Because of such understandings, in the display the concept is rendered 'work for God'.

you labor *in order to help people because you love* **them** The Greek is τοῦ κόπου τῆς ἀγάπης 'the labor of love'. As already mentioned, commentators connect the preceding genitive pronoun ὑμῶν 'your' with 'work of faith' and 'labor of love' and 'endurance of hope'. Thus, all three phrases have the agent 'you'. This second of the phrases is interpreted as was the first: the Thessalonians labored because of their love. Though Bruce says that Paul meant no substantial difference of meaning between κόπος 'labor' here and ἔργον 'work' in the preceding phrase, many commentators say that κόπος 'labor' stresses the cost or exertion involved (also GW, JBP, and TEV).

The object of 'love' is unexpressed. One interpretation is that the Thessalonians labored because of their love for the Lord (Lenski), which parallels the thought in the preceding phrase. Other commentators say the Thessalonians labored because they loved others (Best, Frame, Morris) or because they loved both others and the Lord (Marshall, Wanamaker). But in Paul's writings he speaks much less of men's love for God or Christ than of the love of God or Christ for men (Best, p. 70; Frame, p. 132). In this epistle especially (3:12, 4:9-10, 5:13), and elsewhere (see 2 Thess. 1:3), he speaks of love for fellow believers and others. Therefore the object of the Thessalonians' love is taken to be people. Like 'work' in the previous construction, 'labor' is qualified: 'in order to help people'. If in the receptor language the meaning is not clear, it may be necessary to supply more information: 'in order to help fellow believers and other people because you love them'.

The activities implied by κόπος 'labor' here may include some of the same spiritual ministries implied by ἔργον 'work' in the previous phrase. It may also include manual labor to support their ministry (Frame).

you endure *people persecuting you because you confidently expect* The Greek is τῆς ὑπομονῆς τῆς ἐλπίδος 'the steadfastness of the hope'. Like the two preceding genitive nouns, 'hope' can be interpreted as source (Best, Frame, Wanamaker, Marshall, Morris; NCV): 'your hope causes you to endure'. However, some take 'steadfastness' as modifying 'hope'. Bruce has "your patient hope"; TEV has "firm hope." But since the genitive of source makes good sense here and there is no compelling reason to understand this third genitive differently from the first two, the rendering in the display reflects such a genitive.

It is clear from 2:14 that the Thessalonians experienced severe opposition from their fellow citizens. Hiebert says the steadfastness mentioned here is endurance and constancy when confronted by obstacles, trials, and persecutions. The essence of the situation is expressed by 'people persecuting you'.

The word ἐλπίς in Scripture is 'hope' that is completely certain because it is based on what God has said he will do (Hiebert). It is rendered in the display 'confidently expect'.

that our(inc) Lord Jesus Christ *will return from heaven to rescue you* Lenski is one of very few who connect the objective genitive phrase τοῦ κυρίου ἡμῶν Ἰησοῦ Χριστοῦ 'of our Lord Jesus Christ' with all three preceding genitives: your faith, love, and hope are all directed toward our Lord Jesus. But because Paul so infrequently speaks of people loving Christ, it is better to connect 'of our Lord Jesus Christ' with only the contiguous genitive noun, 'hope'. The implied content of 'hope' is that Jesus 'will return from heaven to rescue you'. This is based on references to the fact that the Thessalonians are awaiting Jesus' return from heaven (1:10), that they have encountered persecution (1:6, 2:14, 3:3), that they are to put on the hope of salvation (ἐλπίδα σωτηρίας, 5:8), and that Jesus will return to rescue them both from God's wrath (1:10, 5:9) and from their persecutors (2 Thess. 1:6-7): "their hope was in Jesus, whom they believed would soon return from heaven to bring about their deliverance" (Wanamaker).

1:4 Verses 4-10 constitute an embedded paragraph. (See "Intent" for an explanation.)

Fellow believers The kinship term ἀδελφοί 'brothers' is used in a metaphorical or secondary sense by Paul to indicate affection for his readers as well as the group identity and unity he and they have as Christians. In the display it is rendered here and elsewhere as 'fellow believers'.

whom God loves The perfect tense of the participle ἠγαπημένοι 'loved' is appropriate in this context (and in 2 Thess. 2:13), in which Paul speaks of God's choosing the Thessalonians. God's love for the Thessalonians existed in the past when he chose them and continues in the present (Best, Hiebert). The English rendering 'whom God loves' does not bring out this nuance, but it seems better than 'whom God has loved', which fails to capture the idea of God's continuing love.

I(&S&T) also thank God because* we(exc) know The participle εἰδότες 'knowing' at the beginning of 1:4 is parallel to μνημονεύοντες 'remembering' in 1:3. It gives a second reason (*situation*) for the thanksgiving of Paul and his companions in 1:2. Some understand it to be the ultimate or primary reason (e.g., Best, Frame, Hendriksen). This seems correct, for it is the last participle in the series and the concept that it introduces is developed more fully in the rest of the paragraph.

God* chose you *to be people who trust in him The implied agent of the event of choosing in τὴν ἐκλογὴν ὑμῶν 'the choice of you' is God. Various suggestions have been made regarding the purpose of the choosing: to be God's people (Marshall, Wanamaker; CEV, NLT); to be like Christ (Bruce); or to receive salvation (Frame, Hendriksen, Hiebert, Marshall, Morris, Wanamaker). The last has merit because of its similarity to 2 Thess. 2:13. There, although he uses a different verb, αἱρέω 'to choose', Paul explicitly says that it was εἰς σωτηρίαν 'for salvation' that God chose the Thessalonians. In some languages it is difficult to translate the concept of spiritual salvation. The rendering in the display, 'God chose you to be people who trust in him', is a suggestion for translating this concept. An alternative rendering would be 'God chose you to be his people/children'.

1:5a since With the word ὅτι 'because' Paul introduces grounds (two *minor premises*) for the conclusion (*INFERENCE*) in 1:4 that he knows God chose the Thessalonians (Frame, Hiebert, Wanamaker, Morris). First, Paul knows this because spiritual power was present in the messengers' presentation of God's word to the Thessalonians (v. 5). Second, he knows this because of the extraordinary response and witness of the Thessalonians (vv. 6–10).

***when* we(exc) told the gospel to you** The phrase τὸ εὐαγγέλιον ἡμῶν 'the gospel of us' is interpreted by most as 'the gospel that we (Paul and companions) preach/preached'. But because the collocation of 'our gospel' with ἐγενήθη εἰς ὑμᾶς 'came to you' is unnatural in many languages, it is here rendered 'we(exc) told the gospel to you'.

The Greek for 5a–c is one clause. Because of the complex functions of that clause some versions (CEV, JB, REB) describe the event of proclaiming the gospel in an initial circumstance clause (using 'when') and the manner in which Paul and his companions preached in a subsequent clause or clauses. Because manner is emphasized in v. 5 (Frame, Wanamaker), it does indeed seem appropriate to background the event of proclaiming the gospel by considering the relation of 5a to 5b–c to be circumstance-nucleus.

1:5b–c we(exc) did not speak only words. More than that [1:5b], *we(exc) spoke* **powerfully/effectively** When Paul says τὸ εὐαγγέλιον ἡμῶν οὐκ ἐγενήθη εἰς ὑμᾶς ἐν λόγῳ μόνον ἀλλὰ καὶ ἐν δυνάμει 'our gospel did not come to you in word only but also in power', he is saying that the preaching consisted of both the words spoken and the power manifested to the Thessalonians (Wanamaker). The construction οὐκ ... μόνον ἀλλὰ καί 'not ... only but also' is a conjoining relation in which the second proposition is emphasized as something more than expected. Thus 5c has marked prominence. For that reason the second NUCLEUS label is in uppercase letters, but not the first. The phrase ἐν δυνάμει 'in power' indicates manner, hence 'powerfully/effectively'.

Paul's ministry, not the response of the Thessalonians, is the primary focus of 5a–c. This is supported by the fact that the grounds proposition 5d refers to the manner in which he and his companions ministered when they were in Thessalonica. Also, v. 6 has the fronted pronoun 'you', which indicates that the subject matter changes to the Thessalonians and their response to the message.

An issue here is whether Paul *spoke* powerfully or *acted* powerfully. Marshall and Wanamaker see the phrase 'in power' as a possible reference to miracles, but this view is rejected by Best and Frame. There is nothing specifically in the context or in Paul's extended discussion of his ministry in 2:1–12 to indicate that he means miracles here. In fact, Paul's use of πληροφορίᾳ πολλῇ 'much assurance' in the immediate context accords better with an inner energizing by the Spirit.

When Paul says that the proclaimers spoke powerfully, he does not mean that they spoke in a loud voice or even that they spoke eloquently, but rather that they were effective in persuading their audience. Hiebert says, "As they spoke the preachers were keenly conscious of the presence of this supernatural power behind their words, producing spiritual persuasiveness and penetrating conviction."

by means of the Holy Spirit's enabling us(exc), and we(exc) were strongly assured by him The prepositional phrase 'in power' is followed by another, or two others, depending on how one evaluates the manuscript evidence for καὶ ἐν πνεύματι ἁγίῳ καὶ [ἐν] πληροφορίᾳ πολλῇ 'and in Holy Spirit and in much assurance'. The preposition 'in' that precedes 'much assurance' in MJTGNT is in brackets in UBSGNT, indicating that it is not present in some older manuscripts. If the preposition was absent in the original, the words then constitute one phrase, 'in the Holy Spirit and much assurance'. This strengthens the position of those commentators and versions that say the Holy Spirit produces the full assurance (Morris, Best, Bruce, Frame; CEV, DGN, EHP, JBP, NLT).

Commentators also relate the phrase 'in the Holy Spirit' to the phrase that precedes it, 'in power'. Best views the phrase as semantically coordinate with 'in power': God empowered the gospel message and the Holy Spirit made the speech wise and effective. This distinction between the activity of God and of the Spirit seems contrived, however. More preferable is the interpretation that 'Holy Spirit' is mentioned after 'power' here because he is its source (Bruce, Marshall, Morris, Wanamaker; CEV, REB). This understanding is compatible with one of the potential functions of ἐν 'in' phrases, namely, means: 'we spoke powerfully/effectively by means of the Holy Spirit's enabling us'.

It seems best to relate the second phrase, 'in the Holy Spirit', both to the preceding phrase, 'in power', and to the phrase that follows, 'in strong assurance'. This is the view of Bruce, Frame, Hiebert, Morris, CEV, and JBP.

The term πληροφορία has been translated 'conviction, assurance, certainty'. (Another meaning of the word, 'fullness', is rejected by commentators as inappropriate for this context.) Commentators disagree as to whether the assurance is produced in the proclaimers of the message (Best, Frame, Marshall, Morris, Wanamaker) or in the hearers (Bruce). The view of the majority seems preferable because the focus in 5a–c is on the ministry of Paul and his companions.

that God was powerfully working through the gospel which we(exc) told Commentators variously define the content of 'conviction': that the gospel was true, that it was from God, or that God was using the gospel as they preached it. Though any of the three would be acceptable, the third is most appropriate in this context. Assurance that God was working through the gospel would contribute to Paul's conviction that God had chosen the Thessalonians.

1:5d *You can verify this* [1:5c] since you know how I(&S&T) spoke and conducted myself/ourselves With the words καθὼς οἴδατε 'as you know' Paul introduces the grounds for statements in v. 5 about his ministry (Frame, Wanamaker): the Thessalonians knew that what Paul just said was true because they saw how he and his companions conducted themselves. The phrase οἷοι ἐγενήθημεν [ἐν] ὑμῖν 'what kind we were among you' speaks primarily of the manner of ministry that Paul has just mentioned but also of his total life-style (Bruce, Hiebert).

in order that we(exc) might help you Paul and his companions taught and lived for the benefit of the Thessalonians: δι' ὑμᾶς 'for the sake of you'. They didn't preach for their own selfish interests (Frame, Hiebert). The benefit could have been the salvation of the Thessalonians (Marshall) or the messengers' example, consistent with their message, an example that the Thessalonians could follow (Bruce, Morris, Wanamaker). It is rendered here with a general expression, not specifying the benefit.

1:6a And *I(&S&T) know that God chose you since* The conjunction καί 'and' at the beginning of v. 6 has a dual function. It primarily indicates that 6–10 is a conjoined grounds (second MINOR PREMISE) for knowing that God chose the Thessalonians (Best, Frame, Morris, Wanamaker). It also indicates, with the fronted pronoun 'you', that the subject matter changes to the Thessalonians and their response to the ministry of Paul and his companions just mentioned in v. 5 (Best, Wanamaker). NAB, REB, and TNT translate this change of focus as "you, in turn."

you reacted in the same way that *you know we(exc) did and the Lord Jesus Christ did when people persecuted us(exc)* The Greek is ὑμεῖς μιμηταὶ ἡμῶν ἐγενήθητε καὶ τοῦ κυρίου 'you became imitators of us and of the Lord'. Propositional cluster 6a–c is in a reason-result relation with v. 7 (see the note there). Because of the finite verb ἐγενήθητε 'you became' and the forefronting of the comment μιμηταὶ ἡμῶν 'imitators of us', the 6a proposition has marked prominence. Therefore its label, REASON, is in uppercase letters in the display, as is the label RESULT for v. 7.

Most commentators agree that the Thessalonians imitated the way Paul and Jesus responded to persecution. They had heard of Jesus' suffering and had seen how Paul reacted to persecution. However, this was probably not a conscious imitation. Thus the phrase 'you reacted in the same way' is used in the display.

1:6b *Specifically, although* **people persecuted you greatly** *because* **you believed the gospel** *which we(exc) taught* The participial phrase δεξάμενοι τὸν λόγον ἐν θλίψει πολλῇ 'having received the word in much affliction' has been understood in one of two ways. It either specifies *in what way* the Thessalonians became imitators ('you became imitators by joyfully receiving the gospel in spite of tribulation', following Best, Frame, Marshall, Morris); or it specifies the *time* when they became imitators ('you became imitators when/after you joyfully received the gospel in spite of tribulation', following Bruce, Wanamaker). Just as the messengers experienced the Holy Spirit's power as they delivered the gospel message (1:5a-c), so the Thessalonians experienced the Holy Spirit's joy in spite of persecution (1:6b-c). This corresponds to the joy of Paul and Jesus despite persecution and thus is the way they were imitators. Therefore the former interpretation is preferable, taking 6a and 6b-c to be in a generic-specific relation.

Implicit in the seemingly mutually exclusive concepts of persecution and joy is the concession-contraexpectation relation, which versions indicate by "in spite of" (NIV) in the concession proposition or by "but" (CEV, NCV) or "yet" (REB) in the contraexpectation.

The word δέχομαι 'to receive' can also mean 'to welcome'. Here τὸν λόγον 'the word' refers to the gospel message that Paul preached (Frame, Hiebert). To receive or welcome a message is figurative; the nonfigurative meaning is to believe and appropriate it.

The phrase ἐν θλίψει πολλῇ 'in much affliction' refers to opposition and persecution from non-Christians aroused by the Thessalonians' faith in Christ (Bruce). The noun phrase 'much affliction' represents an event and agent and is here rendered 'people persecuted you greatly'.

1:6c you were joyful because the Holy Spirit caused you to be joyful The phrase μετὰ χαρᾶς πνεύματος ἁγίου 'with joy of (the) Holy Spirit' indicates the manner with which the Thessalonians endured persecution: they were joyful. The genitive 'of the Holy Spirit' indicates that he was the source of their joy.

1:7 As a result The conjunction ὥστε 'so that' introduces the result of the Thessalonian believers' response mentioned in v. 6.

all the people who trust *in God* **and who live in Macedonia and Achaia** *provinces* **have seen or heard how firmly you trusted in God when people persecuted you, and so they know that they should firmly trust in God as you do** The Greek is ὥστε γενέσθαι ὑμᾶς τύπον πᾶσιν τοῖς πιστεύουσιν ἐν τῇ Μακεδονίᾳ καὶ ἐν τῇ Ἀχαΐᾳ 'so that you became an example to all the (ones) believing in Macedonia and in Achaia'. The Thessalonians were an 'example' or 'model' for other believers in that their joyful suffering for the gospel they believed (Best, Bruce, Hiebert, Frame, Marshall) and their fearless witness to the gospel (Bruce) encouraged other believers to do the same. As Marshall says, "The way in which the Thessalonian Christians had joyfully received the message despite the opposition which they faced would thus have been both an incentive to these other Christians and also a pattern for them to follow." MJTGNT has the plural form, τύπους 'examples'. If the singular form 'example' (UBSGNT) is accepted, it could indicate that it was the Thessalonian group of believers as a whole that modeled behavior to other believers (Morris).

The word πᾶσιν 'all' in the phrase 'to all the (ones) believing' could be hyperbole. However, considering the few places we know of in the provinces of Macedonia (Philippi, Thessalonica, Berea) and Achaia (Athens, Corinth) where there were probably congregations, and a few possible other ones, it is not impossible that believers in all of them would have heard of the persevering faith of the Thessalonians.

The object of the faith of believers living in Macedonia and Achaia as well as of the Thessalonians themselves is most likely 'God' (implicit), because Paul states explicitly in 8b that the Thessalonians trust in him.

1:8a I(&S&T) know this [1:7] since Here γάρ 'for' introduces the grounds for Paul's statement that the Thessalonians have become an example.

people have watched you and heard you tell the message *that originates from* **the Lord** *God,* **and then they have proclaimed the message to people who live throughout Macedonia and Achaia** *provinces* The Greek is ἀφ' ὑμῶν γὰρ ἐξήχηται ὁ λόγος τοῦ κυρίου οὐ μόνον ἐν τῇ Μακεδονίᾳ καὶ [ἐν τῇ] 'Αχαΐᾳ 'for from you has been sounded forth the word of the Lord not only in Macedonia and in Achaia'. The verb ἐξηχέω means "*cause to resound* or *be heard*" (BAGD, p. 276). Here it indicates a sound that spreads out from a central point in all directions (Best, Marshall, Wanamaker). The sound spreading from Thessalonica is the gospel message and story of the Thessalonians' faith. The dissemination of this news was more easily accomplished because Thessalonica was on a major trade route, the Egnatian Way. Frame points out that it is ἀφ' ὑμῶν 'from you (Thessalonians)' not ὑφ' ὑμῶν 'by you' that the news spread; other people, whether Christians or non-Christians, primarily spread the word. This interpretation is supported by the passive voice of the verb, 'has been sounded forth'. The perfect tense indicates that it was a continuing process. Though fairly detailed propositions are needed to represent the meaning of the verb, the translator should recognize that "this verse is concerned not with the method by which the news of the gospel and of the faith of the readers is brought everywhere, . . . but with the fact that the word of the Lord and their faith have actually spread" (Frame).

The phrase ὁ λόγος τοῦ κυρίου 'the word of the Lord' is used by Paul only here and in 2 Thess. 3:1, but it is used often in the OT. The majority of commentators consulted understand its use in 1:8 to be a subjective genitive or genitive of source: the Lord sends or inspires the message. The TEV, however, renders it as an objective genitive: the message is about the Lord. Those commentators who comment on the term 'Lord' understand it to refer to Jesus, because this is Paul's customary usage. However, in the OT 'Lord' referred to God, and when used in this phrase in the OT it meant that God inspired the message. Paul, as a scholar of the OT, would have had this understanding of the phrase. In 2:13 Paul refers to his message explicitly as the λόγον τοῦ θεοῦ 'word of God' and says that the Thessalonians received it as the word from God, not from men. Thus from the context and Paul's understanding of the OT phrase, it seems preferable to understand 'the word of the Lord' in 1:8 as referring to 'the message that originates from the Lord God'. The content of the message is most likely the gospel. If 'Lord' refers to Christ, as the majority of commentators consulted understand it, the rendering of the TEV seems preferable, "the message about the Lord Jesus."

In MJTGNT the words ἐν τῇ 'in the' occur before 'Achaia'. The UBSGNT (which uses brackets) and commentators consider the occurrence uncertain. Without the words 'in the' Macedonia and Achaia could be viewed as a unity rather than as distinct provinces. This textual difference does not affect the rendering in the display.

1:8b And not only that [1:8a], they told *people who live* in many faraway places that you trust in God The construction οὐ μόνον . . . ἀλλά 'not only . . . but' in 8a–b indicates a conjoining relationship in which the second proposition has marked prominence because more happened than might be expected: word of the Thessalonians' faith had spread farther than could be imagined.

The idea in ἀλλ' ἐν παντὶ τόπῳ ἡ πίστις ὑμῶν ἡ πρὸς τὸν θεὸν ἐξελήλυθεν 'but in every place your faith, the (faith) toward God, has gone out' is similar to 'has been sounded forth the word of the Lord' in 8a. Thus it is rendered as an additional part of what people reported: 'they told people that you trust in God'. Now the focus is on reports about the Thessalonians' faith rather than about the message itself.

The phrase 'in every place' is hyperbole. Because of the context, which speaks of the spread of the news beyond Greece, the hyperbole probably includes extent of distance as well as number of places.

1:8c As a result, I(&S&T) do not need to tell people *that you trust in God* The conjunction ὥστε 'so that' indicates the result of the dissemination of news about the Thessalonians: Paul and his companions need not say anything. The general phrase λαλεῖν τι 'to say anything' has been taken variously to mean anything about the Thessalonians generally (Best, Wanamaker); about Paul's mission to Thessalonica (Hiebert, Morris); or about their faith (Bruce, Marshall; CEV, NCV, NIV, NLT, REB). This last view has been used in the display because the Thessalonians' conversion is prominent in the next verse.

1:9a because Here γάρ 'for' introduces the reason (Best, Marshall, Wanamaker) for Paul's statement in 8c: he didn't need to say anything because those other people were already reporting what had taken place in Thessalonica.

1:9b concerning how we(exc) spoke and conducted ourselves when we(exc) were with you These people reported about two things: they reported about Paul's ministry in Thessalonica (ὁποίαν εἴσοδον ἔσχομεν πρὸς ὑμᾶς 'what sort of entrance/reception we had to you') here in 9b and about the Thessalonians' response in 9c. The term εἴσοδος literally means "(*a way of*) *entering, entrance, access*" (BAGD p. 233.1). Figuratively it can mean "find entrance (=welcome) w. someone . . . but [it] can also mean visit" (ibid.). The term is used here and again in 2:1. In 2:1 most versions translate it "visit" (NCV, NIV, NJB, NLT, REB, RSV, TEV, TNT); CEV has "our time with you." But in 1:9 it is translated with the idea of welcoming, receiving, or accepting (CEV, GW, NAB, NCV, NIV, NLT, RSV, TEV) more often than "visit" (REB, TNT; see also NJB). However (following Best, Frame, Hiebert, Marshall, Morris), the rendering in the display is based on the meaning 'visit' for two reasons. First, in v. 9 the phrase περὶ ἡμῶν 'concerning us (they report)' is fronted for emphasis, and the report is about 'what sort of entrance we had to you', not "what kind of reception you gave us," as the NIV has it. The emphasis on and repetition of first person plural pronouns indicate that people first reported about the ministry of the messengers themselves. (Some mss. have περὶ ὑμῶν 'concerning you' instead of περὶ ἡμῶν 'concerning us', but UBSGNT, MJTGNT, and commentators reject this.) Another reason for preferring the meaning 'visit' is that Paul's pattern in this division of the letter is to speak first of the ministry of the messengers (1:5, 1:9a; 2:1–12) and then of the response of the Thessalonians (1:6, 1:9b; 2:13–14).

1:9c And *they report* that you stopped worshiping things that you considered gods and began to worship God As pointed out in the previous note, the second thing these people told about was the Thessalonians' response to the message. The word πῶς 'how' does not speak here of manner but of the content of what was reported, namely that the Thessalonians turned to God (Best, Frame). The verb ἐπιστρέφω 'to turn' is used figuratively for their conversion from worshiping idols, symbolizing the totality of their religious experience before their conversion (Wanamaker), to worshiping the real God. In the LXX the word εἴδωλον 'idol' (which Paul uses here) referred not only to images but also to the gods they represented (Marshall).

1:9d *As a result*, you serve The infinitive δουλεύειν 'to be a slave to' is rendered 'serve' in the display. It could be taken as either the purpose for turning to God or the result of turning to God. This infinitive is joined to the infinitive ἀναμένειν 'to wait for' in v. 10 by καί 'and'. The infinitive in v. 10 is more appropriately result (CEV, EHP, JBP, NLT, TNT): you turned to God and as a result you wait for His Son from heaven. And as there is no indication in the text that the two infinitives have a different relation to the 9c proposition, both are interpreted as result (following Marshall, EHP, JB, NCV, NJB).

While the result proposition of a result-reason relation is usually more prominent, in 9c–10a the reason occurs first and has natural prominence. This is signaled by a nonsubordinate verb, 'you turned', in the 9c reason and subordinate infinitives, 'to serve' and 'to wait', in the 9d and 10a result propositions. Thus in the display the labels REASON and RESULT are all in uppercase letters.

The infinitive δουλεύειν 'to be a slave to' is understood as a live metaphor by Morris: as a slave obeys and serves his master, so you obey and serve God. However, Paul uses this term over and over in contexts such as this where the comparison with a slave is not pertinent. Thus it is most likely a dead metaphor.

the God who is alive and who is the real God One aspect of the nature of the God they serve is indicated by the participle ζῶντι 'living'. "'Living' means not only alive but active, as we see from Acts 14:15. It contrasts sharply with dead idols, 'gods' who can do nothing (Pss. 96:5; 115:4–7)" (Morris). Another aspect of the nature of God is indicated by the adjective ἀληθινός 'true', which means that God is the real God in contrast to false gods (Bruce). To better capture the meaning of 'living and true God' an alternative translation to that in the display might be 'you serve the God who is alive and acts powerfully and who is the real God'.

1:10a and you wait expectantly The infinitive ἀναμένειν 'to await' introduces the second result of the Thessalonians' turning to God: they look forward to Jesus' return to earth. REB has "to wait expectantly," which appropriately expresses the positive aspect and hope of this waiting.

for his Son Translators should realize that the noun υἱός 'son' here is used as a live metaphor. While a specific ground of comparison may be difficult to decide, it most likely includes the idea that as a son Jesus Christ has all his father's divine attributes. Since in the NT 'Son of God' is a title referring to the Messiah, commentators see allusions in the term 'Son' here to Jesus as the Messiah (Frame, Wanamaker). The expression 'his Son' indicates the close relation between God, in whom the Thessalonians were trusting, and Jesus Christ as God's agent for bringing about eschatological salvation (Wanamaker).

***to return to earth* from heaven** In his letters Paul uses both the singular form of οὐρανός 'heaven' (4:16, 2 Thess. 1:7) and the plural form, as here. The plural form may reflect Jewish thought (i.e., it may be a Hebraism), in which heaven was divided into several levels (Wanamaker). There is no difference of meaning, however, between Paul's use of the singular or plural. Here the word specifically refers to the place to which Jesus ascended after his resurrection and from which he will return to earth.

1:10b God raised his Son to live again after he died The Greek is ὃν ἤγειρεν ἐκ [τῶν] νεκρῶν 'whom he raised from the dead'. This description, expressed as a relative clause, is appropriate to the context. Paul perhaps wanted to identify the one who was to come from heaven as the one whom God raised from the dead (Wanamaker). Also, Jesus' resurrection by God gives confidence that he is now with God and that God will bring him back to earth (Marshall). By using brackets UBSGNT indicates that the inclusion of the article τῶν (which is in MJTGNT) is questionable. Paul most often uses the phrase without the article (Frame), but its inclusion or exclusion does not affect the meaning.

1:10c *His Son is* **Jesus, who** *will* **rescue** *all of* **us(inc)** *who trust in God* **from** *God's punishing us(inc)* **when** *God* **punishes people** *who do not trust in him* The relative clause in 10b interrupts the flow of thought regarding the future return of God's Son. Paul returns to this topic now by stating the name 'Jesus'. This may be a syntactical device enabling Paul to continue his description of Jesus and at the same time mark him as prominent; the use of a pronoun would not indicate as much prominence. Best says the Thessalonians are waiting for full deliverance, which might indicate that this proposition is the purpose for 10a: you wait for his Son from heaven in order to deliver us. However, as it is deliverance from punishment that is in view here rather than salvation in its more positive aspects, it seems best to take this proposition as a second descriptive comment on 'his Son' in 10a.

The participle in the attributive phrase τὸν ῥυόμενον ἡμᾶς 'the (one) rescuing us' is present tense. Some understand this as connoting Jesus' timeless characteristic as savior/deliverer (Hiebert; REB). Others take it as a process of saving that has already begun and will later be completed (Best). However, the idea of future deliverance is given prominence by the mention of the return of Christ earlier in the verse. The very next phrase, ἐκ τῆς ὀργῆς τῆς ἐρχομένης 'from the coming wrath' reinforces this idea: 'coming' in itself indicates a future occurrence. Thus the proposition in the display uses the future tense, 'who will rescue'. The object of the deliverance, ἡμᾶς 'us', includes the messengers and the readers of the letter, but it also includes all believers.

In Colossians 3:6 there is a phrase similar to 'the coming wrath' that Paul uses here, namely, 'God's wrath is coming'. J. Callow (1983:176) interprets 'wrath' in Colossians 3:6 as a metonymy for punishment, the cause being substituted for the effect. "It has been observed that when Paul uses the word ['wrath'] it generally means not an emotion felt by God but the unpleasant measures which are taken against sinners" (Marshall). Commentators understand the phrase to refer to the future day of judgment. Other texts (Rom. 1:18, Col. 3:6) make explicit what is implicit here: it is God who will punish people on that day.

If the proposal in the note on 9d is correct (that 'living God' means both 'alive' and 'powerfully active'), Paul may here be giving an illustration in reference to God's Son. He also is alive, raised to life by God, and he acts powerfully in rescuing believers from the coming judgment of God.

BOUNDARIES AND COHERENCE

The initial boundary of 1:2–10 was discussed under 1:1 ("Boundaries"). As to the terminal boundary, there are several factors indicating the beginning of a new unit at 2:1: (1) The forefronted emphatic pronoun αὐτοί 'you yourselves' in 2:1 contrasts with the forefronted αὐτοί 'they themselves' in 1:9 and indicates discontinuity in the discourse. (2) A new orienter, οἴδατε 'you know', occurs. (3) The vocative, ἀδελφοί 'brothers', is present. (4) The Greek that underlies proposition 1:9b, ὁποίαν εἴσοδον ἔσχομεν πρὸς ὑμᾶς 'what sort of entrance/reception we had to you', is restated in slightly different words in 2:1: τὴν εἴσοδον ἡμῶν τὴν πρὸς ὑμᾶς 'our entrance/coming to you (has not been in vain)'. This repetition creates a type of tail-head linkage.

In the Greek 1:2–10 consists of one sentence. Since it is so long, some versions and commentators have divided it in two, but different divisions have been suggested. Some divide between

1:3 and 1:4; some, between 1:4 and 1:5; and some, between 1:5 and 1:6. There is evidence both for and against each of these.

Hendriksen, NBV, NCV, NIV, NJB, and NLT probably place a boundary between 1:3 and 1:4 for three reasons: (1) A vocative, ἀδελφοὶ ἠγαπημένοι ὑπὸ θεοῦ 'brothers loved by God', occurs in v. 4; and a vocative often indicates a boundary in 1 Thessalonians (see 2:1, 17; 4:1, 13; 5:1, 12), though not always (cf. 2:9; 3:7). (2) They consider vv. 4–10 an embedded paragraph with a different intent (to affect ideas) than the encompassing paragraph 1:2–10 (to affect emotions). (3) The participles μνημονεύοντες 'remembering' in v. 3 and εἰδότες 'knowing' in v. 4 are in parallel subordinate relationships to the main verb of the unit, εὐχαριστοῦμεν 'we thank', in v. 2. Thematically, the second of these participles is more prominent in that the main ideas of the paragraph and the epistle develop from it. However, that second participle occurs first in its phrase, indicating continuity of the discourse between vv. 3 and 4. Thus, despite the presence of the vocative, the change of intent and the prominence of the second participle, a boundary between these verses is probably not justified.

Morris places a boundary between 1:4 and 1:5, based perhaps on the discontinuity of the discourse indicated by the forefronting of a new topic, τὸ εὐαγγέλιον ἡμῶν 'our gospel', in 1:5. However, v. 5 is the grounds of v. 4, with ὅτι 'because' at the beginning of v. 5; and this grammatical coherence seems to override the discontinuity factor and militate against a boundary here.

Bruce, DGN, GW, and REB place a boundary between 1:5 and 1:6 based perhaps on the discontinuity of the discourse at v. 6 where a new referent, ὑμεῖς 'you', is forefronted. Also, Paul's statement at the end of v. 5, 'you know how we spoke and conducted ourselves when we were with you', may possibly be viewed as parenthetical and indicative of discontinuity. Third, Paul leaves the topic of his ministry conduct at this point to resume it in the next unit, 2:1–12. However, the conjunction καί 'and' in v. 6 conjoins the very closely related grounds (v. 5 and vv. 6–10) of the v. 4 conclusion. Paul says he knows that God chose the Thessalonians (v. 4) since the Holy Spirit empowered the proclamation of the gospel (v. 5) *and* since in spite of persecution, the Thessalonians responded with joy (v. 6).

A boundary between 1:5 and 1:6 has better support than one between 1:3 and 1:4 or between 1:4 and 1:5. Yet the relational coherence established by parallel participles and by conjunctions that tie the elements of Paul's thought closely together support the majority view that 1:2–10 is a unit.

PROMINENCE AND THEME

There are two *situations* in the 1:2–10 unit that cause Paul to be thankful to God. They are introduced by participles in 1:3 and 1:4. The second of these (vv. 4–10) begins with a vocative, and its development continues through the end of the unit. Thus it is the more prominent of the two *situations* and is labeled in uppercase letters in the display. However, as Paul's purpose is to affect the emotions of the Thessalonians through his praise of them, the first *situation* (v. 3) is also included in the theme. This is summarized in more generic terms ("the way you live as believers") than the second SITUATION because the first is the less prominent of the two.

In the embedded paragraph (1:4–10), the *INFERENCE* (v. 4) is prominent. So, too, is the second *MINOR PREMISE* (vv. 6–10), which is developed more fully than the first (v. 5). That makes the first less prominent. However, because the mention of the ministry of the messengers in Thessalonica in 1:5a–d (and again in 1:9b) is setting the stage for a fuller discussion in 2:1–12, the first *minor premise* is also included in the theme ("the Holy Spirit enabled us to powerfully tell you the gospel").

In the second *MINOR PREMISE* both the REASON (v. 6) and the RESULT (v. 7) are prominent (see the note on 6a). Thus parts of both propositions are also included in the 1:2–10 theme.

SECTION CONSTITUENT 2:1-12
(Descriptive Paragraph: Rapport Basis₂ of 1:2-16)

THEME: You and God know it is true that I behaved in a very virtuous, upright, and irreproachable manner toward you. You know also that I continually exhorted, encouraged, and urged that you behave in the way that God's people should.

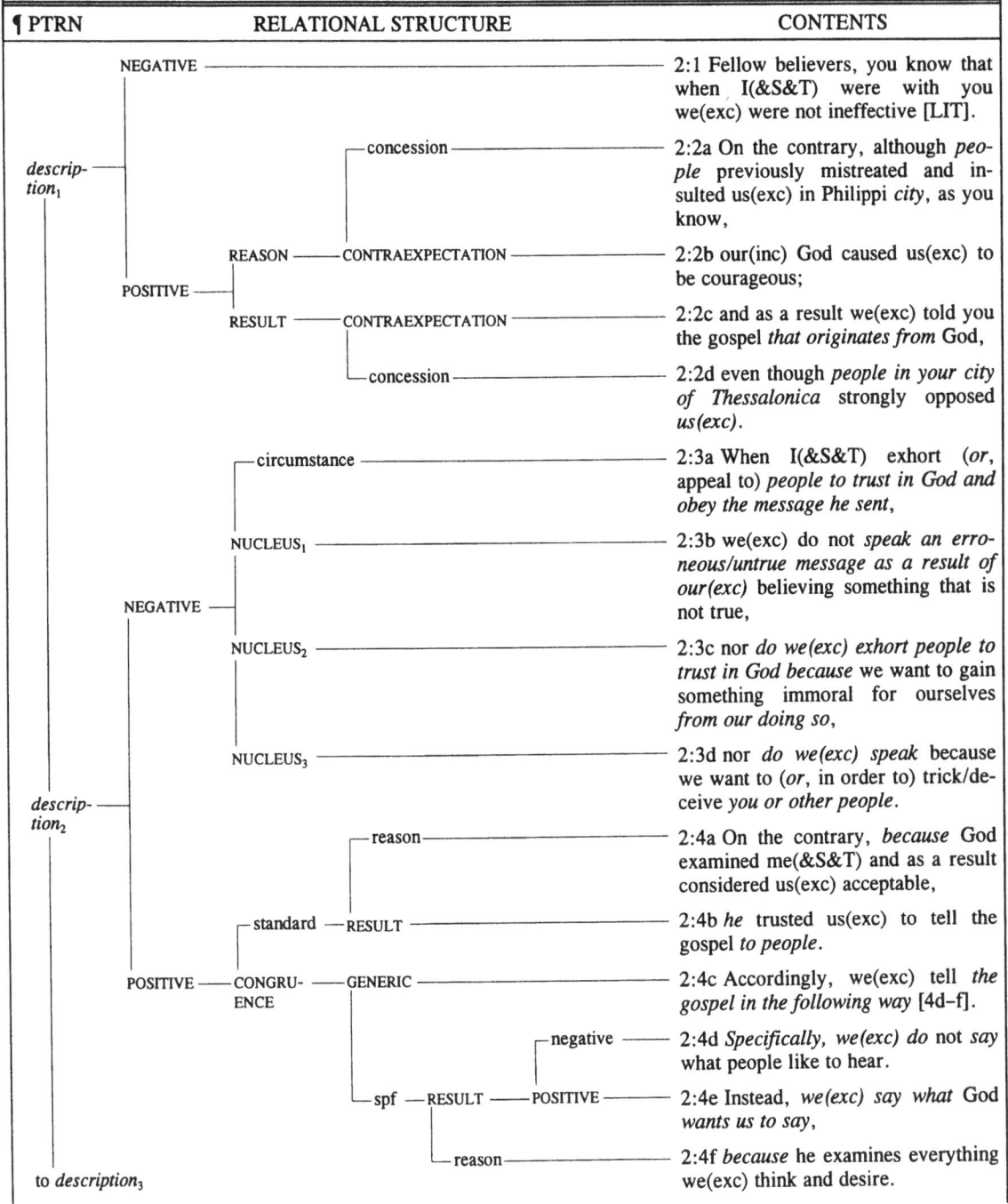

SECTION CONSTITUENT 2:1–12

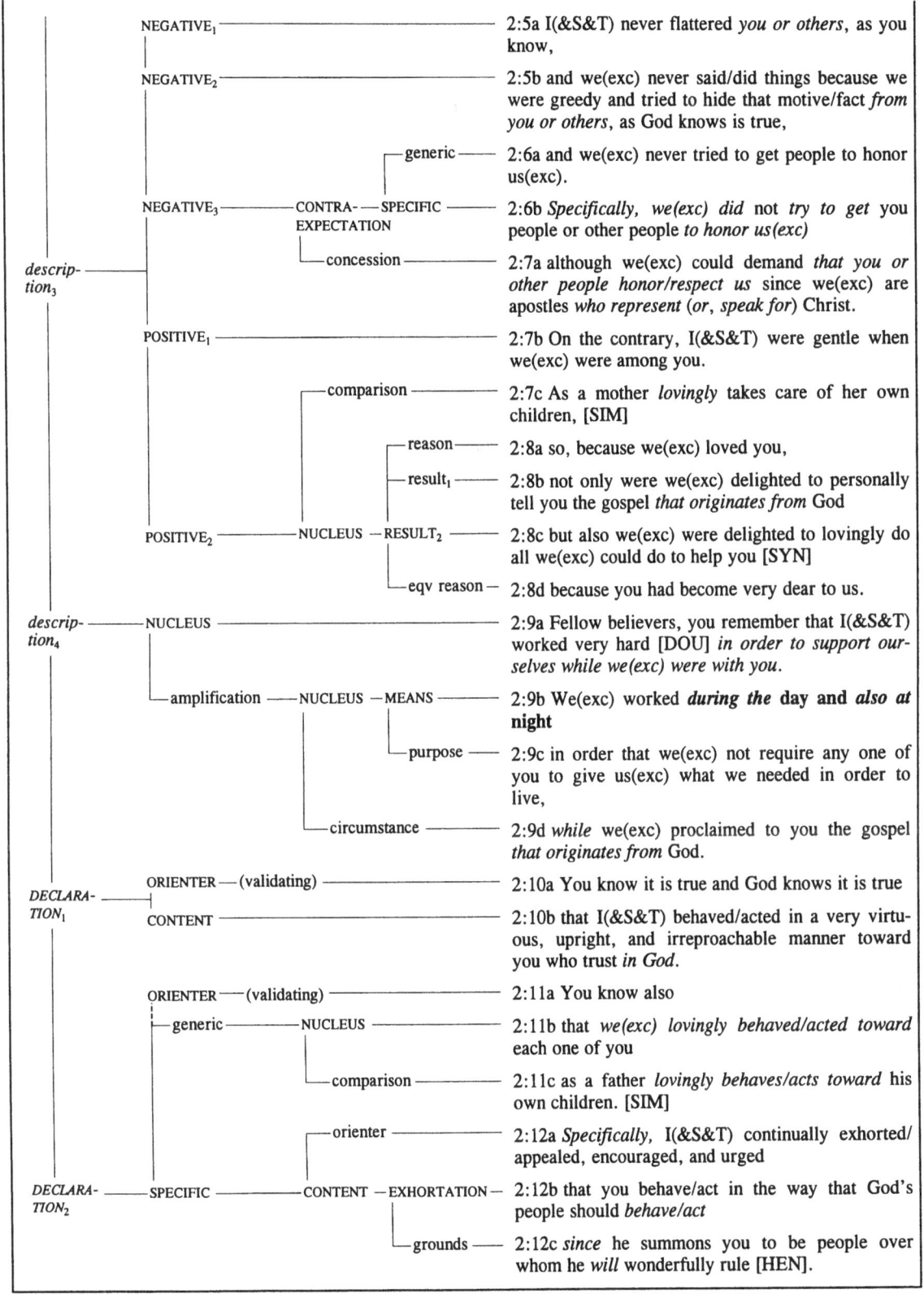

INTENT AND PARAGRAPH PATTERN

In the 2:1-12 paragraph Paul's primary intent is to affect the emotions of the Thessalonians and thus continue to build rapport. In the preceding paragraph, 1:2-10, Paul's words οἴδατε οἷοι ἐγενήθημεν [ἐν] ὑμῖν δι' ὑμᾶς 'you know what kind we were among you for the sake of you' in 1:5d function as a general preview for the specific statements that Paul makes here. Now he wants his readers to recognize that he ministered in order to benefit them, not himself, because he cares deeply for them. He involves them by the repetition of personal references like 'you know'. He uses a series of emotive denials and affirmations. He also uses two similes with emotional images to describe his concern for the Thessalonians: a mother's care for her children (vv. 7-8) and a father's training of his children (vv. 11-12). The personal references, emotive statements and similes, and lack of appeals signal that the genre is emotive, of the descriptive type because Paul sequentially builds toward a climax, the summary DECLARATIONS in vv. 10-12.

The 2:1-12 paragraph, which is the first peak unit of 1:2-3:13 (see "Intent" under 1:2-2:16), is composed of six conjoined propositional clusters: 1-2d, 3a-4f, 5a-8d, 9a-d, 10a-b, and 11a-12c. By means of these Paul advances his goal of convincing the Thessalonians of his integrity and love for them. The structure and intent signal a paragraph pattern subtype of volitionality. The constituents of the volitionality subtype of a descriptive paragraph are labeled *description* and *DECLARATION*.

In the context of the letter as a whole Paul most likely has a secondary intent in this paragraph, that is, to prepare for 4:1-5:24, in which he seeks to affect the behavior of his addressees. "In ancient rhetoric and epistolography role models were given in order to provide the audience with examples of moral behavior," says Wanamaker (p. 91). The antithetical approach used by Paul here was often used for moral examples in the Greco-Roman world (ibid.). Paul mentions specific aspects of the conduct of his and his co-workers' ministry as a way of exhorting his readers to follow his example and teachings. His purpose in writing the letter is the same as his purpose while in Thessalonica; as he says at the climax of this unit, we 'urged that you behave in the way that God's people should behave' (2:12).

NOTES

2:1 The conjunction γάρ 'for' in 2:1 (also in 2:3a, 5a, and 9a) signals that Paul is going to discuss further something he has previously mentioned. There is clear reference to 1:9 through repetition of the words εἴσοδον πρὸς ὑμᾶς 'entrance/coming to you'. "It may be that by picking up these words 2:1 is intended to offer an explanation concerning the type of visit that Paul had with his readers. To a certain extent this is true, but the real emphasis in 2:2-12 is on the nature of Paul's ministry in Thessalonica" (Wanamaker). For that reason commentators (Best, Bruce, Frame, Hiebert, Marshall, Wanamaker) also see reference in 2:1-12 to 1:5, where Paul declares that the Thessalonians know the type of persons he and his companions were and how they ministered. Because the propositions in the previous chapter upon which this and the following propositional clusters most likely expound are not contiguous, γάρ 'for' in this verse is not rendered in the display. Neither is it translated in most versions, with the exception of KJV, NASV, NBV, and RSV.

you know that when I(&S&T) were with you The pronoun αὐτοί 'you' is fronted. The same form is also fronted in 1:9, but there it functions as third person plural. Its discourse function in 2:1 is to differentiate the Thessalonian readers, who know of Paul's ministry by firsthand experience, from the people mentioned in 1:9 whose reports of that ministry and the conversions in Thessalonica were secondhand. Many versions translate αὐτοί here as 'you yourself' to express the emphasis.

The words τὴν εἴσοδον ἡμῶν τὴν πρὸς ὑμᾶς 'our entrance/reception the (one) to you' represent an event, agent, and undergoers and are thus rendered as a circumstantial clause, 'when I(&S&T) were with you'. (See the note on 1:9b for a discussion of εἴσοδος 'entrance/reception'.) The context of 2:1-9 indicates that Paul is not writing here of the reception of the message or merely of his initial time in Thessalonica but of the conduct of his ministry during his total time there.

we(exc) were not ineffective The phrase ὅτι οὐ κενὴ γέγονεν 'that it (our visit) has been not empty' is a litotes, in which the affirmative idea of effectiveness of ministry is expressed by the negation of its antonym. The figure is retained in the display to maintain the point of contrast with 2:2, which begins with ἀλλά 'but'. The term κενός literally means "*empty*" (BAGD, p. 427.1). Its figurative use in this passage has been understood to mean lack of ministry results (BAGD, p. 427.2aβ; Best; Wanamaker; JB, REB), lack of content and power (Frame, Hiebert), or lack of character or earnestness (Marshall, Morris). The first of these three interpretations fits in the immediate context of 2:1-2 and is the one used in the display. Paul says that despite persecution he accomplished his goal of proclaiming the gospel (v. 2); he was effective in that he proclaimed the gospel in difficult circumstances. In the second interpretation of lack of content and power the words 'were not empty' in 2:1 are taken as semantically parallel to 1:5b-c, 'we did not speak only words but we spoke powerfully'; here in 2:2 Paul writes of telling with God's enabling the gospel which God sent. This interpretation also fits the context of 2:1-2; it can be rendered 'we did not speak an ordinary message in an ordinary way'. The third interpretation of not being without character or earnestness seems to fit the larger context of 2:1-9 even better than the first or second, because Paul speaks not only of the courage of the preachers (2:2) but also of their integrity (2:3-7) and affection (2:8). The rendering according to this interpretation would be 'we were not insincere'. But this was not chosen for the display because 2:1 is viewed as relating specifically to 2:2 and not to the total unit.

2:2a On the contrary The adversative ἀλλά 'but' introduces the POSITIVE component of the negative-positive construction in 2:1-2.

although *people* previously mistreated and insulted us(exc) in Philippi *city* The participles in προπαθόντες καὶ ὑβρισθέντες 'having suffered previously and having been shamefully treated' are understood by most commentators and versions to be concessive rather than temporal. The concessive relation is appropriate because one would not ordinarily expect that Paul and his companions, having suffered physically and emotionally, would have the courage to continue ministering in another city. The terms together most likely refer to their physical suffering when people dragged them through the city of Philippi to the authorities, who had them publicly flogged, imprisoned, and put in stocks (Acts 16:19-24). It may also refer to the humiliation of having their Roman citizenship disregarded as well (Acts 16:35-39). The generic term 'people' is supplied as the implied agent of the mistreating and insulting of Paul and his companions. Philippi, a Roman colony, is designated 'city'.

2:2b-c our(inc) God caused us(exc) to be courageous and as a result we(exc) told you the gospel *that originates from* God The Greek is ἐπαρρησιασάμεθα ἐν τῷ θεῷ ἡμῶν λαλῆσαι πρὸς ὑμᾶς τὸ εὐαγγέλιον τοῦ θεοῦ 'we had courage in our God to speak to you the gospel of God'. The phrase 'in our God' indicates the means or cause of the messengers' courage (Best, Bruce, Frame, Wanamaker; CEV, JB, JBP, NCV, NIV, TEV, REB). In spite of their having been mistreated, God caused them to courageously tell the gospel, whether from their sense of God's approval of their work (Wanamaker) or from his indwelling power (Frame). When Paul speaks of 'our God' the pronoun primarily refers to the messengers who were experiencing God's sufficiency, but it was probably not meant to exclude the Thessalonians who now knew him as their God as well (Hiebert). In some languages it may not be possible to use the possessive pronoun 'our' with God; then a phrase such as 'the God whom we(inc) worship' should be used.

The verb παρρησιάζομαι means "*speak freely, openly, fearlessly*" (BAGD, p. 631.1), but when used with an infinitive, as here, it has the meaning "*have the courage*" (ibid., p. 631.2). Thus, with the infinitive λαλῆσαι 'to tell' in 2c it means 'had the courage to tell'. God's causing his messengers to be courageous was the reason that the gospel was proclaimed in Thessalonica. The genitive in 'the gospel of God' is understood by most commentators as a subjective genitive or genitive of source: God was the source of their message. (See the note on 'the message that originates from the Lord' in 1:8a.)

It is difficult to determine whether the reason (2b) or result (2c) proposition is more naturally prominent here. Speaking (the infinitive λαλῆσαι 'to tell' in 2c) is certainly prominent and thematic, but the auxiliary concept (ἐπαρρησιασάμεθα 'we had the courage' in 2b) also seems important. Thus reason and result are considered equally prominent and the labels for both are in uppercase letters in the display.

2:2d even though *people in your city of Thessalonica* strongly opposed *us(exc)* The phrase ἐν πολλῷ ἀγῶνι 'in much opposition' relates by concession to 2c (CEV, NIV, NRSV, TEV). The noun ἀγών 'opposition, struggle' has been understood to mean either strong external opposition, the effort of preaching the gospel, or the internal anxiety of the messengers. Because outward persecution in Thessalonica has already been mentioned in 1:6 and will be mentioned again in 2:13-16, most commentators understand ἀγών to refer to the conflict Paul and his colleagues had with the opponents of the gospel there (see Acts 17:5-9).

2:3a Here γάρ 'for' occurs for the second time in the paragraph. It could be interpreted (with Marshall, Morris, Wanamaker) as introducing the grounds for vv. 1-2. But because the 3a-4f propositional cluster has a grammatical structure similar to the other clusters in 2:1-9 (see "Boundaries"), and because the semantic relationship of vv. 3-4 with vv. 1-2 is not obviously conclusion-grounds, a different interpretation is followed here, namely that 3a-4f is a second description of the manner in which the messengers ministered. (Frame holds this view; EHP and GW start a new paragraph at v. 3, suggesting a similar understanding.) As in v. 1, γάρ 'for' is not rendered here (nor in CEV, EHP, GW, JBP, NAB, NCV, NJB, REB, TEV, and TNT).

When I(&S&T) exhort (*or*, appeal to) *people to trust in God and obey the message he sent* The noun phrase ἡ παράκλησις ἡμῶν 'the appeal of us' represents an event and is rendered in the display as a circumstantial clause. The 3a-4f cluster is the only cluster in 2:1-9 that does not state that the Thessalonians know the truth of what Paul is saying. This is appropriate, however, as Paul in vv. 3-4 seems to be speaking of his ministry to people generally, whether in Thessalonica or elsewhere, and of character traits and internal motives which only God knows for sure (4f).

Although v. 3 has no verb in the Greek, present-tense verbs (habitual aspect) are used in the display in 3a-d because this is a general discussion of the messengers' characters and motivations. Also, these verbs accord with the present-tense verb λαλοῦμεν 'we tell/speak' in 4c. The undergoer of 'exhort' that is supplied is 'people' rather than the more specific 'you Thessalonians' because this is a general discussion of character and motivation.

The noun παράκλησις can mean 'appeal', 'exhortation', 'encouragement', or 'consolation'. Since Paul uses the verb λαλέω 'to tell' in reference to the messengers telling the gospel in 2c and again in 4c, either of the first two meanings, 'exhort' or 'appeal', seems appropriate here. In some languages the nature of the appeal or exhortation needs to be made explicit as in the display.

2:3b we(exc) do not *speak an erroneous/untrue message as a result of our(exc) believing something that is not true* The nouns in this and the following two Greek phrases represent states or events and are rendered as clauses in the display. The preposition ἐκ 'from' in the phrase οὐκ ἐκ πλάνης 'not from error/deceit' indicates source: the message did not originate from people who were deluded or deceived. The noun πλάνη can mean either '(in) error, delusion' or 'deception, deceit'. Later in this verse Paul uses another noun, δόλος, which specifically means 'deception, trickery'. To emphasize a point Paul often uses synonyms (as in 2:12a); here he may intend that his readers understand the meaning 'deception' for both words. If, however, Paul is seeking to be comprehensive he may intend that the words be understood as different in meaning. The latter view fits with Paul's extensive defense of his ministry in 2:1-12. Therefore (with the majority of commentators and versions consulted), πλάνη here is taken to mean '(being) deluded/deceived' and δόλος in 3d as '(practicing) deception, trickery'. In this context Paul mentions that the messengers are not deluded in order to implicitly make the point that the message itself is not in error or untrue. "Paul thus asserts that his understanding of the gospel and his presentation of it to the Thessalonians was not an intellectual mistake on his part" (Wanamaker).

2:3c nor *do we(exc) exhort people to trust in God because* we want to gain something immoral for ourselves *from our doing so* The Greek is οὐδὲ ἐξ ἀκαθαρσίας 'nor from uncleanness'. Here ἐκ 'from' indicates source, as it does in the immediately preceding phrase. This source is the messengers' character or motive: "impure motives" (NAB, NIV, NJB, NRSV, TEV), "sordid motive" (REB). Some commentators (Bruce, Frame, Morris) understand the noun ἀκαθαρσία 'uncleanness' to refer specifically to sexual impurity, but others (Best, Hendriksen, Marshall, Wanamaker) understand it to refer to general moral impurity: greed, ambition, pride, and perhaps sexual misconduct. The fact that Paul uses the same term in a discussion of sexual purity in 4:3-8 gives a slight edge to the former view, but he does write of motives such as greed later in 2:5-9.

2:3d nor *do we(exc) speak* because we want to (*or, in order to*) trick/deceive *you or other people* A different preposition, ἐν 'in', is used here: ἐν δόλῳ 'in deception'. It can be understood as indicating the reason for exhorting people. However, implicit in the phrase is also the idea of purpose, or intent, to trick or deceive. This is recognized and translated as such by most versions consulted, for example, NIV's "trying to trick you."

2:4a–b On the contrary A positive contrast to the negative statements of v. 3 is introduced by ἀλλά 'but'. Also, the conjunction καθώς 'as' occurs here. It is paired with the adverb οὕτως 'thus, so' in 4c to form a relation of standard-congruence between 4a–b and 4c–f: in accordance with God's approval and commissioning, the messengers proclaim the gospel in a strict and godly way in order to please him. In the display this relationship is expressed by 'accordingly' at the beginning of 4c.

because* God examined me(&S&T) and as a result considered us(exc) acceptable, *he* trusted us(exc) to tell the gospel *to people The Greek is δεδοκιμάσμεθα ὑπὸ τοῦ θεοῦ πιστευθῆναι τὸ εὐαγγέλιον 'we have been approved by God to be entrusted with the gospel'. The form of the verb δοκιμάζω is passive, but it is rendered as active in the display. It can mean 'to examine, test', as in 4f, or 'to approve on the basis of such a test', as here. The latter meaning involves a reason-result relationship. Proposition 4a is taken to be the reason for 4b; the infinitive phrase 'to be entrusted with the gospel' in 4b expresses the result of God's examining the messengers (Hiebert): he appoints them to tell the gospel. In this context it is more normal in English to use past tense ('examined' and 'considered') rather than the perfect tense as the Greek has it: δεδοκιμάσμεθα 'we have been approved'. There is no essential difference in meaning.

'To be entrusted with the gospel' is to be trusted as someone worthy of proclaiming it. (In Gal. 2:7 a similar phrase is used of Paul's divine commission to take the gospel to the Gentiles.) The passive infinitive is rendered as active in the display. As God is the one who approved Paul and his companions (4a), he is semantically the agent who entrusted them with the gospel.

2:4c Accordingly, we(exc) tell *the gospel in the following way* [4d–f] The Greek is οὕτως λαλοῦμεν 'so we speak'. This is the conclusion of the standard-congruence relation begun in 4a (see the note there). The relative adverb ὡς 'as' in the following clause, οὐχ ὡς ἀνθρώποις ἀρέσκοντες 'not as pleasing men' (4d), seems best understood as indicating the manner of ministry or "the characteristic quality" of the messengers (BAGD, p. 898.III). The words 'in the following way' are intended to convey this.

2:4d *Specifically, we(exc) do* not *say* what people like to hear The phrase οὐχ ὡς ἀνθρώποις ἀρέσκοντες 'not as pleasing men' introduces a specific description of the messengers' way of ministering. They spoke not to please men (4d) but to please God (4e), who trusted them to proclaim the gospel (4a–b) and who continues to examine even their innermost thoughts (4f). In 4d Paul is "thinking of the kind of action involving flattery (2:5) and similar devices which superficially pleases other people but is really dictated by self-interest and thus stands in sharp contrast with pleasing God, in the sense of serving his purpose" (Marshall).

2:4e Instead, *we(exc) say what* God *wants us to say* The conjunction ἀλλά 'but' introduces the positive component of the 4d–e negative-positive construction. The messengers speak not in order that people will be pleased, but in order that God will be pleased. There is an ellipsis in the original, which has only ἀλλὰ θεῷ 'but (as pleasing) God'. The rendering in the display supplies what was omitted.

2:4f *because* he examines everything we(exc) think and desire The construction τῷ δοκιμάζοντι τὰς καρδίας ἡμῶν 'the (one) testing our hearts' is appositional. It is an integral part of Paul's reasoning in this verse. Here in 4f Paul uses the same verb, δοκιμάζω, as in 4a, where he states that God has tested and approved the messengers to proclaim the gospel. In 4e he says they minister in a way that pleases God, and in 4f they minister this way *because* (implicit) God continues to test, or examine, their hearts. Though it is a well-known theme of the OT that God examines the hearts of all people, it is the hearts of the messengers that are primarily in focus here (Frame, Hiebert), 'heart' being used figuratively. To examine the heart is to lay open the center of the inner life, the emotions, thoughts, and motives that determine outer conduct.

2:5a Here γάρ 'for', occurring for the third time in the paragraph, could be interpreted as introducing grounds or explanation for vv. 3–4 (Hiebert, Marshall), especially what is represented by the 4c–d propositions (Wanamaker). But because the 5a–8d propositional cluster has a structure similar to the other clusters in 2:1-9 (see "Boundaries"), 2:5-8 is interpreted as a further explanation of the way in which Paul and his companions ministered (Best, Bruce, Frame, Morris). As in 2:1 and 2:3a, the relater γάρ 'for' is not rendered in the display.

I(&S&T) never flattered *you or others* The clause οὔτε γάρ ποτε ἐν λόγῳ κολακείας ἐγενήθημεν 'for neither at any time we were with word of flattery' states that the messengers never ministered with flattering words. Louw and Nida gloss κολακεία as "praise as a means of gratifying someone's vanity" (33.367). It may be excessive or insincere praise, often with motives of self-interest. In v. 6 the general terms 'people . . . you . . . others' are explicit in the original as those from whom Paul and his companions did not seek honor. Therefore it is appropriate to use those general terms here also (and in 5b): 'I(&S&T) never flattered you or others'.

2:5b and we(exc) never said/did things because we were greedy and tried to hide that motive/fact *from you or others* The main verb phrase in v. 5 is οὔτε ἐγενήθημεν 'we were not'. It is complemented by 'with word of flattery' in 5a and by ἐν προφάσει πλεονεξίας 'with pretext of greed' here. The genitive in 'pretext of greed' can be interpreted as subjective: "a pretext which greediness . . . uses or inspires" (Frame). The pretext in this passage is ministering the gospel; the ulterior motive is greed. The first noun in the construction, πρόφασις, could have the meaning: "*actual motive* or *reason*" (BAGD, p. 722.1) or "*falsely alleged motive, pretext, ostensible reason*" (ibid., p. 722.2). BAGD and all versions and commentaries consulted (except Wanamaker) prefer the second meaning. Wanamaker says that in the context it makes no sense to say "nor did we act with an *ostensible motivation* of greed." He prefers the first meaning and suggests a rendering such as 'we did not act with a motive which is greed'. The idea of cover-up is inherent in the idea of 'pretext' and is implied in Wanamaker's 'motive which is greed', so in any case the difference between the two views seems insignificant. (If the translator prefers the meaning 'motive' to 'pretext', the phrase 'and tried to hide that motive/fact from you or others' in 5b of the display should be disregarded.)

Wanamaker feels that greed for money, specifically, is in view here. Others (Frame, Marshall, Morris) say the meaning is more general.

as God knows is true The clause θεὸς μάρτυς 'God (is) witness' is best interpreted not as an oath but as a solemn statement parallel to 'as you know' in 5a (CEV, EHP, NCV). Paul is writing here of hidden motives, which only God can and does know (see 4f).

2:6a and we(exc) never tried to get people to honor us(exc) The Greek is οὔτε ζητοῦντες ἐξ ἀνθρώπων δόξαν 'nor seeking from men honor'. Some propagandists of the day required respect and subservience, but God's messengers to the Thessalonians did not. The verb ζητέω has the primary meaning of "*seek, look for* in order to find" (BAGD, p. 338.1) and the secondary meanings of "*try to obtain, desire to possess* τὶ *someth.*" (ibid., p. 339.2a), "*strive for, aim (at) desire, wish*" (ibid., p. 339.2b), and "*ask for, request, demand* τὶ *someth.*" (ibid., p. 339.2c). The rendering in the display is based on the first of the three secondary meanings. Frame and maker prefer the third meaning 'to demand, to require' because of the statements that follow in 7a–b.

The noun δόξα 'honor' represents an event and is rendered as an infinitive in the display. In other biblical contexts it can mean 'radiance, glory', but here it has its classical meaning, 'honor', 'fame'. "There is no evidence that it is equivalent to *honor* in the later sense of *honorarium*" (Frame). (Such a meaning could radically affect the interpretation of the statements that follow.)

2:6b *Specifically,* we(exc) did not *try to get* you people or other people *to honor us(exc)* At the end of v. 6 Paul adds οὔτε ἀφ' ὑμῶν οὔτε ἀπ' ἄλλων 'neither from you nor from others'. This addition makes specific from whom he didn't seek honor and gives prominence to the denial. Paul and his companions didn't seek honor from the Thessalonian converts or from any other people, whether Christians or not.

2:7a although The 7a participial phrase is concessive. The majority of commentators and versions consulted relate it to the proposition that precedes rather than to the one that follows. This seems correct because the proposition that follows (7b) begins with ἀλλά 'but'. In two previous occurrences in chapter 2, ἀλλά introduces positive propositional clusters (2a–d and 4a–f) that contrast with preceding negative ones (1 and 3a–d). A similar function of ἀλλά in 7b signals that the 7b–8d positive propositions contrast with the 5a–7a negative ones. (If the 7a concessive phrase were related primarily to the 7b proposition, Paul would be using ἀλλά differently here.)

we(exc) could demand *that you or other people honor/respect us* The participial phrase, δυνάμενοι ἐν βάρει εἶναι 'being able to be with weight', has been variously interpreted as 'having authority which requires respect or obedience' (Best, Frame, Marshall, Wanamaker; NASB, NCV, REB), 'having the right to be supported with provisions' (Bruce, Morris; CEV, DGN, NIV), or both (Hiebert). The first of these meanings can be verified lexically from other Greek sources; that is, βάρος elsewhere may mean "*weight* of influence which someone enjoys or claims" (BAGD, p. 134.2; see also Schrenk, pp. 553–56). This first meaning seems more appropriate than the second to the immediately preceding and following propositions. In 2:6 Paul said that the messengers did not try to get people to honor and praise them; it was not a question of trying to get them to supply material provisions. In 7b–8d he says that the messengers were gentle and loving toward the Thessalonians. The contrast between 6a–7a and 7b is better taken as between the right to wield authority and acting in a gentle, loving way rather than between the right to demand provisions and being gentle. On the other hand, the second meaning (having the right to be supported with provisions) does seem to fit 5b, which says the messengers were not greedy, and could lead up to the statement in 2:9 that the messengers worked hard not to be a burden to the converts. However, if Paul were referring to demanding funds here, he certainly would have stated 7a immediately following 5b. Therefore the first meaning seems more contextually appropriate and is given in the display.

since we(exc) are apostles *who represent* (*or, speak for*) *Christ* The conjunction ὡς 'as' introduces the grounds (ὡς Χριστοῦ ἀπόστολοι 'as apostles of Christ') for the previous proposition. Paul uses the term 'apostles', not in the narrow sense of the original Twelve that Christ commissioned, but in the broader sense of that wider group who were later accepted and recognized as apostles, including Paul himself (Bruce). If the first person plural is more than epistolary (and refers to Silas and Timothy in addition to Paul, the author), then here all three would be designated as apostles. The genitive in '(apostles) of Christ' is understood as a genitive of role relationship: Christ chose them to represent and speak for him.

2:7b On the contrary, I(&S&T) were gentle when we(exc) were among you A positive contrast to the preceding negative statements is introduced by ἀλλά 'but'. The fourth edition UBSGNT accepts the textual variant νήπιοι 'infants' as almost certain, whereas the third edition accepted the reading with considerable doubt. The MJTGNT reading is ἤπιοι 'gentle'. Concerning the two readings Metzger (p. 562) says, "Despite the weight of external evidence [for νήπιοι 'infants'], only ἤπιοι seems to suit the context, where the apostle's gentleness makes an appropriate sequence with the arrogance disclaimed in ver. 6." Frame suggests that νήπιοι 'infants', being a noun, contrasts appropriately with the noun ἀπόστολοι 'apostles'; rather than demanding things as authoritative apostles they were as unassuming as babies. The reading 'gentle' is used in the display for several reasons: (1) It seems to fit better with the preceding propositions, and it does not create a difficult mixed metaphor; being like infants is quite different from the following comparison, being like a mother. (2) The term 'gentle' is used just one other time in the NT; 'infant' is much more common. A scribe creating a new manuscript would be more likely to accidentally or deliberately change the text from the less common 'gentle' to the more common 'infants' than the other way around. (3) 'Gentle' leads appropriately into the comparison of a loving mother in 7c–8d. (4) Nowhere else does Paul refer to himself and his colleagues as 'infants'.

2:7c As A comparison is introduced here by ὡς ἐάν 'as if'. The comparison can be taken as relating either to what precedes in 7b (Bruce, Wanamaker; KJV, JBP, NAB, NIV, NRSV, REB, TEV, TNT) or to what follows in v. 8 (Best, Frame, Marshall, Morris; NJB). Here it is taken as relating to v. 8 for the following reasons: (1) The fronting of τροφός 'nurse, mother' in 7c creates discontinuity between 7b and 7c. Fronting indicates that τροφός is the topic of a new discourse constituent, 7c–8d. (2) The adverb οὕτως 'so, thus' occurs at the beginning of v. 8 and can function to complete the comparison of Paul lovingly caring for the Thessalonians as a mother cares for her children.

a mother *lovingly* **takes care of her own children** In 7c–8d Paul uses a simile in which 'mother' is the image; Paul, Silas, and Timothy's ministry to the Thessalonian believers is the topic; and the ground of comparison is loving care for those entrusted to them. The noun τροφός can mean either 'mother' or 'nurse, one who takes care of others' children'. This particular term emphasizes the element of loving care (Marshall). The use of the reflexive pronoun ἑαυτῆς 'her own' infers that even if τροφός means 'nurse' in this context, the nurse is most likely also the mother and it is *her own* children that she cherishes more than other children in her charge (Best, Frame, Wanamaker), hence 'mother' in the display.

2:8a so Those who understand the comparison in 7c to relate to what precedes it take οὕτως 'so' here in 8a to indicate degree (Bruce; NIV, NRSV, REB): we loved you *so much*. However, it seems better to understand 7c as relating to v. 8, in which case οὕτως 'so' corresponds to ὡς 'as' in 7c and introduces the application of the comparison.

because we(exc) loved you The participial phrase ὁμειρόμενοι ὑμῶν 'loving you' is a reason for the following propositions. The verb ὁμείρομαι 'to have an affectionate feeling for, to long for' expresses the deep affection the messengers felt for their converts. The present tense here indicates that the affection continued up to the time when Paul wrote. However, it is rendered past tense in the display to agree with the imperfect tense (past continuous) of the main verb 'we were delighted' in 8b.

2:8b not only were we(exc) delighted to personally tell you the gospel *that originates from God* The Greek is εὐδοκοῦμεν μεταδοῦναι ὑμῖν οὐ μόνον τὸ εὐαγγέλιον τοῦ θεοῦ 'we were pleased to share with you not only the gospel of God'. The verb εὐδοκέω can mean 'to consider good, resolve' or 'to be well pleased, take delight'. The latter meaning involves emotion and seems more appropriate in this context which twice speaks of the love the messengers have for the Thessalonians. By using μεταδίδωμι 'to share, impart' rather than a verb such as λαλέω 'to speak, tell' Paul most likely intends to communicate the personal and loving way in which he proclaimed the gospel and ministered to the needs of the Thessalonians. The genitive in the phrase 'the gospel of God' is considered a subjective genitive or genitive of source: the gospel originates "from God" (TEV).

2:8c but also The construction οὐ μόνον . . . ἀλλὰ καί 'not only . . . but also' conjoins propositions 8b and 8c. The construction gives emphasis to 8c as something which is more than expected. To indicate this prominence the second RESULT label is in uppercase letters in the display, but not the first.

we(exc) were delighted to lovingly do all we(exc) could do to help you The verb μεταδίδωμι 'to share' in 8b is complemented by 'the gospel' there and also by τὰς ἑαυτῶν ψυχάς 'our own souls' here in 8c. To share one's own soul is synecdoche, in which a part represents the whole person. The term ψυχάς 'souls' encompasses the totality of the messengers' lives—their time, energy, health, will, and emotions. Bruce says, "The meaning is not simply 'we were willing to give (lay down) our lives for you' but 'we were willing to give ourselves to you, to put ourselves at your disposal, without reservation.'" The rendering in the display is an attempt to convey this idea of total, loving commitment.

2:8d because you had become very dear to us The clause διότι ἀγαπητοὶ ἡμῖν ἐγενήθητε 'because you became dear to us' is an equivalent reason repeating the sense of 8a. As such, it emphasizes the love of the messengers for these new believers.

2:9a The conjunction γάρ 'for' here has been understood as introducing grounds or explanation for 7c-8d by Wanamaker; for 6a by Frame; and for 5b-8d by Marshall. It should be noted that the 9a-d propositional cluster does not have the γάρ . . . ἀλλά 'for . . . but' construction common to the preceding three clusters (1-2d, 3a-4f, and 5a-8d), and therefore γάρ 'for' could signal grounds for a preceding statement(s). However, because a conclusion-grounds relation with a particular proposition is not immediately apparent, it seems better to consider 9a-d as parallel in function to the preceding propositional clusters. As in v. 1, 3a, and 5a, γάρ 'for' is not rendered in the display.

you remember The verb form μνημονεύετε can be either indicative ('you remember') or imperative ('Remember'). The former seems preferable here (following most versions consulted) because other verbs in the unit with similar meaning ('you know' in v. 1, 'as you know' in 2a and 5a) are in the indicative mood.

that I(&S&T) worked very hard *in order to support ourselves while we(exc) were with you* The nouns κόπος 'work' and μόχθος 'labor', collocated here and also in 2 Cor. 11:27 and 2 Thess. 3:8, form a doublet emphasizing how hard the messengers had worked. Because the doublet represents an event, it is rendered in the display as a clause, 'I(&S&T) worked very hard'. It is obvious from the context that the messengers labored manually to earn money to support themselves during the time that they preached the gospel. Paul could even have proclaimed the gospel to individuals while he worked in the shop as a tentmaker or leatherworker (cf. Acts 18:3). The phrase 'while we were with you' is implied information about the communication situation.

2:9b We(exc) worked *during the day and also at night* The main verb of 9b–d is ἐκηρύξαμεν 'we proclaimed' in 9d, to which the participle ἐργαζόμενοι 'working' here in 9b is subordinate. Since the phrase νυκτὸς καὶ ἡμέρας 'night and day' is fronted for emphasis, most translations make 9d, rather than 9b, the circumstantial clause: 'we worked night and day . . . while we preached the gospel to you'. In the display this emphasis is indicated by likewise making 9d the circumstantial clause and using bold type for 'during the day and also at night'.

The propositional cluster 9b–d is best understood as an amplification of 9a. MJTGNT has γάρ 'for' here, which would explicitly indicate this relationship. Although this reading is not mentioned by UBSGNT and thus rejected, the relationship is still valid.

The phrase νυκτὸς καὶ ἡμέρας 'night and day' does not mean that Paul and his colleagues worked all night and all day. It emphasizes the long hours they worked. That 'night' precedes 'day' in the Greek may or may not emphasize the fact that they worked even at night. The usual order for the phrase in the LXX is "day and night," but in his writings Paul uses the order "night and day" only (2:9; 3:10; 2 Thess. 3:8; and 1 Tim. 5:5). We do not know whether or not this was Paul's set order (not meant to emphasize night over day), since in every context where he uses it, it functions as an intensive marker. The rendering in the display uses the more common English order, *day and night*, and communicates the long hours by adding 'also (at night)'.

2:9c in order that we(exc) not require any one of you to give us(exc) what we needed in order to live The phrase πρὸς τὸ μὴ ἐπιβαρῆσαί τινα ὑμῶν 'in order not to burden any of you' gives what is in effect the ultimate purpose for the hard manual labor of the messengers. Commentators agree that the burden for the Thessalonians would have been the responsibility of providing for the needs of Paul and his companions.

2:9d *while* we(exc) proclaimed to you the gospel *that originates from* God The nonsubordinate verb and clause that express this proposition are rendered here as circumstantial to preserve the emphasis of the original on the hard work of the messengers (see the note on 9b). For τὸ εὐαγγέλιον τοῦ θεοῦ 'the gospel of God' see the note on 2:2c.

2:10a You know it is true and God knows it is true The clause ὑμεῖς μάρτυρες καὶ ὁ θεός 'you (are) witnesses and God' states in an emphatic and different way what Paul has already said several times in vv. 1–9 concerning the Thessalonians (and once concerning God); he will say it again in the next verse ('you know also'). The Thessalonians and God are witnesses, not in the sense that Paul is calling on them to testify to the truthfulness of his claim (REB), but in the sense that they have seen Paul's conduct, God has examined his service and motives, and both parties know that what Paul says is true. The 10a orienter serves to validate Paul's claim of righteous behavior, and not merely to introduce content, which orienters usually do. Thus the label ORIENTER is in uppercase letters in the display here (and in 11a). There are no verbs in the Greek, but 'know(s) it is true' is used in both clauses of 10a to convey the content of 'witness', which is in focus here.

2:10b that I(&S&T) behaved/acted in a very virtuous, upright, and irreproachable manner In the Greek, three adverbs (ὁσίως καὶ δικαίως καὶ ἀμέμπτως 'devoutly and uprightly and blamelessly') modify the verb ἐγενήθημεν 'we were', even though adjectival forms would be more appropriate. The use of adverbs with ἐγενήθημεν shows that it represents an event rather than a state: it has the meaning of 'behaved, conducted ourselves' in this context. Since manner is explicitly represented in these adverbial forms, the word 'manner' is made explicit in the display. Marshall differentiates the meaning of the adverbs as follows: 'Holy' (ὁσίως) "expresses an attitude of piety and reverence toward God which affects a person's conduct." 'Uprightly' (δικαίως) "is used of conduct which accords with justice, a universally recognised standard but one which for Paul was based on God's revelation of how men ought to live." 'Irreproachably' (ἀμέμπτως) "refers to conduct which is free from any accusation that it falls below the standard of justice." Since in English *holy* connotes a person's relationship to God, and since the context here speaks primarily of the messengers' relationship to people (vv. 11-12), ὁσίως is rendered 'virtuous' in the display.

The Greek clause that expresses 10b begins with ὡς, which can be understood either as introducing the content after the orienter (you and God are witnesses 'that') or as indicating degree of the behavior characteristics ('how' devoutly). Either meaning seems appropriate here. But as ὡς occurs also in 11b, most likely with the meaning 'that', it seems good to take it with the same meaning in this first occurrence also. In the Greek the three adverbs are fronted for prominence, which in the display is indicated by placing 'very' before the three adjectives. The same would be done if ὡς were taken to mean degree ('how').

toward you who trust *in God* The dative phrase ὑμῖν τοῖς πιστεύουσιν 'to you the (ones) believing' has been variously understood: (1) It can mean 'in the sight or opinion of you who believe' (Frame). In this sense focus would be on the truth that the Thessalonians are believers because only believers would be qualified to judge the messengers' behavior. (2) It can mean 'among you who believe' (Marshall, Wanamaker; NCV, NIV). In this sense it would be stating that the messengers behaved uprightly when they were with the Thessalonians. (3) It can mean 'toward you, for the benefit of you who believe' (Best, Bruce; CEV, JB, NRSV, REB, TEV). In this sense it would indicate that the messengers behaved uprightly toward the Thessalonians. This is appropriate to the context because in 2:11-12 Paul speaks of having encouraged and urged the Thessalonians as a father would his children. Even in 2:1-9 it seems Paul is primarily speaking of his ministry to the Thessalonians. For these reasons the third meaning, 'toward you', may be slightly preferable. In 1:8 Paul speaks of the Thessalonians' faith in God as being reported everywhere. Thus 'God' is made explicit in the display as the object of their faith.

2:11a You know also The Greek is καθάπερ οἴδατε 'as you know'. Some take καθάπερ 'as' as introducing grounds for Paul's statement in v. 10 (Hiebert, Marshall), in which case the sense would be 'it is true that we lived righteously since you know that we did the following things'. Others (Bruce; CEV) take it as an additional statement, that is, a second *DECLARATION*. This interpretation is preferable. Verse 10 speaks generally of the messengers' righteous conduct, which corresponds to statements in 2:1-7a; vv. 11-12 speak more specifically of a father's concern and love for his children, like the simile of a mother in 2:7c-8d. Thus vv. 11-12 do not seem to relate to v. 10 as grounds, and 11a is simply another orienter validating Paul's claims (see the note on 10a).

2:11b-c that *we(exc) lovingly behaved/acted toward* each one of you as a father *lovingly behaves/acts toward* his own children The Greek is ὡς ἕνα ἕκαστον ὑμῶν ὡς πατὴρ τέκνα ἑαυτοῦ 'how each one of you as a father his children'. The first ὡς 'how', which follows the orienter οἴδατε 'you know', introduces the content and is rendered 'that' in the display. The second ὡς 'as' establishes a comparison (simile) using the term 'father' (cf. 'mother' in the simile of 7c-8d). Here the image is a father dealing with his children; the topic is Paul, Silas, and Timothy ministering to the Thessalonian believers. The participles in v. 12 indicate that the ground of comparison here is the same as in 7c-8d. Just as a father's earnest concern and love cause him to instruct his children and exhort them to behave properly and wisely, so Paul and his companions lovingly urged the Thessalonians to conduct themselves as God's people should (Marshall). It is probable that 'each one of you' "means giving attention to the individual needs of those converted through the public preaching" (Morris).

Apart from the orienter 'you know' there is no other verb in v. 11. Thus the event or state in both parts of the comparison is implicit. The rendering 'behave/act toward' follows most versions consulted; they use a general verb such as 'treat' or 'deal with' to express the event. Just as the main verb ἐγενήθημεν 'we were' in 10b takes its meaning, 'behaved', from the adverbs 'devoutly and uprightly and blamelessly', so the participles of 12a suggest the wording of the event that is implied here in 11b-c. The adverb 'lovingly' is supplied in the rendering because it is an important aspect of the ground of comparison.

The UBSGNT and most versions end v. 11 at this point, and the next three participles are in v. 12. But MJTGNT, NASB, and RSV include the participles at the end of v. 11. Different verse breaks, however, affect only the numbering of propositions, not the semantic analysis.

2:12a *Specifically*, **I(&S&T) continually exhorted/appealed, encouraged, and urged** As there is no main verb in vv. 11–12, the three participles here (παρακαλοῦντες ὑμᾶς καὶ παραμυθούμενοι καὶ μαρτυρόμενοι 'exhorting you and encouraging and urging') function to state specifically what behavior Paul was referring to in the 11b–c comparison. They are rendered as nonsubordinate verbs in place of the missing verb.

Most versions and commentators consulted understand 12b ('that you walk worthily of God') to be the content of one or more of the participles here in 12a. Some (Marshall; CEV, REB) take 12b as relating to all three participles. Frame takes the first participle in 12a, 'exhorting', as the orienter for 12b, with the other participles indicating how the messengers exhorted: exhorting you by encouraging and urging. GW, NCV, and TEV take only the third participle, 'urging', as related to 12b. The first option is the one chosen for the display. The three verbs are very close in meaning, and it seems Paul adds participle to participle to emphasize the urging of a loving and caring father to his children. In some languages such verbs for appealing, encouraging, and urging require that the content of the appeal and encouragement be explicit, and 12b is appropriate content for all three of the verbs.

The meanings of the verbs παρακαλέω 'to exhort' and παραμυθέομαι 'to encourage' overlap. Often both admonition and comfort are meant where either of these verbs is used. If they function as orienters for 12b, the meaning 'to admonish' is primary. The third verb μαρτύρομαι 'to urge' has the connotation of a solemn, authoritative injunction. The three participles here occur in the present tense, indicating that it was the continual practice of Paul and his companions to exhort, encourage, and urge, hence the adverb 'continually'.

2:12b that you behave/act in the way that God's people should *behave/act* The Greek is εἰς τὸ περιπατεῖν ὑμᾶς ἀξίως τοῦ θεοῦ 'that you walk worthily of God'. The construction εἰς τό with the infinitive περιπατεῖν 'to walk' indicates purpose (Bruce, p. 69; Morris): we urged in order that you would walk. However, in English the relation of such a clause to the particular verbs in 12a is normally represented by an orienter-content construction. This is the way most versions consulted render it: we urged that you walk. The verb 'to walk', when used in an ethical sense as here, was a dead metaphor relating to behavior, whether good or bad.

The adverb ἀξίως 'worthily' indicates the manner in which the Thessalonians were to behave. The meaning of the adverb depends on the phrases that follow it here and in 12c, worthily 'of God the one calling you to his own kingdom and glory'. The sense is that since God summons/chooses them as people over whom he will rule, they are to conduct themselves in the way that God's people should behave.

2:12c *since* **he summons you to be people over whom he** *will* **wonderfully rule** The relation between 12b and 12c is reported exhortation-grounds; using a relative phrase (τοῦ καλοῦντος ὑμᾶς εἰς τὴν ἑαυτοῦ βασιλείαν καὶ δόξαν 'the (one) calling you to his own kingdom and glory') Paul reminds his readers of the motivation he previously gave for their living a righteous life. UBSGNT and MJTGNT both have the present-tense participle of the verb καλέω 'to call', but some text traditions, such as the Textus Receptus, have the aorist tense. The UBSGNT indicates that the former is almost certain, giving it a B rating. According to Metzger (p. 562), the texts with the aorist form were apparently influenced by the fact that the same verb in Gal. 1:6 is an aorist. Paul uses the aorist tense of this verb later in this letter (1 Thess. 4:7), which could also have influenced the copyists who wrote the aorist tense here. Most versions accept the present-tense form, translating it 'who calls (you)'. Since it has strong manuscript support, it is the one chosen for the display. Commentators explain the use of the present tense in various ways: (1) It is continuous (Marshall); even after the initial conversion experience God continually calls believers to respond to his kingdom and glory. (2) It is timeless (Morris, Frame); though some people were called to salvation in the past, God keeps on calling new people. Since 'call' has the primary sense of 'cry aloud', it is rendered 'summon' in the display, following J. Callow's suggestion (1982:79) that this word conveys "the ideas of (a) authority and (b) effectiveness, both of which components are involved in the Pauline use of this verb when God is the agent."

Some interpret the phrase εἰς τὴν ἑαυτοῦ βασιλείαν καὶ δόξαν 'to his own kingdom and glory' as a hendiadys (Best; Bullinger, p. 668; Ellingworth and Nida; Findlay; JB, JBP, NCV, TNT). A hendiadys expresses a single complex notion with two conjoined words: he "calls you into his glorious Kingdom" (TNT). This interpretation seems best because the terms 'kingdom' and 'glory' are closely linked by a common preposition and a common article, and the one reflexive pronoun 'his own' modifies them both. "[T]here is so much in common between the meanings of the two nouns that where Mark 10.37 reads 'in your glory', the parallel in Matthew 20.21 has 'in your kingdom'" (Ellingworth and Nida). In view of the word 'glory' here the phrase is taken as a reference to the future manifestation of God's kingdom, following all commentators consulted.

The noun 'kingdom' may refer to God's act of ruling, the subjects over whom he rules, or a location where he rules. As the focus here is on the summoning of people, the first two ideas seem preeminent, hence the rendering in the display 'to be people over whom he will wonderfully rule'. The future tense ('will') supplied in the display makes it clear that Paul has a future reign in mind. The rendering allows for a reign either in heaven or on earth.

BOUNDARIES AND COHERENCE

The initial boundary of 2:1–12 was discussed under 1:2–10 (see "Boundaries"). The closing boundary between 2:12 and 2:13 is well established. At 2:13 Paul returns to the matter of thanksgiving for the Thessalonians' response to the messengers' proclamation. Verse 13 begins with a cataphoric reference, καὶ διὰ τοῦτο καί 'and because of this also', which looks ahead to the expression of Paul's additional thanksgiving. The clause ἡμεῖς εὐχαριστοῦμεν τῷ θεῷ ἀδιαλείπτως 'we thank God unceasingly' in v. 13 is very similar to 'we thank God always' in 1:2 and serves to reintroduce the topic of thanksgiving. It is noteworthy that Paul concludes the 2:1–12 paragraph with an eschatological reference in v. 12 just as he ended the previous paragraph, 1:2–10, with an eschatological reference.

The 2:1–12 paragraph is unified by repeated references to the fact that the Thessalonians knew the truth of Paul's claim: 'you know' (vv. 1, 2, 5, 11); 'you remember' (v. 9); 'you are witnesses' (v. 10). God is called a witness in vv. 5 and 10. There are repeated references to 'the gospel', particularly its proclamation (vv. 2, 4, 8, 9), and to expressions of ministry: exhortation and exhorting (vv. 3, 12), encouraging (v. 12), and urging (v. 12). There are two related comparisons, one to a mother caring for her children (vv. 7–8), the other to a father training his children (vv. 11–12). Two triads of negative ministry characteristics (3a–d, 5a–7a) are balanced by the three positive characteristics mentioned in 10b.

Parallel grammatical structures and repetition create strong relational coherence. The first four propositional clusters (1–2d, 3a–4f, 5a–8d, 9a–d) all begin with the conjunction γάρ 'for'. Initial negative statements in the first three of these clusters are followed by positive statements introduced by ἀλλά 'but' in 2a, 4a, and 7b. (The fourth cluster, 9a–d, has only positive statements.) Three of the four clusters state in some form that the Thessalonians know that what Paul is writing is true: 'you know' in v. 1; 'as you know' in 2a; 'as you know' in 5a; and 'you remember' in 9a. While versions and commentators have interpreted one or more occurrences of the conjunction γάρ 'for' in this unit as grounds for an immediately preceding statement, the antithetical and structural parallelism of the propositional clusters seem to indicate that they are instead parallel descriptions regarding manner of ministry.

The two declarations of 2:10–12 likewise cohere with what precedes. The three characteristics of ministering in 10b summarize Paul's statements in 3a–4f and 5a–7b. The comparison to a father in v. 11 corresponds to the comparison to a mother in 7c–8d. The messengers' exhortation and urging (v. 12) echo the several references to proclamation in previous propositions (2b–c, 4b–e, 8b, and 9d).

Versions and commentaries have divided 2:1–12 at different places: between 2:2 and 2:3 (EHP, GW), 2:3 and 2:4 (NLT), 2:4 and 2:5 (Bruce; CEV), 2:6 and 2:7 (EHP, NIV), 2:7a and 2:7b (GW, JB, NCV), and 2:8 and 2:9 (Bruce; CEV, EHP, NBV, NLT, NRSV). Each of these boundaries either separates a propositional cluster beginning with γάρ 'for' from the other such clusters in vv. 1–9, or it disrupts the unity of a γάρ ... ἀλλά 'for ... but' negative-positive construction. For that reason they are rejected in this analysis.

A boundary between 2:9 and 2:10 (NCV, NIV, REB, and TEV), however, does merit discussion. First, in support of this, there is parallelism of reference between 2:1–2 and 2:9, resulting in a sandwich structure around the unit: The words in 2:1–2, αὐτοὶ γὰρ οἴδατε, ἀδελφοί, τὴν εἴσοδον ἡμῶν ... λαλῆσαι πρὸς ὑμᾶς τὸ εὐαγγέλιον τοῦ θεοῦ 'for you yourselves know, brothers, our coming ... to tell to you the gospel of God' are echoed in 2:9 by μνημονεύετε γάρ, ἀδελφοί, τὸν κόπον ἡμῶν ... ἐκηρύξαμεν εἰς ὑμᾶς τὸ εὐαγγέλιον τοῦ θεοῦ 'for you remember, brothers, our work . . . we proclaimed to you the gospel of God'. This sandwich structure could set 2:1-9 apart as a separate unit. Second, v. 10 has no beginning conjunction (asyndeton), which can be an indication of a boundary. In addition, vv. 10-12 have a different relational structure than the previous verses. There are no γάρ 'for' connectors, and there are no antithetical negative-positive propositional clusters.

Third, 2:10 begins with an equative clause with no verb: ὑμεῖς μάρτυρες καὶ ὁ θεός 'you (are) witnesses and God'. This clause fulfills the function of the cognitive orienters in 2:1, 'you know', and 2:9, 'you remember'; but being a clause without a verb, it brings discontinuity to the discourse. Finally, the phrase τὸ εὐαγγέλιον τοῦ θεοῦ 'the gospel of God', found three times in 2:1-9, does not occur at all in 2:10-12.

One consideration militates against a boundary between 2:9 and 2:10. Neither 1-9 nor 10-12 is a complete paragraph pattern by itself. Each is only a series of conjoined propositional clusters. But when joined as a unit, 2:1-12, they form a paragraph of *descriptions* and *DECLARATIONS*. This is the view followed here. Others who likewise have not segmented 2:1-12 at all include Best, Frame, Hiebert, Marshall, Wanamaker, UBSGNT, MJTGNT, NASB, and TNT.

PROMINENCE AND THEME

A positive statement is naturally more prominent than its contrastive negative statement. However, the negative clusters in the 2:1-12 paragraph emphasize by structure and repetition how the messengers did not minister. They are formalized denials. They also have the implicit function of exhorting the Thessalonians to avoid such behavior. For these reasons, in the display the relation labels NEGATIVE are in uppercase letters to indicate marked prominence.

The last two constituent clusters (10a-b and 11a-12c) are a recognizable peak of the paragraph. This peak is marked by two validating orienters (10a and 11a) as well as by orienter 12a, which has three participles indicating admonition. Verse 10 begins with the validating orienter ὑμεῖς μάρτυρες καὶ ὁ θεός 'you (are) witnesses and God (also is)'. Next, in 10b, comes a string of three prominent (forefronted) adverbs that declare the righteous way in which the messengers ministered. Also, the three participles in orienter 12a emphasize through repetition the persistent admonition of the messengers. Because of such marked prominence and the fact that these clusters are the goal toward which the preceding constituents build, propositional clusters 10a-b and 11a-12c are labeled *DECLARATIONS*.

Because of the prominence of the *DECLARATIONS* in vv. 10 and 11-12 (and because they summarize well what Paul said in vv. 1-9), they constitute the 2:1-12 theme. Naturally prominent propositions 10b and 12b are included, as are validating ORIENTERS 10a and 11a and orienter 12a.

SECTION CONSTITUENT 2:13–16
(Expressive Paragraph: Rapport Basis₃ of 1:2–2:16)

THEME: I continually thank God also because when you heard the message which we told you, you accepted as true not a message that originates from human beings. Rather, you accepted as true the message that originates from God as evidenced by the fact that you suffered when your own countrymen mistreated you in the same way that Jewish people in Judea who are united to Jesus suffered when Jewish people who are not united to him mistreated them.

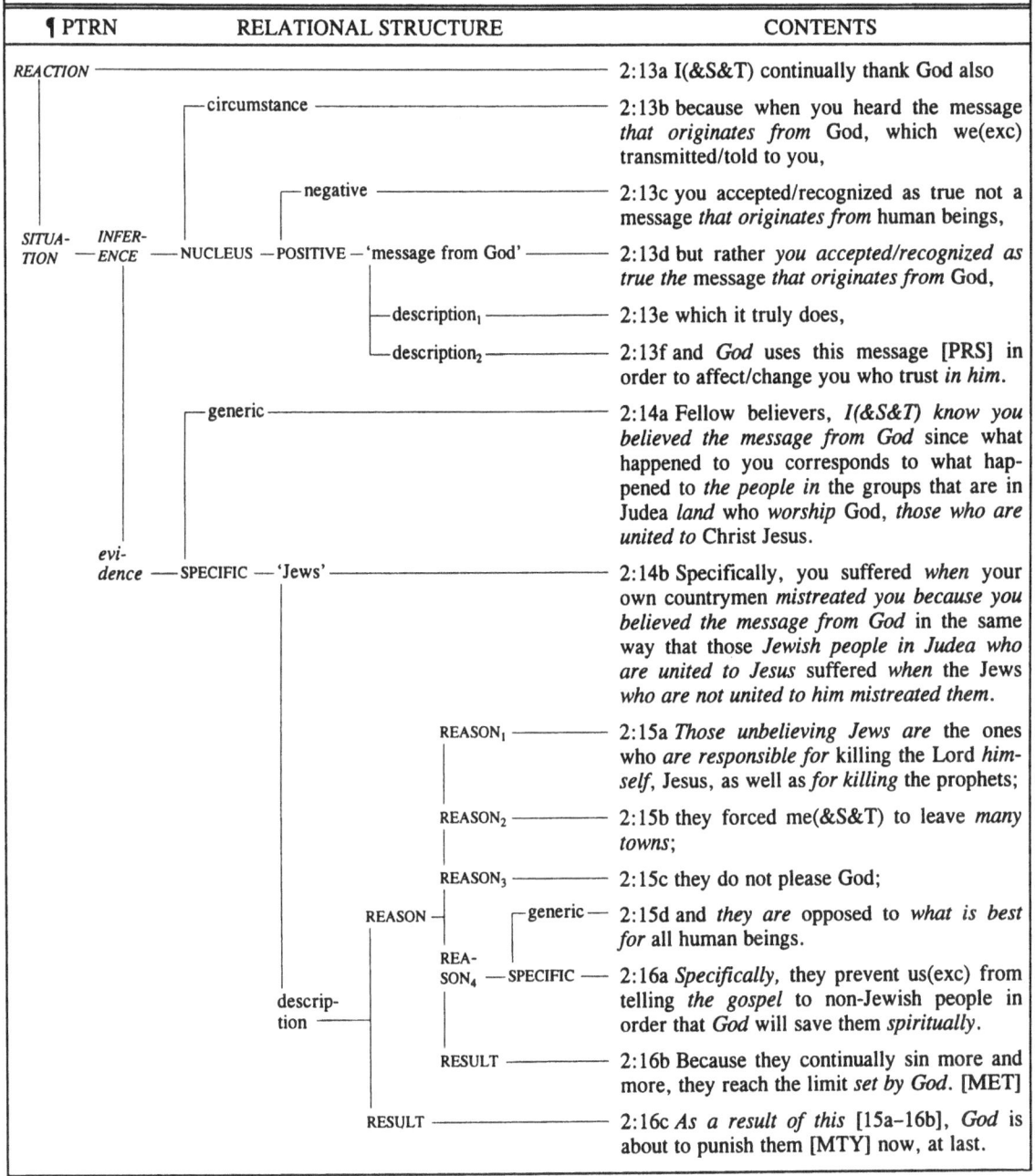

INTENT AND PARAGRAPH PATTERN

In the 2:13-16 paragraph, as in 1:2-10, Paul's intent is to affect the emotions of the Thessalonians by expressing his thankfulness for them. He thanks God for their sincere reception of the gospel message as evidenced by the persecution they endured. The expression of thanksgiving indicates this is emotive discourse. It is an emotive paragraph of the expressive type because Paul develops his thoughts in a result-reason relation rather than in a sequential one.

The paragraph has a result proposition (13a) that is based on a reason (13b-16c, which is introduced by ὅτι 'because'). Paul is not presenting an emotive problem, so this is not a solutionality subtype of paragraph pattern. Neither is he listing his beliefs that result in control of his emotions, which would indicate volitionality. What he is doing is telling the Thessalonians why he is thankful; thus this is the causality subtype. The constituents of the result-reason communication relation in an expressive causality paragraph are labeled REACTION and *situation*.

The *situation* (13b-16c) is composed of an embedded expository paragraph. In it Paul gives grounds (vv. 14-16, introduced by γάρ 'for') for his conclusion (13b-f) that the Thessalonians accepted the message from God as true. Had Paul needed to convince his readers he probably would have used several grounds clusters to support his conclusion. That would be evidence of a volitionality subtype of expository paragraph pattern. Here we have just the one grounds cluster, and it is a statement which is self-evident to the Thessalonians. This most likely indicates the paragraph pattern subtype of causality. Among the labels for that subtype of an expository paragraph are INFERENCE and *evidence*.

Paragraph 2:13-16 is the second peak unit of 1:2-3:13 (see "Intent" under 1:2-2:16).

NOTES

2:13a I(&S&T) continually thank God also Verse 13 begins with καὶ διὰ τοῦτο 'and because of this'. The conjunction 'and' is omitted in MJTGNT, but it is included in the UBSGNT text as certain. Some see 'and' as indicating a close relationship to the preceding unit, 2:1-12 (Best, Hiebert): having just discussed his ministry, Paul turns to the gospel's reception. However, it seems better to view καί 'and' as resumptive, introducing a theme related to 1:2-10. Paul repeats words from 1:2-10 in 2:13-16: 'we thank God' (1:2 and 2:13); 'received the word' (1:6 and 2:13); 'you became imitators' (1:6 and 2:14); and 'in much affliction' in 1:6 is echoed by 'you suffered' in 2:14. Thus the initial καί 'and' introduces a new reason for Paul's thanksgiving (Wanamaker) or an amplification of it (Bruce). The latter is the view of this analysis. As the connection is not with the immediately preceding unit, the initial 'and' is not rendered in the display.

The 1:2-10 paragraph (to which καί 'and' relates) is too remote to be the referent for 'this' in the expression διὰ τοῦτο 'because of this'. Instead, 'this' is a reference to what follows (Bruce, Marshall, Wanamaker), which is confirmed by the presence of ὅτι 'because' later in the verse: we thank God because of this (διὰ τοῦτο), namely, because (ὅτι) you believed our message. The expression διὰ τοῦτο 'because of this' marks prominence on the 13b-16c reason/*situation* in that it provides an additional signal for that relationship. In the display, therefore, SITUATION is in uppercase letters.

A second καί 'and, also' occurs after διὰ τοῦτο in v. 13: καὶ διὰ τοῦτο καὶ ἡμεῖς εὐχαριστοῦμεν τῷ θεῷ ἀδιαλείπτως 'and because of this also we thank God unceasingly'. It has been variously interpreted: (1) as indicating that others beside Paul, Silas, and Timothy gave thanks (Bruce, Frame), in other words, we messengers along with you Thessalonians—or along with other believers in Macedonia and Achaia—thank God; (2) as a means of emphasis (Best, Morris)—we for our part thank God; or (3) as indicating an additional reason for the messengers' thanksgiving (Wanamaker)—besides the previously mentioned reason(s) we thank God. The third interpretation seems most appropriate because Paul in 1:2-10 has already given two reasons for the messengers' thanksgiving and there is no indication in the context that he is thinking of others who are giving thanks. The NJB rendering is based on this interpretation: "Another reason why we continually thank God for you is. . . ."

2:13b because The conjunction ὅτι 'because' introduces the reason (SITUATION) which caused the messengers' reaction of thanksgiving. In some languages this relation may be expressed as content ('we thank God that').

when you heard the message *that originates from* God, which we(exc) transmitted/told to you The participle παραλαβόντες 'having received' introduces a circumstantial phrase (Bruce; NIV, NJB, NRSV, REB, TEV). The verb παραλαμβάνω 'to receive' was used of receiving or learning a body of instruction handed down by tradition (BAGD, p. 619.2bγ; Bruce). It is rendered in the display from the reciprocal perspective of the messengers ('which we transmitted/told to you'), and the next words in the Greek are rendered from the perspective of the Thessalonians ('when you heard the message that originates from God').

What was received was λόγον ἀκοῆς παρ' ἡμῶν τοῦ θεοῦ 'word of hearing (or word which is heard) from us of God'. The genitives in this phrase have been variously understood, but it seems best (following Bruce; also DGN, NCV, NIV, NRSV) to take 'of God' with 'word' (as in λόγον θεοῦ 'word of God' in 13d), and to take 'from us' with 'that which is heard'. The genitive 'of God' is understood as a genitive of source and is rendered as 'that originates from God'. Thus the Thessalonians received (=heard) the message God had given, which the messengers transmitted to them.

In the Greek there is a double signaling of one event (παραλαβόντες 'having received', ἀκοῆς 'of hearing'). It is rendered 'you heard'. The implied event signaled by παρ' ἡμῶν '(heard) from us' is translated by the reciprocal of παραλαβόντες 'having received' in order to more clearly represent the meaning of παραλαβόντες λόγον 'having received (the) word': 'message . . . which we transmitted to you'. This expresses the meaning more clearly than the more literal 'you received the message', which could be wrongly taken to mean 'you accepted the message'; later in the verse Paul uses the verb δέχομαι, which does mean "*approve, accept . . . teaching*" (BAGD, p. 177.3b).

2:13c-d you accepted/recognized as true not a message *that originates from* **human beings, but rather** *you accepted/recognized as true the* **message** *that originates from* **God** The Greek for 13c-e is ἐδέξασθε οὐ λόγον ἀνθρώπων ἀλλὰ καθώς ἐστιν ἀληθῶς λόγον θεοῦ 'you accepted not a word of men but as it is truly a word of God'. The first verb here is δέχομαι 'to accept'. Some (Marshall; KJV) see no significant difference between it and παραλαμβάνω 'to receive' in 13b. However, because παραλαμβάνω occurs in a circumstantial proposition, it seems appropriate to view it as referring to the outward transmission of the message and δέχομαι to the inward acceptance of the message (Bruce, Frame): when you heard the message you accepted it. Paul is expressing the Thessalonians' subjective evaluation of the message (Bruce, Frame, Marshall, Morris, Wanamaker, and most versions consulted): "you accepted it for what it really is, God's message and not some human thinking" (JB). Wanamaker says, " . . . they accepted it because they recognized the divine origin of the missionaries' preaching."

When Paul mentions the divine origin of the message in 13b, it may well be that the unusual order of genitives there gives marked emphasis. Here, with a negative-positive construction he again emphasizes that it is God's message. Paul's reasoning seems to be similar to that in 1:5: ὅτι τὸ εὐαγγέλιον ἡμῶν οὐκ ἐγενήθη εἰς ὑμᾶς ἐν λόγῳ μόνον ἀλλὰ καὶ ἐν δυνάμει καὶ ἐν πνεύματι ἁγίῳ καὶ ἐν πληροφορίᾳ πολλῇ 'because our gospel did not come to you in word only but also in power and in (the) Holy Spirit and in much assurance'. It is not the Thessalonians' response to the message that is emphasized here and in 1:5, but the divine nature of the message. God's working through it affects them; the message, as Paul goes on to say, is at work in the believers (13f), enabling them to imitate the example of those who endure suffering (v. 14; see also 1:6). The focus in v. 13 seems to be on the word of God and its character; in v. 14 the focus switches with the forefronting of 'you' to the Thessalonians' response.

2:13e which it truly does The subordinate clause καθώς ἐστιν ἀληθῶς 'as it is truly' is a description of 'message that originates from God'. It emphasizes the truth of Paul's statement in 13d.

2:13f and *God* **uses this message in order to affect/change you who trust** *in him* The relative clause ὃς καὶ ἐνεργεῖται ἐν ὑμῖν τοῖς πιστεύουσιν 'which/who also works in you the (ones) believing' is a second description of 'message that originates from God'. TEV takes it as the grounds of 13d: "For God is at work in you who believe." This seems an appropriate alternative relationship because Paul's point that the message originates from God, not man, is supported by the supernatural effect it has in the believers' lives.

The verb ἐνεργέω 'to work' here is almost always used in the NT of supernatural work (Frame, Morris). Bruce says it is the word of God, not the word of humans, which "works effectually" in believers. The Greek form can be either passive or middle; but in either case God is still the one who works through the message. It is his work that affects and changes the behavior and personality of the hearers. The personification of λόγον 'word' is so rendered in the display as to make this clear (see CEV, EHP, TEV).

The conjunction καί 'and' in the relative clause may indicate that *additionally* the message changes them (i.e., in addition to simply being heard or in addition to originating from God). Bruce, NIV, REB, and TEV do not render the 'and'. The implied object of the Thessalonians' faith is 'God' (see the note on 2:10b).

2:14a I(&S&T) know you believed the message from God Because 14a is separated from 13d by two descriptions, this summary is supplied to reestablish the context.

since Here γάρ 'for' introduces the grounds either for Paul's statement in 13c–d that the Thessalonians believed the message that originates from God (Best, Bruce, Frame, Marshall) or for the statement in 13f that this message works in them (Hiebert, Morris). The former is preferable because v. 14 speaks of the suffering that resulted from their having believed the message. If the verse *explicitly* talked of their endurance (which some believe is implied), there would be better support for the second interpretation. Thus γάρ 'for' is taken as introducing the 14a–16c *evidence* for the 13b–f INFERENCE.

what happened to you corresponds to what happened The words here, ὑμεῖς μιμηταὶ ἐγενήθητε 'you became imitators', were used also in 1:6a. Here, as there, the imitation is not intentional on the part of the Thessalonians. "Rather they had through circumstances been made imitators of the Judean Christians" (Wanamaker). NCV has "your experiences have been like those of God's churches . . . in Judea." TEV has "Our brothers, the same things happened to you that happened to the churches of God in Judea. . . ."

to *the people in* the groups that are in Judea land who *worship* God, *those who are united to* Christ Jesus The Greek is τῶν ἐκκλησιῶν τοῦ θεοῦ τῶν οὐσῶν ἐν τῇ Ἰουδαίᾳ ἐν Χριστῷ Ἰησοῦ 'of the churches of God the (ones) being in Judea in Christ Jesus'. See the note on 1:1a for a discussion of ἐκκλησία 'church', which is rendered 'group(s)', and for a discussion of ἐν 'in'. The phrase 'in Christ Jesus' is rendered 'who are united to Christ Jesus'; it is taken as in apposition to the semantic representation of τῶν ἐκκλησιῶν τοῦ θεοῦ 'of the churches of God', 'groups who worship God'. The phrase 'groups that are in Judea who worship God' could apply to any Jewish congregations, but Paul makes it clear that these are Christian worshipers by qualifying the phrase with 'in Christ Jesus'. As to the order, Paul uses 'Christ Jesus' more frequently than 'Jesus Christ', but there is no discernible semantic difference between the two orders. The preceding preposition 'in' and Paul's fondness for the phrase 'in Christ' may have influenced the order here.

Here 'Judea' could mean either the land, comprised of Judea, Samaria, and Galilee (Best, Hiebert, Morris, Wanamaker) or just the southern province of that land. The latter may seem contextually more appropriate because it was in Jerusalem in the province of Judea that Jesus was killed and the first believers persecuted and scattered; vv. 14–15 speak of the Lord's death and Christians' persecution and expulsion. However, at this time in history the name Judea also referred to the larger area (see Luke 23:5, Acts 10:37), and the church had extended to the three provinces (Acts 9:31). So for those languages which must make a distinction, 'land' has better commentary support than 'province'. If possible, a term should be chosen that does not denote an independent political entity, as 'country' does in English; Judea at this time was not independent but was a part of the Roman empire.

2:14b Specifically The conjunction ὅτι 'because, in that' here introduces either the grounds for 14a (Hiebert, Wanamaker) or a specific restatement of it (Bruce, Frame; JB, NIV, REB). The latter interpretation seems preferable because 14b expresses the specific way in which the Thessalonians became imitators, not so much the grounds for considering them imitators.

you suffered *when* your own countrymen *mistreated you because you believed the message from God* in the same way that those *Jewish people in Judea who are united to Jesus* suffered *when* the Jews *who are not united to him mistreated them* The Greek is τὰ αὐτὰ ἐπάθετε καὶ ὑμεῖς ὑπὸ τῶν ἰδίων συμφυλετῶν καθὼς καὶ αὐτοὶ ὑπὸ τῶν Ἰουδαίων 'the same things you suffered also from your own countrymen as also they from the Jews'. The propositionalization is an attempt to maintain focus on the verb ἐπάθετε 'you suffered' by rendering the prepositional phrase 'from your own countrymen' with a circumstantial clause. Frame (also Morris) feels it is implied that it was not suffering but "the steadfast endurance manifested under persecution" that made the Thessalonians like the Judean believers; there is nothing in the context, however, that indicates this. It *is* implied that the Thessalonians had suffered because of their acceptance of God's message (Morris). Some say that their persecutors were their gentile countrymen (Bruce, Frame, Wanamaker). Marshall, however, understands 'countrymen' in a local, rather than racial sense, and would include Jewish instigators of the persecutions (see Acts 17:5). This would give a basis for Paul's denunciation of the Jews in vv. 14-15. The words 'the same things you suffered also . . . as also they' establish the comparison; in the display they are rendered 'in the same way that'. The Thessalonian readers would have understood that the believers in Judea were Jews who had been mistreated by their countrymen (other Jews who were not united to Jesus), just as the Thessalonian believers were being mistreated by theirs.

2:15a *Those unbelieving Jews are* **the ones who are responsible for** **killing the Lord** *himself,* **Jesus** This is the first of five parts of a complex relative clause that modifies 'the Jews' in 14b; the first four parts are coordinate and function as descriptions of the sins of those 'Jews'. The objects (patients) in the four parts are prominent because of forefronting. Morris points out that vv. 15-16 do not include all Jews but only those who had been hostile to God's messengers. Here in this first part Paul used the verb ἀποκτείνω 'killed' rather than 'crucified', perhaps because the Jews only plotted and demanded Jesus' death (Best). But in some languages 'killed' would imply that the Jews did physically kill him. This is not historically accurate, so 'who are responsible for' may be a necessary adjustment in those languages.

In the Greek the names 'Lord' and 'Jesus' are separated by the participle 'killed'. Frame says, "By separating τὸν κύριον from Ἰησοῦν, Paul succeeds in emphasizing that the Lord of glory whom the Jews crucified (1 Cor. 2:8) is none other than the historical Jesus, their kinsman according to the flesh (Rom. 9:5)."

as well as *for killing* **the prophets** Commentators (Best, Bruce, Frame, Marshall) take this as a reference to OT prophets rather than Christian prophets of the early church. This seems correct, as Jesus earlier characterized the people of Jerusalem as ones "who kill the prophets" (Luke 13:34). MJTGNT adds ἰδίους 'their own (prophets)', which supports the view that these are OT prophets, but the reading is rejected by UBSGNT.

By a different punctuation of the text 'prophets' can be taken with the verb in 15b instead of 15a (Thomas), giving the sense 'who forced the prophets and us to leave'. However, this would weaken the impact of 15b, which is taken here as a personal reference to Paul's being driven from Thessalonica and Berea. Moreover, UBSGNT, MJTGNT, and all versions consulted place 'prophets' in 15a.

The word καί 'and' occurs before both 'the Lord' and 'the prophets'. Some therefore render the construction 'both . . . and' (e.g., NCV).

2:15b they forced me(&S&T) to leave *many towns* The verb ἐκδιώκω can mean 'to drive out' (Bruce; CEV, NCV, NIV, NRSV, REB) or 'to persecute' (BAGD, p. 239; Best; Morris; DGN, KJV, NAB, NJB, TEV). The former seems preferable as the Thessalonians would quickly recall how Paul and his companions had not only been persecuted but forced by the Jews to leave Thessalonica (Acts 17:5-10) and Berea (Acts 17:13-14); their forcing them to leave curtailed face-to-face ministry to the Gentiles (16a). The pronoun ἡμᾶς 'us' therefore is understood as exclusive, referring to Paul, Silas, and Timothy (Marshall). The exclusive 'us' here fits Paul's use of 'us' in 16a in the statement that the Jews prevent the messengers from telling the gospel.

2:15c they do not please God Paul now switches to present-tense participles to describe how the behavior of these people is viewed. These Jews no doubt think they please God by opposing all who proclaim the gospel and accept it, but Paul says that what they continually do is counter to God's will. Some see 15c as an understatement used to emphasize God's displeasure with them (Hiebert, Thomas). TEV has "How displeasing they are to God!" They displeased God by killing the Lord and driving out his messengers, but primarily they displease him by opposing God's desire to save the Gentiles (16a): "[who] are so heedless of God's will and such enemies of their fellow-men that they hinder us from telling the Gentiles how they may be saved" (REB).

2:15d and *they are* **opposed to** *what is best for* **all human beings** The adjective ἐναντίος in the phrase 'to all men opposed' (with the participle ὄντων 'being' understood) indicates that the Jews are "*opposed, contrary, hostile* τινί *to someone*" (BAGD, p. 262.2), namely, to human beings (ἀνθρώποις 'men'), including the Gentiles. Bruce says, "This sounds like an echo of slanders current in the Greco-Roman world." Paul, however, in 16a defines their hostility, not in terms of feeling cultural superiority or pride as God's people, but in terms of the efforts of these unbelieving Jews to prevent Gentiles from hearing the gospel (Best). As Frame says, the Jews are "against the best interests of humanity, namely, their salvation." This again is not a conscious opposition on the part of the Jews but one indicated to Paul by their actions.

2:16a *Specifically*, **they prevent us(exc) from telling** *the gospel* **to non-Jewish people** The relative clause here is not preceded by καί 'and' as were the four clauses in v. 15. Thus the participle κωλυόντων 'hindering' is not coordinate with the preceding clauses but introduces either a grounds, manner, or specific proposition. Thomas, NJB, and TNT treat it as grounds, which means the Jews are against all people *since* they prevent us. Hiebert, Marshall, and NRSV treat it as manner, which means the Jews oppose all people *by* preventing us. Best, Frame, and Wanamaker treat it as a specific proposition, which means the Jews oppose all people, *that is*, they prevent us. The relation of generic-specific seems most appropriate because 16a (a specific personal example) brings the list of the sins of the Jews to a peak and leads directly into the statements of 16b and c. The verb λαλέω 'to speak' here was used in 2:2c with the object 'the gospel'; that object is implied here in that Paul says salvation was the goal of his speaking.

in order that *God* **will save them** *spiritually* The conjunction ἵνα is best understood as introducing the purpose of Paul's telling the gospel (Best, Bruce, and Wanamaker; CEV, NJB). Proposition 16a is relationally complex (in the Greek and thus in translation) because two different agents are involved, the unbelieving Jews and the messengers. The uninitiated reader may not be able to determine which agent purposes the salvation of the Gentiles. The CEV makes clear that it is the messengers: "They keep us from speaking his message to the Gentiles and from leading them to be saved." The passive verb σωθῶσιν 'they might be saved' is rendered in the display as active with 'God' the implied agent. The two sides of salvation of which Paul is speaking are most likely deliverance from coming punishment (1:10) and entrance into God's glorious kingdom (2:12).

2:16b Because they continually sin more and more, they reach the limit *set by God* The words εἰς τό with the infinitive indicate either purpose or result. Frame, Marshall, Morris, and Wanamaker take the meaning as purpose here: "in order that they might fill up the purposed measure of their sins always" (Frame); it is in accordance with God's purpose that the Jews sin as they do. Best and Greenlee (p. 54) take it as result, which seems preferable. There is no indication in the context that Paul specifically has God's purpose in mind. The sins of the Jews listed in 15a–16a are the reasons that result in the limit of God's patience being reached (16b). In the display the four REASON labels of 15a–16a (as well as the 16b RESULT) are in uppercase letters because the recounting of those sins is prominent in Paul's description.

The phrase ἀναπληρῶσαι αὐτῶν τὰς ἁμαρτίας 'to fill up their sins' expresses a biblical metaphor (see Gen. 15:16; Dan. 8:23; Matt. 23:32). The image is the filling up of a scale or container, and the topic is the large number of sins certain Jews have committed. The ground of comparison is that nothing further can be added when the established capacity is reached. God has set a limit to the sins he will allow a people to commit; the sins they commit accumulate until they reach the limit. Best says it is the implication of 15–16a that this limit is nearly filled up. NJB translates it, "Thus all the time they are *reaching the full extent of* their *iniquity*" (italics in original, indicating a quotation from another part of the Bible).

The adverb πάντοτε 'always' refers to the continual sinning of unbelieving Jews, represented by the persecution of the servants of God that stretched from the time of the OT prophets to the present (Bruce) (as 15a–16a set forth). The noun ἁμαρτία 'sin' represents an event and is rendered as such in the display.

2:16c *As a result of this* **[15a–16b]**, *God* **is about to punish them now, at last** In 16c Paul switches to a finite verb (ἔφθασεν 'came') after the string of nonfinite verbs in 15a–16b. This may be an indication of a minor break and new development in the discourse. He also uses for the first time in the letter the conjunction δέ. This conjunction often functions as "a developmental marker, in the sense that the information it introduces builds on what has gone before and makes a distinct contribution to the argument" (Levinsohn, p. 64). Here the verb 'come' and the conjunction δέ seem to function together to indicate a reason-result relation in the discourse—the accumulation of the heinous sins mentioned in 15a-16b results in the coming of God's punishment. The noun phrase ἡ ὀργή 'the wrath' is understood as a metonymy (as in 1:10c) signifying God's punishment. It can be interpreted as expected punishment in the present for sins that men commit (Rom. 1:18) or punishment in the future (1 Thess. 1:10) or both. It seems best to understand it here as in 1:10, where 'the coming wrath' refers to future judgment.

Paul uses the aorist-tense verb ἔφθασεν 'came' as the predicate of 'the wrath'. Some scholars interpret this as a reference to an event such as the expulsion of the Jews from Rome by Claudius, a massacre in Jerusalem in A.D. 49, or even the destruction of Jerusalem, which some say had already occurred when Paul wrote. Wanamaker says, "The apocalyptic character of the statement, however, warns against insisting that an actual event lies behind the verb." The past tense may mean that in Paul's view God's punishment had drawn so near that it inevitably would come when the measure of the sins of the Jews was filled up (Best, Bruce, Frame, Marshall, Morris). Based on this interpretation, some versions render ἔφθασεν 'came' with the English present perfect: "the wrath of God has come upon them" (NIV). But this rendering, intended to convey the idea of nearness and inevitability, indicates present rather than future punishment. The CEV captures the meaning better: "Now God has finally become angry and will punish them." In the display 'the wrath' is rendered in accordance with the interpretation that this refers to near but future judgment: 'God is about to punish them'.

The final phrase εἰς τέλος 'to (the) end/utmost' is rendered temporally in the display as 'now, at last' (following Best, Frame) because this fits the temporal use of πάντοτε 'always' in 16b. However, εἰς τέλος has also been understood intensively (Bruce, Morris): 'in full, completely'.

BOUNDARIES AND COHERENCE

The initial boundary of 2:13-16 was discussed under 2:1-12 and the final boundary under 1:2-2:16. (See "Boundaries.")

Second person references to the Thessalonians predominate in 2:13-16. This contrasts with the first person references to the ministry of Paul and his companions in 2:1-12.

Most commentators and versions view 2:13-16 as a unit. Some make a boundary between 2:13 and 2:14 (Bruce; EHP, GW, NAB, NLT, WFB), others between 2:14 and 2:15 (CEV).

As to a boundary between 2:13 and 2:14, although v. 14 contains the vocative 'brothers', which sometimes indicates a boundary (see 2:17), in v. 14 it serves to emphasize the forefronted topic 'you'; and although the conjunction γάρ 'for' sometimes occurs at the beginning of a new unit (see 2:1), in v. 14 it performs the same function as ὅτι 'because' in 1:5, closely tying what follows to what precedes. A boundary between v. 13 and v. 14 is thus not justified on relational grounds. In 1:2-6 Paul thanks God that the Thessalonians are chosen as evidenced by the way they received the messengers' message and responded to persecution; paralleling that idea in 2:13-16 Paul thanks God that the Thessalonians truly received the gospel as evidenced by the fact that they were persecuted as other true believers in Judea were. A boundary between v. 13 and v. 14 would separate the conclusion (INFERENCE) from the grounds (evidence).

As to a boundary between 2:14 and 2:15, the shift from second person pronouns to third person in v. 15 (signaling the shift of topic from the Thessalonians to the unbelieving Jews) would support it. However, vv. 15-16 is a complex relative clause that relates to a noun in v. 14, and there is no forefronted noun in v. 15 to indicate that Paul intended to focus on the new topic. A boundary between v. 14 and v. 15 may serve English discourse structure better than it reflects the Greek discourse.

PROMINENCE AND THEME

The theme of 2:13-16 consists basically of Paul's REACTION of thanksgiving (13a) and the prominent propositions from the SITUATION (namely, the INFERENCE-evidence propositions 13b-14b), which cause him to give thanks. In the INFERENCE the 13b circumstance proposition is important in providing necessary background information and thus is included in the theme. The negative-positive contrast in 13c-d is a form of prominence, and thus the 13c negative proposition is included in the theme along with the 13d positive one. The 14a-b generic-SPECIFIC propositional cluster of the evidence is prominent because of the new topic ὑμεῖς 'you', the forefronted noun μιμηταί 'imitators' (which is also prominent because of repetition—it was used first in 1:6), and the vocative ἀδελφοί 'brothers', all in 14a. The 14b SPECIFIC restatement is included in the theme as well.

Grammatically, the propositions in 15a–16c are a description of 'Jews' in 14b. As such, they have little prominence in the discourse. We have to ask, however, why Paul presents such a long and involved description of unbelieving Jews. Perhaps it functions to give added support to 14b. Or perhaps Paul wants to convince the Thessalonians of the sinfulness of some unbelieving Jews among them (see Acts 17:5) and to warn against them.

DIVISION CONSTITUENT 2:17–3:13
(Expressive Section: Rapport Basis₂ of 1:2–3:13)

THEME: When people forced me, Silas, and Timothy to be separated from you for a short time, I strongly desired to be with you because it is you who cause us to be proud and joyful. When I could no longer endure, I sent Timothy to find out whether or not you were still trusting in God. Now Timothy has just returned and has told me the good news that you still trust in God. As a result I have been cheered up and I cannot adequately thank God for what he has done for you. Very frequently I ask God that I will be able to visit you.

MACROSTRUCTURE	CONTENTS
EMOTIVE PROBLEM (peak₃ unit of 1:2–3:13)	2:17–20 When people forced me, Silas, and Timothy to be separated from you for a short time, I strongly desired to be with you because it is because of you that we are proud and are joyful.
seeking	3:1–5 When I could no longer endure, I sent Timothy to you in order to find out whether or not you were still trusting in God.
SOLUTION (climax unit of 1:2–3:13)	3:6–10 Now Timothy has just returned to me from you and has told me the good news that you still trust in God. As a result I have been cheered up and I cannot thank God adequately for what he has done for you and because of my greatly rejoicing because of you. Very frequently I ask God that I will be able to visit you and help you trust him more strongly.
reaction/transition	3:11–13 I pray that God will help us return to you and that the Lord Jesus will help you to love each other and other people more and more, just as we love you.

INTENT AND MACROSTRUCTURE

The 2:17–3:13 section is the last in which Paul primarily intends to affect the emotions of his readers. Here he reaches the climax of the rapport-building division (1:2–3:13) of his letter. He tells the Thessalonians about the great joy they bring him (2:19–20; 3:9), of his deep concern for them since his untimely departure (2:17; 3:1, 5) and of his repeated attempts to find out how they were faring in persecution (2:17–18; 3:1–2, 5). Now that Timothy has returned to Paul from visiting Thessalonica and reported that the believers remain faithful to the Lord, Paul expresses his elation and overwhelming thankfulness (3:7–9). And he prays fervently that he may be able to return to these believers (3:10–11).

Such expressions of deep feeling indicate that the genre is emotive. But is it an expressive or descriptive unit? Although Paul recounts sequentially his strong desire to be with the Thessalonians, his sending of Timothy to learn about their welfare, and his great joy in hearing Timothy's report, this sequence is merely incidental to the emotive problem that is expressed and solved in the section. Moreover, the constituent paragraph 3:1–5 begins with διό 'therefore', which signals a reason-result relation with the preceding paragraph, not a sequential one. In view of all this, 2:17–3:13 is seen as an expressive section of the solutionality subtype. The first paragraph of this section states an emotive problem, which is Paul's intense desire to be with the Thessalonians because of his love and concern for them. The second paragraph gives the resulting action—Paul's seeking, through his emissary Timothy, to find out how the Thessalonians were faring. The third and fourth paragraphs each begin with the developmental marker δέ (see the note on 2:16c). The third paragraph thus moves the discourse to an emotive solution, which consists of Timothy's report and Paul's overwhelming thankfulness at hearing this good news. The fourth and final paragraph adds a concluding wish-prayer, which is a reaction of Paul to the emotive solution but also a transition to the next division of the book.

With regard to the overall discourse structure, the 2:17–20 paragraph ends with two rhetorical questions in 2:19 (the first of which is complex, having three nuclei). They express the joy and pride that the Thessalonians bring to Paul and his companions. These are the first rhetorical questions in the epistle, and they appear to bring prominence and heightened emotive expression to the 2:17–3:13 section as well as to the 1:2–3:13 division. Thus it seems appropriate to consider 2:17–20 a peak of the division.

Next, in the 3:1–5 paragraph Paul briefly backs off from the emotional buildup in 2:17–20.

He seems to be setting the stage for the climactic unit (3:6-10) that follows.

Then, in the 3:6-10 paragraph Paul verbalizes his emotions, perhaps with some difficulty (see the note on 3:9a), in response to the good report concerning the Thessalonians. He exclaims νῦν ζῶμεν 'now we live' (3:8). Using a rhetorical question, he asks τίνα γὰρ εὐχαριστίαν δυνάμεθα τῷ θεῷ ἀνταποδοῦναι περὶ ὑμῶν ἐπὶ πάσῃ τῇ χαρᾷ ᾗ χαίρομεν δι' ὑμᾶς 'for what thanks are we able to give back to God concerning you because of all the joy (with) which we rejoice because of you' (3:9). Such heightened expression and the concentration of referents (Paul, Timothy, and the Thessalonians) signal that 3:6-10 is the climax of 1:2-3:13, the rapport-building division of the epistle. The opening of 3:6-10 with ἄρτι δέ 'and now' contributes to the impression that this is a climax.

Finally, the 3:11-13 paragraph is a post-climax unit. This wish-prayer closes the 2:17-3:13 section and provides a transition to the next division, 4:1-5:24.

The labels for the 2:17-20 and 3:6-10 paragraphs are in uppercase letters in the display because of the prominence of these units in the section—and in the 1:2-3:13 division as well.

BOUNDARIES AND COHERENCE

The initial boundary of 2:17-3:13 was discussed under 1:2-2:16, the final boundary under 1:2-3:13. (See "Boundaries.")

Repeated concepts bring referential coherence to 2:17-3:13: 'joy' (2:19, 20; 3:9); the verb παρακαλέω ('encourage' in 3:2 and 'cheered up' in 3:7); 'to see each other' (2:17, 18; 3:6, 10); 'your faith' (3:2, 5, 6, 7, 10); 'affliction' (3:3, 4, 7). There are words which express deep emotion: 'being orphaned' (2:17); 'were very eager' (2:17); 'great desire' (2:17); 'longing' (3:6); 'we live' (3:8).

The final constituent (3:11-13) of the 2:17-3:13 section exhibits referential coherence with its other constituents. The phrase 'clear the way' in 3:11 relates to the obstacle of Satan's 'hindering us' in 2:18; that is, Paul prays in 3:11-13 that God will overcome the obstacles and clear the way for him to visit the Thessalonians. There is also a sandwich construction between the first section constituent (2:17-20) and the final one (3:11-13) as follows:

'before our Lord Jesus at his coming' (2:19)
'before God . . . at the coming of our Lord Jesus' (3:13)

There is another pair of similar phrases that bring coherence between 3:11-13 and what precedes: 'just as also we you' in 3:6 and 'just as also we to you' in 3:12.

There is also relational coherence in 2:17-3:13, seen in the resolution of a problem: Paul and his companions are concerned about the Thessalonians but cannot return; then Timothy is sent and brings back a good report. The particle δέ, which functions here as a developmental discourse marker, also brings relational coherence. It occurs in the initial verses (2:17, 3:6, 3:11) of three of the four constituent units and again in 3:12. (Paul used δέ only once, in 2:16, in the entire preceding section, 1:2-2:16.)

PROMINENCE AND THEME

In 2:17-3:13 what is prominent is Paul's expressions of strong desire, pride, joy, and thanksgiving concerning the Thessalonians. Many of these occur in the emotive solution constituent, 3:6-10, which is naturally prominent. Others, however, occur in 2:17-20, the emotive problem constituent. Therefore both of these labels, *EMOTIVE PROBLEM* and *SOLUTION*, are in uppercase letters in the display.

The theme of 2:17-3:13 is derived primarily from the themes of its prominent constituents, 2:17-20 and 3:6-10. Background information from 3:1-5 about Paul's sending Timothy is also included.

SECTION CONSTITUENT 2:17-20
(Expressive Paragraph: Emotive Problem of 2:17-3:13)

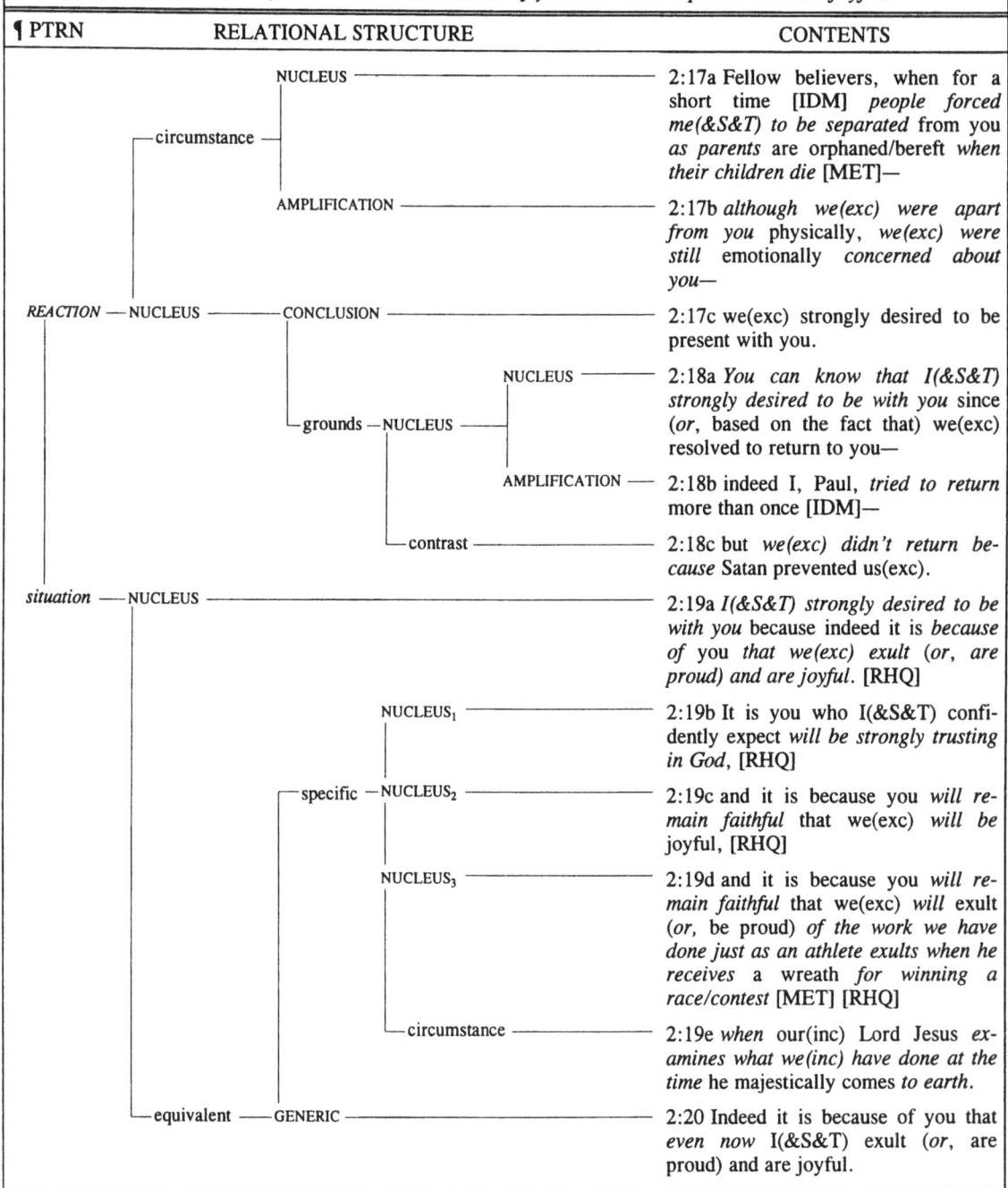

INTENT AND PARAGRAPH PATTERN

In the 2:17-20 paragraph Paul's intent is to affect the emotions of his readers. He continues to build rapport by telling them how much they mean to him and his companions (v. 17). He wants the Thessalonians to recognize that it was not a lack of affection or desire that caused him to stay away; rather, he was prevented by Satan from returning (v. 18). The fact that the Thessalonians continue to trust Christ despite strong persecution brings him, and will bring him, much joy and pride (vv. 19-20). Such expressions indicate the genre is emotive. Because Paul develops his thoughts in a result-reason relation rather than a sequential one this is an emotive paragraph of the expressive type.

The paragraph consists of two propositional clusters, a result (17a–18c) and a reason (19a–20, introduced by γάρ 'for'). In the first cluster Paul states an emotive problem, but the second doesn't move toward a resolution; therefore this is not a solutionality subtype pattern. It is also not a volitionality subtype because in vv. 17–18 Paul is expressing strong desire to be with the Thessalonians. Thus 2:17–20 is a simple causality subtype, the constituents of which (in an expressive paragraph) are labeled REACTION and *situation*.

The 2:17–20 paragraph is the third peak unit of 1:2–3:13 (see "Intent" of 2:17–3:13).

NOTES

2:17a The conjunction δέ could be taken as indicating contrast: the affection of the messengers is a contrast to the behavior of the unbelieving Jews in vv. 14–16 (Morris; also NBV, NIV, NRSV, TEV). However, it seems best to understand its primary function to be a high-level developmental marker indicating a transition to new subject matter in the discourse (Best, Bruce, Frame, Hiebert, Marshall, Wanamaker). It could be translated with the transitional 'now', but that would be misleading if understood temporally. It is best left untranslated in the display (as in CEV, GW, NAB, NCV, NJB, NLT, REB), but how it is translated in another language will depend on the types of high-level markers used in the language.

when for a short time *people forced me(&S&T)* **to be separated from you** *as parents are orphaned/bereft when their children die* The participle ἀπορφανισθέντες 'being made orphans' here is very probably a live metaphor expressing the depth of Paul's feeling. The word referred to parents bereaved of their children as well as to children whose parents had died (Marshall, Wanamaker). Here the topic of the metaphor is Paul and his companions; the image is being orphaned. The ground of comparison is pain caused by loss: just as parents are bereaved when children die, the messengers to the Thessalonians were painfully affected when they were suddenly forced to leave the city and couldn't return to the new believers. NJB has "we had been deprived of you"; NIV, "we were torn away from you." The emphasis is on the separation itself, not the length of the separation. The passive participle has been rendered actively in the display, with the agent 'people' supplied. The participle most likely indicates circumstance (Best, Frame; DGN, NAB, NBV, NIV, NRSV, REB, TEV) and is rendered 'when' in the display.

The idiom πρὸς καιρὸν ὥρας 'for a time of an hour' emphasizes the fact that the time between the messengers' leaving Thessalonica and Timothy's contacting the believers again was short. Paul wants them to know that it was difficult to wait even a very short time to reestablish contact and learn of their condition.

2:17b *although we(exc) were apart from you* **physically,** *we(exc) were still* **emotionally concerned about you** The phrase προσώπῳ οὐ καρδίᾳ 'in face not in heart' is characteristic of traditional friendship letters (Wanamaker). Here it is an amplification interjected to emphasize the messengers' emotions. The 17b AMPLIFICATION is given equal prominence with the 17a NUCLEUS in the display because of the contribution of the former to Paul's expression of emotional longing in the paragraph. The relation within proposition 17b is one of concession-contraexpectation. The word πρόσωπον 'face' here is presumably part of a dead figure (synecdoche), in which a body part represented the whole person. The meaning is that the messengers and Thessalonians were physically apart from each other. The word καρδία 'heart' signifies either emotions (NJB has "deprived of you ... in body but never in affection") or thoughts (CEV has "we never stopped thinking about you"). It is best taken here as emotional concern because Paul speaks in vv. 17–18 of the strong desire he had to see the Thessalonians and in 3:2–5 of the concern he had that their faith would remain strong in spite of persecution.

2:17c we(exc) strongly desired to be present with you The Greek is περισσοτέρως ἐσπουδάσαμεν τὸ πρόσωπον ὑμῶν ἰδεῖν ἐν πολλῇ ἐπιθυμίᾳ 'very much we were eager, or tried, to see your face with great desire'. The adverb περισσοτέρως may have either a comparative sense such as 'the more abundantly' (Bruce; NBV) or an intensified sense such as 'very hard' (Frame, Morris, Wanamaker; CEV, DGN, GW, NCV, NIV, NLT, TEV). As there is nothing in the context with which a comparison is being made, it seems best to understand it as intensified. The verb σπουδάζω may signify either the desire the messengers felt (Frame; NAB, NASB, NJB, NRSV REB, TNT) or the effort they made to see the Thessalonians

(Best, Marshall, Morris, Wanamaker; CEV, EHP, GW, NBV, NCV, NIV, NLT, TEV). The former seems more appropriate to the context. In v. 17 Paul is emphasizing the desire he had to see the Thessalonians. In the next verse he speaks of his resolve and attempts to return. The preceding adverb 'very much' and the following prepositional phrase, 'with great desire', fit the meaning of 'we longed, desired' for the verb σπουδάζω in v. 17. The phrase 'to see your face' probably contains a dead figure of synecdoche as in 17b, in which 'face' signifies the whole person. In the display it is rendered 'to be present with you'.

2:18a *You can know that I(&S&T) strongly desired to be with you* **since (*or*, based on the fact that)** The conjunction διότι 'because, therefore' can be interpreted as introducing either grounds for the preceding statement (BAGD, p. 199.3; Best, Bruce, Frame, Marshall, Wanamaker) or result (NKJV, NAB, REB, TNT). TNT has "for that reason." The former seems preferable. Paul uses the communication relation of grounds to say that his resolve and his several efforts to return demonstrated his strong desire to see the Thessalonians.

we(exc) resolved to return to you The verb θέλω here can mean a general desire (Frame; CEV, NIV, NRSV, TEV, TNT) or a wish with a resolve to do something (Best, Marshall, Wanamaker), as in REB's "we made up our minds." Since Paul speaks in 18c of being prevented from going to the Thessalonians, the idea of resolve does seem to be involved; and this meaning also fits well with the aorist tense of the verb.

Paul and his companions had been in Thessalonica previously, so in the display the infinitive of ἔρχομαι 'to come' is rendered 'to return' (also TEV).

2:18b indeed I, Paul, *tried to return* The particle μέν emphasizes the subject (BAGD, p. 503.2). There is no verb in the Greek. In 18a Paul says the messengers desired or resolved to return to the Thessalonians; in 18c he says that Satan prevented them from doing so. It must be that Satan somehow prevented them physically rather than just hindering their resolve, so Paul must have 'tried to return'. The 18b proposition can be understood either as amplification of the strong desire Paul had to see the Thessalonians again or as the goal of Paul's resolve in 18a. The amplification relation has been chosen for the display because here the progression is from mind (resolve) to action. (The move-goal relation would be more appropriate to narrative where one action leads to another.) In the display the 18b AMPLIFICATION is given equal prominence with the 18a NUCLEUS because of the role the former plays in emphasizing and substantiating Paul's strong desire.

more than once The idiom καὶ ἅπαξ καὶ δίς 'both once and twice' has been variously interpreted as more than once (Bruce, Morris; NAB, NCV, NJB, REB, TEV), more than two times (Best; CEV, NAB, NJB, REB), or many times (Frame; DGN, NIV, NRSV, TNT). The first is chosen for the display because the second and third can be inferred from it.

2:18c but *we(exc) didn't return because* **Satan prevented us(exc)** The conjunction καί introduces a contrast (Bruce; CEV, NAB, NCV, NIV, NJB, NRSV, REB, TEV, TNT): we resolved to return but we didn't. The reason (the implied relation within 18c) they didn't return is that Satan prevented them in some way. In using the first person plural pronoun (Satan prevented 'us') Paul may be referring only to himself (Morris, Wanamaker). Or he may be referring to himself and Silas (Bruce) or to himself and Silas and Timothy (Frame). Either of the latter two possibilities seems preferable to the first. Paul uses the first person singular pronoun in 18b when making a statement about his personal efforts to return; at 18c the first person plural pronoun refers back to the plural pronoun in 18a: we resolved to return to you but we didn't. It is improbable that Paul would use a literary 'we' (meaning 'I') in 18c, when he had just used 'I' in 18b.

In some languages 'but we didn't return' may need to be made explicit if it is not understood from the phrase 'Satan prevented us'.

The verb rendered 'prevented' in the display is ἐγκόπτω 'to break up'. The word was used of soldiers breaking up a road to prevent the enemy from reaching them. NRSV has "Satan blocked our way;" REB, "Satan thwarted us."

2:19a *I(&S&T) strongly desired to be with you* **because** Here γάρ 'for' introduces the reason for the messengers' desire to see the Thessalonians again (Bruce, Frame, Marshall, Wanamaker). Proposition 17c is the nuclear statement in the 17–18 REACTION and is supplied here in the nuclear proposition of the 19–20 *situation* to make the paragraph pattern clear.

indeed it is *because of* **you** *that we(exc) exult (or, are proud) and are joyful* Verse 19 consists of two rhetorical questions. The second one (ἢ οὐχὶ καὶ ὑμεῖς 'is (it) not also/even you?') is embedded in the first (τίς γὰρ ἡμῶν ἐλπὶς ἢ χαρὰ ἢ στέφανος καυχήσεως . . . ἔμπροσθεν τοῦ κυρίου ἡμῶν Ἰησοῦ ἐν τῇ αὐτοῦ παρουσίᾳ 'for what (is) our hope or joy or wreath of boasting . . . before our Lord Jesus at his coming?'), and it answers the first. The word οὐχί, a strong negative, implies a definite affirmative answer to the embedded question. Paul repeats the answer with a declarative statement in v. 20, in which he forefronts the pronoun 'you'. This forefronting, repetition, and use of two rhetorical questions are prominence devices to focus on the answer. To indicate this prominence, in the display the answer is given first (in 19a) and rendered with a cleft construction, 'it is because of you'. (This follows the TEV, which is one of the few translations to render the rhetorical questions as declarative.) The answer cannot be brought forward, however, without the question, which is represented by the content clause 'that we exult and are joyful'. The meaning of 2:19a is equivalent to 2:20.

The particle ἢ can be a disjunctive 'or' or a comparative 'than'. Paul uses it twice as a disjunctive in the first rhetorical question of v. 19: 'What is our hope or joy or wreath of boasting'. It also occurs at the beginning of the embedded question, which Hendriksen renders "or are not also you." Bruce suggests the last occurrence has the wrong accent and should read ἦ, which is an interrogative particle. Alternatively, BAGD lists examples of ἢ which introduce and add rhetorical questions (p. 342.1dα) or which introduce a question that is parallel to a preceding one or that supplements it (342.1dβ). The display does not render the particle as 'or'.

The καί in the embedded question ἢ οὐχὶ καὶ ὑμεῖς 'not also/even you?' has been understood in two ways: (1) It means 'also' and includes the idea of Paul's other converts (Best, Frame): TEV has "it is you—you, no less than others!" (2) It means 'indeed, even' and gives emphasis to the answer (Bruce, Wanamaker): "what indeed but you?" (REB). The second seems more appropriate in this passage where Paul has not mentioned others of his converts but instead is emphasizing what the Thessalonians mean to him.

2:19b It is you who I(&S&T) confidently expect *will be strongly trusting in God* In view of the fact that v. 20 is the declarative answer to Paul's rhetorical questions in v. 19, propositions 19b–e are understood as contributing specific information for the 2:20 generic answer.

There is no verb in v. 19 in the Greek; the tenses of the supplied verbs here and in the following two propositions are dependent on the relationship of the three propositions to the final phrase of the verse, 'before our Lord Jesus at his coming' (19e). 'Crown of boasting' in 19d is in the same semantic domain as the Lord's coming in 19e (implying judgment and rewards), so 19d most likely refers to that future time. Marshall, Morris, and Wanamaker relate 19b, c, and d to that future event (also NAB, CEV, REB, TNT), but others render 19b and c as present hope and joy (Best; NCV, NJB). Though Paul does speak of the messengers' joy with a present-tense verb in v. 20, in v. 19 it seems best to relate the hope and joy, as well as the crown, to the return of Christ. Paul is writing of his present hope, which will be fulfilled at the time of Christ's return, and of a future joy to be experienced at that time (NLT).

The noun phrase ἡμῶν ἐλπίς 'our hope' represents a cognitive event and is rendered in the display by a clause. Hope is a present confidence that looks forward to future fulfillment, here at the time of Christ's return. Thus, 'hope' is rendered as present tense ('confidently expect'), but the content of that hope is future tense ('will be strongly trusting in God'). Paul was concerned that the Thessalonians continue to trust in the Lord despite persecution (3:5), and so Timothy was sent back to encourage them (3:2–3). Thus it fits the context to say that Paul hoped that they would still be faithful when Christ returned. Bruce says it is "hope that the divine work so well begun in them will increase to maturity."

2:19c and it is because you *will remain faithful* **that we(exc)** *will be* **joyful** The noun χαρά 'joy' here is preceded by the disjunctive conjunction ἢ 'or', as is στέφανος καυχήσεως 'crown of boasting' in 19d. Paul is not saying, however, that one or the other of the three things in 19b–d will be true; they will all be true. The conjunction functions as a copulative, 'and' (Best, Frame, Morris, Wanamaker; CEV, NJB, TEV); it conjoins propositions 19b–d.

The pronoun 'our' which modifies 'hope' in 19b also modifies 'joy' and 'crown of boasting'. The noun phrase 'our joy' represents a state and is rendered by a clause in the display. That this is a future joy is implied by the mention of the return of Christ (19e) and the sandwiching of 'joy' between 'hope' and 'crown of boasting', which are both related to the return of Christ. Paul will be joyful in the presence of Jesus because the

Thessalonians will represent lasting effectiveness of the messengers' work (Marshall).

2:19d and it is because you *will remain faithful* that we(exc) *will* exult *(or,* be proud) *of the work we have done just as an athlete exults when he receives* a wreath *for winning a race/contest* The noun στέφανος 'crown' here is the laurel wreath that victorious military commanders or winners of athletic competitions received (Bruce, Frame, Wanamaker). It is the image of a live metaphor: just as a wreath was awarded at the end of a successful campaign or race, so rewards will be given to the faithful when Christ returns and examines their work (19e). At that time the continued faithfulness of the Thessalonians will indicate that the work of Paul and his companions was a success. Just as a military commander or athlete exulted in the wreath, so Paul will exult in the continuing faithfulness of the Thessalonians; they will be evidence of the messengers' successful ministry (Bruce, Marshall, Wanamaker; TEV, TNT). "The Thessalonians are Paul's 'hope, joy, and crown of boasting' at the public manifestation of Christ because they are the fruit of his ministry as an apostle of Christ. They thus demonstrate his faithfulness in carrying out the mission given to him by the risen Christ" (Wanamaker, p. 123). Because this context implies Christ's judgment (see the note on 19e), Paul may also have had in mind the reward this evidence of faithful ministry would bring him (Wanamaker).

The second noun in στέφανος καυχήσεως 'crown of pride/boasting' is a genitive expressing a general relationship (Greenlee, p. 27). It indicates that the crown is something about which Paul will boast (Frame; TEV) or that will bring exultation (Bruce, Marshall, Morris; NAB) or pride (Wanamaker; NCV). Paul uses the verbal form of this same noun root in 2 Thess. 1:4 when he says the messengers boast about the perseverance and faith of the Thessalonians to other churches. But considering the reference in the present passage to a future time of examination, 'boasting' seems inappropriate; at that time Paul would have no one to boast to, though he could feel pride in the good sense of the word. Scripture denounces 'pride' in the senses of conceit and arrogance. Here, however, Paul is speaking of the delight or elation he will feel within himself because of his work for and relationship with the Thessalonian believers. The noun form 'pride' represents a cognitive event and is thus rendered in the display as a clause 'we will exult, or, be proud'.

Banker understands στέφανός μου 'my crown' in Phil. 4:1 as a dead figure, and he gives a nonfigurative meaning for στέφανος: "pride, glory, honor" (p. 157). If it is a dead figure here as well, 2:19d would be 'and it is because you *will remain faithful* that we(exc) *will* exult *(or,* be proud)'. Banker's caution for translating the figure in Phil. 4:1 applies here: "It needs to be remembered that this verse is very emotive. This should be maintained in translation. A rendering [of the figure] that is too involved would detract from its emotive power" (ibid.).

2:19e *when* our(inc) Lord Jesus *examines what we(inc) have done at the time* he majestically comes *to earth* The implied relation of ἔμπροσθεν τοῦ κυρίου ἡμῶν Ἰησοῦ ἐν τῇ αὐτοῦ παρουσίᾳ 'before our Lord Jesus at his coming' to what precedes is best understood as circumstance: "when we stand before our Lord Jesus at his coming" (REB). It relates to the three preceding propositions (see the second paragraph of the note on 19b). There is also a circumstantial relation within the proposition: when he comes. This relation is rendered in the display 'at the time' for stylistic variation.

The idea of Christ's tribunal, a time of final review and reward, may be inferred from the phrase 'before our Lord Jesus' (Bruce, Marshall, Frame; NLT, REB). Paul has just mentioned the wreath given to the victor in a contest, indicating the idea of reward. In 3:13, where he uses similar wording, Paul speaks of the Thessalonians' being blameless and holy 'before our God and father at the coming of our Lord Jesus'. The idea of being blameless implies examination. For the Thessalonians and all believers this will not be punishment for sin (from which Christ has already delivered them as stated in 1:10 and 5:9), but an occasion for evaluating work or deeds done (see 1 Cor. 3:12-15, 2 Cor. 5:10). It is rendered 'examines what we have done', which has less negative connotations in English than 'judges us'. The first person plural pronouns in 19e are understood as inclusive because Jesus is the Lord of the Thessalonians as well as of the messengers, and they will also stand before him when he comes.

The Textus Receptus and many manuscripts add Χριστοῦ 'Christ' after 'our Lord Jesus', which is a more frequent Pauline usage. The UBSGNT does not mention this variant reading, and the MJTGNT text doesn't include it.

In this verse is one of the earliest Scripture usages of the technical term παρουσία 'coming'. In the Hellenistic world it referred to the visit of a god or to the visit of a human ruler or high official to a city, with appropriate ceremonies held and honors bestowed (Bruce, Wanamaker). It was adopted by Paul and other NT authors to speak of Christ's coming as sovereign Lord to earth.

2:20 Indeed Here γάρ 'for' could be taken in one of two ways, either as introducing grounds for the implied affirmative answer to the second rhetorical question in v. 19, 'Is it not you?' (so Marshall, Wanamaker), or as providing emphasis (so Bruce, Frame). The second, rendered 'indeed' in the display, is preferable as 2:20 is the declarative form of the answer to Paul's rhetorical question in v. 19, and as such, emphasizes the point that the Thessalonians provide the messengers much pride and joy. For reasons of prominence this answer is first presented in proposition 19a. Proposition 2:20 then functions as an equivalent proposition to the 19a NUCLEUS.

it is because of you that *even now* I(&S&T) exult (*or*, are proud) and are joyful The Greek of 2:20 is ὑμεῖς γάρ ἐστε ἡ δόξα ἡμῶν καὶ ἡ χαρά 'for/indeed you are the glory of us and the joy'. Because they have remained faithful to the Lord despite considerable persecution, the Thessalonians cause the messengers to have glory and joy. The meaning of 'glory' here can focus either on (1) that which brings praise to the messengers (BAGD, p. 204.3, has "*you bring us renown*") or (2) that in which the messengers exult or take pride (Bruce, Wanamaker; EHP, NAB, NJB, NLT, TEV). Although elements of both are probably involved, the second meaning seems more appropriate to the immediate context as Paul has just said that the Thessalonians will be 'a crown of exultation/pride' (19d), and this interpretation fits as well Paul's statement in 2 Thess. 1:4. In addition to having pride Paul is filled with joy because of the strong faith of the Thessalonians.

The verb ἐστε 'you are' here is present tense. As future-tense verbs were made explicit in 19b–d because of the future event in 19e, the change to present is shown in the display by 'even now'.

BOUNDARIES AND COHERENCE

The initial boundary of 2:17–20 was discussed under 1:2–2:16 (see "Boundaries"). The terminal boundary is between 2:20 and 3:1, as shown by the resumption, after the rhetorical questions of v. 19 and the answer of v. 20, of Paul's discussion of his attempts to learn about the Thessalonians. The change is indicated by the particle διό 'therefore' in 3:1. There is also a change from the present tense, with which Paul speaks of the Thessalonians in v. 20, to the aorist tense in 3:1. In 2:20 the Thessalonians are the topic of the sentence; in 3:1-5 it is the messengers. In 3:1 Paul uses a participle, στέγοντες '(no longer) enduring', which is similar in form and emotional impact to the participle with which he began the previous paragraph, ἀπορφανισθέντες 'being made orphans' (2:17).

Some see a boundary between 2:18 and 2:19 (Morris; GW, WFB). This is no doubt based on the fact that 2:19 is a rhetorical question, which somewhat breaks the continuity of the discourse. Also, v. 19 does not have a verb, and when the first verb does appear (v. 20) it is present tense, which contrasts with the aorist tense of the verbs of 2:18. However, v. 19 is in a support relation to what precedes, as indicated by the conjunction γάρ 'for'. That relation of reason provides the *situation* for the REACTION of 2:17–18 and makes the semantic paragraph complete. Thus 2:17–20 is best taken as a single unit.

This unit has referential coherence in that its freestanding pronouns refer to the messengers (ἡμεῖς 'we' in v. 17; ἡμᾶς 'us' in v. 18; ἡμῶν 'our' in v. 19; ἡμῶν 'our' in v. 20; and ἐγώ 'I' in v. 18) and the Thessalonians (ὑμῶν 'you/your' in v. 17 twice; ὑμᾶς 'you' in v. 18; ὑμεῖς 'you' in v. 19; and ὑμεῖς 'you' in v. 20). In addition, there are emotional terms that bring unity: ἀπορφανισθέντες 'orphaned', καρδία '(in) heart', ἐσπουδάσαμεν 'we were eager', and ἐν πολλῇ ἐπιθυμίᾳ 'in much desire' (all in v. 17); ἠθελήσαμεν 'we resolved' (v. 18); χαρά 'joy' and καυχήσεως 'of pride/boasting' (v. 19); δόξα 'glory' and χαρά 'joy' (v. 20).

PROMINENCE AND THEME

The theme of 2:17–20 consists of three elements: the 2:17a circumstance proposition, which supplies necessary background information; the 2:17c NUCLEUS of the naturally prominent REACTION; and the *situation*'s 2:19a NUCLEUS, which contains the information in the prominent rhetorical questions and answer of 2:19-20.

A SEMANTIC AND STRUCTURAL ANALYSIS OF 1 THESSALONIANS

SECTION CONSTITUENT 3:1-5
(Expressive Paragraph: Seeking of 2:17-3:13)

THEME: *When I could no longer endure, I sent Timothy to you in order to find out whether or not you were still trusting in God.*

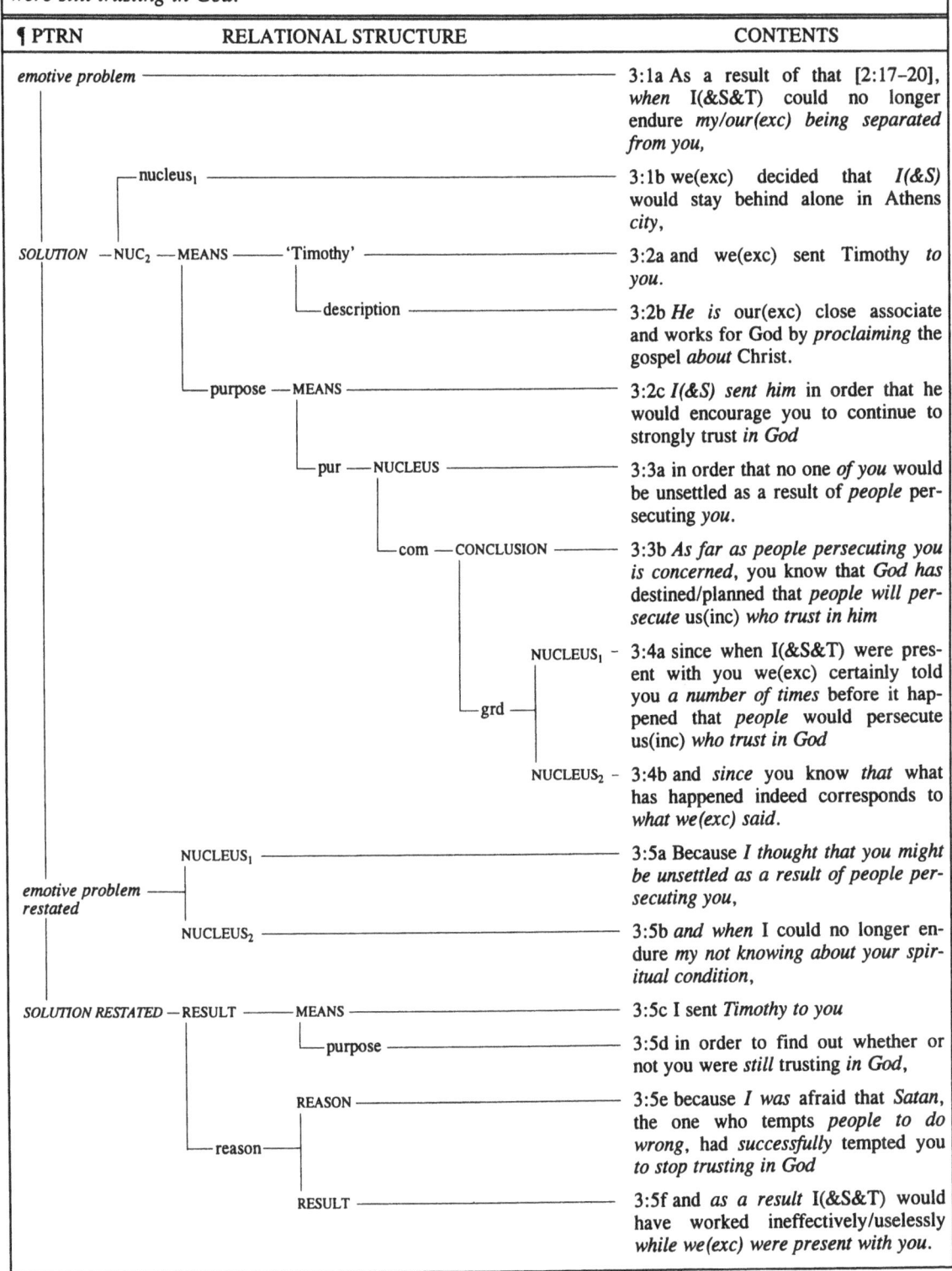

INTENT AND PARAGRAPH PATTERN

In the 3:1–5 paragraph Paul's intent is to affect the emotions of his readers. To do this he demonstrates his great interest in and concern for them. Twice he says that he and his companions couldn't endure (vv. 1, 5). While separated from the Thessalonians he was anxious to know if they were still believing (v. 5), because he was fearful that afflictions (v. 3) or Satan (v. 5) had caused them to fall. He cared enough to send Timothy to them. The purpose propositions of the paragraph show this concern and care: Paul sent Timothy back in order to encourage the Thessalonians to continue to trust in God (2c), in order that none of them would be unsettled by persecution (3a), and in order to learn whether or not they were still trusting in God (5d). Such expressions of interest and concern indicate that the genre is emotive. The paragraph structure of statements and restatements is not sequential development; the sequence in the account of sending Timothy is only incidental to the emotive problem Paul is seeking to solve, as indicated in the multiple means-purpose relations. Thus this is an emotive paragraph of the expressive type.

Paul and his companions had an emotive problem; that is, they were not able to endure separation from the Thessalonians. This problem is stated in the 1a proposition. An attempt at resolution (in 1b–4b) was to send Timothy to Thessalonica. In 5a–b and c Paul restates the problem and solution. Thus 3:1–5 is an example of the solutionality subtype of the expressive paragraph pattern, in which the constituents are labeled *emotive problem, seeking,* and SOLUTION. (It should be noted that the label SOLUTION is used in the display of this paragraph for what is actually a *seeking* constituent on the next higher level, as seen in the display for 2:17–3:13.)

Perhaps Paul also has a secondary intent in this unit, as suggested by the 3:2b description. This description gives Timothy's credentials for ministry and indicates to the Thessalonians that he, as Paul's representative, had Paul's full support. Also, Paul may have intended that Timothy would carry this letter back to Thessalonica, and the description would then have influenced the readers to accept him and his ministry to them.

NOTES

3:1a As a result of that [2:17–20] The conjunction διό 'therefore' functions on the next higher discourse level to relate this paragraph to the previous one in the section. It introduces the result (Bruce, Frame, Marshall) of Paul's strong desire to return to the believers in Thessalonica—Timothy was sent to find out how they were.

when I(&S&T) could no longer endure my/our(exc) being separated from you The participle στέγοντες 'enduring' can be interpreted as introducing either reason, 'because' (Best, Bruce, Frame; TEV), or circumstance, 'when' (Hiebert; NAB, NCV, NIV, NJB, NRSV, REB, TNT). Either fits the context, but the latter is chosen for the display because a present-tense participle is more commonly used this way when it precedes the main verb (as here). What Paul and his companions could not endure was the separation (Frame; also EHP, JBP), which prevented them from ministering to these people who were their pride and joy and left them ignorant of how they were doing in the midst of persecution (Best, Wanamaker).

3:1b we(exc) decided that I(&S) would stay behind alone in Athens *city* The referent of the bound first person plural pronoun in εὐδοκήσαμεν 'we decided' is uncertain. It could be a literary 'we' meaning 'I'. In 3:5 Paul uses 'I', and because of the similarity of 3:1b and 3:5, some have interpreted the plural pronoun of 1b as a literary plural meaning 'I, Paul' (Morris, Thomas, Wanamaker). Alternatively, 'we' could well refer to Paul and his co-workers. However, we don't know if Silas and Timothy came to Athens when Paul sent for them (Acts 17:15–16). Acts 18:5 says they came from Macedonia to Corinth when Paul was there, but assuming that Paul sent Timothy back to Thessalonica from Athens in person as the text indicates (and not by a letter to him in Berea telling him to go), Timothy was in Athens and very possibly Silas as well. So it seems best to take the referent in 3:1b to be plural. The agent of 'decided', namely 'we(exc)', refers at least to Paul and Silas (Bruce, Frame) and possibly Timothy as well (Hiebert, Marshall). In regard to the infinitive καταλειφθῆναι 'to remain', both Hiebert and Marshall suggest that the decision was for Paul to remain behind alone, Silas, too, having departed. However, this is conjecture. We know only that Timothy could not be included in those left behind. The display rendering 'I(&S) would stay behind' leaves open the possibility that Silas remained behind with Paul. The use of 'I' in 3:5 can be explained as Paul's way of emphasizing his prominent part in this decision (Frame).

The passive of the infinitive καταλείπω here means "*remain behind*" (BAGD, p. 413.1a). The infinitive introduces the content of the decision.

3:2b He is our(exc) close associate This description of Timothy is in the form of an appositional phrase. Paul says Timothy is our ἀδελφός 'brother' (rendered elsewhere in the displays as 'fellow believer'). Paul is not speaking here so much of Timothy's faith as of the authority with which he is being sent as a representative of the senior messengers, Paul and Silas. Marshall says 'brother' is a term "Paul often uses of his colleagues in missionary work and which underlines the closeness of the relationship between them."

and works for God There are various textual readings for the phrase καὶ συνεργὸν τοῦ θεοῦ 'and co-worker of God' (UBSGNT). Some manuscripts omit the words 'of God' so that the text reads 'our brother and co-worker'. Instead of 'co-worker', some manuscripts have διάκονον 'minister' (accepted by Hiebert, Morris, NJB, RSV): "Timothy, who is God's helper" (NJB). MJTGNT has both 'minister of God' and 'our co-worker' (accepted by CEV, KJV, NCV, NKJV): "He works with us as God's servant" (CEV). The UBSGNT reading has a B rating, indicating near certainty; Metzger (p. 563) says this reading best accounts for the origin of the others. The following accept the UBSGNT reading: Bruce, Marshall, Frame, Wanamaker; NAB, NASB, NIV, NRSV, REB, TEV, and TNT. It is the reading on which the rendering in the display is based. Some interpret the phrase to mean that Timothy is Paul and Silas' co-worker (NRSV, TEV, TNT). Since that idea is already made clear in the display rendering by 'close associate', the second part of the proposition focuses on Timothy's role as one who will minister in Paul's stead to the Thessalonians. He is a 'co-worker of God' in that he is involved in God's enterprise and as such he works "for God" (NRSV, TEV, TNT).

by *proclaiming* the gospel *about* Christ The way in which Timothy is God's co-worker is expressed by the means phrase ἐν τῷ εὐαγγελίῳ τοῦ Χριστοῦ 'in the gospel of Christ'. Implied is the idea that he "preaches" (CEV, NAB, TEV), "tells" (NCV), or "proclaims" (NRSV) the gospel. Previously the word 'gospel' was associated with the genitive 'of God' (2:2, 8, 9), which is a genitive of source: 'the gospel that originates from God'. The genitive 'of Christ' here is viewed as expressing content (Hiebert, Wanamaker; CEV, NCV, TEV), 'the gospel about Christ'.

3:2c I(&S) sent him in order that he would encourage you to continue to strongly trust *in* God The words εἰς τό 'in order', linked with two infinitives, give Paul's primary purpose for sending Timothy (Frame): εἰς τὸ στηρίξαι ὑμᾶς καὶ παρακαλέσαι ὑπὲρ τῆς πίστεως ὑμῶν 'in order to strengthen you and to encourage for the sake of your faith'. The first infinitive is used in the secondary sense of strengthening inwardly or spiritually. A study of the ten times it is used figuratively in the NT yields the meaning "cause someone to continue (in some state/activity)" (J. Callow 1982:84). The second infinitive is better translated 'encourage' than 'exhort' or 'comfort' because the Thessalonians were experiencing trials (v. 3) and needed encouragement to remain strong in their faith. (Most versions render it as 'encourage'.) Marshall says Christian teaching is to be the means Timothy uses to encourage them. The strengthening and the encouraging were "'for the sake of your faith', i.e. to reinforce and strengthen it amid their afflictions" (Bruce). Most versions translate these infinitives as two separate events. However, it seems that strengthening is the purpose and encouraging is the means to that purpose (Hiebert). (In 2 Thess. 2:17 the order of the same verbs is reversed, which better indicates a logical progression.) The display rendering is similar to REB and TNT, which recognize a means-purpose relation: "to encourage you to stand fast in your faith" (TNT).

The noun 'faith', which represents an event, is rendered 'to trust' in the display; 'to strengthen' is rendered as an adverb, 'strongly'. Paul has previously written of the Thessalonians' faith in God (1:8), so 'God' is supplied in the display as the object of their trust.

3:3a in order that no one *of you* would be unsettled A third infinitive here introduces a result (Bruce, Marshall) or an additional purpose. It is appropriate as the purpose for Timothy's encouragement of the Thessalonians (Best, Hiebert, Wanamaker). Timothy's ministry of encouragement by teaching was to help the Thessalonians endure the persecutions that came to them as a result of their conversion. The passive infinitive of σαίνω (which verb is used only here in the Greek Bible) has been understood by some to mean 'to be deceived' (Frame, Morris; TEV). However, the ancient versions and early interpreters took the verb to mean "*move, disturb, agitate*" (BAGD, p. 740), and this meaning has been found in an extrabiblical manuscript (Bruce).

This latter meaning (accepted by BAGD, Best, Bruce, Marshall, Wanamaker, CEV, DGN, NAB, NCV, NIV, NJB, REB, and TNT) seems preferable here as the context gives no indication of who or what might have deceived the Thessalonians.

as a result of *people* persecuting *you* The noun in the phrase ἐν ταῖς θλίψεσιν ταύταις 'in these afflictions' represents an event and is rendered here as a verbal phrase. The relation of the phrase to the main clause of 3a can be understood either as reason-result or as means-result. However, because we do not know exactly what the persecutors were doing or what their intentions were, it is difficult to determine whether the relation is reason or means. (The latter requires intention according to the definition in SSWC, which theory underlies SSAs.) The Greek demonstrative 'these' indicates that Paul is referring to persecutions of the Thessalonians previously mentioned in 1:6 and 2:14 (Bruce, Frame, Morris, Wanamaker; JBP, NLT), or to persecutions of the messengers (2:2), or of both (Best, Marshall) with the emphasis on the trials of the Thessalonians. The first of these is preferable since Paul uses the same term for afflictions in 1:6 that he uses here; also it is more likely that the Thessalonians would be unsettled by being persecuted themselves than by hearing of Paul's being persecuted.

3:3b *As far as people persecuting you is concerned* The Greek that expresses the 3b and 4a propositions contains the conjunction γάρ 'for' in each. Whereas v. 4 obviously is grounds for 3b, the relation of 3b to what precedes is less clear. But it seems best to take γάρ here as introducing a digression (Wanamaker). Thus 3b–4b is labeled a comment because in these propositions Paul briefly departs from the main topic of the paragraph, Timothy's mission to Thessalonica. Those versions which do not render γάρ (CEV, NAB, NCV, NIV, NJB, REB, TEV, TNT) may likewise understand 3b–4b to be a digression. Paul's purpose in making the comment may be to fortify the believers (by reminding them that God's plan includes their being persecuted) just as Timothy sought to do when he visited.

you know that *God* has destined/planned that *people will persecute* us(inc) *who trust in him* The Greek of 3b is αὐτοὶ γὰρ οἴδατε ὅτι εἰς τοῦτο κείμεθα 'for you yourselves know that to this we are appointed'. 'To this' refers to the persecution mentioned in 3a. The passive form 'we are appointed' conceals the agent, God. It is God who has determined that suffering will be a part of the experience of believers (Best, Bruce, Hiebert, Morris, Wanamaker; TEV): "such persecutions are part of God's will for us" (TEV). Paul is most likely saying that this is the lot not just of the Thessalonians and the messengers, but of all believers (Best, Frame, Hiebert, Wanamaker; NLT), including those in Judea mentioned in 2:14.

3:4a since . . . we(exc) certainly told you *a number of times* before it happened Verse 4 begins with two conjunctions, καὶ γάρ 'and for'. The conjunction 'for' introduces grounds (in 4a–b) for Paul's previous statement (Best; CEV, REB, TEV); 'and' is best understood as an intensifier, variously translated as 'indeed' (Bruce; NJB) or 'in fact' (NIV, NRSV). In the display the intensive concept is expressed by 'certainly'.

The prefix προ- on the verb προλέγω 'tell beforehand' indicates that something is spoken of before it happens. The phrase 'a number of times' renders the imperfect tense of the verb προελέγομεν 'we were telling beforehand'. NIV has "we kept telling you." Since the content of the telling is unpleasant experiences to come, some (Bruce; NAB, NJB, NLT, REB, TNT) translate it "we warned". A similar rendering may be appropriate in other languages as well.

that *people* would persecute us(inc) *who trust in God* By using the words μέλλομεν θλίβεσθαι 'we are to be afflicted', Paul indicates he is repeating the idea in v. 3 that this affliction is by divine decree (BAGD, p. 501.1cδ; also Morris, Wanamaker). Here, as there, the passive form is rendered as active in the display. That this persecution will happen to those who trust in God is implicit in 3b and here as well, and therefore is supplied in the display.

3:4b and *since* you know *that* what has happened indeed corresponds to *what we(exc) said* The Greek is καθὼς καὶ ἐγένετο καὶ οἴδατε 'just as indeed it happened and you know'. The first καί 'and/indeed' is emphatic (Frame has 'indeed'; TEV has 'exactly'); the second καί indicates that this is a conjoined proposition in Paul's grounds for the Thessalonians' knowing that persecution was about to come. In the display the two clauses of the Greek have been changed into an orienter-content construction (as in NCV, TNT). The word καθώς 'just as' indicates congruence and is rendered 'corresponds to what we said'.

3:5a Because *I thought that you might be unsettled as a result of people persecuting you* The phrase διὰ τοῦτο 'because of this' can be taken either as referring back to what Paul said earlier (Best, Marshall, Wanamaker; also NAB, NJB, TEV, TNT) or as referring ahead to what he says in this verse: "my reason for sending . . . was to learn of your faith" (Bruce). A reference backward such as "that is why" (TEV) could target references to persecution in the immediately preceding verses (Hiebert, Marshall, Wanamaker) or even in 2:17–3:4 (Best, Hendriksen). A back reference fits the context well, and because 3b–4b is a comment, it seems best to take διὰ τοῦτο as referring back to 3a. However, there is not much difference of meaning between a back reference and a forward reference in this context. Paul in v. 3 speaks of concern that the Thessalonians not be unsettled by the persecutions they were experiencing, and in v. 5 he expresses his concern that Satan might have caused their faith to waver by means of those same persecutions.

The similarity of form between the Greek of 3:5a–c and 3:1a and 2a indicates that Paul here restates his unit topic. Propositions 5a–b restate the emotive problem first mentioned in 1:a; propositions 5c–f restate the solution mentioned in 1b–4b.

3:5b *and when* **I could no longer endure** *my not knowing about your spiritual condition* The participial phrase μηκέτι στέγων 'I no longer enduring (it)' has been understood as circumstance (CEV, KJV, NAB, NCV, NIV, NJB, NLT, NRSV), as was the participial phrase in 1a. In the display both 1a and 5b are represented as constituents of the *emotive problem*. Regarding the implied content of 'enduring', in 1a it is implied (from the preceding paragraph 2:17–20) that the messengers were not able to endure the forced separation. That could be true here as well (Frame, Morris). However, the immediate context indicates that Paul and his companions were concerned that they didn't know how the Thessalonians were faring under persecution, so the rendering in the display seems a better choice (following Hiebert, Marshall; also NAB, NCV, TNT). NAB has "I sent to find out about your faith when I could stand the suspense no longer."

3:5c I sent *Timothy to you* The contraction κἀγώ 'and I' is a freestanding form of the same agent in the verb ἔπεμψα 'I sent' here. The contraction can be taken as explicitly emphasizing Paul's personal feelings (Best, Bruce, Hiebert, Marshall, Morris): 'I for my part'. Or it may indicate that Paul's sentiments are those of others as well (Frame; NASB). But since this is not indicated in the context, the first interpretation is followed in the display. Note that in addition to the explicit first person singular pronoun bound to the participle in 5b and the explicit κἀγώ 'and I' here in 5c, 'I' is supplied in 5a and 5e to emphasize that Paul was personally concerned for the Thessalonians. Paul might have been the one most responsible for sending Timothy (Best, Bruce), although the plural 'we' in 3:1–2 probably indicates that Silas, at least, was also involved in the decision (see the note on 1b).

3:5d in order to find out whether or not you were *still* **trusting** *in God* This is the second purpose in sending Timothy (the first is in 2c–3a): εἰς τὸ γνῶναι τὴν πίστιν ὑμῶν 'in order to know your faith'. The noun phrase 'your faith' represents an agent and event and is rendered in the display as a clause. Paul did not want the Thessalonians to be unsettled by persecutions (3a) and he was concerned that Satan may have caused them to waver in their faith (5e). He sent Timothy to find out "how their faith was holding up under persecution" (Hiebert). The phrase 'whether or not' in the display renders the feeling of apprehension indicated by the conjunctions μή πως 'lest' at the beginning of the next proposition.

3:5e because *I was* **afraid that** The Greek is μή πως 'lest'. BDF, §370(2); BAGD, p. 519.1b; and Louw and Nida 89.62 indicate that these conjunctions are used in contexts where apprehension is implied. The display follows those versions in which is expressed the idea of fearing (DGN, NAB, NASB, NCV, NIV, NJB, NLT, NRSV, REB). NIV, for example, has "I was afraid that." The result-reason relation is appropriate between 5c–d and 5e–f: Paul sent to find out about the Thessalonians' faith because he was afraid persecution might have weakened their commitment to the Lord.

Satan, **the one who tempts** *people to do wrong*, **had** *successfully* **tempted you** *to stop trusting in God* Satan is referred to in terms of his characteristic behavior of tempting people. "[H]ere the thought is clearly of encouraging somebody to do what is evil and contrary to the will of God" (Marshall). The purpose of the temptation was most likely to get the Thessalonians to abandon their faith (so Marshall). TNT has "whether your faith had resisted the tempter." Paul assumed the temptation had already occurred as indicated by the aorist indicative tense of ἐπείρασεν 'tempted' (Hiebert, Frame, Marshall,

Morris). What he feared, but didn't know, was that Satan had been *successful* in getting them to abandon their faith (Bruce, Frame, Wanamaker), so he sent Timothy to find out.

3:5f and *as a result* **I(&S&T) would have worked ineffectively/uselessly** *while we(exc) were present with you* The Greek is καὶ εἰς κενὸν γένηται ὁ κόπος ἡμῶν 'and in vain would become our labor'. The noun κόπος 'labor, toil' represents an event and is rendered as a clause in the display. The same word occurs in 1:3 and 2:9a. It denotes hard work. The subjunctive verb γένηται 'would become' indicates that if Satan had successfully tempted the Thessalonians, this would have resulted in nullifying the effectiveness of the messengers' work in Thessalonica (Best, Bruce, Frame, Marshall, Wanamaker; NCV). The word rendered 'ineffectively/uselessly' in the display is κενός. The same word was used in 2:1 (see the note there). Here it is forefronted for emphasis.

Propositions 5e and 5f are in a reason–result relationship. It seems the reason proposition (that the believers could have been successfully tempted) is at least as prominent as the result proposition (that the messengers' work was in vain). Paul connects the two propositions with καί 'and', which may indicate that they are equally prominent in his thinking or that they state the same idea in different ways. In the display both labels are in uppercase letters to indicate equal prominence.

BOUNDARIES AND COHERENCE

The initial boundary of 3:1–5 was discussed under 2:17–20 (see "Boundaries"). The terminal boundary is between 3:5 and 3:6. Verses 1–5 present one topic: Paul's sending Timothy back to Thessalonica and his reasons for doing so. (Also, v. 5 is the second part of a lexical/grammatical repetition, forming a type of sandwich structure with 3:1–2). Then at 3:6 the adverb ἄρτι 'now' indicates the start of a new topic. The time frame changes because Timothy has returned from his trip to Thessalonica. In vv. 6–10 Paul exults in the news that Timothy brings. At 3:6 there is also the developmental particle δέ, which occurs at the beginning of three of the four constituents of the 2:17–3:13 section (in 2:17, 3:6, 3:11). At 3:6 the participial phrase ἐλθόντος Τιμοθέου 'Timothy having come' marks a new development in the narrative, as did the participles at 2:17 and 3:1.

EHP places a boundary between 3:3a and 3b; NBV and NLT place one between 3:4 and 3:5. The first of these could be justified by a head-tail linkage between θλῖψις 'oppression, affliction' in 3a and the passive of θλίβω 'to be afflicted' in 4a. Also, the forefronted αὐτοί 'you' and Paul's comment at 3b bring discontinuity to the discourse. A boundary between 3:4 and 3:5 could be justified because 3:1–4 and 3:5 can be considered separate paragraph patterns. However, because of its referential coherence (discussed below) it seems best to recognize 3:1–5 as a unit (as do all commentaries and most versions consulted).

The referential coherence of 3:1–5 derives from its repetitive structure. Some lexical items and grammatical structures of 3:1–2 are repeated in 3:5 as follows:

1a διό therefore
    μηκέτι στέγοντες . . . no longer enduring
2a ἐπέμψαμεν . . . we sent
2c εἰς τὸ στηρίξαι ὑμᾶς . . . to strengthen you
    ὑπὲρ τῆς πίστεως ὑμῶν concerning your faith

5a διὰ τοῦτο . . . because of this
5b μηκέτι στέγων no longer enduring
5c ἔπεμψα I sent
5d εἰς τὸ γνῶναι τὴν πίστιν ὑμῶν to know your faith

The 3:1–5 paragraph has two terms from the same root: θλίψεσιν 'afflictions' in 3a and θλίβεσθαι 'to be afflicted' in 4a. These also lend referential coherence.

PROMINENCE AND THEME

Prominence in the 3:1–5 paragraph is indicated by repetition: That Paul could no longer endure is in 1a and 5b. That he sent Timothy is in 2a and 5c. The purpose of his sending Timothy is in 2c, 3a, and 5d.

The theme for 3:1–5 is derived from naturally prominent propositions 5b and 5c and purpose proposition 5d, all of which are in the restatements.

SECTION CONSTITUENT 3:6–10
(Expressive Paragraph: Solution of 2:17–3:13)

THEME: Now Timothy has just returned to me from you and has told me the good news that you still trust in God. As a result I have been cheered up and I cannot thank God adequately for what he has done for you and because of my greatly rejoicing because of you. Very frequently I ask God that I will be able to visit you and help you trust him more strongly.

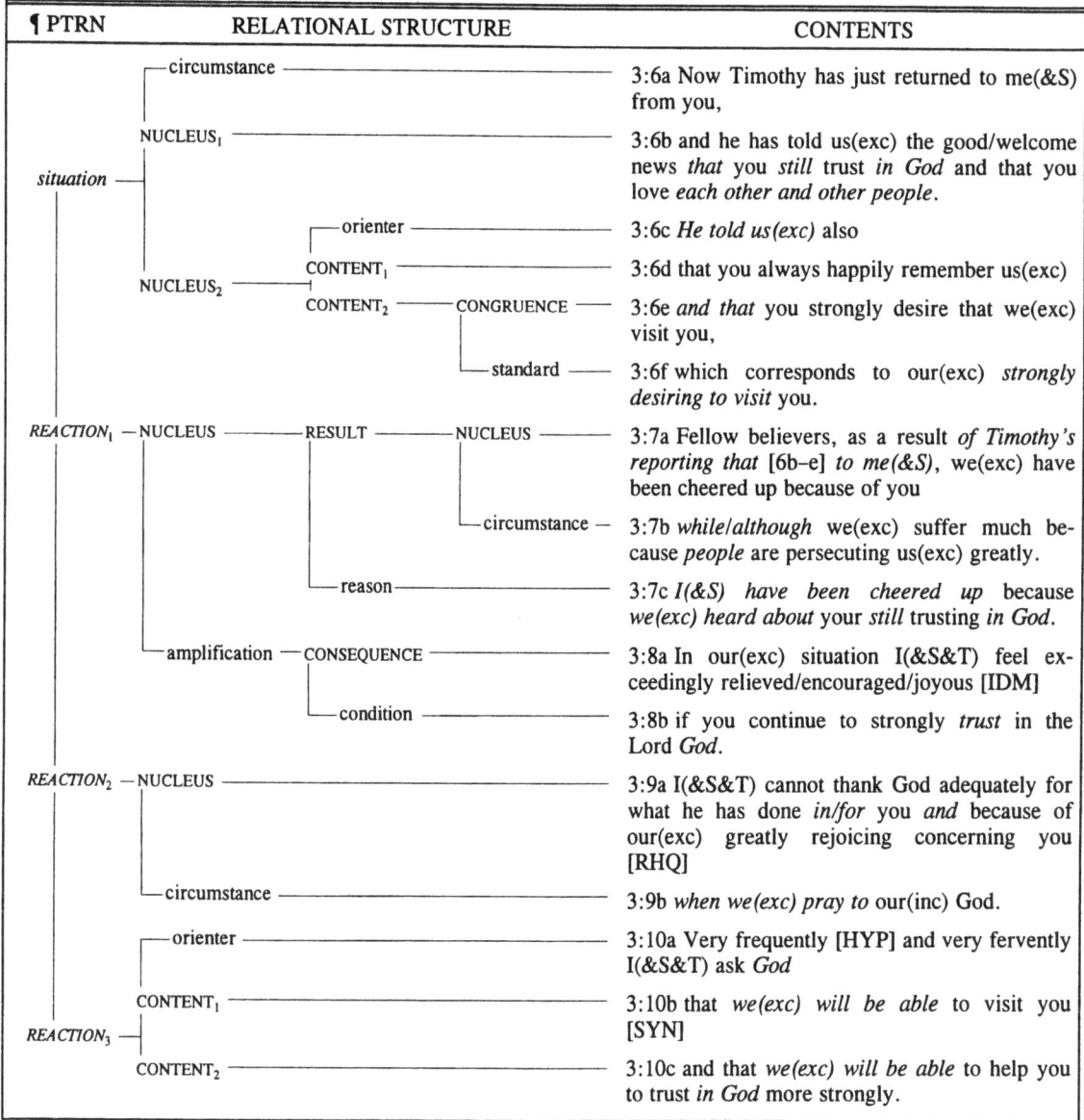

INTENT AND PARAGRAPH PATTERN

In the 3:6–10 paragraph Paul's intent is to affect the emotions of the Thessalonians. That this is emotive genre is clear from the 8a statement about feeling exceedingly encouraged, the very emotional rhetorical question in 9a with repetition of words for joy, and the 10a hyperbole with a forefronted adverb of intense feeling. Each of these expressions should indicate to Paul's readers his love and concern for them and should powerfully affect their emotions. Paul expresses his feelings in reason-result relations rather than sequential ones, so this is an emotive paragraph of the expressive type.

The paragraph consists of four propositional clusters. The second (7a–8b) begins with διὰ τοῦτο 'because of this', which indicates that it is in a reason-result communication relation with the first cluster (6a–f). The third cluster (9a–b) begins with γάρ 'for', which is taken as introducing an explanation or amplification of v. 7 (see the note on 9a). Thus it is a second result of Timothy's report. The last cluster (10a-c) is a participial phrase in the Greek. Since Paul often appends participial phrases that are prayers to expressions of thanksgiving, this cluster is best understood, not as subordinate, but as a third result. This series of three results (emotional responses) to Timothy's report signals the paragraph pattern subtype of causality, the constituents of which for an expressive paragraph are labeled *situation* and *REACTION*: Timothy's report (v. 6) is the *situation*, and the expressions of Paul's personal joy (vv. 7-8), his almost inexpressible thanksgiving to God (v. 9), and his prayer (v. 10) are three REACTIONS to it.

Paragraph 3:6-10 is the climactic unit of 1:2-3:13 (see "Intent" under 2:17-3:13).

NOTES

3:6a Now Timothy has just returned to me(&S) from you The 3:6-10 paragraph begins with ἄρτι δὲ ἐλθόντος Τιμοθέου πρὸς ἡμᾶς 'and/but now Timothy having come to us'. Here the particle δέ 'and/but' is taken by many as introducing a contrast with what precedes (Hiebert; NAB, NBV, NCV, NIV, NJB NRSV, REB, TNT). It is not so much a contrast, however, as a new point in the discourse (Frame), namely the resolution of the emotional turmoil Paul refers to in 3:1-5. As a transitional particle, δέ could be translated "*now, then*" (BAGD, p. 171.2). But the idiomatic sense of 'now' for δέ is likely to be confused with 'now' in the temporal sense, which is the meaning of ἄρτι here in 6a. Therefore the particle δέ is not translated in the display (also CEV, JBP, NLT, TEV).

The adverb ἄρτι 'now' modifies the participle 'having come' (Best, Frame); it does not modify 'cheered up, reassured' in 7a, from which it is too far removed. The forefronting of this adverb may emphasize the idea that Timothy very recently returned, hence 'now . . . just' in the display (following Bruce, Frame; also JBP, NLT, REB, TNT, NIV, NRSV). By writing so soon after Timothy's return Paul communicates to the Thessalonians his concern and warm affection (Wanamaker).

The participles ἐλθόντος 'having come' in 6a and εὐαγγελισαμένου 'having told good news' in 6b are best interpreted as reason for what follows (Frame, Wanamaker). NAB has "since Timothy has returned and told us." This interpretation is supported by the presence of διὰ τοῦτο 'because of this' in 7a. The reason-result communication relation is conveyed by the words 'as a result' in 7a. A reason-result relation often indicates a causality type of paragraph pattern. Here v. 6 is the *situation* that leads to three REACTIONS, the first of which is Paul's encouragement in v. 7. There is a syntactical problem in that διὰ τοῦτο 'because of this' begins a new sentence at v. 7 with Paul's thought in v. 6 uncompleted—there is no nonsubordinate verb in v. 6 to which the participles in 6a and 6b relate. The meaning, however, is unaffected, as διὰ τοῦτο 'because of this' makes it clear that Timothy's report on his return (v. 6) is the reason Paul and Silas are encouraged (v. 7). The Greek participles are rendered in 6a, b, and c as nonsubordinate verbs.

Within the 6a-f *situation* the participle 'having come' in 6a establishes the setting. It was the news Timothy told that triggered a reaction; his return was only incidental. Therefore, in the display 6a is labeled circumstance and is not one of the NUCLEI of the *situation*. The participle 'having come' is rendered 'has returned' because Timothy had come back to the one(s) who sent him.

The Greek pronouns 'we' and 'us' in vv. 6-7 could be taken to refer to Paul alone or to Paul and Silas. With the latter understanding they may need to be rendered as dual pronouns for languages that have that distinction.

3:6b and he has told us(exc) the good/welcome news The verb εὐαγγελίζω 'to tell good news' is normally used in the NT of proclaiming the gospel. Here it is not used in that technical sense (Bruce, Frame, Wanamaker); instead it means that what Timothy told Paul and Silas was welcome news to them. Morris says it is the term that could best express Paul's emotions.

that* you *still* trust *in God* and that you love *each other and other people The content of Timothy's news is expressed by the nouns πίστις 'faith' and ἀγάπη 'love', which are both modified by the pronoun ὑμῶν 'your'. These noun phrases represent agents and events and are rendered in the display as clauses. That the Thessalonians were still believing was good news because Paul had been concerned that Satan might have caused them to stop believing (5c-e). The implicit object of their faith is considered to be 'God', as it has been throughout the letter. In 1:3 the object of 'love' was supplied as 'people'. Here it is more specific, 'each other and other people', because in

3:12 Paul will state his desire that their love will "increase and overflow for each other and for everyone else" (NIV). Some (including Bruce) feel that Paul was here speaking also of the Thessalonians' love for him and his companions; however, in 6d-e he speaks specifically of that affection, and as 6b exhibits a parallel to 1:3, love for the messengers is most likely not in focus in 6b.

3:6c *He told us(exc) also* The conjunction καί 'and' indicates that 6c-f form a coordinate aspect of Timothy's report. Since Paul uses an explicit ὅτι 'that' in 6d and changes from using noun phrases as the content in 6b to a content clause in 6c-f, the latter cluster is labeled a second NUCLEUS.

3:6d *that you always happily remember us(exc)* The Greek is ὅτι ἔχετε μνείαν ἡμῶν ἀγαθὴν πάντοτε 'that you have good remembrance of us always', meaning that the Thessalonians had friendly and happy memories of the messengers (Bruce; CEV, GW, NJB, NLT). Wanamaker glosses the clause "you always think of us affectionately." The noun 'remembrance' represents an event and is thus rendered in the display '(you) remember'. This affectionate remembrance indicated to Paul that the Thessalonians had not rejected him as a result of his not having returned to Thessalonica or harbored bitterness because the messengers were "visitors who brought them nothing but trouble" (Bruce). Concern for such rejection may explain Paul's defensive statements in 2:17-18 (Wanamaker).

3:6e *and that you strongly desire that we(exc) visit you* The participial phrase ἐπιποθοῦντες ἡμᾶς ἰδεῖν 'longing to see us' is best taken as coordinate to 6d (following Bruce; also CEV, NAB, NCV, NIV, NJB, NRSV, REB, TEV, TNT), though it has also been understood as the grounds (Best, Frame) or result (Eadie) of 6d. The verb εἶδον 'to see' is used in a secondary sense here, *"visit someone"* (BAGD, p. 221.6).

3:6f *which corresponds to our(exc) strongly desiring to visit you* The Greek is καθάπερ καὶ ἡμεῖς ὑμᾶς 'just as also we you', which involves an ellipsis. The implied information is supplied from 6e. The words 'just as also' indicate the relation of congruence-standard with the preceding proposition.

3:7a *as a result of Timothy's reporting that* [6b-e] *to me(&S), we(exc) have been cheered up because of you* The 7a proposition is a result (the first REACTION) of Timothy's good report (see the note on 6a). It is introduced by the phrase διὰ τοῦτο 'because of this'

The main clause is παρεκλήθημεν, ἀδελφοί, ἐφ' ὑμῖν 'we were encouraged, brothers, about, or because of, you'. If the preposition ἐπί is taken to mean 'about' (Bruce; CEV, NIV, NRSV, REB, TEV), then Paul is saying that he was cheered in his difficult situation by Timothy's report that the Thessalonians were remaining faithful. If ἐπί is taken to mean 'because of' (Best, Frame, Hiebert, Marshall, Morris, Wanamaker; JBP, NAB, NJB, NLT, TNT, WFB), then Paul is saying that he was encouraged because he heard that his converts were remaining faithful. The focus may be slightly different, but both renderings would have the same components of meaning: (1) Paul and his co-workers are in a difficult situation, stated in 7b; (2) their reaction is joy; and (3) the cause of the joy is the news that the Thessalonians remain faithful to the Lord, which is made explicit in 7c. The focus of the second rendering of ἐπί ('because of') seems to fit the immediate context better, so that is the one chosen for the display.

The passive of the verb παρακαλέω 'to encourage, to comfort' here means to be emotionally uplifted in difficult circumstances. It is rendered 'have been cheered up' (also JBP). TNT is similar: "distressed and afflicted though we are, the news of your faith has greatly cheered us." The aorist tense of the Greek verb is rendered with the English present perfect as apparently Paul is writing soon after Timothy's return and Timothy's report still cheers him.

3:7b *while/although we(exc) suffer much because people are persecuting us(exc) greatly* The Greek is ἐπὶ πάσῃ τῇ ἀνάγκῃ καὶ θλίψει ἡμῶν 'in/concerning all the distress and affliction of us'. The preposition ἐπί can mean 'concerning' (Best, Frame), indicating that the messengers were cheered up concerning the troubles they were experiencing. The more common interpretation is that it means 'in' and introduces the circumstances in which the messengers were cheered up (Bruce, Marshall, Wanamaker; NAB, NIV, NJB, NRSV, REB, TEV). This latter interpretation is rendered in the display as 'while'. It seems more appropriate than 'concerning (the messengers' troubles)' because Paul says that he had been unsettled, not concerning his own afflictions, but about those of the Thessalonians, and the recent news from Timothy banished his fears about them even while he himself suffered distress. This proposition has also been understood as concession (CEV, NCV, TNT), which is an acceptable alternative. TNT has "distressed and afflicted though we are, the news of your faith has greatly cheered us."

Moore (p. 25) takes the nouns ἀνάγκη 'distress' and θλίψις 'affliction' as near-synonymous doublets (also Bruce, Marshall, Wanamaker). Most commentators understand the terms to refer to external circumstances confronting Paul and his companions, but we have no specific reference to indicate what distress these messengers may have been experiencing at the time Paul wrote the letter. The use of two near-synonyms emphasizes the suffering they were experiencing and could be rendered in the display by a single term, but both are retained; they represent events and thus are rendered by clauses. The second term 'affliction' explains why the messengers are in 'distress', and thus it is rendered as reason.

The word πᾶς 'all' may indicate that the suffering and persecution are to be viewed as a unit (NAB, NJB). NAB has "throughout our distress and trial." On the other hand, it may indicate intensification (Best; CEV, NCV, NIV, NRSV, REB, TEV). CEV has "a lot of trouble and suffering." This is the basis for the rendering in the display: 'much' and 'greatly'. (Each verb is intensified because the word 'all' and the definite article modify both nouns in the Greek.)

3:7c because *we(exc) heard about* your *still trusting in God* The meaning of ἐφ' ὑμῖν 'because of you' in 7a is made clear here by the phrase διὰ τῆς ὑμῶν πίστεως 'because of, or through, your faith'. Some take this phrase as reason (NCV, NIV); others take it as means (Best, Bruce, Frame, Hiebert, Wanamaker; NRSV). Because means implies intent, this phrase is best taken as reason: Paul heard the report and was cheered up, whether or not that was Timothy's intent in reporting it. The word 'still' is supplied here as "it is the steadfastness of the Thessalonians' faith which is primarily in Paul's mind as the cause of thanksgiving" (Marshall). Paul does not mean their initial act of trusting in God.

3:8a In our(exc) situation I(&S&T) feel exceedingly relieved/encouraged/joyous Some take the conjunction ὅτι 'because' here as signaling a reason (Best, Hiebert, Marshall; TEV). However, the verb in 8a is present tense and the preceding verb in 7a is aorist tense; it is unlikely that a present state is the reason for a past state. Although ὅτι is the principal causal conjunction, often the subordination is very loose. BDF, §456(1), suggests the gloss 'for' (also Frame, Wanamaker; KJV, NASB, NIV, NRSV), but that rendering usually indicates a grounds or causal relationship as well. It seems best to take 8a as an amplification of 7a, which says 'we have been cheered up because of you'. Thus the conjunction ὅτι is not rendered in the display (also Bruce; CEV, JBP, NJB, NLT, REB, TNT) because it is taken as introducing an amplification.

The amplification is νῦν ζῶμεν 'now we live'. These words are not meant to emphasize the present, but rather νῦν 'now' is to be understood as the situation at a given moment, "*as the situation now is, we live if*" (BAGD, p. 545.2). Hearing of the steadfastness of their converts is what would bring Paul and his co-workers relief and joy.

Paul uses the verb ζῶμεν 'we live' idiomatically here. Bullinger says, "'To live' is used not merely of being alive, or having life, but of having all that makes life worth living, flourishing and prospering" (p. 829). Before Timothy had been sent to find out how they were, Paul's separation from the Thessalonians had distressed him (2:17, 3:1). He was especially concerned that they might have given up faith in Christ (3:5). Timothy's report after the visit revitalizes Paul. Morris says the faith of the Thessalonians was "[t]he thing that really made [Paul] rejoice, the thing that really strengthened him, the thing that gave him life." The NIV and TEV render the verb "really live"; NAB has "shall continue to flourish." The connotation is relief, joy, and renewed vigor.

3:8b if you continue to strongly *trust* in the Lord *God* The clause ἐὰν ὑμεῖς στήκετε ἐν κυρίῳ 'if you stand in (the) Lord' is the condition for the messengers' joyful reaction in 8a. The conjunction ἐάν 'if' can denote "a general, often-repeated condition when no actual instance is being considered" (Greenlee, p. 62); this fits with 8a–b, which is a generally valid statement. This conjunction normally occurs with a verb in the subjunctive mood, but here the verb is indicative. The indicative is normally used with a different conjunction (εἰ 'if') in conditions of fact. However, the indicative here may indicate "something of Paul's certainty that the converts stood firm" (Morris). The conjunction ἐάν 'if' should not be rendered 'since' (as it is in CBW, NIV) or 'as' (NJB) because 8a–b is a statement that is generally valid.

The verb στήκω 'to stand' is used figuratively. "Though this might be called a dead metaphor in English, the sense . . . is built on the idea of not retreating but standing one's ground" (Banker, p. 158). In 3:2-3 Paul says Timothy was sent to encourage the Thessalonians to remain strong in their faith in order that they wouldn't be unsettled by persecution. Here he says he is delighted if they stand in the Lord. Given the context of chapter 3, 'to stand' here means to be steadfast, to continue to do what they did when Paul was with them.

The preposition ἐν 'in' has been understood to indicate the sphere in which the Thessalonians stand firm (Best, Hiebert, Marshall). TEV has "stand firm in your life in union with the Lord." It has also been understood as instrumental (Frame, Wanamaker). Frame says, "[T]heir faith stands unwavering in virtue of the indwelling power of Christ." This phrase, 'stand in the Lord', is used in Phil. 4:1 in a summary statement reminiscent of things Paul says in 1 Thess. 2:17-20: "Therefore, my brothers, you whom I love and long for, my joy and crown, that is how you should stand firm in the Lord, dear friends!" (NIV). (The words "that is how" refer back to Paul's statements that the Philippians should follow his example and live according to the teaching he gave them in Phil. 3:1-21). With regard to the Thessalonians, their initial reception of the message is prominent in the first two chapters of 1 Thessalonians (1:6, 9; 2:13). In 3:1-10 Paul expresses concern that that faith continue (3:2, 5, 6, 7, and 10). Thus it seems appropriate to render the verb and prepositional phrase here 'continue to strongly trust in the Lord God'. CEV has "your strong faith in the Lord."

3:9a Verse 9 is a rhetorical question in the Greek. It contains the conjunction γάρ 'for', which can be taken as introducing reason or grounds for v. 8 (Bruce); this would mean we live if you stand firm 'because that is what we are exceedingly thankful and rejoice about'. Frame understands it as a coordinate reaction of the messengers to Timothy's report; this would mean that hearing about the Thessalonians' faith (v. 7) brought the messengers not only life (v. 8) but also joy (v. 9). A third interpretation is that γάρ indicates result (Best, Marshall); this would mean we live if you stand firm 'and as a result we rejoice'. Frame's interpretation, that γάρ in 9a introduces a coordinate statement, seems correct; however, instead of v. 9 being coordinate with v. 8 (as Frame says) it seems better to take it as coordinate with v. 7. There are similarities in grammatical structure between v. 7 and v. 9 (Best, Bruce):

(7) παρεκλήθημεν . . . ἐφ' ὑμῖν
we were encouraged . . . concerning you

ἐπὶ πάσῃ τῇ ἀνάγκῃ . . . ἡμῶν
in all the distress . . . of us

διὰ τῆς ὑμῶν πίστεως
because of your faith

(9a) τίνα . . . εὐχαριστίαν . . . περὶ ὑμῶν
what . . . thanksgiving . . . concerning you

ἐπὶ πάσῃ τῇ χαρᾷ ᾗ χαίρομεν
in all the joy with which we rejoice

δι' ὑμᾶς
because of you

Thus 9a, with its similar structure, is parallel to v. 7; and just as v. 7 is the first *REACTION* to Timothy's report, so v. 9 is the second. However, v. 9 is not adjacent to the *situation* (v. 6). Therefore, γάρ in 9a is not rendered in the display (also CEV, NAB, NCV, NIV, NJB, NRSV, REB, TNT).

I(&S&T) cannot thank God adequately for what he has done *in/for* you The Greek is τίνα γὰρ εὐχαριστίαν δυνάμεθα τῷ θεῷ ἀνταποδοῦναι περὶ ὑμῶν 'for what thanks are we able to give back to God concerning you?'. This rhetorical question implies that Paul "was profoundly thankful for the continuing faithfulness of the Thessalonians" (Wanamaker). NCV has "We cannot thank [God] enough. . . ." The noun 'thanks' represents an event and is rendered as a verb in the display.

The verb ἀνταποδίδωμι 'give back' has the meaning component of returning what is due. Paul cannot adequately give God the thanks that are his due (Frame, Marshall, Morris). REB renders this meaning "What thanks can we give to God in return for you?" Paul feels that thanks are due to God for his working to bring about the spiritual vitality of the Thessalonians. The information 'for what he has done' is therefore given in the display.

Some manuscripts have return thanks 'to the Lord' rather than 'to God', a variant which could have arisen because 'Lord' occurs at the end of v. 8. This reading is not mentioned by UBSGNT or MJTGNT and is not accepted by any version consulted.

***and* because of our(exc) greatly rejoicing concerning you** The prepositional phrase ἐπὶ πάσῃ τῇ χαρᾷ ᾗ χαίρομεν δι' ὑμᾶς 'for all the joy (with) which we rejoice because of you' is most commonly understood as a reason (or *the* reason) why Paul desired to thank God (Frame; Marshall; Wanamaker; BAGD, p. 285.III1bγ). This is a legitimate interpretation, as the preposition ἐπί 'for' can express the basis of an action like thanksgiving. Some versions render this phrase as the sole basis of the thanksgiving in v. 9 (CEV, NAB, TNT). TNT has "How can we thank our God sufficiently for all the joy we have on your account in his presence?" Other versions render it as an additional or appositional basis of the thanksgiving (NCV, NIV, NJB, NLT, NRSV, REB, TEV). NJB has "how can we thank God enough for you, for all the joy we feel before our God on your account." The rendering in the display is based on the latter understanding.

There is, however, another possible understanding of the phrase. Verses 7 and 9 have a similar structure, as has been noted earlier, and in v. 7 the phrase that begins with ἐπί is a circumstance. This could be the appropriate relation in v. 9 as well (Best), for the following two reasons: (1) In the first part of 9a Paul has already stated his reason for giving thanks (i.e., περὶ ὑμῶν 'concerning you'): he couldn't adequately thank God for what God had done in or for the Thessalonians. That Paul and his companions couldn't thank God enough for their own joy seems less appropriate. That joy was based on the report they had heard about the Thessalonians; it was for the Thessalonians, not their own joy, that they gave thanks. (2) In the first part of 9a Paul, using a rhetorical question with strong emotion, says he and his companions could not thank God adequately for what he had done in the lives of the Thessalonians. They were emotional because of the inadequacy of their thanksgiving while they were rejoicing. A suggested alternative based on this interpretation would be as follows:

> 3:9a I(&S&T) cannot thank God adequately for what he has done *in/for* you [RHQ]
>
> 3:9b *while* we(exc) greatly rejoice concerning you
>
> 3:9c *when we(exc) pray to* our(inc) God.

The second half of 9a (9b in the alternative suggestion) is also emotional, combining the noun 'joy', which is modified by the adjective 'all', with a relative clause containing the verb 'we rejoice'. 'All' indicates the intensity of the joy (Marshall). The phrase δι' ὑμᾶς 'because of you' indicates that the Thessalonians are the reason that the messengers rejoice. It is rendered 'concerning you' in the display.

Proposition 9a is semantically complex. The relations are difficult to understand and chart in a logical way because Paul is expressing the intensity of his emotion by combining the reactions of thanksgiving and joy, piling them on top of one another in idiomatic speech. For this reason, the rendering in the display is probably more appropriate than the more logical alternative suggested.

3:9b *when we(exc) pray to* our(inc) God The phrase ἔμπροσθεν τοῦ θεοῦ ἡμῶν 'before our God' refers to the present time, as did the similar phrase in 1:3. (A similar phrase is used in 3:13 with regard to Christ's coming.) It echoes the Hebrew expression 'before the LORD your God', which was first used in Lev. 23:40 and Deut. 12:12, 18. Moses speaks there of people rejoicing before God when they worshiped at the tabernacle where he dwelt. The meaning here is similar; Paul worships through prayer in God's presence. This meaning is confirmed by references in the context which are in the same semantic domain: 'to repay thanks to God' (9a) and 'asking God' (10a). Proposition 9b is related to 9a as circumstance. Since God is the God of the Thessalonians as well as of the messengers, 'our' is understood to be inclusive.

3:10a Grammatically, v. 10 is subordinate to v. 9 in that it is a participial phrase linked to it. The participle is δεόμενοι 'asking'. When Paul combines thanksgiving and prayer in a passage, the thanksgiving is often in a finite clause and the prayer in a participial clause (see 1:2). Thus, although v. 10 could be viewed as circumstantial (Best; JBP, NAB, NASB, REB), it is better taken as a third REACTION to Timothy's report in 3:6. Paul is simply employing a customary convention and not intending to indicate subordination. Verse 10 has prominence because of the forefronted adverbial phrases 'night and day' and 'very earnestly', which serves to raise it above the level of an ordinary subordinate construction. Having heard the report, Paul has an even greater desire to see the Thessalonians again (10b). Also, he now knows the things they need to be taught (10c).

Very frequently and very fervently I(&S&T) ask *God* The Greek is νυκτὸς καὶ ἡμέρας ὑπερεκπερισσοῦ δεόμενοι 'night and day most earnestly asking'. The phrase 'night and day' is rendered 'very frequently' here. It is a hyperbolic expression that speaks of the frequent nature of Paul's prayers. The adverb ὑπερεκπερισσοῦ 'most earnestly' is "the highest form of comparison imaginable" (BAGD, p. 840) and expresses Paul's earnestness. It "communicates the intensity of Paul's prayer as well as the intensity of the desire that lies behind his prayer request" (Wanamaker). NCV and TEV render it figuratively, "with all our heart."

The verb δέομαι means 'to ask'. Morris says it signifies a want or lack and shows Paul's need to see the Thessalonians again. The CEV, NCV, NIV, NJB, NRSV, REB, and TNT versions render it with a form of the verb 'to pray'. If rendered as 'ask', 'God' is the implied object (NLT, TEV).

3:10b that *we(exc) will be able* to visit you The clause εἰς τὸ ἰδεῖν ὑμῶν τὸ πρόσωπον 'in order to see your face' gives part of the content of Paul's prayers. Some understand it as expressing purpose also (Best, Bruce, Marshall), but the relation of content seems to be the basic one, at least for 10b. The synecdoche 'to see your(pl) face(sg)', in which 'face' signifies the whole person, is rendered as 'see you face to face' by the NAB, NJB, NRSV, and TNT, and as 'visit you' in the display.

3:10c and that *we(exc) will be able* to help you to trust *in God* more strongly The Greek is καὶ καταρτίσαι τὰ ὑστερήματα τῆς πίστεως ὑμῶν 'and to complete the deficiencies of your faith'. The phrase relates to the words εἰς τό 'that, in order to', which occur at the beginning of 10b. The conjunction καί 'and' suggests that this phrase is a second CONTENT coordinate with 10b. Alternatively, it would be appropriate semantically as the purpose of the hoped-for return visit mentioned in 10b (Best, Marshall, Wanamaker).

The phrase 'to complete the deficiencies of your faith' has been understood in a couple ways. It could mean that the Thessalonians needed teaching in matters that the messengers were unable to cover on their first visit (Bruce, Hiebert, Marshall, Wanamaker). Or it could mean that some things they believed or were doing needed correction (Best, Morris). Some commentators say that it could mean both of these (Frame). The first view seems preferable. Thus far in the letter Paul has only commended the Thessalonians for their faith and the practical expressions of it. In the second half of the letter he tells them they are following his previous teaching and encourages them to continue (4:1, 10). Even in his expositions and exhortations in chapters 4 and 5, Paul does not chide them as people who are in error but instructs them as perhaps ignorant (4:13). The versions that follow the first meaning render it in various ways: CEV has "help you to have an even stronger faith"; NCV has "give you all the things you need to make your faith strong."

BOUNDARIES AND COHERENCE

The initial boundary of 3:6–10 was discussed under 3:1–5 (see "Boundaries"). As for the terminal boundary, there is good support for its being between 3:10 and 3:11. In 3:10 Paul writes that he asks (God) for two things: that he be able to visit the Thessalonians and help strengthen their faith. Beginning at 3:11 he expresses his thoughts in wish-prayer form, changing to the optative mood. The primary referents change at v. 11, as indicated by the forefronted phrase αὐτὸς δὲ ὁ θεὸς καὶ πατὴρ ἡμῶν καὶ ὁ κύριος ἡμῶν Ἰησοῦς 'and/now he our God and Father and our Lord Jesus'. The conjunction δέ 'and/now', which occurs at the beginning of previous units (2:17, 3:6), also occurs at 3:11. It helps to signal the switch to the new referents and the development of the discourse. There may also be head-tail linkage between 3:10b ('to see your face') and 3:11 ('may he direct our path to you').

CEV has a boundary between 3:6 and 3:7. This, however, is unacceptable as it separates the reason (*situation*) from the three results (*REACTIONS*). Moreover, neither of these subunits would be a semantic paragraph.

Morris, EHP, GW, NAB, NBV, NLT, and WFB have a boundary between 3:8 and 3:9. This could be justified by the switch to an interrogative (the v. 9 rhetorical question) and the forefronting of new subject matter, thanksgiving. However, the relational coherence brought about by the structural similarity between v. 7 and v. 9 (see the note on 3:9a) seems to unite the verses. Thus it is improbable that there is a boundary between 3:8 and 3:9.

As to lexical coherence, the referents bring unity to this paragraph: Timothy, who has recently returned from Thessalonica; the Thessalonians, about whom he reports; and Paul and most likely Silas, who responded to the report. The noun phrase πίστις ὑμῶν 'your faith' occurs three times (vv. 6, 7, 10). The emotive statements also bring referential unity: 'we have been cheered up' (7a), 'we live' (8a), 'how can we thank God enough' (9a), 'we greatly rejoice' (9a), and 'very frequently and fervently' (10a).

Relational coherence between the report (v. 6) and what follows (vv. 7–10) is established by διὰ τοῦτο 'because of this' in 7a. There is structural parallelism (see the note on 3:9a) between the first REACTION (v. 7) and the second (v. 9); the latter is introduced by γάρ 'for'. Although v. 10 is a subordinate participial phrase, it was a convention by which Paul customarily expressed the reaction of prayer after giving thanks. Thus v. 10 is taken as a third REACTION conjoined to the first two.

PROMINENCE AND THEME

In 3:6-10 the three REACTIONS are prominent. The theme is drawn from the NUCLEUS or CONTENT propositions in each of the REACTIONS (7a, 9a, 10a-c). However, the REACTIONS are dependent for meaning on the *situation* (v. 6). Thus the 6a circumstance and part of the 6b NUCLEUS of the *situation* are included in the theme. Timothy's report that the Thessalonians were still trusting in God is included because references to their faith occur three times in the paragraph and are thus prominent.

SECTION CONSTITUENT 3:11–13
(Expressive Paragraph: Reaction/Transition of 2:17–3:13)

THEME: I pray that God will help us return to you and that the Lord Jesus will help you to love each other and other people more and more, just as we love you.

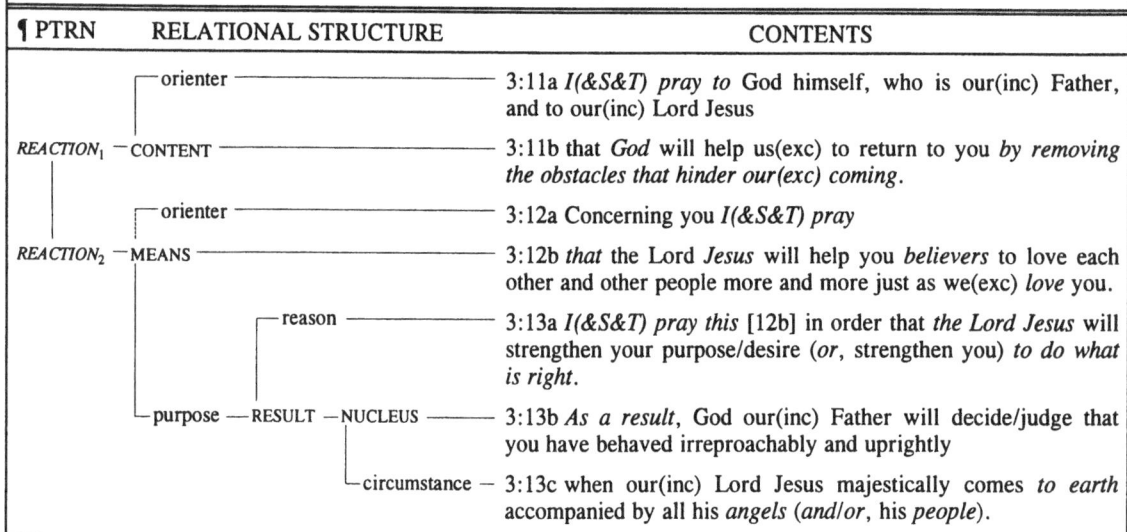

INTENT AND PARAGRAPH PATTERN

In the 3:11–13 paragraph Paul expresses his desires in what Wiles has called a "wish-prayer" (pp. 22–107). God is referred to in the third person and the verbs are in the optative mood, used to express a wish. Yet the language approaches that of a prayer.

In this wish-prayer Paul's primary intent is to affect the emotions of his readers. He does this by expressing to them his desire that God will facilitate a reunion between him and them ('may our God . . . clear the way for us to come to you') and that God will bring about spiritual health in them ('may the Lord make your love increase . . . in order that you will be blameless and holy'). Its genre is not expository. Neither is it hortatory: Paul is not appealing to his readers to do something. Nor is he directly appealing to God to act; the main relationship is still between author and readers as shown by Paul's use of second person plural pronouns four times in the three verses. Rather, the genre is emotive of the expressive type as shown by the intent to affect emotions and the lack of sequential development in the paragraph. As to subtype, it is not solutionality: no emotive problem is stated. Neither is it volitionality in that Paul does not list beliefs that bring about control of his emotions. Thus it seems best to consider this a causality subtype, the constituents of which (in the expressive type of emotive genre) are labeled *situation* and REACTION.

The paragraph consists of two propositional clusters, 11a–b and 12a–13c. The second begins with the developmental particle δέ, which here signals a conjoining relationship. Each of the two constitutes a REACTION; the *situation*, however, is not mentioned in this paragraph. Paul's REACTIONS are the result of Timothy's report that the Thessalonians are still trusting in God.

From the content of the wish-prayer it is obvious that Paul also has a strong secondary intent. He prays that the Lord will help the Thessalonians to love people more in order that they will live in a righteous way. Paul's intent in the next division (4:1–5:24) is to affect his readers' behavior, and that intent, although secondary, is present in this prayer as well.

The 3:11–13 paragraph seems to function on two levels. First, it is a fitting reaction at the close of the 2:17–3:13 section, in which Paul recounts how he has missed the Thessalonians, how he has unsuccessfully tried to return to them, and how he repeatedly prays that he might see them again. Therefore, in 3:11 Paul asks that God would clear the way for him to return. In 3:10 Paul wrote that he would like to help the Thessalonians; here in 3:12 he asks the Lord to help them to love each other and other people more.

The second function of 3:11–13 is on the division level, as a closing to 1:2–3:13 and as a transition to 4:1–5:24. (It parallels the wish-prayer in

5:23-24, at the end of the next division of the BODY.) Paul in 3:12 expresses his desire that the Thessalonians' love for each other will abound as his love does for them; this recalls 2:1-12, which describes his ministry to them as an expression of love (see also 3:6). As a transitional unit, 3:11-13 introduces concepts to be developed in the next division: The ideas in 3:12 of abounding more and more and love for fellow believers are echoed in 4:1, 9-10 and 5:8, 13. The ideas in 3:13 of holiness and the Lord's coming are echoed in 4:3-4, 7, 4:13-18 and 5:1-11, 23.

NOTES

3:11a The conjunction δέ 'and/now' here is not adversative but developmental or transitional (Best, Frame, Morris). It signals the switch on the paragraph level to the divine agent(s)—God and Christ. (It fulfills the same function in Paul's other wish-prayers in the Thessalonian letters at 5:23 and 2 Thess. 2:16; 3:5, 16). Some render it 'now' (Bruce, Frame; also KJV, NASB, NCV, NIV, NRSV). However, because 'now' can be understood as a temporal reference, it seems best in the display to follow those versions which do not render it at all (CEV, NAB, NJB, REB, TEV, TNT).

I(&S&T) pray to The optative mood of the three verbs in vv. 11-12 implies the orienter 'I(&S&T) pray to'. In 10a-b Paul says that he asks God to enable him to visit the Thessalonians and help them; vv. 11-13 expand upon this desire.

God himself, who is our(inc) Father The Greek is αὐτὸς δὲ ὁ θεὸς καὶ πατὴρ ἡμῶν 'and/now he/himself the God and Father of us'. The first pronoun, αὐτός, is best understood as a marker of prominence on the noun(s) that it agrees with, rather than on itself. Related to this interpretation is the understanding that this way of beginning a wish-prayer ('God himself') echoed synagogal language, which was taken from the language of the psalms (Wiles, p. 30); this observation seems valid because the same form appears in other Thessalonian passages (5:23; 2 Thess. 2:16; 3:16). The prominence-marking function of the pronoun αὐτός in this formalized wish-prayer beginning is difficult to render in English; it is not translated by CEV.

Some take the second pronoun, ἡμῶν 'our', to modify both 'God' and 'Father', resulting in the rendering 'our God and Father' (NCV, NIV, NKJV, NRSV, REB, TNT). However (comparing the wish-prayer in 2 Thess. 2:16, where there is no καί 'and' between 'God' and 'Father'), it is more meaningful to take 'and' here as introducing a comment and 'our' as modifying only 'Father': God, who is our father (also JBP, NJB, NLT). (See 1:3, where the phrase 'before God and our Father' is rendered 'God our Father'.) Marshall thinks that the use of καί 'and' in this phrase is a Hebraism.

When God is referred to as 'our Father', it is in the metaphorical sense of a parent-child relationship (Wanamaker). He is 'our Father' in that he has summoned believers to be part of the family of which he is the head and for which he provides. In turn his children have a relationship with one another that entails love and commitment.

3:11b that *God* will help us(exc) to return to you *by removing the obstacles that hinder our(exc) coming* This proposition is the first content of Paul's wish-prayer. The Greek is κατευθύναι τὴν ὁδὸν ἡμῶν πρὸς ὑμᾶς 'may he make straight our path to you'. Paul has just mentioned God the Father and the Lord Jesus (11a), but the bound pronoun of the verb in 11b is third singular. In the Greek NT it is not unusual for compound subjects to occur with singular verbs. Commentators suggest that the singular verb here indicates that Paul thinks of the Father and the Lord Jesus as a unity (Morris) or as intimately associated (Best, Bruce, Marshall, Wanamaker). However, the fact that 'God' and 'Lord (Jesus)' each occur with the definite article indicates that Paul also views them as distinct personalities (Wanamaker). Wanamaker elsewhere (p. 141) says that this passage and 2 Thess. 2:16-17 are "evidence of the profound change in prayer language that took place in Christianity as the early Christian community moved away from traditional Jewish prayers, where God alone was addressed or invoked, to the address and invocation of both God and Jesus Christ."

It seems best to understand the third person pronoun in 11b as referring to God the Father. In 12b it is the Lord (Jesus) that Paul mentions. Thus the order of mention in 11b and 12b follows the order in the orienting proposition 11a. The alternative would be to render 11b 'that they will help us'.

The phrase 'make straight our path to you' is probably a dead metaphor. It has been understood to mean either that God would direct the way of the messengers back to the Thessalonians in the sense of permitting them to return (CEV) or that God would smooth the way in the sense of removing obstacles (Bruce, Hiebert, Marshall, Morris; also NIV, NJB, REB, TEV). Given the context of 2:17–3:13, the second understanding seems preferable. The verb κατευθύνω was used of removing detours or obstacles so that quicker progress could be made toward a destination. Paul and his companions needed divine help in overcoming Satanic hindrances (2:18) in order to return to Thessalonica. The REB renders it "open the way" for us to come to you; the NIV, "clear the way."

3:12a Concerning you *I(&S&T) pray* Verse 12 begins with ὑμᾶς δὲ 'and/now you'. The developmental marker δέ along with the pronoun 'you' indicates a change of beneficiaries in the wish-prayer from Paul and his companions to the Thessalonians. The change is highlighted by the forefronting of 'you'. The 12a prayer orienter begins a second *REACTION*.

3:12b *that* the Lord *Jesus* When Paul uses the term 'Lord' he normally means Jesus (Marshall). He explicitly mentions 'our Lord Jesus' in 11a and 13c, which supports the interpretation that 'Lord' here means 'Lord Jesus' (Best, Bruce, Frame, Marshall, Wanamaker).

will help you *believers* to love each other and other people more and more The Greek is πλεονάσαι καὶ περισσεῦσαι τῇ ἀγάπῃ εἰς ἀλλήλους καὶ εἰς πάντας 'cause to increase and cause to abound in love to one another and to all (people)'. The verbs πλεονάζω 'to cause to increase' and περισσεύω 'to cause to abound' are synonyms (Best; Frame; Marshall; Moore, p. 25; Morris; Wanamaker). The use of this doublet emphasizes the meaning: "make you greatly abound" (Marshall). Paul desired that the Thessalonians would greatly increase 'in love'. Bruce and NAB take this prepositional phrase with περισσεύω only, the second of the verbs: "may the Lord increase you and make you overflow with love" (NAB). However, in 2 Thess. 1:3 Paul collocates the first verb, πλεονάζω, with love in a similar passage: "the love every one of you has for each other is increasing" (NIV). Thus it seems that here in 3:12, 'in love' was intended to modify both verbs. The phrase 'in love' represents an event and is rendered in the display by the infinitive 'to love'. The two verbs of the doublet have a causative and adverbial meaning here, which is rendered 'help you to love more and more'.

Paul desired the love of the Thessalonians to grow 'for one another and for all'. (The same expression recurs in 5:15). 'One another' means people within the community of believers; 'all' signifies nonbelievers outside the fellowship, namely "all mankind" (Bruce).

just as we(exc) *love* you There is an ellipsis in καθάπερ καὶ ἡμεῖς εἰς ὑμᾶς 'as also we to you'. Wanamaker completes the ellipsis: "just as we *abound in love* for you." Paul has already given the Thessalonians examples of the messengers' love for them (2:7–8, 11–12, 17–20; 3:5). The words καθάπερ καί 'as also' indicate that this proposition is either in a comparison or congruence relation to what precedes. If it is comparison, Paul is assuring the Thessalonians of his love for them; if congruence, as seems preferable, Paul is praying that the Lord will help the Thessalonians to follow the example of his and his companions' love (Best, Frame, Marshall, Morris, Wanamaker). The word 'love' is supplied in the rendering of the display to fill out the ellipsis.

3:13a *I(&S&T) pray this* [12b] in order that The words εἰς τό plus the infinitive στηρίξαι 'to strengthen' indicate that v. 13 relates to the preceding as purpose (Best, Frame, Hiebert, Marshall, Morris, Wanamaker). Wanamaker says that even though this is a purpose clause, it constitutes the additional wish of Paul that "his converts be blameless when they stand in the presence of God at the judgment." This may be the understanding of versions which do not have a purpose relational at the beginning of v. 13 (CEV, NAB, NCV, NIV, NJB, NRSV, REB, TNT). Rendering the verse without an introductory conjunction, however, gives the impression that it is another coordinate request in Paul's prayer. But it is not (Best), as shown by εἰς τό plus the infinitive, which indicates a change of subordination and relation.

the Lord Jesus* will strengthen your purpose/desire (*or*, strengthen you) *to do what is right The Greek is στηρίξαι ὑμῶν τὰς καρδίας 'to strengthen your hearts'. The 'Lord Jesus', the agent who helps their love to grow (12b), is the agent also of strengthening their hearts (Best, Frame, Hiebert). Best says, "The strengthening does not come directly from the loving: rather loving creates the kind of person whom the Lord can strengthen. . . ." Paul uses the term καρδία 'heart' here as in 2:4, where the heart is said to be tested by God; the meaning in 2:4 is that God examines all thoughts and motives. In 3:13a 'heart' likewise represents the inner being: the thoughts, will, feeling, and motives (Bruce, Frame, Morris, Wanamaker). These purposes and desires are to be strengthened 'to do what is right', as the word 'holy' in 13b shows. Marshall says Paul has in mind "the establishing of a firm and steady Christian character." Alternatively, 'heart' here can be understood as synecdoche, that is, 'the Lord Jesus will strengthen you'. In many languages some word other than 'heart' expresses the meaning of the Greek here.

3:13b *As a result* An implicit relation connects 13a with the rest of the verse; 13b-c is the result of the Lord's strengthening the Thessalonians' purposes and desires (Bruce, Frame, Marshall; NCV, NIV, REB, TNT). Frame says the purpose of the prayer for love is that Christ may strengthen "their hearts, their inward purposes and desires, with the result that these hearts may be blameless (*cf.* 2¹⁰) in the realm of holiness."

God our(inc) Father will decide/judge that you have behaved irreproachably and uprightly The Greek is ἀμέμπτους ἐν ἁγιωσύνῃ ἔμπροσθεν τοῦ θεοῦ καὶ πατρὸς ἡμῶν 'blameless in holiness before the God and Father of us'. In 2:10b Paul said he and his companions behaved 'blamelessly' (an adverbial form of the first word here); here in 13b he says he desires that the Thessalonians behave likewise ('irreproachably') so that they will be blameless at the judgment. The word ἁγιωσύνη 'holiness' that is here in 13b is used in 2 Cor. 7:1 to mean living in a holy way: "let us purify ourselves from everything that contaminates body and spirit, perfecting holiness out of reverence for God" (NIV). Of its use in 13b Wanamaker says, "[T]o love as Paul desired his converts to love would result in their living sanctified lives, placing them beyond any opprobrium at the judgment." Since the noun 'holiness' represents a state the phrase 'in holiness' is rendered 'you have behaved . . . uprightly'.

Because of the reference to Jesus' coming to earth in 13c, the phrase 'before the God and Father of us' is understood to refer to God's judgment at that time (Best, Bruce, Frame, Marshall, Wanamaker). The Thessalonians will be blameless before God when he judges them. (A similar phrase occurs in 2:19e, where it refers to Christ's future judging.) The rendering in the display 'will decide/judge' reflects the idea that God's judgment is in view. For the rendering of 'the God and Father of us' see the notes on 1:3 and 3:11.

3:13c when our(inc) Lord Jesus majestically comes *to earth* accompanied by all his angels (*and/or*, his people) Proposition 13c is related to what precedes as its circumstance (Marshall). The phrase ἐν τῇ παρουσίᾳ τοῦ κυρίου ἡμῶν Ἰησοῦ 'at the coming of our Lord Jesus' is rendered as was the similar phrase in 2:19e (see the note there). Here Paul adds that Christ comes μετὰ πάντων τῶν ἁγίων αὐτοῦ 'with all his holy ones'. The term ἅγιοι 'saints, holy ones' could mean people who have believed in Christ and lived a life of devotion to him (Hendriksen, Hiebert; CEV). Or it could mean angels (Best, Marshall, Wanamaker); angels were called 'holy ones' in the OT (see Job 15:14-15; Ps. 89:6-7). Or it could mean both (Bruce, Morris, Williams); Morris understands 'all' to be inclusive of both angels and believers. The meaning is hard to decide. Although 'believers' is the normal meaning of ἅγιοι 'saints' in Paul's letters, it seems likely that Paul had in mind OT passages describing this event such as Zech. 14:5, "Then the LORD my God will come, and all the holy ones with him" (NIV), where 'holy ones' were understood to be angels. Paul explicitly states in 2 Thess. 1:7 that the Lord Jesus will be revealed from heaven "with his powerful angels" (NIV).

One solution is to use an ambiguous term or phrase which could refer to either angels or believers; JBP and TEV have "all who belong to him." If 'angels' or 'people' is used, however, it would be good to mention the other interpretation in a footnote.

The additional/alternative rendering retains the possessive 'his people'. For languages in which 'people' cannot be possessed, it could be rendered 'people who trust in him'. This description of 'people' follows 2 Thess. 1:10, where "his holy people" and "all those who have believed" (NIV) are in parallel propositions.

Some manuscripts include the word 'Amen' at the end of v. 13. MJTGNT does not have it; UBSGNT includes it in brackets and gives it a C rating, indicating that the UBS committee had difficulty deciding which variant to place in the text. The evidence for or against the inclusion is fairly evenly divided. Metzger (p. 563) says it is difficult to decide whether it was dropped by scribes who thought it inappropriate in the body of a letter or whether it was added as the appropriate ending for a prayer, which this unit resembles. "'Amen' is a transliteration of the Hebrew word for 'truth'. It is a seal of sincerity and fervency added to the doxology" (Smith and Beekman, p. 110). If a translator wishes to retain 'Amen', he may render it with whatever vernacular expression closes prayers or phrases such as 'we desire this' or 'may it be so'.

BOUNDARIES AND COHERENCE

The initial boundary of 3:11-13 was discussed under 3:6-10. The terminal boundary was discussed under 1:2-3:13. (See "Boundaries.")

Referents that give lexical coherence to the unit are God the Father (in vv. 11, 13), the Lord Jesus (in all verses), and the beneficiaries of the prayer (the Thessalonians), referred to by the second person pronoun (in all verses).

Relational coherence is established by a coordinating particle δέ between the two REACTIONS (11a-b and 12a-13c) and a subordinate purpose statement introduced by εἰς τό 'in order that' in 13a. A lexical sandwich construction is created by repetition of the phrases 'God and our Father' and 'our Lord Jesus' in the beginning and ending propositions, 11a and 13b-c.

PROMINENCE AND THEME

Propositions 11b and 12b contain the three nonsubordinate verbs of 3:11-13 and are the most naturally prominent parts of the paragraph. Thus they are central to the 3:11-13 theme. The initial part of the 11a orienter is included in the theme as well.

PART CONSTITUENT 4:1–5:24
(Hortatory Division: Appeal of 1:2–5:24)

THEME: God wants you to be distinct people who behave right in every way. Be sexually pure. Love each other. Be vigilant and self-controlled as you wait for the Lord Jesus to return. Esteem and love your leaders and do good deeds to each other and to all people. Always rejoice and thank God.

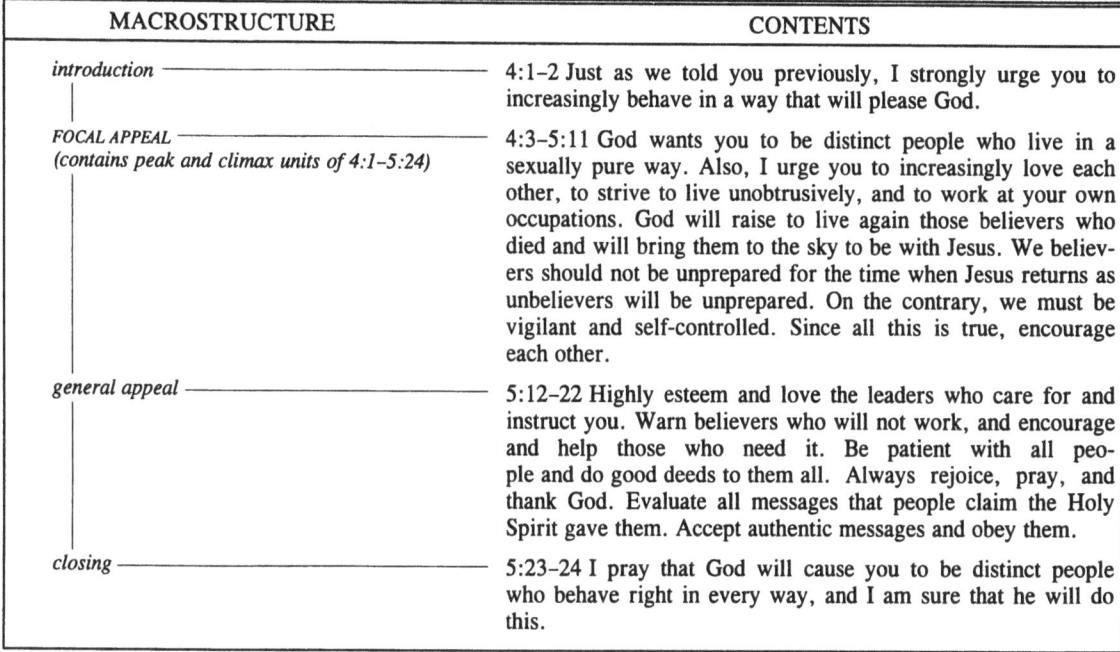

MACROSTRUCTURE	CONTENTS
introduction	4:1–2 Just as we told you previously, I strongly urge you to increasingly behave in a way that will please God.
FOCAL APPEAL *(contains peak and climax units of 4:1–5:24)*	4:3–5:11 God wants you to be distinct people who live in a sexually pure way. Also, I urge you to increasingly love each other, to strive to live unobtrusively, and to work at your own occupations. God will raise to live again those believers who died and will bring them to the sky to be with Jesus. We believers should not be unprepared for the time when Jesus returns as unbelievers will be unprepared. On the contrary, we must be vigilant and self-controlled. Since all this is true, encourage each other.
general appeal	5:12–22 Highly esteem and love the leaders who care for and instruct you. Warn believers who will not work, and encourage and help those who need it. Be patient with all people and do good deeds to them all. Always rejoice, pray, and thank God. Evaluate all messages that people claim the Holy Spirit gave them. Accept authentic messages and obey them.
closing	5:23–24 I pray that God will cause you to be distinct people who behave right in every way, and I am sure that he will do this.

INTENT AND MACROSTRUCTURE

Paul's intent in the 4:1–5:24 division is to affect the behavior of the Thessalonians. In the opening paragraph and the two major sections Paul exhorts his readers; exhortation is a strong secondary purpose of the closing expressive paragraph as well. Paul exhorts the Thessalonians to do more and more in the areas of morality, relationships, and spiritual attitudes and disciplines. This extensive exhortation signals that the genre is hortatory.

The 4:1–5:24 division consists of four conjoined units. The second begins with the conjunction γάρ, which signals a generic-specific relation to the first; the third and fourth units begin with the developmental marker δέ. The first unit (4:1–2) is an *introduction*; it contains a discourse orienter for this second half of the epistle body. It also contains a general appeal and motivational and authoritative bases, which are appropriate for the appeals in the whole 4:1–5:24 division. The second unit (4:3–5:11) deals with matters that the Thessalonians raised or that Timothy discerned to be their needs when he was in Thessalonica. This section is thus labeled FOCAL APPEAL. In the third unit (5:12–22) Paul makes more general appeals, similar to appeals in the Gospels or in lists in the Epistles. This section is labeled *general appeal*. The *closing* (5:23–24) is a wish-prayer that also focuses on what Paul desires the Thessalonians to become.

The 4:3–5:11 section of the 4:1–5:24 division contains the division's peak and climax units (see "Intent" under 4:3–5:11). For that reason the label FOCAL APPEAL is in uppercase letters in the display.

BOUNDARIES AND COHERENCE

The initial boundary of 4:1–5:24 was discussed under 1:2–3:13, and the closing boundary under 1:2–5:24. (See "Boundaries.")

Referential coherence in 4:1–5:24 is established by several factors: (1) Paul uses the speech orienters ἐρωτάω 'to ask' (4:1, 5:12) and παρακαλέω 'to urge' (4:1, 5:14). The latter also occurs in 4:10 with the same meaning. In 4:18 and 5:11 it occurs with the meaning 'to encourage or comfort'. (2) 'God' and 'the Lord Jesus' are mentioned in each of the constituent units. 'Holy Spirit' is added in the second and third units and is represented by the Spirit's work of sanctification in the closing wish-prayer. (3) Terms for sanctification and holiness are used in the second and fourth units (see "Prominence" below), and 'peace' occurs as a noun or verb in the last three units in 5:3, 13, 23. (4) The phrase 'for this is the will of God' occurs in the second and third units (in 4:3, 5:18), with only slight variation in the Greek.

Some commentators and versions separate the 5:23-24 wish-prayer from the preceding units and designate it part of the epistle closing (Best, Morris, Wanamaker; NAB, NJB). However, the wish-prayer repeats themes of the preceding units: sanctification, peace, blamelessness, the return of the Lord Jesus, and God as the caller of his people. Thus it seems more appropriate to take it as a closing or summary for 4:1-5:24. As such, it is parallel to the 3:11-13 wish-prayer that closes 2:17-3:13.

PROMINENCE AND THEME

In 4:1-5:24 and in the preceding 3:11-13 wish-prayer Paul emphasizes the fact that God wants the Thessalonians to be distinct people by their behaving in a righteous way. Five times he uses three related terms (all from the root ἁγι- 'holy'). In the wish-prayer, which closes the preceding unit and provides a transition to the present one, Paul prays that God may "strengthen your hearts in holiness [ἁγιωσύνη]" (3:13). (This and the following four references are from NRSV.) Now, here in the 4:1-5:24 unit this is echoed with the words "the will of God, your sanctification [ἁγιασμός]" (4:3); "control your own body in holiness [ἁγιασμός]" (4:4); "God did not call us to impurity but in holiness [ἁγιασμός]" (4:7); and, in the prayer that closes the unit, "sanctify [ἁγιάζω] you entirely" (5:23). The kind of behavior Paul urges should be motivated by the expectation of Christ's return (4:13-5:11) and the expectation of being declared blameless by God at that time (3:13, 5:23).

Righteous behavior is thus a prominent concept of the unit. The first sentence of the 4:1-5:24 theme ("God wants you to be distinct people who behave right in every way") is taken from the theme of the *closing*, which restates the concept developed in the division. That first sentence is also a modification of renderings used for 'sanctification' in propositions throughout the division.

The 4:3-5:11 section is prominent because it contains peak and climactic paragraphs (4:3-8 and 5:1-11) of the 4:1-5:24 division. Elements of the themes of those paragraphs are used in the second, third, and fourth sentences in the division theme. Section 5:12-22 is less prominent, and so the themes of its constituent paragraphs are merely summarized in the last two sentences of the division theme.

DIVISION CONSTITUENT 4:1-2
(Hortatory Paragraph: Introduction of 4:1-5:24)

THEME: Just as we told you previously, I strongly urge you to increasingly behave in a way that will please God.

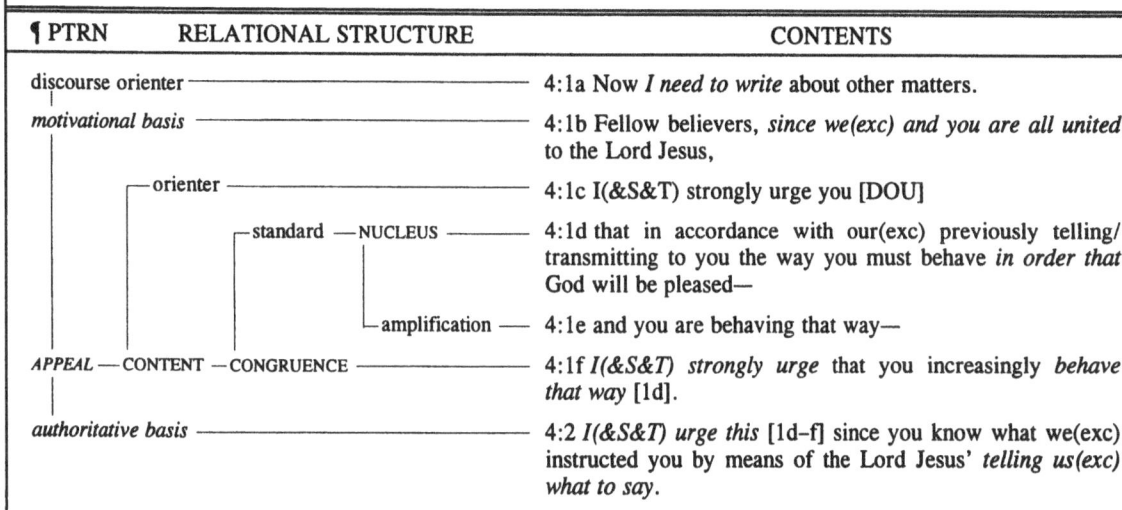

INTENT AND PARAGRAPH PATTERN

Paul's intent in the 4:1-2 paragraph is to begin the process of affecting the behavior of the Thessalonians. He urges them to do more and more the things that he and his companions told them previously. Such an exhortation indicates that the genre is hortatory.

Proposition 4:1a expresses the words λοιπὸν οὖν 'in addition then', which function as a discourse orienter for the last half (4:1-5:24) of the epistle's BODY. There are three other constituents in the 4:1-2 paragraph: proposition 1b, propositional cluster 1c-f, and proposition 4:2. Since no problem is mentioned, this is not a solutionality subtype of paragraph pattern; and since Paul does not support his APPEAL by giving means to accomplish it, it is not the volitionality subtype. Instead, he uses the exhortation-grounds relation, indicated by the conjunction γάρ 'for' in 4:2. Thus this is a causality subtype of paragraph pattern, the constituents of which (in the hortatory genre) are APPEAL and basis. Verse 2 is an *authoritative basis* for the 1c-f APPEAL. Also, early in the first verse are the vocative ἀδελφοί 'brothers' and the adverbial phrase ἐν κυρίῳ Ἰησοῦ 'in (the) Lord Jesus', which appear to function as a *motivational basis* (1b).

NOTES

4:1a Now *I need to write* about other matters The first words in v. 1 are λοιπὸν οὖν 'in addi-tion then'. The word λοιπόν is an adverbial expression which functions here as a transition to the remaining matters in the body of Paul's letter (Best, Frame, Wanamaker); it is a discourse orienter for 4:1-5:24. The second word οὖν 'therefore, so' sometimes functions as an inferential particle. If that is the case here, Paul may be referring back to the *rapport basis* that he developed in the first division (1:2-3:13) for the APPEALS he will give in this second division (4:1-5:24). Or he may be referring to the 3:11-13 wish-prayer that closes the first division and the desires he expressed for the Thessalonians to conduct themselves irreproachably and righteously. Some understand οὖν as merely a transitional particle (Bruce, Williams). This seems preferable because of its association here with λοιπόν 'in addition'. (The οὖν is absent from some early mss., but UBSGNT and MJTGNT include it without comment.) These opening transitional words have been translated "finally" by NIV, NJB, RSV, and TEV. However, in English 'finally' could indicate that the unit occurs near the end of the book, which is not the case here—there are two full chapters to come.

4:1b-c Fellow believers, *since we(exc) and you are all united* to the Lord Jesus, I(&S&T) strongly urge you Although the phrase ἐν κυρίῳ Ἰησοῦ 'in (the) Lord Jesus' is rendered in 1b, in the Greek it actually follows the verbs of 1c.

Following the vocative 'brothers' are the two conjoined verbs ἐρωτῶμεν 'we ask, request' and παρακαλοῦμεν 'we urge, exhort, encourage', which in this context are virtually synonymous (Frame, Marshall, Moore, Wanamaker). The repetition is for emphasis, rendered 'strongly urge' in the display. If such a doublet is unnatural in the receptor language, a single verb meaning 'urge' will adequately convey the emphasis. Proposition 1c functions as the orienter for 1d–f.

The Greek verbs of 1c are modified by the adverbial phrase ἐν κυρίῳ Ἰησοῦ 'in (the) Lord Jesus', the meaning of which is difficult to determine. It could refer to the authority of Paul as an apostle of the Lord (Wanamaker). In that case the phrase might be a contraction of 'in the name of the Lord Jesus'. A similar phrase in 2b, διὰ τοῦ κυρίου Ἰησοῦ 'through the Lord Jesus', does imply authority (see the note there). However, in v. 1 Paul addresses his readers as ἀδελφοί 'brothers', and he asks and urges/encourages them 'in the Lord Jesus'. The kinship term and phrase perhaps indicate that the 1c-f APPEAL is personal and mitigated, based on the oneness Paul and the Thessalonians have in the Lord (Best, Bruce). The communication situation as a whole was not one in which Paul had to appeal to his authority. Thus the phrase is rendered in 1b adjacent to the vocative 'brothers', and together they speak of the bond between the author and the readers who are both united to the Lord. By this understanding, 'fellow believers in the Lord Jesus' is a *motivational basis* for Paul's 1c-f APPEAL. What Paul is saying is, since it is the case that we are all united to the Lord Jesus and want to maintain that unity by obeying him, I urge you. REB has "And now, friends, we have one thing to ask of you, as fellow-Christians."

4:1d that in accordance with our(exc) previously telling/transmitting to you the way you must behave *in order that* God will be pleased The Greek is ἵνα καθὼς παρελάβετε παρ' ἡμῶν τὸ πῶς δεῖ ὑμᾶς περιπατεῖν καὶ ἀρέσκειν θεῷ 'that as you received from us how it is necessary (for) you to walk and to please God'. The content of Paul's urging (1c) is indicated here by the conjunction ἵνα 'that'. 'As you received from us' is the first part of a standard-congruence relation with 1f. The passive-like idea is rendered actively in the display. The verb παραλαμβάνω is a technical term that refers to the reception of authoritative tradition; Paul first used it in 2:13b (see the note there). The messengers had received the teaching from the Lord, and they passed it on to the Thessalonians. This is a reference to Paul's teaching when he and his companions were in Thessalonica, not a reference to the earlier part of this letter.

The content of what Paul previously told the Thessalonians is given in the clause 'how it is necessary for you to walk and to please God'. (For περιπατέω 'walk', see the note on 2:12b.) The conjoined infinitives most likely are not two distinct teachings: how to behave *and* how to please God. Rather, the second is either the purpose or result of the first. Bruce and Bullinger (p. 671) call the construction a hendiadys; Best and Frame call it a καί consecutive. The resulting meaning is the same. Paul called the Thessalonians to a lifestyle that would please God. The rendering in the display indicates a relation of purpose. The relation of result also seems appropriate: 'the way you must behave with the result that God will be pleased'.

4:1e and you are behaving that way Paul affirms the obedience of the Thessalonians in an amplification: καθὼς καὶ περιπατεῖτε 'as indeed you are walking'. The presence of a second καθώς 'as' here suggests that 1e is also in a standard-congruence relation with 1f. Thus the label of amplification is appropriate. This clause is absent in MJTGNT, but UBSGNT accepts it as certain. Early manuscript support for the reading is strong; also, Paul's statement in the next proposition (1f) that his readers should do more and more presupposes the mention here that the Thessalonians were following his teaching (Metzger, p. 564).

4:1f I(&S&T) strongly urge that you increasingly *behave that way* [1d] Paul now gets to the main CONTENT of his exhortation. It is ἵνα περισσεύητε μᾶλλον 'that you abound more'. Because of the disruptive intervening clauses 1d and 1e, he repeats the conjunction ἵνα 'that'; similarly, the display repeats 'I(&S&T) strongly urge' from 1c. In 3:12a Paul uses this same verb περισσεύω to say that he wants the Thessalonians' love to increase. Here he wants them to do more of what he instructed when he visited Thessalonica and what he has heard from Timothy that they are now doing.

4:2 *I(&S&T) urge this* [1d-f] since you know what we(exc) instructed you by means of the Lord Jesus' *telling us(exc) what to say* The Greek is οἴδατε γὰρ τίνας παραγγελίας ἐδώκαμεν ὑμῖν διὰ τοῦ κυρίου Ἰησοῦ 'for you know what instructions we gave you through the Lord Jesus'. Marshall interprets γάρ as indicating a statement equivalent to what precedes, especially 1d. However, it seems better to take γάρ as introducing grounds (Frame, Hiebert, Wanamaker). Verse 2 is an *authoritative basis* for Paul's 1c-f APPEAL; the Thessalonians should follow Paul's present urging since they knew the specific instructions that he and his companions had given earlier, and these instructions came from the Lord Jesus himself. The word παραγγελία can mean 'command' or 'instruction'. It was used for commands given by a military officer to his men. It is appropriate here where authoritative instruction comes from the Lord Jesus through Paul, Silas, and Timothy. Note the similarity of v. 2 to 2 Thess. 3:6, where Paul uses the cognate verb παραγγέλλω 'to command' or 'to instruct' along with the phrase 'in the name of the Lord Jesus Christ'.

The phrase 'through the Lord Jesus' indicates that the instructions actually came from the Lord Jesus. Paul is not appealing to his own authority as Christ's representative. Rather, he appeals here to the authority of the Lord Jesus himself; in 4:3 he will appeal to the authority of God; and in 4:8 to the authority of God and the indwelling Holy Spirit. Here in 4:2 it is the indwelling Lord Jesus who has given the orders and prompted the messengers (Frame). (Note that this meaning is different from that of the similar phrase in 1b, 'in the Lord Jesus', because of the different prepositions and contexts.) Wanamaker says that the preposition "διά with the genitive of the person frequently indicates the originator of an action. . . . Thus the thought, but not the grammar, is very similar to 1 Cor. 7:10, where Paul writes, 'To those who are married I command (παραγγέλλω), not I but the Lord. . . .'" The TNT renders it as "You know the instructions we gave you from the Lord Jesus." This emphasis on the divine authority in Paul's ministry is similar to 1:5, where Paul said the Holy Spirit empowered his words, and to 2:13, where he said the Thessalonians accepted not a human message, but a divine one.

BOUNDARIES AND COHERENCE

The initial boundary of 4:1-2 was discussed under 1:2-3:13 (see "Boundaries"). The terminal boundary is taken to be between 4:2 and 4:3, but is much disputed. No boundary is indicated here either by UBSGNT or MJTGNT. None of the versions consulted place a boundary here, with the exception of CBW, JB, NIV AND NJB. The primary reason for the omission of a boundary seems to be grammatical coherence. Verses 3-8 are related to the preceding verses by the conjunction γάρ 'for'. The same conjunction relates v. 2 to v. 1 and vv. 1-2 are a unit. Thus the repetition of the γάρ in v. 3 may indicate continuation of the unit begun in v. 1.

But several commentators (Best, Bruce, Frame, Morris, Wanamaker) and the versions just mentioned do place a boundary between 4:2 and 4:3, and there are good reasons for starting a new paragraph at this point. First, vv. 1-2 constitute what seems to be a general exhortation and 3-8 are a specific exhortation regarding sexual purity. They seem to have an affinity; however, vv. 1-2 can be considered an introductory paragraph that relates not only to 3-8 but to paragraph 9-12 and the remaining paragraphs in 4:1-5:24 as well. If this is the case it is best to represent 4:1-2 as a distinct unit. The fact that 4:1-2 relates to 4:9-12 (at least) is supported by the use in each of lexical items of the same root: 'you know what instructions [παραγγελία] we gave you' in v. 2 and 'as we instructed [παραγγέλω] you' in v. 11; 'how it is necessary for you to walk [περιπατέω]' in 1d and 'in order that you walk [περιπατέω]' in v. 12.

Second, 4:3 begins with an unusual orienter, a stative expression (τοῦτο γάρ ἐστιν θέλημα τοῦ θεοῦ 'for this is the will of God') and an abstract noun phrase (ὁ ἁγιασμὸς ὑμῶν 'your sanctification'). This seems to create semantic distance between v. 3 and v. 2.

Finally, according to the theory underlying this analysis, 4:1-2 constitute a complete paragraph pattern, as do 4:3-8.

PROMINENCE AND THEME

In 4:1-2 the APPEAL is the prominent constituent. The theme for the paragraph is derived from the prominent CONTENT proposition (1f) of the APPEAL. Information is supplied from the orienter (1c) and standard (1d) propositions, where necessary, to give the complete meaning.

DIVISION CONSTITUENT 4:3–5:11
(Complex Section: Focal Appeal of 4:1–5:24)

THEME: God wants you to be distinct people by your behaving in a sexually pure way. Also, I urge you to increasingly love each other, to strive to live unobtrusively, and to work at your own occupations. God will raise to live again those believers who died and will bring them to the sky with Jesus. We believers should not be unprepared for the time when Jesus returns as unbelievers will be unprepared. On the contrary, we must be vigilant and self-controlled. Since all this is true, encourage each other.

MACROSTRUCTURE	CONTENTS
FOCAL APPEAL₁ —————— (contains peak unit of 4:1—5:24) | FOCAL APPEAL₂ —————— (contains climax unit of 4:1—5:24)	4:3–12 God wants you to be distinct people by your behaving in a sexually pure way. Also, I urge you to increasingly love each other, to strive to live unobtrusively, and to work at your own occupations. 4:13–5:11 God will raise to live again those believers who died and will bring them to the sky with Jesus. We believers should not be unprepared for the time when Jesus returns as unbelievers will be unprepared. On the contrary, we must be vigilant and self-controlled. God has destined us believers to be saved from being punished in the future and to be able to live together with our Lord Jesus after he returns. Since all this is true, encourage each other.

INTENT AND MACROSTRUCTURE

Paul's intent in the 4:3–5:11 section is to affect the behavior of the Thessalonians. He exhorts his readers in four specific areas: sexually pure behavior, loving conduct toward fellow believers, hope concerning Christians who have died, and self-control and vigilance in the light of Christ's future return. Such exhortations indicate that the genre is hortatory. However, because the second constituent is considered complex (see "Intent" under the 4:13–5:11 subsection), this larger unit, a section, is also considered complex.

The section consists of two subsections (4:3–12 and 4:13–5:11). The second subsection begins with the developmental marker δέ, which conjoins it to the first.

Paul may have seen the need to write about the matters in this section after Timothy's report on his time in Thessalonica, or some of the issues may have been raised in correspondence from the Thessalonians. Thus the constituent units are labeled *FOCAL APPEALS*.

The 4:3–12 subsection contains a peak paragraph (4:3–8) in the discourse. The introductory paragraph (4:1–2) that precedes it is a rather gentle start to the hortatory division (4:1–5:24), but in 4:3–8 Paul writes with fervor. The appeal in 4:3–8 has five bases: authoritative (3a), warning (6b-c), axiomatic (7a-c), a second authoritative (8a-d), and a second axiomatic (8e). Of all exhortations in the letter only those in the 5:1–8 climactic paragraph approach this level of support. It is obvious from the strong wording of the appeal and bases in 4:3–8 that righteous moral behavior is a nonnegotiable issue for Paul. The concept of sanctification is an important one in the letter (see "Prominence" under 4:1–5:24). Five times in 1 Thessalonians Paul uses terms from the root ἁγι- 'holy', three of which are in the 4:3–8 peak paragraph: ἁγιασμός 'sanctification, holiness' in v. 3, v. 4, and v. 7.

The 4:13–5:11 subsection contains the climactic unit of the epistle, the 5:1–8 paragraph. The following features signal that 5:1–8 is the climax:

(1) In 5:1–8 Paul changes the pace of the discourse. Whereas in 4:1–12 he primarily uses orienters and present-tense infinitives to exhort his readers, he uses no such exhortations in 5:1–8 (nor in the 4:13–18 pre-climax unit). Instead he uses four first person plural subjunctive verbs in mitigated appeals: μὴ καθεύδωμεν 'let us not sleep' in 6a, γρηγορῶμεν καὶ νήφωμεν 'let us keep awake and let us be sober/self-controlled' in 6c, and νήφωμεν 'let us be sober/self-controlled' in 8b. Paul then adds a participial construction in 8c-f, which takes on the function of νήφωμεν 'let us be sober/self-controlled', the finite subjunctive verb that precedes it: ἐνδυσάμενοι θώρακα πίστεως καὶ ἀγάπης καὶ περικεφαλαίαν ἐλπίδα σωτηρίας 'having put on a breastplate of faith and of love and a helmet (that is) hope of salvation'. After the 5:1–8 climactic unit Paul switches almost exclusively to second person imperatives, which are unmitigated appeals. Mitigated appeals are appropriate for the climax of 1 Thessalonians. They show Paul's fatherly love for the Thessalo-

nians in gently encouraging and appealing to them to follow appropriate Christian behavior rather than in authoritatively demanding as an apostle that they change their pagan lifestyle.

(2) Paul's liberal use of figurative speech in 5:1-8 creates heightened vividness. He develops an extended metaphor (with the contrasting images of day and night, light and dark, awake and asleep, sober and drunk, and salvation and disaster/wrath), and he uses similes with images of a thief (twice) and a pregnant woman.

(3) Paul also gives prominence to 5:1-8 by using two major negative-positive constructions (5a-b, 6a-c) in the unit. (There is also one in the post climax paragraph 5:9-11, in 9a-b.)

Paul's intent in using all of these features is to impress on the Thessalonians the uniqueness of their Christian identity and destiny and the need for them to live differently from unbelievers around them.

The two FOCAL APPEAL labels are both in uppercase letters in the display because constituent units of each contain peak or climax units of 4:1-5:24.

BOUNDARIES AND COHERENCE

The initial boundary of 4:3-5:11 was discussed under 4:1-2 (see "Boundaries"). The terminal boundary is between 5:11 and 5:12, where the topic changes. At 5:12 Paul leaves the topic of the second coming of Christ and the three extensively developed exhortations in 4:3-5:11 to begin a series of shorter, general exhortations. This is a strong indication for a boundary between 5:11 and 5:12. Also the performative ἐρωτῶμεν 'we ask' and the conjunction δέ 'now' in 5:12 can both indicate a boundary: δέ here indicates continuity with the exhortations that have preceded, yet with a new, distinct contribution. The vocative 'brothers' also contributes to the evidence for a boundary between 5:11 and 5:12.

Referential coherence in 4:3-5:11 is established by the words περὶ δέ 'now concerning'. They occur in the first verses of three of the four paragraphs in the two constituent subsections. In two of the verses (4:9, 5:1) the words are verse initial. In the third (4:13) περί follows the vocative 'brothers' and the initial statement 'now (δέ) we do not want you to be ignorant'. The two words περὶ δέ are important, because they designate the new topics as ones that Paul had specific reason to mention (see the note on 4:9a). The topic of the first paragraph (4:1-8), sexual purity, is in the same category even though it is not introduced by περὶ δέ; this is obvious from the fact that Paul issues strongly worded appeals and bases against such behavior.

Referential coherence is also established by the rhetorical device of paralipsis ('you do not need . . .') in verses 4:9 and 5:1 of each of the subsections.

PROMINENCE AND THEME

The 4:3-5:11 section comprises two subsections. The second one, 4:13-5:11, is the more prominent of the two because it contains the climactic paragraph of 4:1-5:24. The first, 4:3-12, is also prominent, however, because it contains the peak paragraph. Thus the theme for 4:3-5:11 is a combination of the themes of both constituents.

SECTION CONSTITUENT 4:3–12
(Hortatory Subsection: Focal Appeal₁ of 4:3–5:11)

THEME: God wants you to be distinct people by your behaving in a sexually pure way. Also, I urge you to increasingly love each other, to strive to live unobtrusively, and to work at your own occupations.

MACROSTRUCTURE	CONTENTS
APPEAL₁ (peak unit of 4:1–5:24)	4:3–8 God wants you to be distinct people by your behaving in a sexually pure way.
appeal₂	4:9–12 I urge you to increasingly love each other, to strive to live unobtrusively, and to work at your own occupations.

INTENT AND MACROSTRUCTURE

Paul's intent in the 4:3–12 subsection is to affect the behavior of his readers in the areas of sexual purity and of love and consideration for each other. His exhortations indicate that the genre is hortatory.

The subsection consists of two paragraphs, 3–8 and 9–12. The second paragraph begins with the developmental marker δέ, which functions to conjoin it to the first.

Because 4:3–8 is a peak unit in 4:1–5:24 (see "Intent" under 4:3–5:11), the first APPEAL label is in uppercase letters.

BOUNDARIES AND COHERENCE

The initial boundary of 4:3–12 was discussed under 4:1–2 (see "Boundaries"). The terminal boundary is between 4:12 and 4:13. It is well established. At 4:13 Paul switches to a new topic, the Lord's coming as it relates to believers who have died. The discourse genre also changes, to expressive, though within this next subsection is embedded an extensive expository paragraph (4:14–17). The vocative 'brothers' in 4:13 adds to the evidence for the beginning of a new unit.

There are a couple of usages in 4:3–12 which give referential coherence. Both constituent paragraphs have references (in 6c and 11d) to Paul's previous instructions to the Thessalonians. Also, the concepts of not sinning against one's brother (6a) and loving one's brother (9a–10c) give referential coherence.

PROMINENCE AND THEME

The first APPEAL (4:3–8) of the 4:3–12 subsection is a peak unit in 4:1–5:24 (see "Intent" under 4:3–5:11). It is more thoroughly developed and supported than the second. Therefore it is more prominent. However, the second *appeal* (4:9–12) contains a strong *trust basis* (9a–10a). Thus the themes of both are combined, with only slight modification, to form the theme of 4:3–12.

SUBSECTION CONSTITUENT 4:3-8
(Hortatory Paragraph: Appeal$_1$ of 4:3-12)

THEME: God wants you to be distinct people by your behaving in a sexually pure way.		
¶ PTRN	RELATIONAL STRUCTURE	CONTENTS
generic appeal	——(summary of 4:1-2)——	[4:1-2 *I strongly urge that you increasingly behave in such a way that God will be pleased.*]
authoritative basis$_1$	——(ORIENTER)——	4:3a *Specifically,* God wants the following:
SPECIFIC APPEAL — GENERIC		4:3b *he wants* you to be distinct people by your behaving in a morally pure way.
└─ specific — MEANS — NUCLEUS		4:3c *Specifically, he* does not want you to do any sexually immoral things (*or,* to act/be sexually immoral in any way).
└─ eqv — NUCLEUS		4:4a *That is, he wants* each one of you to know how to control your own sexual passions, [EUP]
└─ eqv ┬ POSITIVE		4:4b by *behaving in* a morally pure and respectable way,
└─ NEG — NUC		4:5a not by lustfully desiring *and doing* immoral things
└─ cpr		4:5b as the people *do* who do not worship (*or,* obey) God.
└─ purpose		4:6a *God wants each one of you to control your sexual passions in order that* no one of you sin against and take advantage of your fellow believer by doing such things [3c–5b].
warning basis — CONGRUENCE		4:6b *I(&S&T) exhort this* [3a–6a] *since* the Lord *Jesus* will punish *people who do* such sexually immoral things
└─ standard		4:6c in accordance with what we(exc) strongly warned you previously [HEN].
┌─ grounds — MEANS		4:7a *God wants this* [3a–6a] *since* he did not summon us(inc) *believers*
├─ negative		4:7b to *be people who* behave in a sexually immoral way.
└─ purpose — POSITIVE		4:7c On the contrary, *he summoned us* to be distinct *people who* behave in a morally pure way.
axiomatic basis$_1$ and authoritative basis$_2$ ┌─ condition		4:8a Therefore, if anyone disregards *this appeal* [3a–6a],
├─ negative		4:8b he is not disregarding a human being.
CONCLU- ─ CONSE- ┬ POSITIVE CONCLUSION		4:8c On the contrary, *that person is disregarding* God
SION QUENCE └─ implied grounds		4:8d *since God commanded it.*
axiomatic basis$_2$		4:8e *I(&S&T) exhort that you do this* [3a–6a] *since* God gives his Spirit, who is **holy**, *to live* in you.

INTENT AND PARAGRAPH PATTERN

In the 4:3-8 paragraph Paul seeks to affect the behavior of the Thessalonians. The strong wording of the exhortations and grounds creates a striking contrast to the expressive, emotionally warm units of the first half of the letter. Therefore, Wanamaker (pp. 158-59) may be correct when he hypothesizes that Paul was dealing with an actual problem in the Christian community at Thessalonica that concerned him greatly. Paul wanted the moral lives of the Thessalonians to be qualitatively different from those around them who did not acknowledge God. The exhortations indicate that the genre is hortatory.

The paragraph consists of three propositional clusters (3a-6a, 6b-c, 7a-8d) and a proposition (8e). The first cluster is Paul's exhortation. (In the display the label of the 3a orienter is moved left to the paragraph pattern level in order to better indicate its function and prominence as the first *authoritative basis*. However, it relates to the 3b-6a content propositions of the first cluster.) The second cluster is introduced by διότι 'because', and the third, by γάρ 'for'. These conjunctions signal that the second and third clusters are in an exhortation-grounds communication relation with the first. The final proposition (8e) is taken as having the same relation to the first.

Although there may have been a problem in Thessalonica that Paul was addressing, he does not mention it, so this is not a solutionality subtype of paragraph pattern. Neither is it volitionality because support for the specific appeal is not the means (enablement) to accomplish it. Rather, it is the grounds (basis) to justify carrying out the appeal. Thus this is a simple result-reason causality subtype, the constituents of which (for the hortatory genre) are APPEAL and *basis*.

Paragraph 4:3-8 is a peak unit of 4:1-5:24 (see "Intent" under 4:3-5:11).

NOTES

4:3a Specifically Using the conjunction γάρ 'for', Paul introduces an explanation of what precedes (Marshall, Wanamaker). The conjunction indicates that the 3a-6a appeal details or specifies an important aspect of Paul's more general appeal in vv. 1-2. The γάρ ties vv. 1-2 and vv. 3-8 so closely together that it is difficult to decide if 4:1-8 is one or two units (see "Boundaries" under 4:1-2). To show that close relationship, Paul's appeal in the preceding paragraph (4:1-2) is summarized in this display and is labeled *generic appeal*; the 3b-6a exhortation is labeled SPECIFIC APPEAL. Because the 4:1-2 *generic appeal* relates as well to other appeals in 4:1-5:24, the line in the display connecting it to the SPECIFIC APPEAL is a broken line.

God wants the following The SPECIFIC APPEAL begins with an orienter and a generic proposition: τοῦτο γάρ ἐστιν θέλημα τοῦ θεοῦ, ὁ ἁγιασμὸς ὑμῶν 'for this is (the) will of God, your sanctification' (3a-b). Whether or not τοῦτο 'this' is a fronted comment or merely the topic, the Greek surface form of the orienter, 'this is the will of God', gives prominence to the orienter and indicates that it is an *authoritative basis* of the exhortations to follow. (Frame calls it the "divine sanction.") Thus 3a has a dual role as *authoritative basis* and ORIENTER, which is indicated in the display. The noun θέλημα 'will' represents a verbal idea, hence '(God) wants'. The lack of an article before 'will of God' may indicate that it was a formula well known to Paul and his readers (Wanamaker), or that it marks the predicate (Bruce), or that it refers to an aspect, not the total will of God (Frame). The pronoun τοῦτο 'this' is rendered 'the following' in the display to make the cataphoric (forward) reference clear.

4:3b *he wants* you to be distinct people by your behaving in a morally pure way The noun ἁγιασμός 'sanctification' is a technical term that refers to setting apart objects or people for a distinct purpose, ministry, or conduct. Here it may refer either to the process whereby the Thessalonians dedicate themselves to God by separating from immorality (Bruce, Frame, Wanamaker) or the outcome of that process. In 4b Paul uses the term to exhort his readers to a holy manner of sexual conduct, and in 7c he uses it as the antithesis of ἀκαθαρσία 'immorality, impurity'. Bruce says that "not even in LXX does it bear the strong ethical sense which it has here [in the earliest Christian occurrence] and in later Christian literature." Thus in vv. 3-8 it seems the meaning of ἁγιασμός focuses on the process of the Thessalonians' consecration, that of their being a unique people because they live a life of moral purity. 'Sanctification' represents a stative verbal predicate and is rendered in the display as 'to be distinct people . . . behaving in a morally pure way'. 'Distinct' speaks of separateness. Morally pure behavior makes believers different in nature and quality from those in the society around them.

4:3c *Specifically, he* does not want you to do any sexually immoral things (*or*, to act/be

sexually immoral in any way) There is a subordinate infinitive phrase here giving a specific explanation of Paul's exhortation in 3b. The specific thing is ἀπέχεσθαι ὑμᾶς ἀπὸ τῆς πορνείας '(for) you to abstain from sexual immorality'. The term πορνεία "refers to all sexual intercourse other than that which takes place within the marriage relationship" (Marshall; also BAGD, p. 693).

4:4a *That is, he wants* **each one of you to know how to control your own sexual passions** Verse four consists of a second infinitive phrase: εἰδέναι ἕκαστον ὑμῶν τὸ ἑαυτοῦ σκεῦος κτᾶσθαι ἐν ἁγιασμῷ καὶ τιμῇ 'each one of you to know (how) to possess his own vessel in sanctification and honor'. This could be understood as coordinate with the one in 3c (Wanamaker), in which case it would relate to 3b as a second specific proposition. However, it seems better to understand it as explanatory (Frame, Marshall) and as equivalent to 3c (Morris); to abstain from illicit sexual intercourse is to control one's bodily passions. (Alternative interpretations are that each man should know how to acquire a wife or respect and honor the wife he has.)

Throughout church history v. 4 has been a problem to interpreters. The difficulty is determining the meaning of the figure σκεῦος 'object, vessel' and of the verb κτάομαι 'to acquire, get'. Those who focus on the normal meaning of the verb feel that 'acquiring' or 'respecting a wife' is the meaning of the figure (Best, Frame; CEV, DGN, RSV, TEV). The difficulty with this view is that σκεῦος 'vessel' is an obscure way of referring to a wife; Greek has the unambiguous term γυνή, which Paul could have used if he had meant this. (There is evidence, however, according to Wanamaker, that rabbis referred to women with the Hebrew equivalent of σκεῦος 'vessel' when speaking euphemistically of sexual intercourse.) Others have focused on the noun and think that here it refers to a person's body (Bruce, Hiebert, Morris; JBP, NCV, NIV, NJB, NLT, NRSV, REB, TNT) or that it is a euphemism for the genitalia (Louw and Nida 23.63, Marshall, Wanamaker; NAB). In this view the noun and verb together speak of controlling one's body, or more specifically, sexual passions. The difficulty with this interpretation is that 'to control' was not the normal meaning of the verb κτάομαι, although a few examples from papyri documents indicate it was beginning to be used colloquially to mean 'to take possession' in the sense of 'use properly' or 'control' (Morris).

That the noun and verb are a euphemism for controlling sexual passions seems the best interpretation for several reasons: (1) Paul's appeal in this passage seems to be to all Thessalonians, since in 4a 'each one of you' probably means men and women, married and unmarried. Thus this is not an admonishment to only unmarried men to take wives or to only married men to live honorably with wives. (2) In v. 5 Paul says pagans perform in a lustfully passionate manner what he is speaking of in 4a. This comment fits 4a better if 4a is taken as referring to controlling one's bodily passions rather than to acquiring a wife. (3) Paul nowhere uses σκεῦος to refer specifically to a wife, but he does use it figuratively of human beings or the body, as in 2 Cor. 4:7. (4) Finally, the LXX in 1 Sam. 21:5 uses σκεῦος of men's bodies (perhaps genitals) that have not been ceremonially defiled by sexual intercourse.

Because versions divide on the understanding of this verse it is wise to include a footnote in the translation indicating the interpretation not rendered in the text.

4:4b by *behaving in* **a morally pure and respectable way** Using two prepositional phrases Paul states what it means for a believer to control his or her sexual passions. Here in 4b is the first of these phrases, ἐν ἁγιασμῷ καὶ τιμῇ 'in sanctification and honor'. It is propositionalized as 'by behaving in a morally pure and respectable way' and appears to be parallel in meaning to 4a (εἰδέναι ἕκαστον ὑμῶν τὸ ἑαυτοῦ σκεῦος κτᾶσθαι, he wants 'each one of you to know how to control your own sexual passions'). The second of the two propositional phrases is in 5a: μὴ ἐν πάθει ἐπιθυμίας 'not in passion of evil craving'. It is propositionalized as 'not by lustfully desiring and doing immoral things' and appears to be parallel to 3c (ἀπέχεσθαι ὑμᾶς ἀπὸ τῆς πορνείας, he does not want 'you to do any sexually immoral things'). This shows that propositions in 3c–5a are for the most part equivalent to each other and thus the labels in the display.

The first of the two prepositional phrases, 4b, is positive: ἐν ἁγιασμῷ καὶ τιμῇ 'in sanctification and honor'. Some commentators say that the preposition ἐν 'in' indicates the sphere (Hiebert) or atmosphere (Frame) in which 4a takes place, that is, as people consecrated to God. However, in the corresponding negative phrase in 5a, which also begins with ἐν 'in', it is obvious that Paul is speaking of ethical behavior. Thus it is appropriate to take 4b as speaking of manner of behavior as well (as do NCV, NIV, NJB, and TEV). Marshall says the phrase tells how the sexual side of life is to be conducted.

The noun ἁγιασμός 'sanctification', the first noun in this phrase, is discussed in the note on 3b. The second, τιμή 'honor', could refer to sexual behavior that is respectful toward one's own body, toward other people, and toward God (Wanamaker), all of which are applicable in this context. The nouns 'sanctification' and 'honor' represent abstract descriptions of the manner of behavior and are rendered as attributes in the display.

4:5a not by lustfully desiring *and doing* immoral things The negative counterpart of 4b is in this second prepositional phrase, μὴ ἐν πάθει ἐπιθυμίας 'not in passion of evil craving'. The first noun, πάθος, here signifies *"passion . . . esp. of a sexual nature"* (BAGD, p. 603.2). The second noun, ἐπιθυμία, was used in a good sense in 2:17c. In this context, however, it is a desire for something forbidden (BAGD, p. 293.3). It is in the genitive case, which emphasizes the evil quality of the passion; TEV has "a lustful desire." Since the noun πάθος 'passion/desire' represents a state, it is rendered in the display as a verb. Paul's point is probably that the heathen not only desired these immoral things but that they also did those things. REB has "not giving way to lust like the pagans," and NJB and TNT are similar. As this proposition appears to have equal prominence with the preceding POSITIVE one, its label is also in uppercase letters in the display.

4:5b as the people *do* There is a comparison here, introduced by καθάπερ καί 'as also/even'. The words together probably have a comparative function; no versions consulted except KJV separately render the second term, 'also/even'. The next terms are τὰ ἔθνη, which most often mean 'the Gentiles, non-Jewish people,' in the NT; that was the meaning in 2:16a. Here the focus is on the immoral lifestyle of people who do not follow God's standards. NIV and TEV have 'heathen'; REB has 'pagans'. In the display it is rendered simply 'people' because the following restrictive relative clause, which gives the connotation of ungodly lifestyle, makes any further characterization unnecessary.

who do not worship (*or*, obey) God The phrase τὰ μὴ εἰδότα τὸν θεόν 'those not knowing God' has its roots in the OT. NRSV renders Ps. 79:6 as "Pour out your anger on the nations [ἔθνη in the LXX] that do not know you, and on the kingdoms that do not call on your name." What causes sinful behavior is not so much ignorance of God as a refusal to acknowledge or worship him (Rom. 1:21-28). In 2 Thess. 1:8 Paul makes disobedience explicit: "He will punish those who do not know God and do not obey the gospel of our Lord Jesus" (NIV). Thus the rendering in the display.

4:6a *God wants each one of you to control your sexual passions in order that* Verse 6 begins with two coordinate infinitives preceded by the neuter article τό. This construction differs from the infinitives in 3c and 4a, which do not have the article. The different surface structure here probably indicates that 6a is not a second or third specific proposition parallel to 3c, although some view it as such (Hiebert, Wanamaker; CEV, NAB, NIV, NRSV). Nor is it in apposition to 4a-5b as others hold (Best, Marshall; REB). Instead, it seems best to understand v. 6 as expressing purpose (Bruce, Frame). (An articular infinitive in 3:3a similarly, and less ambiguously, indicates purpose.)

The referential phrase ἐν τῷ πράγματι 'in the matter', which follows the infinitives, most likely indicates that 6a is a continuation of the topic in 3c-5b. This is the view on which the display is based. However, some commentators have proposed quite a different understanding of 6a. They say that the change to articular infinitives and the use of verbs and a noun which were used in extrabiblical commercial texts, indicate a switch to a new topic: defrauding a brother in business matters. This is unlikely, however, because Paul seems to continue the topic of sexual purity in the very next verse, even repeating the noun ἁγιασμός 'sanctification' that he has already used twice in this paragraph.

no one of you sin against and take advantage of your fellow believer by doing such things [3c-5b] Here καί 'and' joins the infinitives ὑπερβαίνειν 'to wrong' and πλεονεκτεῖν 'to defraud'. It is translated *und* 'and' by DGN and 'or' by Bruce, NAB, NCV, NIV, NRSV, REB, TEV, and TNT (i.e., to not wrong *or* defraud his brother). In English usage such an 'or' is ambiguous. It can indicate that one thing and not the other is intended, or it can be an idiomatic way of conjoining things with the same or similar meaning. It is this latter usage and meaning that seems to fit the words here; therefore καί is rendered 'and' in the display. Paul may be emphasizing the evil of such sin by adding the second verb (Ellingworth and Nida).

In its figurative use the verb ὑπερβαίνω means "*overstep, transgress, break* (laws and commandments . . .)" (BAGD, p. 840.2). The second verb, πλεονεκτέω, means "*take advantage of, outwit, defraud, cheat* τινά *someone*" (BAGD, p. 667.1). The object 'his brother' follows the second verb. Other than that there is no mention of what was transgressed. However, it seems appropriate to take the phrase 'his brother' as the object of the first, as well as the second, verb (following Frame, Morris; NCV, NIV, NRSV, REB, TEV).

A specific area is in view here: ἐν τῷ πράγματι 'in the matter', that is, in the matter of illicit sexual relations (Bruce, Frame), which was just discussed in 3c–5b. Best, Marshall, and others understand this prepositional phrase as a euphemism, much like "an affair." The phrase is rendered in the display 'by doing such things'.

The term ἀδελφός 'brother' probably refers to a fellow believer here (Best, Bruce, Frame, Marshall, Wanamaker; CEV, REB, TEV). Paul was primarily concerned with sexual immorality in the Christian community (Marshall, Wanamaker), though commentators point out that Paul's point would also be true if the offended were a nonbeliever. A Christian who would use his familiarity and friendship to gain sexual favors from a member of another Christian's family would be taking advantage of that fellow believer (Wanamaker). It would be sexual behavior to which he or she had no right, whether with the believer's spouse, betrothed, or an unmarried member of their family.

4:6b I(&S&T) exhort this [3a–6a] since the Lord *Jesus* will punish *people who do* such sexually immoral things The Greek is διότι ἔκδικος κύριος περὶ πάντων τούτων 'because (the) avenger (is the) Lord concerning all these'. The conjunction διότι 'because' introduces grounds, but it is debatable whether it is grounds for the immediately preceding proposition (Morris, Wanamaker) or for the whole 3a–6a APPEAL (Frame, Hiebert, Marshall). The second view is preferable. Paul here says the Lord is the avenger 'concerning all these', and the plural demonstrative 'these' seems to refer to the broader appeal to abstain from all forms of sexual immorality. Also, 4:6b is very similar to 2 Thess. 1:7–8, which says the Lord Jesus will avenge 'those who do not know God', the same words used earlier in 5b. Propositions 6b and c are a powerful *warning basis* for the 3a–6a APPEAL.

Even though the OT normally speaks of YHWH as the avenger (e.g., in Ps. 94:1), it seems best to understand 'Lord' here as referring to Jesus (Bruce, Frame, Marshall, Wanamaker). This is the normal Pauline meaning of 'Lord' (see 4:1b and 4:2). In 2 Thess. 1:7–8 Paul says Jesus is the one who avenges wrong. That Jesus is in view here in 4:6b is confirmed by the fact that when the agent is changed in 4:7 'God' is explicitly mentioned.

The Lord is here said to be the ἔκδικος, "*the avenger, the one who punishes*" (BAGD, p. 238). NJB captures the meaning with "The Lord always pays back sins of that sort." When the Lord avenges evil, however, he does so with justice, not as man often does, with personal vindictiveness. In the display 'punish' is used because it conveys the idea of deserved retribution. The Greek for 'avenger' is a noun, but it represents an event and so is rendered as a verb with its implied object. Most commentators feel that Paul is referring to retribution when Jesus returns, an idea made explicit in 2 Thess. 1:7–8, but it can also refer to punishment in the present life. The phrase περὶ πάντων τούτων 'concerning all these' is rendered 'such sexually immoral things' in the display to make the reference to the preceding appeal clear.

4:6c in accordance with what we(exc) strongly warned you previously The words καθὼς καί 'as also' introduce the second proposition in a congruence-standard relation. Frame calls the second word a comparative καί. Since the comparison idea is included in the first word, καθώς 'as', it would be redundant to render the second. The display therefore does not render the 'also', following most versions.

The first of the two verbs is προεῖπον 'to tell beforehand' or 'to have said something previously', the latter being preferable here. Earlier (in 4:1d and 4:2) Paul alluded to what he taught when he and his companions were in Thessalonica, and that idea is appropriate here as well. Also, the retribution Paul told the Thessalonians about most likely had not yet happened by the time Paul was writing, so he is not emphasizing fulfillment (as in 3:4). The second verb διαμαρτύρομαι means 'to solemnly testify' or 'to warn'. The meaning here is best expressed "solemnly warned you" (NRSV) or "strongly warned you" (TEV). The two verbs are joined by 'and', which creates either a hendiadys (Marshall) or conjoins the second, more forceful verb simply for emphasis (Hiebert, Wanamaker). REB renders it "As we impressed on you before"; NJB has "as we told you before emphatically." In the display the verbs are considered a hendiadys and rendered as a single verb phrase.

4:7a God *wants this* [3a–6a] since The conjunction γάρ 'for' introduces another *basis* for Paul's APPEAL in 3a–6a (Best, Frame, Marshall, Morris). A few commentators say it is grounds for 6b–c (Hendriksen, Hiebert). The only factor favoring this latter interpretation is the juxtaposition of v. 7 with what precedes. The term ἁγιασμός 'sanctification' in 7c is used twice in the APPEAL itself (in 3b and 4b). Thus v. 7 is a fitting first *axiomatic basis* for the APPEAL: abstain from all forms of immorality since God has called you to live distinctive, moral lives. Verse 7 also functions as the grounds for v. 8 (see the note on 8a).

he did not summon us(inc) *believers* The verb καλέω 'call' is rendered 'summon' here, as it was in 2:12c. God chooses people for salvation through his Spirit, who sets them apart as distinct, and through belief in the gospel (2 Thess. 2:13–14). It is believers that God has called to live holy lives (Frame), and the pronoun 'us' includes the readers as well as the senders of the letter (Marshall, Wanamaker).

4:7b to *be people who* behave in a sexually immoral way The Greek is a prepositional phrase, ἐπὶ ἀκαθαρσίᾳ 'to, or on the basis of, immorality'. All the versions consulted and some commentators (Bruce, Frame, Morris, Wanamaker) understand the preposition to indicate purpose: "God did not call us to live in immorality" (TEV). Best, Hiebert, and Marshall say it indicates what the basis on which God called believers is *not*: "God did not call us on the basis of our uncleanness, as if this was something to be maintained . . ." (Marshall). But the implied meaning of this second view seems close to that of purpose: God called people in order that they not continue in an immoral lifestyle. Thus purpose is taken as the appropriate relation.

The noun ἀκαθαρσία was used also in 2:3c. Its literal meaning is "*impurity, dirt,*" but here it has its figurative meaning of "*immorality,*" especially with reference to sexual sins (BAGD, p. 28.2). The noun represents the verbal idea of behaving in a particular manner, thus the rendering in the display.

4:7c On the contrary, *he summoned us* to be distinct *people who* behave in a morally pure way This is the POSITIVE counterpart of 7b. It is introduced with the conjunction ἀλλά 'but'. The rest of the proposition is the translation of another prepositional phrase, ἐν ἁγιασμῷ 'in sanctification'. The preposition is different from the one in the preceding phrase; it is, however, the same preposition used with the word 'sanctification' in 4b. Some propose that ἐν 'in' here means the distinct sphere in which Christians live out their lives (Best; Hiebert; Morris; Turner, p. 263; Wanamaker), as some say it does in 4b (see the discussion there). Others feel it indicates purpose (Bruce, Frame), as did ἐπί 'to' in the preceding phrase. Purpose seems to be the appropriate relation here just as in 7b because 7b and 7c are corresponding negative-positive propositions. The grammar here is similar to Col. 3:15, where ἐν 'in' introduces the purpose of the verb καλέω 'call': you were chosen (lit., called) by God in order that you should be at peace with one another (Callow 1983:189–91). Paul may have changed prepositions here to emphasize the contrast between the negative and the positive alternatives (Wanamaker). Or he may have used ἐν because he previously collocated it with 'sanctification' in 4b. For the meaning of ἁγιασμός 'sanctification' in this passage see the notes on 3b and 4b. It is a noun which represents the state of being distinct people and the event of behaving in an ethical manner, thus the rendering in the display.

4:8a Therefore The conjunction τοιγαροῦν 'therefore' introduces a conclusion. Some say it is the conclusion of Paul's statement in v. 7 (Morris, Wanamaker). Others say it is related to all that Paul has said in vv. 3–7 (Bruce, p. 81; Frame). Marshall says both views are correct, and this is probably right. Because of its juxtaposition with v. 7 it is appropriately the CONCLUSION of 7a–c. However, because v. 7 is so closely tied with Paul's APPEAL in 3a–6a, it is appropriate to view v. 8 as related to the APPEAL as well. In v. 8 Paul amplifies the *authoritative basis* he gave previously in 3a. If God wants believers to be distinct, holy people (3a–b), then to reject the teaching and live immorally is to reject God's command. With a slightly different understanding, Wanamaker says v. 8 is an implied threat (i.e., an implied warning basis) relating to Paul's APPEAL in 3–6 and reinforcing the reasons given in 6–7. The display shows the lower-level relation of v. 7 and v. 8 to each other (grounds-conclusion) as well as the upper-level relations of first *axiomatic basis* (v. 7) and second *authoritative basis* (8a–d) to the APPEAL (3a–6a).

if anyone disregards *this appeal* The Greek has only an articular participle, ὁ ἀθετῶν 'the one rejecting/disregarding'. The participle is a condition (CEV). The implied object of the rejection is the appeal to moral purity (Bruce, Wanamaker; CEV, NAB, NCV, NIV, REB, TEV, TNT).

4:8b he is not disregarding a human being The word ἄνθρωπος 'man' here does not necessarily mean a 'male' but an individual 'human being'. Some think it could be an obscure reference to Paul himself, the human instrument making the divine appeal (Frame, Marshall, Wanamaker; CEV).

4:8c On the contrary, *that person is disregarding* God The conjunction ἀλλά 'but' introduces this POSITIVE proposition. The Greek construction is an ellipsis, having only the articular noun phrase τὸν θεόν 'the God'. In the display the verb is supplied from 8b.

4:8d *since God commanded it* This is the implied grounds for Paul's statements in 8b and 8c; that is, it is the implicature of the argument.

4:8e I(&S&T) exhort that you do this [3a–6a] since God gives his Spirit, who is holy, to live in you Paul closes this unit with a description of God: τὸν [καὶ] διδόντα τὸ πνεῦμα αὐτοῦ τὸ ἅγιον εἰς ὑμᾶς 'the (one) indeed giving his Spirit, the holy (one), to/into you'. The construction 'his Spirit, the holy one' emphasizes the distinct, holy nature of the Spirit (Bruce, Morris). JBP has "It is not for nothing that the Spirit God gives us is called the *Holy* Spirit." The normal construction is found in 1:5 and 1:6: πνεῦμα ἅγιον 'Spirit holy'. The one here seems elevated from a mere description to a second *axiomatic basis* of Paul's APPEAL: you should live in a holy, morally pure way since God gives his Spirit, who is holy, to you. (See Frame and Wanamaker.)

Here Paul uses the preposition εἰς, which basically means 'in' or 'into'. It is the preposition he uses in Gal. 4:6 when he writes that "God sent the Spirit of his Son into our hearts" (NIV). This preposition is appropriate to the idea of the Spirit's indwelling and consecrating individuals to live holy lives, thus the rendering in the display.

The MJTGNT has καί 'and/indeed' before the participle διδόντα 'giving'. The UBSGNT includes it in brackets but without comment on the manuscript evidence. The Westcott Hort text rejects the reading. Frame says those texts which include it are emphasizing the new point that Paul makes here. The display follows the majority of versions consulted in not translating the conjunction. KJV, NKJV, and NRSV translate it as 'also', which indicates conjoining. Others translate it to indicate emphasis. Bruce and Morris have "indeed," TNT "the very God." Either conjoining or emphasis fits the context, but emphasis is perhaps better because Paul is emphasizing that the indwelling Spirit is holy.

The MJTGNT has an aorist participle, δόντα '(one who) gave (his Spirit)', instead of the present-tense διδόντα '(one) giving'. The UBSGNT has the latter and doesn't mention the other reading. Of the versions consulted, only the DGN, KJV, and NKJV accept the former. Perhaps a scribe changed the tense to agree with the tense of 'called' in the previous verse or with the idea that God has already given his Spirit to believers at conversion. Supporting this latter possibility, the Textus Receptus has 'gave to us' rather than 'to you' as in UBSGNT and MJTGNT. But Paul is thinking of the purity of Thessalonian believers ('you'), not the conversion of believers in general. The present tense is appropriate here where Paul seems to be thinking of the Spirit's activity of helping believers on a regular basis to be morally pure. The present tense also could be timeless, characterizing God as the bestower of the Spirit (Frame, Wanamaker).

BOUNDARIES AND COHERENCE

The initial boundary of 4:3–8 was discussed under 4:1–2 (see "Boundaries"). The closing boundary is between 4:8 and 4:9 and is well established; all versions and commentaries consulted place a boundary here. In v. 9 Paul introduces a new subject with the fronted phrase περὶ δὲ τῆς φιλαδελφίας 'now concerning brotherly love'. This is a grammatical construction that he also uses in 1 Corinthians (7:25; 8:1; 12:1; 16:1, 12) when he changes the subject.

PROMINENCE AND THEME

The *SPECIFIC APPEAL* of 4:3-8 is its most prominent constituent, and the 3b GENERIC proposition is the *SPECIFIC APPEAL*'s naturally prominent part. The form of the Greek underlying the 3a ORIENTER (τοῦτο γάρ ἐστιν θέλημα τοῦ θεοῦ 'for this is the will of God') marks it as prominent also. The fact that the ORIENTER is also one of the *authoritative bases* adds prominence.

The theme of 4:3-8 is derived from the 3a ORIENTER and the 3b GENERIC and the 3c specific propositions of the *SPECIFIC APPEAL*.

SUBSECTION CONSTITUENT 4:9-12
(Hortatory Paragraph: Appeal₂ of 4:3-12)

THEME: I urge you to increasingly love each other, to strive to live unobtrusively, and to work at your own occupations.

¶ PTRN	RELATIONAL STRUCTURE	CONTENTS
trust basis —	CONCLUSION	4:9a Next, you do not need that *I/anyone* write to you about *how you should* love *your* fellow believers [MET]—*although I will now do so*— [PLP]
	grounds₁	4:9b since God has already taught *you* the *way* to love each other
	grounds₂	4:10a and since you already are *showing love* to fellow believers [HYP] who live in every part *of your province* of Macedonia.
	orienter	4:10b Nevertheless, fellow believers, I(&S&T) urge you
	MEANS₁	4:10c to increasingly *love each other*.
APPEAL —	MEANS₂ — NUCLEUS	4:11a We(exc) urge you also to eagerly strive to live unobtrusively,
	equivalent	4:11b *that is*, to attend to your own affairs [IDM].
	MEANS₃ — CONGRUENCE	4:11c And *we(exc) urge you* to work at your own occupations
	standard	4:11d in accordance with what we(exc) instructed you.
	purpose₁	4:12a I(&S&T) urge these things [10c-11d] *in order that* you will cause unbelievers [MTY] to acknowledge that you behave decently/properly
	purpose₂	4:12b and *in order that* you will not need anything (*or*, anyone to help you) *in order for you to live/survive*.

INTENT AND PARAGRAPH PATTERN

In the 4:9-12 paragraph Paul's intent is to affect the behavior of the Thessalonians. The series of exhortations in 10b-11d indicates that the genre of this paragraph is hortatory.

The paragraph consists of two propositional clusters, 9a-10a and 10b-12b. In this context the conjunction δέ at the beginning of the second cluster indicates a concession-contraexpectation relation between the two clusters. As in the previous paragraph (4:3-8), there may well have been a problem in Thessalonica that Paul was addressing. However, rather than mentioning the problem, Paul affirms the Thessalonians, so this is not a solutionality subtype of paragraph pattern. Neither is it a volitionality subtype; Paul does not support his appeal by stating means to accomplish it but by stating grounds for the Thessalonians to carry out the appeal. In the first cluster Paul uses the rhetorical device of paralipsis (see the note on 9a). Because paralipsis was a way of confirming the Thessalonians in their good conduct, the first propositional cluster functions as grounds for the exhortations in the second cluster. Thus this is a causality subtype, the constituents of which (in hortatory genre) are labeled *basis* and APPEAL.

With regard to the discourse structure of the epistle, after the strong appeal and bases of 4:3–8 Paul backs off in 4:9–12 and reestablishes rapport with his readers. He uses paralipsis as a way of affirming what they are doing right and of motivating them to progress even more.

NOTES

4:9a Next Paul opens unit 4:9–12 with a discourse orienter, περὶ δέ 'now/but concerning', which indicates change of subject (Best, Wanamaker; see "Boundaries" for 4:3–8). In 1 Cor. 7:1 and in other passages of 1 Corinthians, Paul uses this same form to introduce responses to inquiries from the Corinthians. Some commentators (Frame included) think that Paul here is answering a letter, as when he wrote 1 Corinthians. However, in 1 Cor. 7:1 Paul explicitly states that he is responding to written inquiries; and here there is no such indication. On the other hand, the need to discuss the issues here and in succeeding units could have been ascertained from Timothy's report.

In some versions (KJV, NLT, RSV) δέ is taken as having an adversative function: 'but'. However, because of its recurring use in opening propositions of units and in appeals in this hortatory part of the letter (here and in 4:10b, 13a; 5:1a, 12a, 14a, 23a), it seems best to view δέ as a developmental marker, maintaining the continuity of the discourse (see the note on 2:16c). The conjunction is not rendered in CEV, NCV, REB, TEV, and TNT; it is rendered 'now' in NIV and NRSV. However, because 'now' can be understood with a temporal sense, the conjunction is rendered 'next' in the display (following JBP).

you do not need that *I/anyone* **write to you . . . —***although I will now do so*— Paul uses a rhetorical device called paralipsis here and in 5:1. In paralipsis the writer or "orator pretends to pass over something which he in fact mentions" [BDF, §495(1)]. This was a way of confirming people in their good conduct (Wanamaker). The agent of γράφειν 'to write' is unspecified. It could be the sender(s) of the letter. Based on this, KJV, NAB, NLT, and REB have a form of first person singular ('I', 'me', or 'mine'), and CEV, NCV, and NIV have 'we'. Alternatively, the agent could be a general 'anyone' (JB, NRSV). (If the latter option is taken the translator should make sure that 'anyone' includes Paul and his companions. In some languages the indefinite third person pronoun would not include them; it would mean 'anyone other than us'.) The display has 'although I will now do so', which supplies what was implied in the paralipsis.

about *how you should* **love** *your* **fellow believers** In classical Greek and the LXX the nouns φιλαδελφία (feminine) and φιλάδελφος (masculine), meaning 'love for brothers and/or sisters', were used almost exclusively of mutual love between blood brothers and sisters. Christian writers like Paul, however, used them metaphorically to encourage love between members of God's family, those who are fellow believers (Best, Bruce, Frame, Wanamaker; NCV, NLT, TEV, TNT). The feminine noun φιλαδελφία 'brotherly love' here in 4:9a represents an event and is rendered in the display as a clause.

Propositions 4:9a–10a are the *trust basis* for Paul's APPEAL in 10b–12b. By expressing his assurance that the Thessalonians already know how to love and are doing it, Paul intends to motivate them to continue and improve in their behavior.

4:9b since God has already taught **you** *the way to love each other* The Greek is αὐτοὶ γὰρ ὑμεῖς θεοδίδακτοί ἐστε εἰς τὸ ἀγαπᾶν ἀλλήλους 'for you yourselves are God-taught to love one another'. The conjunction γάρ 'for' marks this as grounds for 9a (Frame, Wanamaker). Paul apparently coined the term θεοδίδακτος 'God-taught'; it is not found elsewhere in the LXX or NT. The concept may come from Isa. 54:13, particularly Jesus' quotation of it in John 6:45: "They will all be taught by God" (NIV). The term 'God-taught' represents an event plus agent and is rendered in the display as a clause. Paul adds the intensive pronoun 'yourselves'; this perhaps is to emphasize that God has not only taught the sender(s) of the letter, but he has also taught the Thessalonian believers to love (Best, Frame). This emphasis is conveyed in the display by bold type. An alternative is to retain the passive of the Greek and use the intensive pronoun 'yourselves': 'since you yourselves have already been taught by God the way to love each other'.

The content and/or purpose of God's teaching is indicated by εἰς τό plus the infinitive ἀγαπᾶν 'to love'. Whichever relation label is used, the meaning is basically the same. Bruce thinks God may teach believers to love each other both through the Spirit he gives them (4:8) and through Jesus' teaching (e.g., Mark 12:31, John 13:34). Marshall says the point is probably that God teaches them not just the need to love but *how* to love, thus the display rendering 'the way to love each other'.

In 9b–10a Paul uses an argument from the greater to the less. "Paul had evidence that they loved all the brethren throughout Macedonia, and from this he rightly deduced that the same spirit prevailed among members of the church" (Marshall). This nuance is rendered in the display by 'already'.

4:10a and since The words καὶ γάρ 'and for/indeed' in 10a are interpreted as introducing a second grounds for 9a (Wanamaker; CEV, JBP, NAB, REB, TEV). Others interpret them as introducing grounds for 9b (Frame, Hiebert) or a comment on 9b (Bruce, Marshall, Morris; TNT). TNT has "Indeed this is how you behave towards all your fellow-Christians throughout Macedonia." But, in support of the first interpretation, 9b and 10a are both very appropriate grounds for 9a: no one needs to write to the Thessalonians about brotherly love since God has already taught them and since they already love fellow believers throughout Macedonia. The grammatical structure γάρ . . . καὶ γάρ 'for . . . and for' in 9b and 10a fits this interpretation well.

you already are *showing love* to fellow believers *who live* in every part *of your province* of Macedonia The Greek is ποιεῖτε αὐτὸ εἰς πάντας τοὺς ἀδελφοὺς [τοὺς] ἐν ὅλῃ τῇ Μακεδονίᾳ 'you do it toward all the brothers, the (ones) in all Macedonia.' The reference to what they are doing ('showing love') is supplied in the display. 'All the brothers . . . in all Macedonia' could be hyperbole. Omitting the first 'all' of the hyperbole, as in the display, expresses the probable meaning that the Thessalonians were showing love to *many* believers from all over the province. This also implies that they love all the believers as far as their feelings or intentions are concerned. Thessalonica was in the province of Macedonia, and the readers, who lived there, would have known this, of course; in the display this fact is supplied: 'your province'.

Several commentators say the Thessalonians' love may have been demonstrated by the hospitality they offered fellow believers who passed through the major port city of Thessalonica. Marshall adds that they also may have given material gifts to the poor or contributed means for the spread of the gospel.

4:10b Nevertheless The particle δέ 'now/but' could be taken as functioning to continue the discourse and build on what precedes. (CEV has "Brothers, now we encourage you to love them more and more.") However, Paul has just written that the Thessalonians didn't need to be told to love each other and his first appeal (10c) concerns just that; therefore commentators and versions interpret the particle as an adversative (Bruce, Hiebert; CEV, KJV, NAB, NIV, NJB, NRSV, REB). More specifically, it indicates contraexpectation.

I(&S&T) urge you Proposition 10b is the orienter for the exhortations that follow. The verb παρακαλέω 'to urge' that is here was used previously in 2:12 and 4:1.

4:10c to increasingly *love each other* The APPEAL's first content proposition (i.e., MEANS) is indicated by the infinitive phrase περισσεύειν μᾶλλον 'to abound more'. Most take this as a reference back to Paul's commendation of the Thessalonians' love for each other in 9b–10a (Bruce, Marshall, Wanamaker, JBP, NCV, NIV, NLT, NRSV). JBP has "we urge you to have more and more of this love." This back-reference seems very appropriate because Paul uses these words also in 4:1f to refer back to a previous commendation (4:1e).

4:11a We(exc) urge you also In the Greek, 10c–11c is a series of four, seemingly parallel, infinitive phrases joined by three identical conjunctions (καί 'and'). Viewed semantically, however, the relations are more complicated. Many commentators (Best, Bruce, Frame, Marshall, Morris, Wanamaker) feel that the last three phrases (11a–11c) are related to the first: they express how the Thessalonians were to grow in love for each other. However, NCV and NIV begin a new paragraph at 11a, indicating perhaps that what follows is a new subject or only remotely related to what precedes; other versions (CEV, NAB, REB, TEV, TNT) may take a similar view, as their wording and punctuation show. Some (Marshall, Morris, Wanamaker; REB) feel that 11a and 11b are closely related to each other. The best understanding seems to be that 11a, 11b, and 11c have to do with the mutual love of people in Christian community, but the connection is not obvious enough to label them as specifics of 10c. Propositions 11a and 11b seem to be closely related to each other, as do 11c and 11d. In the display the 11a–b propositions are the second content constituent (i.e., a second MEANS) of the orienter 10b.

to eagerly strive to live unobtrusively The Greek is φιλοτιμεῖσθαι ἡσυχάζειν 'to aspire to be quiet'. The verb φιλοτιμέομαι implies "strong ambition for some goal" (Louw and Nida 25.78). The second verb ἡσυχάζω 'to be quiet' does not mean 'to be silent' in this context, as it does in Acts 11:18. Nor does it mean 'to abstain from work', as it does in Luke 23:56. Frame understands it to be inner quiet or calmness, surmising that some Thessalonians were so excited about the Lord's return that they couldn't work; and NEB has "to keep calm." However, Paul does not explicitly make that connection. A better understanding is that this word describes a believer's life in relation to others (Bruce, Marshall, Wanamaker; also perhaps NAB). The word "was used in Classical Greek of looking after one's own business and keeping out of public life" (Marshall). Paul probably states the meaning of 'to live quietly' in the next proposition, that is, 'to attend to your own affairs'. Thessalonians who were not living quietly may have been agitating (Bruce) or meddling in the affairs of others or the church (Frame, Morris). (In 2 Thess. 3:11-12 Paul also raises the issue addressed here. In 3:12 he uses a noun from the same root to say what Thessalonians who are idle and busybodies should do: μετὰ ἡσυχίας ἐργαζόμενοι τὸν ἑαυτῶν ἄρτον ἐσθίωσιν 'with quietness working may they eat their own bread'. TEV translates the phrase "to lead orderly lives and work to earn their own living.") In the display ἡσυχάζω 'to be quiet' is rendered 'to live unobtrusively'. The meaning could be conveyed by an idiom such as 'keep your nose out of the affairs of others'. Paul's equivalent statement in 11b is such an idiom.

4:11b *that is*, to attend to your own affairs The Greek is καὶ πράσσειν τὰ ἴδια 'and to do (one's) own things'. It was probably an idiom like the English 'to mind one's own business'. Marshall says this proposition has the same meaning as the previous one; that is, it is an equivalent proposition. Frame, however, understands 11b to be a distinct exhortation, necessitated by the inner restlessness of the Thessalonians (see the note on 11a). Marshall's position is viewed as preferable because 11b then can give the figurative equivalent of 'to be quiet' in 11a.

4:11c And *we(exc) urge you* to work at your own occupations This is the beginning of the third content constituent (i.e., the third MEANS) of the *APPEAL*. The Greek is καὶ ἐργάζεσθαι ταῖς [ἰδίαις] χερσὶν ὑμῶν 'and to work with your own hands'. The word glossed 'own' is in MJTGNT. The UBSGNT committee had difficulty deciding whether or not to include it. Whether it was in the original manuscript or was added by a copyist influenced by its occurrence in 11b is unknown. In any case, the context indicates continuity between this and the preceding proposition. From 1 Thess. 5:14b and 2 Thess. 3:6-12 we know that Paul was concerned with those in Thessalonica who were idle. The primary aim of 11c seems to be to correct that situation. The mention of 'hands' refers to manual labor, skilled or unskilled. The meaning is that believers should work in order to earn a living (cf. 12b).

4:11d in accordance with what we(exc) instructed you The word καθώς 'as' introduces the second constituent of a congruence-standard relation. Proposition 11d could relate to all of the preceding exhortations (Best, Marshall, Wanamaker) or just 11c (Frame, Hiebert; NAB, REB). What Paul and his companions had instructed the believers was that a person should work to provide for his own daily needs. It seems slightly more preferable to connect 11d with what immediately precedes simply because of juxtaposition and what we know from 2 Thess. 3:10.

The verb παραγγέλλω 'to instruct' that is here echoes 4:2, where Paul used a noun from the same root.

4:12a *I(&S&T) urge these things* [10c-11d] in order that Here a two-part purpose statement is introduced by ἵνα 'in order that' (Frame, Marshall, Wanamaker). The two parts (12a and b) are conjoined by καί 'and'. Some (Hiebert; NAB, REB) think that these propositions relate primarily to the last of Paul's appeals in 11c. It is true that 12b seems especially appropriate to 11c. However, 12a is interposed between 11c-d and 12b, and it seems to be a more general purpose that is appropriate to all the preceding exhortations (10c-11d). Thus it seems better to connect 12a and b either with all the preceding exhortations as in the display (following Best, Frame, Wanamaker) or with at least the three in v. 11 (following Morris and NIV).

you will cause unbelievers to acknowledge that you behave decently/properly The Greek is περιπατῆτε εὐσχημόνως πρὸς τοὺς ἔξω 'you may walk decently toward the (ones) outside'. (See the note on 2:12b-c for a discussion of περιπατέω 'walk'.) Paul is speaking of behavior that is decent or fitting. The expression 'ones outside' is a metonymy. Here a location, 'outside', stands for a relationship (used also in 1 Cor. 5:12, Col. 4:5). These are people who were not part of the group of believers in Thessalonica. It is rendered 'unbelievers' in the display; it could also be rendered 'people who do not believe in God'. With the preposition πρός 'toward' this behavior can be interpreted either as circumspect behavior *toward* unbelievers (Wanamaker; KJV, NRSV) or as proper behavior *with a view to the opinion of* unbelievers (Frame, Marshall, NAB, NCV, NIV, REB, RSV, TEV, TNT). NJB has "so that you may earn the respect of outsiders." The latter seems more appropriate in a unit in which Paul is speaking of love toward fellow believers (9a), not specifically toward outsiders. Paul wants his readers to consider the "effect their behavior had on non-Christians" (Hiebert). By proper behavior within the Christian community believers will not bring disrepute on themselves or their cause.

4:12b and *in order that* **you will not need anything (***or,* **anyone to help you)** *in order for you to live/survive* The Greek is καὶ μηδενὸς χρείαν ἔχητε 'and you may have need of nothing/no one'. The word μηδενός may be understood as neuter 'nothing' (Bruce; KJV) or masculine 'no one' (Marshall; DGN, NCV, NIV, NJB, NRSV, TEV). In either case the meaning is that Thessalonian believers are to live unobtrusively and work at their occupations in order that they and their dependents will not need material assistance from fellow believers (Frame, Morris) or possibly from society (Marshall).

BOUNDARIES AND COHERENCE

The initial boundary of 4:9-12 was discussed under 4:3-8, and the terminal boundary under 4:3-12. (See "Boundaries.")

Some position a boundary between 4:10 and 4:11 (Morris; NCV, NIV); CBW places one between 10a and 10b. They do this perhaps because they feel Paul is changing the topic from loving the brothers to settling down and earning a living. Morris justifies a division by saying that what follows "deals with the practical outworking of Christian love rather than with love itself" (p. 130). This is true, but the series of four conjoined infinitives in 10c-11c seems too closely united grammatically to separate them with a boundary. In addition, 9a-10a is semantically tied to 10b-12b: the former is the *trust basis* for the latter *APPEAL*.

PROMINENCE AND THEME

The *APPEAL* of 4:9-12 is naturally prominent. Thus the theme is derived from the *APPEAL*'s orienter (10b) and three MEANS propositions (10c, 11a, 11c).

SECTION CONSTITUENT 4:13–5:11
(Complex Subsection: Focal Appeal₂ of 4:3–5:11)

THEME: God will raise to live again those believers who died and will bring them to the sky with Jesus. We believers should not be unprepared for the time when Jesus returns as unbelievers will be unprepared. On the contrary, we must be vigilant and self-controlled. God has destined us believers to be saved from being punished in the future and to be able to live together with our Lord Jesus after he returns. Since all this is true, encourage each other.

MACROSTRUCTURE	CONTENTS
nucleus₁	4:13–18 God will raise to live again those believers who died and will bring them to the sky with Jesus. Encourage each other by telling this message.
NUCLEUS₂ (climax unit of epistle)	5:1–8 We believers should not be unprepared for the time the Lord Jesus returns as unbelievers will be unprepared. On the contrary, we must be vigilant and self-controlled.
NUCLEUS₃	5:9–11 God has destined us believers to be saved from being punished in the future and to be able to live together with our Lord Jesus after he returns. Since this is true, encourage each other.

INTENT AND MACROSTRUCTURE

The 4:13–5:11 subsection consists of three paragraphs: 4:13–18, 5:1–8, and 5:9–11. The second paragraph begins with the developmental marker δέ, which conjoins it to the first one. The third begins with ὅτι 'for', which in this context ties it loosely to the preceding paragraphs. The third paragraph functions as a restatement or amplification of an exhortation and truths that Paul has given previously, in 4:13–5:8 and also in the first half of the letter.

Paul's primary intent in 4:13–5:11 is to affect the behavior of the Thessalonians. This intent is especially clear in the second paragraph (in 5:6–8), where he exhorts the believers to be vigilant and self-controlled and to believe, love, and hope in order that they be prepared for the Lord's coming.

Paul also has strong secondary intents in 4:13–5:11. The intent to affect ideas is evident in the first paragraph, which contains the 4:14–17 embedded paragraph giving information about the Lord's return. The intent to affect emotions is seen in the closing exhortation of the first paragraph (in 4:18) and the closing exhortation of the third paragraph (in 5:11), in which the Thessalonians are urged to encourage and comfort each other with truths about the Lord's return and the part believers will play in it. Because Paul's intent in the constituent paragraphs is to affect behavior, ideas, and emotions and because the paragraphs are in conjoined relationships, 4:13–5:11 is labeled a complex subsection.

The 5:1–8 paragraph is the climactic unit of the hortatory division of Paul's letter, and thus the climactic unit of the epistle as well (see "Intent" under 4:3–5:11). Paragraph 4:13–18 is a pre-climax unit, in which Paul introduces and discusses aspects of the Lord's return to comfort his readers and builds toward the appeal in the climax. Paragraph 5:9–11 is a post-climax unit, in which he again exhorts the Thessalonians to encourage and comfort each other with truths concerning the Lord's return. The fact that 5:9–11 is a restatement gives prominence to it. (The idea of future salvation from God's wrath first stated in 1:10 is restated in 5:9, and the exhortation first given in 4:18 is amplified in 5:11.) Thus the NUCLEUS label of the postclimactic 5:9–11 paragraph is in uppercase letters in the display, just as that of the climactic 5:1–8 paragraph is.

BOUNDARIES AND COHERENCE

The initial boundary of 4:13–5:11 was discussed under 4:3–12, and the terminal boundary under 4:3–5:11. (See "Boundaries.")

All three of the paragraphs in 4:13–5:11 concern the return of the Lord, and this brings strong referential coherence. Additional coherence comes from the use of the following: ἐλπίς 'hope' (4:13d; 5:8f); ἀποθνῄσκω 'to die', used of Jesus' death (4:14a; 5:10a); ζάω 'to live, be alive' (4:15b, 17a; 5:10b); καθεύδω 'to sleep' (5:6a, 7a); euphemisms for death, namely κοιμάω 'to sleep' (4:13a, 14b, 15b) and καθεύδω 'to sleep' (5:10b); and the phrases σὺν κυρίῳ ἐσόμεθα 'we shall be with (the) Lord' (4:17d) and ἅμα σὺν αὐτῷ ζήσωμεν 'we (shall) be able to live together with him' (5:10b).

The parallel exhortations in 4:18 and 5:11 give relational coherence.

PROMINENCE AND THEME

In the 4:13–5:11 subsection the 5:1–8 paragraph is naturally prominent in that it contains all the hortatory appeals of 4:13–5:11. (The expressive exhortations at the end of the first and third paragraphs of 4:13–5:11 function differently). The 4:13–18 paragraph is preclimactic and basically sets the stage with its extensive embedded expository unit. However, its function of introducing the topic of the Lord's return is important to the larger unit. The 5:9–11 paragraph is postclimactic; it basically restates truths previously mentioned. The restatements give prominence to 5:9–11.

The theme of 4:13–5:11 is derived from the themes of the constituent paragraphs, but with the parallel closing exhortations in the themes of 4:13–18 and 5:9–11 represented by just one exhortation at the end of the 4:13–5:11 theme.

SUBSECTION CONSTITUENT 4:13–18
(Expressive Paragraph: Nucleus₁ of 4:13–5:11)

THEME: God will raise to live again those believers who died and will bring them to the sky with Jesus. Encourage each other by telling this message.

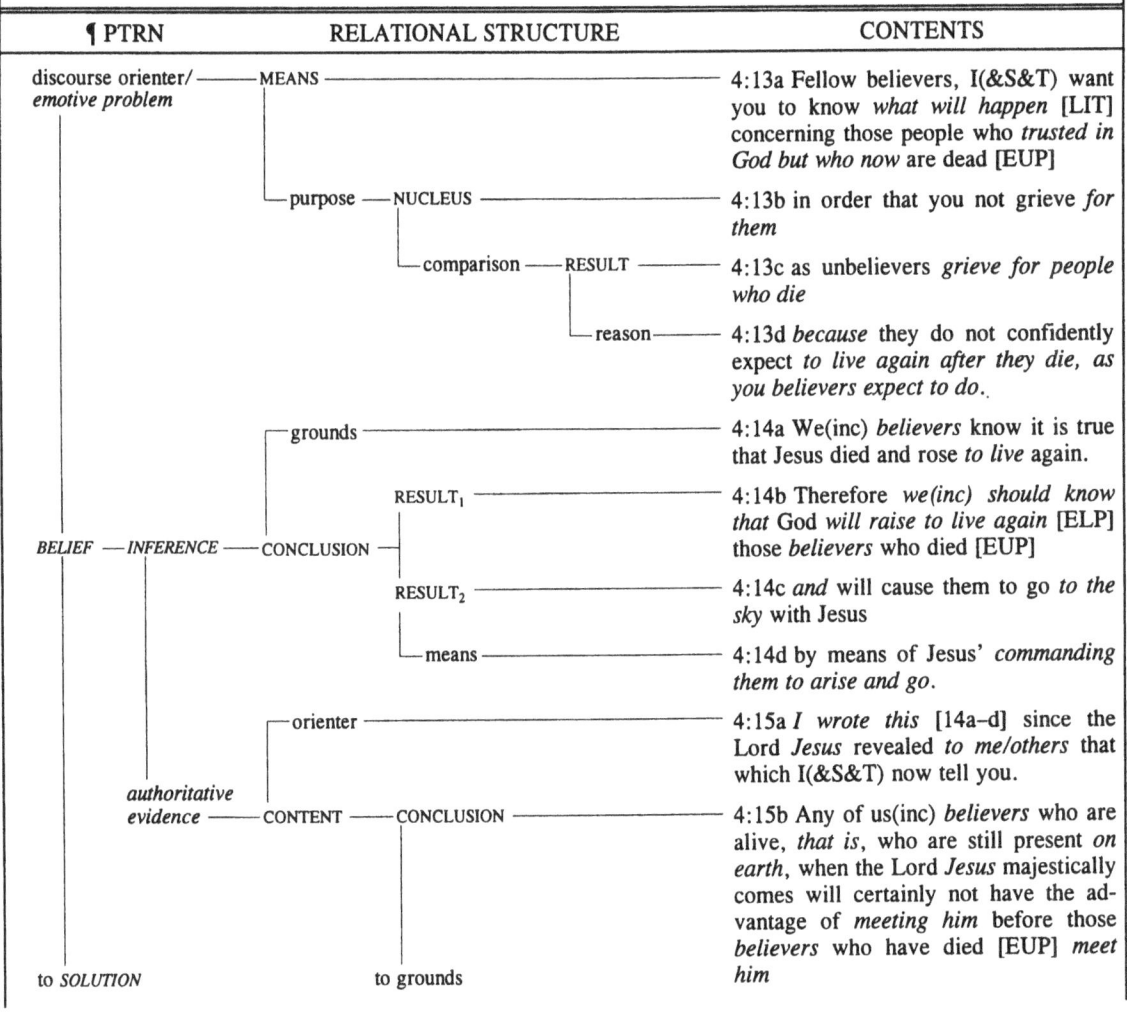

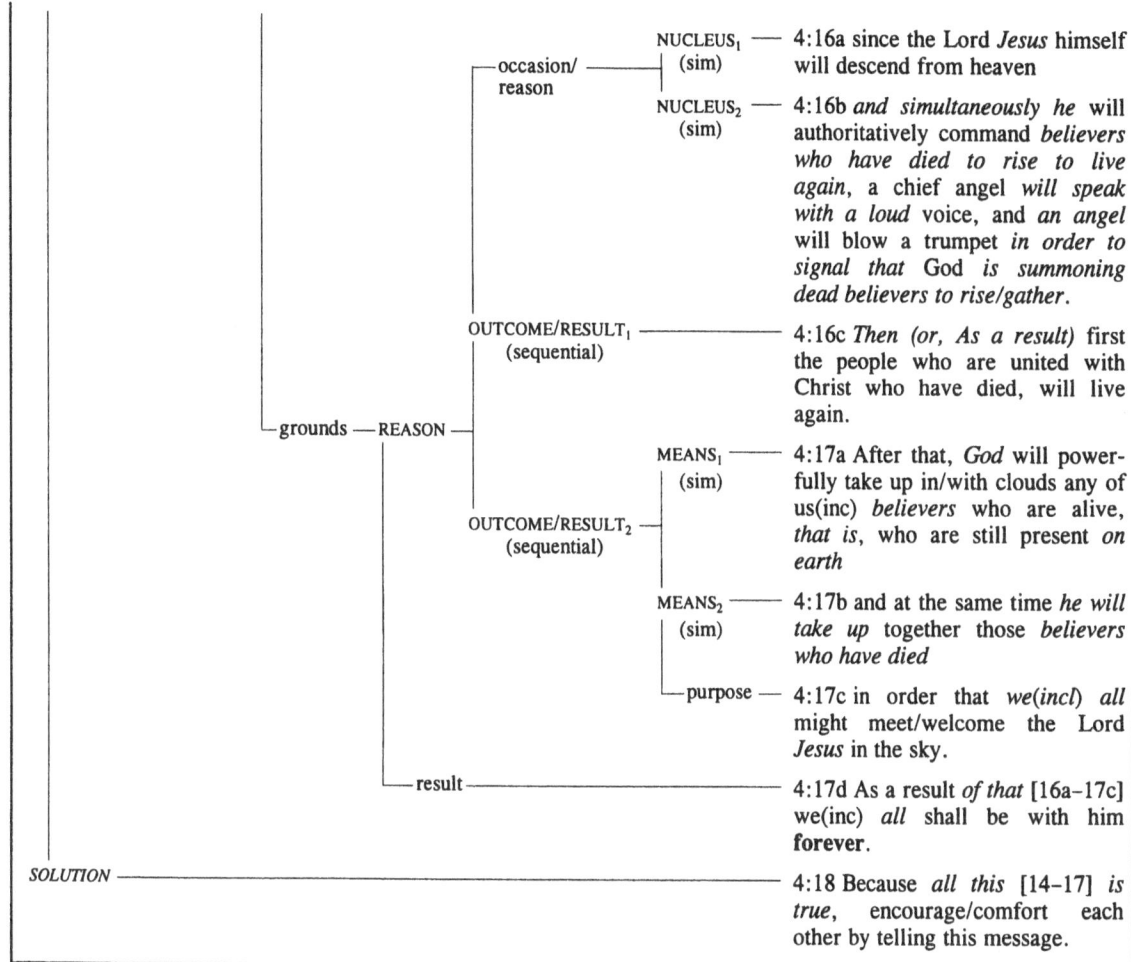

INTENT AND PARAGRAPH PATTERN

Paul's primary intent in the 4:13-18 paragraph is to affect the emotions of his readers. This intent is clear from the 4:13b purpose proposition: ἵνα μὴ λυπῆσθε 'in order that you not grieve'. The exhortation in v. 18 likewise reveals Paul's intent: ὥστε παρακαλεῖτε ἀλλήλους 'therefore encourage/comfort one another' by telling this message. The genre is emotive of the expressive type, because Paul develops his thoughts primarily with conclusion-grounds relations rather than sequential relations.

The paragraph has three constituents. Paul begins with a discourse orienter (13a-d) that expresses an *emotive problem*. Because the Thessalonians didn't know what would happen to fellow believers who had died, they were grieving as unbelievers who have no hope grieve. Paul then expresses his *BELIEF* in the main constituent of the paragraph, which is the 14a-17d embedded paragraph. He tells the Thessalonians what will happen to believers who are dead and believers who are alive when the Lord Jesus returns. The third constituent (v. 18) is an exhortation for the Thessalonians to 'encourage/comfort one another with these words' (παρακαλεῖτε ἀλλήλους ἐν τοῖς λόγοις τούτοις). This is the emotional *SOLUTION* to the problem Paul mentions in 13a-d. Thus the paragraph pattern of 4:13-18 is a solutionality subtype.

Paul's intent in the 14-17 embedded paragraph is clear from his opening statement in v. 13: οὐ θέλομεν δὲ ὑμᾶς ἀγνοεῖν, ἀδελφοί 'we do not want you to be ignorant, brothers', which is a litotes indicating that Paul intends to affect the ideas of his readers. He goes on to describe how believers who have died will be raised to life and taken up in the clouds together with believers who are alive when Jesus returns. The genre of the embedded paragraph is ideational of the expository type, because Paul develops his thoughts primarily with conclusion-grounds relations rather than sequential relations.

The embedded paragraph consists of two propositional clusters, 14a-d and 15a-17d. The first cluster begins with γάρ 'for', which indicates that it is in a special orienter-content relation with the v. 13 discourse orienter. The second cluster also begins with γάρ 'for', and in this case the conjunction indicates that the second cluster is in a conclusion-grounds communication relation with the first. There is no problem stated in the embedded paragraph, so the subtype of solutionality is ruled out. Neither does it seem that Paul is trying to amass evidence in vv. 15-17 that will prove to his readers his conclusion of v. 14; this is the authoritative evidence revealed by the Lord, which should be unquestioned, and therefore the subtype of volitionality is ruled out. Rather, this is the paragraph pattern subtype of causality, in which Paul's conclusion in v. 14 is naturally proved by the authoritative grounds of vv. 15-17. For the causality subtype of the expository genre the labels that best reflect what is happening here are INFERENCE and evidence.

The exhortation in v. 18 begins with ὥστε 'therefore'. It is thus in a grounds-conclusion relation with the 14-17 embedded paragraph. This relation signals its function as SOLUTION in the main paragraph.

The SOLUTION (v. 18) of 4:13-18 is naturally prominent. The 14-17 embedded paragraph has marked prominence because its topic is developed extensively. Thus its label BELIEF is in uppercase letters in the display also.

NOTES

4:13a Some understand the conjunction δέ to indicate a contrast here (KJV, NASB, NRSV). However, it is best interpreted as a developmental marker (transitional 'now/next') as in 2:17a (see the note there). Together with περί 'concerning', which occurs later in the sentence, it marks a change of subject (Frame, Marshall, Wanamaker). The conjunction is not translated in the display, because 'now' can be misinterpreted as temporal. TNT makes the change of subject obvious by fronting the phrase "Concerning the dead."

I(&S&T) want you to know *what will happen* Paul uses a litotes in this discourse orienter proposition: οὐ θέλομεν δὲ ὑμᾶς ἀγνοεῖν 'now we do not want you to be ignorant'. The litotes here may be intended to emphasize the change to the expository genre in the embedded paragraph, the beginning of a new section or subject (Best, Marshall, Frame), or new information (Morris). It may also be an indication that the following information is important (Best, Morris). The figure is expressed positively in the display (as in CEV, NAB, NCV, NJB, TEV). Because Paul speaks in this unit of future events rather than the present state of believers who have died, the implicit object of 'know' in the display is 'what will happen'. "The brethren were in grief not because they did not believe in the resurrection of the saints, but because they feared that their dead would not have the same advantages as the survivors when the Lord came" (Frame, p. 164; also see Wanamaker's discussion of Plevnik's theory, p. 166).

The Textus Receptus has the alternative reading 'I do not want'. This first person singular pronoun would fit the supposition that Paul is the principal author of the book, but it is not found in the earliest manuscripts. UBSGNT and MJTGNT have 'we do not want'.

concerning those people who *trusted in God but who now* **are dead** The topic of the unit is περὶ τῶν κοιμωμένων 'concerning the (ones) sleeping'. The euphemism of 'sleeping' to refer to 'being dead' was used by the Hebrews and Greeks even before NT times (Bruce, Frame, Wanamaker). So it probably was not Paul's intent to convey such nuances as the impermanence of death for the believer or an intermediate state before the resurrection (Marshall, Wanamaker). He simply meant that they were dead. In 16c he refers to the 'dead in Christ', which is an indication that throughout the unit he is speaking of believers who had died (Best, Bruce). That is made explicit in translations of v. 13 by CEV and NLT and in the display also.

4:13b in order that you not grieve *for them* The purpose for 13a is introduced by ἵνα 'in order that' (Frame, Wanamaker). Paul was not speaking of general grief but of grieving for believers who had died. Morris says that the verb λυπέω here denotes primarily inward grief, not outward expressions of grief, and the present tense points to a continuing sorrow. Specifically, this is grief which laments the sad fate of a loved one. It is not grief for loss, which is normal (Marshall).

4:13c as unbelievers *grieve for people who die* This is a comparison proposition introduced by καθὼς καί 'as also' (Bruce, Frame, Wanamaker). A similar usage of καί 'also' with καθάπερ 'as' is in 4:5b, where it likewise indicates comparison.

Paul uses οἱ λοιποί 'the rest' here to refer to unbelievers in general (Frame). It is similar to his reference to 'the ones outside' in 4:12a and is rendered 'unbelievers' just as 'the ones outside' is. This meaning is confirmed in the following relative clause.

4:13d *because* **they do not confidently expect** *to live again after they die, as you believers expect to do* The attributive participial phrase οἱ μὴ ἔχοντες ἐλπίδα 'those not having hope' is taken as a reason proposition. See the note on 1:3 for the rendering of ἐλπίς 'hope'. The phrase has been understood to mean that unbelievers have no knowledge of God (Morris), no hope of escaping his wrath in judgment (Wanamaker), no hope of being with Christ after death (Best, Frame), no hope of reunion between the living and the dead (Marshall), no hope for life after death (Ellingworth and Nida, Marshall, Wanamaker), or no hope for resurrection (Best, Bruce, Hiebert). Either of the last two understandings is probably preferable here. Of course it is true that unbelievers have no true basis for any hope they may have for the afterlife. In this context it is possible that Paul means to say that any hope they do have would not include the resurrection and, therefore, there is nothing to alleviate their grief when their loved ones die. Frame correctly points out that the comparison in 13b-d is also an antithesis: unbelievers, who grieve, do not confidently expect to live again *as believers expect to do*.

4:14a-d We(inc) *believers* **know it is true that Jesus died and rose** *to live* **again** The Greek is εἰ γὰρ πιστεύομεν ὅτι Ἰησοῦς ἀπέθανεν καὶ ἀνέστη 'for if we believe that Jesus died and rose again'. Most commentators (including Best, Frame, Marshall, Wanamaker) say that the γάρ 'for' introduces the reason for 13b, that is, the reason why believers should not grieve about those who have died. While this connection is possible, it does not seem the best interpretation. Rather, v. 14 is better taken as a continuation of the whole unit's topic, which was introduced in v. 13. Verse 13 is a discourse orienter in which Paul says he is going to tell the Thessalonians what will happen to those believers who have died in order that they not grieve for them. Verse 14 states in essence what Paul wants them to know. Verses 15-17 lay out the evidence for Paul's statement based on what the Lord Jesus has said. Thus it seems most appropriate to take γάρ 'for' in 14a as signaling a continued discussion of the topic rather than as grounds or reason for it. It may be an example of BAGD's "*expressing continuation or connection*" (p. 152.4) and probably is what the versions that do not render γάρ have in mind (CEV, JBP, NCV, NIV, NJB, REB, TEV, TNT). Because γάρ is not taken as introducing a reason or grounds proposition, it is not glossed in the display.

In 14a the Greek appears to signal a condition of fact consisting of εἰ 'if' together with a verb in the indicative mood. The Greek for 14b-d is οὕτως καὶ ὁ θεὸς τοὺς κοιμηθέντας διὰ τοῦ Ἰησοῦ ἄξει σὺν αὐτῷ 'thus/so also God the (ones) having fallen asleep through Jesus will bring with him'. This clause is not the typical apodosis for a condition of fact because it begins with οὕτως 'thus/so', which often introduces the second part of a comparison (e.g., 2:8a) or congruent relation (e.g., 2:4c). Some take v. 14 as a conditional sentence (Wanamaker); others take it as a comparison (Eadie). Frame refers to its parts as if it were a condition but renders it as a comparison. However, none call 14b-d a consequence, which is normally associated with a condition, nor do any call it a comparison. Instead, commentators refer to 14b-d as an inference, implication, or deduction. Therefore, it seems best to understand the relation of 14a to 14b-d as grounds-conclusion, the grounds being a *true* condition of fact, based on the historical events of Jesus' death and resurrection. Some (Best, Bruce, Wanamaker) say that Paul was probably quoting a credal formula of early Christians, statements of which typically began 'We believe that'. 'We believe that' here has the connotation of conviction and is equivalent to 'we know it is true that', the rendering in the display. The 'we' is inclusive of Paul and his readers (Wanamaker) and of other believers as well (Best). The grounds-conclusion relation is signaled in the display by 'Therefore' at the beginning of 14b.

Frame says of v. 14, "The Greek sentence runs smoothly . . . , but there is an obvious compression of thought." He proposes what Paul might have said: "As we are convinced that Jesus died and that God raised him from the dead, so also must we believe, since the indwelling Christ is the guarantee of the resurrection of the believer, that God will raise from the dead those who died through Jesus and will lead them on along with him." Frame says the advantage of the shorter form (in the text that Paul wrote) is that the conclusion (14b-d) is more objective and direct. However, it makes good translation more difficult.

In the grounds-conclusion argument of 14a–d there is a syllogism. It contains two premises which are accepted by Christians. The major premise is partially expressed in the 14a εἰ 'if' clause (which is a common way of expressing a "given" premise in an argument). The implied part of that premise is probably, as Frame says, "the indwelling Christ is the guarantee of the resurrection of the believer." The Greek does not explicitly focus on the minor premise (the contrast of dead believers with living believers) although that is Paul's definite intention. Paul's statement that God will bring believers who have died to the sky with Jesus (14c) presupposes the conclusion of the syllogism. The syllogism can be expressed as follows:

> *Major premise*: Jesus' own death and resurrection is the guarantee that all believers will resurrect.
> *Minor premise*: The believers who have died are believers nonetheless (i.e., even though they have died).
> *Conclusion*: Therefore God will raise to live again the believers who have died.

The NT (especially the synoptic Gospels) is surprisingly rich in truncated syllogisms like this (James Mignard, personal communication, November 11, 1996).

In the clause 'Jesus died and rose again', the word 'died' (ἀπέθανεν) is used rather than 'slept', possibly because this was the term in the creed Paul was quoting. The second verb is ἀνίστημι, which was used both transitively ('to raise, raise up') and intransitively ('to rise'). It is intransitive here. This is not the verb Paul normally used to speak of Jesus' resurrection. He most often used ἐγείρω 'to raise', frequently with the indication that it was God who raised him (1:10b; also Rom. 6:4; 8:11; 10:9; 1 Cor. 6:14; Gal. 1:1). Again, Paul may have used the intransitive ἀνίστημι 'to rise' in this verse (and again in 16c) because it was in the credal statement. However, the fact that God was the agent who raised Jesus may have been in Paul's mind because he mentions God as agent in 14b, the conclusion of his syllogism. Thus an alternative rendering of 14a is 'Jesus died and God raised him to live again'.

Therefore *we(inc) should know that* In the display 'therefore' shows 14b–d to be the CONCLUSION of the grounds in 14a (see the discussion earlier in this note). Although οὕτως 'thus, so' is often used in comparisons, it also is used in summarizing a thought or drawing an inference from what precedes (BAGD, p. 597.1b). The latter seems to be its function here. Wanamaker says "οὕτως καί ['thus/so also'] marks the inference to be drawn from what precedes and presupposes the words 'we may believe that.'" CEV, NIV, and TEV use a similar phrase. The display has 'we should know that'.

God *will raise to live again* those *believers who died* The Greek for 14b–d is οὕτως καὶ ὁ θεὸς τοὺς κοιμηθέντας διὰ τοῦ Ἰησοῦ ἄξει σὺν αὐτῷ 'thus/so also God the (ones) having fallen asleep through Jesus will bring with him'. The only grammatical subject here is 'God', and the only non-subordinate verb is 'will bring'. Versions that closely follow the form of the Greek have renderings such as "God will bring with Jesus those who have fallen asleep in him" (NIV) See also CEV, GW, KJV, NJB, NLT, NRSV, TEV, and TNT. Some commentators have understood the Greek to mean that God will bring the immaterial souls or spirits of dead believers from heaven with Jesus (Hiebert, Morris). This meaning, however, has no support in this passage. Rather, Paul's statement presupposes that the ones God brings will be resurrected first (Frame, Marshall, Wanamaker). Since Paul's thought in v. 14 is compressed (Frame) and there is an ellipsis (Bullinger, pp. 89–91), the idea of a preceding resurrection is omitted in 14b. What Paul focuses on in vv. 13–18 is Jesus' coming for dead and living believers and their meeting or being with him (vv. 14c, 17c, 17d); his focus is not the resurrection itself. This may be the reason for the ellipsis. Paul gives evidence supporting the idea of dead believers being resurrected before being brought to meet Jesus in his occasion-OUTCOME propositions in vv. 16–17. The idea that the resurrection of dead believers is presupposed in v. 14 is also supported by the grounds-conclusion relation of 14a and 14b. The fact of a preceding resurrection is needed to connect the 14a grounds with the 14b CONCLUSION. Correspondence between what happened to Jesus and what will happen to believers seems to be the only logical tie-in: we know that God raised Jesus after he died, and therefore we conclude that God will raise believers who have died. The conjunction οὕτως 'thus/so', often used in comparisons, supports this correspondence. A few versions include the idea of resurrection in their rendering of the verb ἄγω 'bring'. This is an improvement over more literal renderings: "God will bring forth with him [Jesus] from the dead those who have fallen asleep believing in him" (NAB). See also Bullinger (p. 91), EHP, GHL, and NCV. The ellipsis in the

Greek is supplied in the 14b display rendering: God 'will raise to live again' those who died.

The euphemism 'fallen asleep', meaning 'died', appears here in 14b as in 13a (see the note on 13a).

and will cause them to go *to the sky* with Jesus There are two issues here: Where is God bringing these deceased believers *from*, and where is he bringing them *to*? Some think that God is bringing them from heaven to earth (Best, Marshall, Morris). (Marshall holds that the future destiny of God's people is not in heaven but in a renewed earth.) However, because the idea of resurrection is presupposed in 14b, the better understanding is that God brings believers who have died from the grave. As to the place they are brought to, it is either to the place where Jesus will meet with living believers (Best, Marshall) or all the way to heaven with Jesus after they are joined by believers who are alive at the time (Ellingworth, Frame, Wanamaker). The first view is supported by 17c, which says living and resurrected believers will meet Jesus in the sky. It is probably the preferable view. Wanamaker feels that the clouds and sky are an image of heaven, so the two views are not far apart.

The verb here is ἄγω 'to lead, bring, or take along'. Its meanings could imply that the agent (God) is present to do the bringing. But Marshall says, "The text need not imply of course that God himself will come with the dead and lead them to the earth; 'will bring' means 'will cause to come'." A second consideration is that the verbs 'bring', 'send', 'go', and 'come', in English and in many other languages, represent the perspective of the speaker or author. In English *God will bring them* would mean God will transport them from where he is (heaven) to where Paul and his readers are (earth). But in Greek it could just as well mean God will transport them from where the dead are (grave) to where he is (heaven). Louw and Nida say the term ἄγω means "to direct or guide the movement of an object, without special regard to point of departure or goal" (15.165). The display rendering 'will cause them to go to the sky' tends to favor the second meaning, that God will transport them from the grave to heaven.

by means of Jesus' *commanding them to arise and go* The phrase διὰ τοῦ Ἰησοῦ 'through Jesus' has caused problems for exegetes. It most likely introduces either a circumstance or means proposition. The question is whether it goes with what precedes or with what follows it. Almost all versions take it as circumstance, with the preceding phrase 'those having fallen asleep' (also Bruce, Frame, Marshall, Morris, Wanamaker). Marshall says "the death of believers does not take place apart from Jesus, and hence Paul can conclude that God will raise them up and bring them into the presence of Jesus at the parousia." Bruce agrees with those who call the relation attendant circumstance and who understand that the referents were in a certain relationship with Jesus when they died. This seems to be the understanding of a number of versions: those having fallen asleep or died "in Jesus/him" (KJV, JBP, NIV, NJB); "believing in Jesus/him" (NAB, TEV, TNT); "as Christians" (REB). However, in 16c Paul speaks of the 'dead in Christ', and it seems unusual that he would use the more difficult phrase 'through Jesus' here to communicate the same idea.

The other point of view is held by Best, Moffatt, GW, and RSV/NRSV, who take the phrase as means, with the following verb 'will bring'. Moffatt says, "Jesus is God's agent in the final act, commissioned to raise and muster the dead." NRSV has "through Jesus, God will bring with him those who have died." However, it is grammatically awkward to have 'bring' qualified by both 'through Jesus' and 'with him'.

Deciding this issue is difficult grammatically. But semantically it seems best to understand the phrase 'through Jesus' as modifying the verb of the clause ('will bring'), which represents the whole process of Jesus' resurrecting believers and causing them to go to the sky to be with himself. Support for this interpretation is very possibly found in vv. 16–17.

The first interpretation, which has popular support, can be diagrammed as follows:

```
NUCLEUS₁ ─ 'those people' ──────────────── 4:14b Therefore we(inc) should know that God will raise to live
         │                                       again those people
         └─ identification ── NUCLEUS ──── 4:14c who died [EUP]
                            └─ circumstance ── 4:14d when they were united with Jesus
NUCLEUS₂ ──────────────────────────────── 4:14e and will cause them to go to the sky with Jesus.
```

4:15a *I wrote this* [14a-d] since The conjunction γάρ 'for' here introduces grounds and/or explanation (Frame, Marshall, Wanamaker) for Paul's statement in v. 14. The relation of grounds (*authoritative evidence*) seems the more appropriate one because Paul appeals to the authority of a revelation or teaching of the Lord to support what he has just said. Proposition 15a is the orienter for 15b-17d.

the Lord *Jesus* revealed *to me/others* that which I(&S&T) now tell you The Greek of 15a is τοῦτο γὰρ ὑμῖν λέγομεν ἐν λόγῳ κυρίου 'for this we say to you in a word of (the) Lord'. The demonstrative pronoun τοῦτο 'this' refers to what Paul is about to write in 15b (Bruce, Frame, Marshall, Wanamaker). This forward reference is made clear in the display.

It is difficult to know just what Paul meant by 'in a word of the Lord'. There are no Gospel sayings that can be equated with the statements here. Some feel Paul could be quoting a saying of Jesus (Bruce, Morris), summarizing a saying (Frame), or alluding to an "apocalyptic discourse by Jesus" (Wanamaker) from tradition or from a source we no longer have. Marshall feels there *is* adequate basis in the Gospel tradition for the words here. Others think this could have been a teaching Paul or Silas received by special revelation (Hiebert) or words a prophet of the church spoke (Best, Bruce). Since the phrase represents an event with an agent and patient(s), it is rendered in the display as 'the Lord Jesus revealed to me/others'.

Paul almost certainly is not saying that every word in 15b-17d was spoken by the Lord; just how much is what the Lord actually revealed is an open question. These verses probably give the essence of his words and their implications. They are composed of a 15b CONCLUSION followed by specific statements which support it as grounds. They could all be based on words the Lord spoke, or 15b could be Paul's own conclusion based on the specific teaching of the Lord referred to in vv. 16-17. This latter seems preferable because the CONCLUSION is very much in Paul's epistolary style (Best). Also, 17d (possibly 17c also) seems to be an inference that Paul draws from the Lord's words, which he states to encourage his readers.

4:15b Any of us(inc) *believers* who are alive, *that is*, who are still present *on earth* The 15b-17d CONTENT is introduced by ὅτι '(I tell you) that'. In the display ὅτι is not rendered because 15a is worded in a way that shows it is an orienter. Paul was expecting Christ's return (5:2), although he didn't know when it would take place. He knew that he and many of his contemporaries might still be alive at that time. This possibility is evident in the freestanding Greek pronoun 'we', which is fronted to indicate the topic of Paul's comments and to specify or personalize the participants, rather than refer to them as 'the living'. It is rendered in the display 'any of us(inc)'. The pronoun includes the writer and his readers (Frame, Marshall) and believers generally (Bruce). Two participial phrases identify the pronoun: ἡμεῖς οἱ ζῶντες οἱ περιλειπόμενοι 'we the (ones) who are alive, the (ones) who remain. As the two phrases are not joined by a conjunction, the second can be considered equivalent to the first (Frame), and it is so rendered in the display. The verb of the second phrase, περιλείπομαι, means 'to remain, to be left behind'. Because these believers will not have died they still remain, or are present, on earth when the Lord returns.

when the Lord *Jesus* majestically comes The preposition εἰς 'to, until' introduces a circumstance phrase here. The meaning and rendering of the noun παρουσία 'coming' is discussed in the note on 2:19e. It represents an event and is rendered as a verb in the display.

will certainly not have the advantage of *meeting him* before those *believers* who have died *meet him* The verb φθάνω can mean "*come before, precede*" (BAGD, p. 856.1; Frame; Louw and Nida 15.141; NIV, NKJV, NRSV, TEV). Or it can mean 'to have an advantage over' (Best, Bruce, Marshall, Morris, Wanamaker; NAB, NJB, REB, TNT). Wanamaker says that the Thessalonians may have thought that believers living when the Lord returned would have the advantage of being taken up to heaven while believers who had died would not. The rendering in the display includes both meanings: there is no advantage for believers who are living at the time of Christ's coming because they will not meet the Lord before those who have died meet him. The double negative οὐ μή 'not not' with the aorist subjunctive verb is the same as an emphatic future indicative; it is rendered 'will certainly not' in the display.

4:16a-b since The Greek begins with ὅτι 'because/that'. Since it is the same conjunction that is at the beginning of 15b, Lenski understands it to indicate a parallelism with 15b, making 16a-

17c a second CONTENT of what Paul told the Thessalonians by a word of the Lord. However, these propositions are more appropriate as grounds (Marshall, Wanamaker) or amplification (Frame). The wording and style suggest that they constitute the Lord's saying that leads Paul to his CONCLUSION in 15b, namely that believers who have died will not miss out on anything when the Lord returns.

The Greek for 16a–b is ὅτι αὐτὸς ὁ κύριος ἐν κελεύσματι, ἐν φωνῇ ἀρχαγγέλου καὶ ἐν σάλπιγγι θεοῦ, καταβήσεται ἀπ᾽ οὐρανοῦ 'because the Lord himself with a command, with a voice/ sound of an archangel and with a trumpet of God, will descend from heaven'. Commentators say the three prepositional phrases beginning with ἐν 'with' are circumstantial phrases. A circumstance proposition does not have natural prominence. However, in the Greek the three 'with' phrases are fronted, which gives the propositions of 16b marked prominence. This prominence fits the function of 16a and b as giving events which bring about OUTCOMES (16c and 17a–c). Therefore in the display 16a–b is labeled occasion/ reason. (See the note on 16c for an explanation of the reason part of the label.)

Several versions take the phrases of 16b as circumstances that initiate Jesus' descent, which is stated in 16a (CEV, JBP, NAB, NJB, REB, TEV, TNT). REB has "when the command is given, when the archangel's voice is heard, when God's trumpet sounds, then the Lord himself will descend from heaven." However, the events of the 16b phrases seem to bring about the OUTCOMES in 16c and 17a–c, so it is better to view them as attendant with the Lord's descent (Bruce, Frame, Marshall, Morris, Wanamaker; KJV, NCV, NIV, NLT, RSV), either while he descends or after he descends. Wanamaker says the command of Christ, the voice of the archangel, and the trumpet of God are all intended to call those who are dead to rise. In the display, 16a and b are rendered as having a simultaneous relation to each other. The three 'with' phrases represent agents and events and are rendered as such in the display.

the Lord *Jesus* himself will descend from heaven *and simultaneously he* will authoritatively command *believers who have died to rise to live again* The referent of 'Lord' here is Jesus (Bruce, Marshall, Wanamaker). The intensive pronoun αὐτός emphasizes that it is he, not some deputy or angelic representative, that comes to earth (Bruce, Morris). The first of the three prepositional phrases, 'with a shouted command', immediately follows the word 'Lord' in the Greek. The close proximity suggests that the Lord Jesus is the implicit agent of this event: he, the Lord Jesus, will command (Bruce, Morris, Wanamaker). The fact that a new agent is explicitly mentioned in the next 'with' phrase ('with a voice of an archangel') may be taken as support for this view.

The noun κέλευσμα has been translated "loud command" (NIV) and "shout of command" (TEV), emphasizing the loudness. But since this word was used of commands a military officer gave his troops or that a boatswain gave his oarsmen (Bruce), the meaning is more appropriately rendered 'will authoritatively command'. It is not explicit in the Greek who is commanded or what is said. Most feel that it is believers who have died who are commanded by the Lord to arise (Bruce, Marshall, Wanamaker). This is supported by Jesus' statement in John 5:28–29: "a time is coming when all who are in their graves will hear his voice and come out . . ." (NIV). For the sake of dramatic effect, a translator should leave implicit, if possible, whom Jesus and the chief angel command and what they say. The 16c OUTCOME gives the reader clues to the connection.

a chief angel *will speak with a loud* **voice, and** *an angel* **will blow a trumpet** *in order to signal that* **God** *is summoning dead believers to rise/gather* The last two 'with' phrases in the series are 'with a voice/sound of an archangel and with a trumpet of God'. The third phrase is joined to the second by καί 'and', which may function simply to append the last phrase of the series. This is the way it is rendered in the display and most versions. Some commentators, however, see it as uniting the last two phrases more closely. These phrases could be specifics (Frame), specifying who it is (an archangel) that issues the authoritative command of the first phrase and how it is issued (with a trumpet blast). NJB has "At the signal given by the voice of the Archangel and the trumpet of God. . . ." Alternatively, the last two phrases could be seen as the means by which the Lord Jesus calls the dead to arise—through the archangel's voice and the trumpet sound (Best, Wanamaker).

Because the third phrase has no explicit agent, the one blowing the trumpet could be the chief angel (mentioned in the second phrase), or it could be another angel. (In the Book of Revelation sounding trumpets is a function of angels.)

Decisions on the relationships and meanings of these three 'with' phrases are difficult because much is implicit here and there are no other Scripture passages which give a fuller explanation. Marshall says a real event is being described, but by means of analogy and metaphor, because human language cannot fully describe God's activity.

There is no article with 'archangel', so it is probably a reference to one of several. Jude 9 gives the name of one, Michael, but that is not to say there were not others. The word φωνή can mean either 'voice' or 'sound'. Some have therefore equated the archangel's voice/sound with the blowing of the trumpet and say the two phrases are describing the same event or at least the same summons (Bruce). Because of its association here with the authoritative command and the trumpet blast, the archangel's voice is probably also loud.

'A trumpet of God' probably does not mean a trumpet that belongs to God or even that he himself blows. Hiebert suggests it is a trumpet used in God's service. In OT accounts a supernatural trumpet seems to announce God's presence (Exod. 19:16) or gather people (Isa. 27:13; Zech. 9:14). In Exodus 19 thunder, lightning, a thick cloud, and a very loud trumpet blast summoned Moses to lead the Israelites from their camp in the Sinai desert to meet with God at Mt. Sinai (vv. 16–17). It seems the trumpet sound grew louder and louder as God approached and finally spoke with Moses (v. 19). Two other NT passages associate a trumpet blast with the gathering of the elect at Christ's coming (Matt. 24:31) and with the resurrection (1 Cor. 15:52). In Paul's CONCLUSION earlier (14b–d) he says that God will be very much involved at Christ's coming, and this is supported by the trumpet here, which evidently signals his presence or his activity.

4:16c *Then* (*or, As a result*), **first the people who are united with Christ who have died, will live again** The Greek is καὶ οἱ νεκροὶ ἐν Χριστῷ ἀναστήσονται πρῶτον 'and the dead in Christ will rise first'. Here καί 'and' most likely introduces the results of the descent of the Lord (Frame). Thus the relation of 16a-b with 16c, and also with 17a-c, has been labeled occasion/reason-OUTCOME/RESULT. In the Greek the focus in these verses is on what is happening to the believers, so labeling it occasion-OUTCOME is legitimate. However, the propositionalization of 17a renders a passive verb in the Greek as active and thus changes the focus to God's agency in gathering believers. Such active voice propositions are more appropriately labeled as reason–result relations.)

The meaning of 'dead in Christ' can be viewed from the perspective of the believers' relationship to Christ at the time of their death: who were believing in, or were united with, Christ at the time when they died (Wanamaker; CEV, JBP, NAB, NCV, TEV, TNT). Or it can be viewed from the perspective of the believers' state at death and until the coming of Christ (Bruce, Frame, Marshall): who were united with Christ at the time of death and still are. The latter seems preferable because the text says 'the dead in Christ', not 'those who died in Christ', and the state of death does not separate believers from Christ and his love (Rom. 8:38–39).

The adverb πρῶτον 'first' is best understood temporally (Bruce, Frame, Marshall, Wanamaker; DGN, REB), indicating that this is the first OUTCOME/RESULT of the events that accompany the Lord's coming. It corresponds to ἔπειτα 'then' in 17a. It does not mean dead believers will rise and actually meet Jesus first (before living believers meet him), as the renderings of some versions seem to imply (JBP, NJB). Both those who have died and those who are alive will meet him at the same time (17b). In 14a the verb ἀνίστημι 'to rise' refers to Jesus' resurrection. Here, the same word most likely means the resurrection to life of dead believers (Bruce, Marshall, Wanamaker; CEV, TEV) and not rising in the air. Translators should be careful to avoid that impression. The display rendering is 'will live again'.

4:17a After that A second OUTCOME/RESULT of the Lord's descent and accompanying events is introduced by ἔπειτα 'then'. This word indicates sequence (Bruce, Marshall, Wanamaker). The event in 17a follows the raising to life of the Christian dead.

***God* will powerfully take up in/with clouds any of us(inc)** *believers* **who are alive,** *that is,* **who are still present** *on earth* Here Paul repeats the words he used in 15b, 'we, the ones who are alive, the ones who remain'. They are fronted to signal a switch in referent, from 'the dead in Christ' in 16c to believers who are living at the time. (Some mss. omit the second phrase. However, MJTGNT and UBSGNT both have it; UBSGNT rates it as "certain.") The verb is ἁρπάζω 'to take up', used here in reference to those who are supernaturally taken away to heaven. (It is also used like this in Gen. 5:24 [LXX]; Acts 8:39; 2 Cor. 12:2 and 4; and Rev. 12:5.) The action can connote both speed (Jude 23) and power (Matt. 12:29; John 10:29; Acts 23:10). The meaning of a supernatural, powerful taking seems to be in view here. The passive 'will be taken up' is rendered as active in the display. The implied agent of the event is most likely 'God'. Verse 14 says God will bring believers who have died with Jesus; and that is the purpose of the action in 17b as well, though living believers are also included in the context.

The verb is followed by the prepositional phrase 'in clouds'. Clouds are understood either as the element that surrounds believers (Hiebert; CEV, JBP) or as the instrument by which believers are taken to meet the Lord (Best, Bruce, Frame, Marshall, Wanamaker). Bruce suggests that the clouds are to veil the glory of the God who has come. Support for the instrument role comes from many other passages. In Isa. 19:1 we read "the LORD rides on a swift cloud" (NIV), also in Deut. 33:26. In Ezekiel 1 is a description of an immense windstorm cloud with the LORD in the center. In Dan. 7:13 and Mark 13:26 the Son of Man goes or comes with clouds. Clouds which veil God's or Christ's presence are found in Exod. 19:16, 40:34, Mark 9:7, and Acts 1:9.

4:17b and at the same time *he will take up together those* **believers** *who have died* The Greek is ἅμα σὺν αὐτοῖς 'at the same time with them'. The pronoun 'them' refers to the dead believers who have just been raised (16c). Paul uses both the adverb ἅμα 'at the same time' and the preposition σύν 'with'. BAGD (p. 42.2) says this collocation is "seemingly pleonastic" (redundant). Bruce feels that ἅμα 'at the same time' strengthens the force of σύν 'with'. Frame holds that these two words give the most precise statement possible of the equality of advantage between living believers and those who have died. The meaning is that God will gather at the same time both believers who have died and believers who are alive.

4:17c in order that *we(inc)* **all might meet/welcome the Lord** *Jesus* **in the sky** The Greek is εἰς ἀπάντησιν τοῦ κυρίου εἰς ἀέρα 'for/to a meeting of the Lord in air'. The first preposition 'for/to' introduces the purpose for the taking up of believers (Frame). "The expression εἰς ἀπάντησιν ['for/to a meeting'] was a technical expression in Hellenistic Greek for the departure from a city of a delegation of citizens to meet an arriving dignitary in order to accord the person proper respect and honor by escorting the dignitary back to the city" (Wanamaker). Bruce agrees. The prepositional phrases 'for/to a meeting of the Lord' represent agent, event, and patient and are rendered with a clause in the display.

The meeting will be of the Lord, believers who have been dead, and other believers who are still alive (Best, Bruce). The encouragement that Paul is giving to the Thessalonians in 4:13-18 is that believers who have died will not miss out on this meeting with the Lord. The rendering 'we(inc) all' in the display attempts to make the meaning and encouragement clear.

The place of the meeting is 'in air'. In Jewish cosmology this was the space between the earth and the heavens (Wanamaker). Bruce mentions that there were two different terms for the upper air and the lower air where clouds would be. The word used here was the latter term. In English, 'sky' conveys this meaning.

4:17d As a result *of that* **[16a-17c] we(inc)** *all* **shall be with him** <u>forever</u> The words καὶ οὕτως 'and so' here are taken by Frame as introducing "the result of the resurrection, the rapture, and the meeting of the Lord in the air." Alternatively, this proposition may be taken to connect specifically to the meeting in the sky just mentioned in 17c (Bruce, Wanamaker). While the latter view is possible, it seems unnatural for a result proposition to be directly related to a purpose proposition (17c in this case). The result proposition would better be connected to 16a-17c, which is basically the position of Frame. Thus, in the display 17d is labeled a result of the events in 16a-17c. The result (17d) is not as prominent as the REASON (16a-17d) because the REASON, as the major part of the grounds of CONCLUSION 15b, deals with the issue of the order in which believers are taken up to the Lord, not with their being with the Lord forever. The 17d result states a fact by which Paul intends to further encourage the Thessalonians. The words 'always with (the) Lord' are fronted to emphasize the permanence of the fellowship (Frame). This emphasis is indicated in the display by 'forever' being in bold letters. In 14b-d Paul concluded that God will cause the Christian dead to be with Jesus. Now he adds that they and living believers will be with him forever, an added encouragement.

4:18 Because *all this* **[14-17]** *is true*, **encourage/ comfort each other by telling this message** The exhortation of 4:18 is introduced by the conjunction ὥστε 'therefore, so'. The result Paul intends in writing vv. 14-17 is that the Thessalonians will encourage each other regarding the Lord's return and, in particular, regarding those believers who have died. Verse 18 is thus the SOLUTION to the *emotive problem* in v. 13. The English rendering 'therefore' (NIV, NRSV) usually denotes a relation with what immediately precedes. Because v. 18 relates to much of the preceding material, versions have either omitted the conjunction (CEV, NAB) or have used the less immediate word 'then' in the middle of the verse (NJB, REB, TNT). NJB effectively conveys the relation and meaning by rearranging the order of the verse: "With such thoughts as these, then, you should encourage one another."

The verb παρακαλέω has been used previously to mean 'exhort, urge' (2:12a; 4:1c, 10b) and 'encourage, cheer up' (3:2c, 7a). Here it has the latter meaning. It also has the connotation of comfort because Paul offers consolation regarding believers who have died.

The prepositional phrase ἐν τοῖς λόγοις τούτοις 'with these words' states the means by which the Thessalonians are to encourage each other (Bruce). The term 'words' refers to the teaching of the Lord and Paul's deductions from it.

In some languages it might be necessary or preferable to render 4:18 in another way: 'Because all this is true, tell this message to each other in order that you will encourage/comfort each other (or, in order that you be comforted)'.

BOUNDARIES AND COHERENCE

The initial boundary of 4:13-18 was discussed under 4:3-12 (see "Boundaries"). The terminal boundary is between 4:18 and 5:1 and is well established. At 5:1 Paul introduces a new subject with the distinct grammatical construction περὶ δέ 'now concerning (the times and the seasons)'. He uses the vocative 'brothers', which often indicates the start of a new unit. And he adds οὐ χρείαν ἔχετε ὑμῖν γράφεσθαι 'you have no need to be written to you', an almost identical phrase to the one that begins the 4:9-12 unit: οὐ χρείαν ἔχετε γράφειν ὑμῖν 'you have no need to write to you'.

UBSGNT, MJTGNT, NLT, REB, and TEV place a boundary between 4:14 and 4:15. Such a division may be justified by the fronted demonstrative pronoun τοῦτο '(for) this (we say to you)' in v. 15, a pronoun that refers forward, emphasizing the word of the Lord that Paul will mention. Orienters often begin units, and v. 15 contains the orienter 'we say'. However, the conjunction γάρ 'for' is also present in v. 15. It connects the *authoritative evidence* in vv. 15-17 with Paul's INFERENCE in v. 14. Both INFERENCE and *evidence* are necessary to complete the paragraph pattern of the 14-17 embedded paragraph. Also, in the overall paragraph the *emotive problem* (v. 13) would be separated from the SOLUTION (v. 18) by placing a boundary between 4:14 and 4:15. For these reasons it is preferable not to divide 4:13-18 at this place.

CEV places a boundary between 4:15 and 4:16. However, v. 16 begins with the conjunction ὅτι 'because', which rarely initiates a new unit. Here ὅτι introduces the grounds (16a-17d) for Paul's CONCLUSION in 15b. Thus, a boundary here is not justified.

Referential coherence is established by repetition of participants, events, and descriptions. The primary participant is referred to as 'Jesus' (14a, 14c), 'Lord' (15a, 15b, 16a, 17c, 17d), and 'Christ' (16c). 'God' is mentioned in 14b and 16b. Christians who have died are referred to with participles of the verb κοιμάω 'to sleep' (13a, 14b, 15b), and they are also called 'the dead in Christ' (16c). Living believers are twice referred to as 'the ones who are alive, the ones who remain' (15b, 17a). Just as Jesus rose to live again (14a), so will the Christian dead (16c). The preposition σύν 'with' is repeated three times: The Christians who are alive at Christ's coming will be taken to heaven 'with' those believers who have just been raised (17b); God will bring both groups of believers to be 'with' Jesus (14c); and they will be 'with' him forever (17d). The future tense occurs five times in 4:13-18, but not at all in the adjoining 4:9-12 and 5:1-11 units.

Conjunctions establish relational coherence: The INFERENCE (14) is connected to the *discourse orienter* (13) by γάρ 'for'; the *authoritative evidence* (15-17) is connected to the INFERENCE by γάρ 'for'; the concluding APPEAL (18) is appended with ὥστε 'therefore'.

PROMINENCE AND THEME

The naturally prominent part of the 4:13–18 paragraph is the exhortation that constitutes the *SOLUTION* (v. 18). However, the embedded paragraph (vv. 14–17), being the dominant constituent, has marked prominence. In the embedded paragraph the *INFERENCE* (v. 14) is prominent, as indicated by the fact that the information in its CONCLUSION propositions (14b–14d) is amplified in the grounds propositions (16a–17c) of the *authoritative evidence*.

The theme for the 4:13–18 paragraph is derived from the *INFERENCE*'s two RESULT propositions (14b and 14c) and from the *SOLUTION* (18).

SUBSECTION CONSTITUENT 5:1-8
(Hortatory Paragraph: Nucleus₂ of 4:13-5:11)

THEME: We believers should not be unprepared for the time the Lord Jesus returns as unbelievers will be unprepared. On the contrary, we must be vigilant and self-controlled.

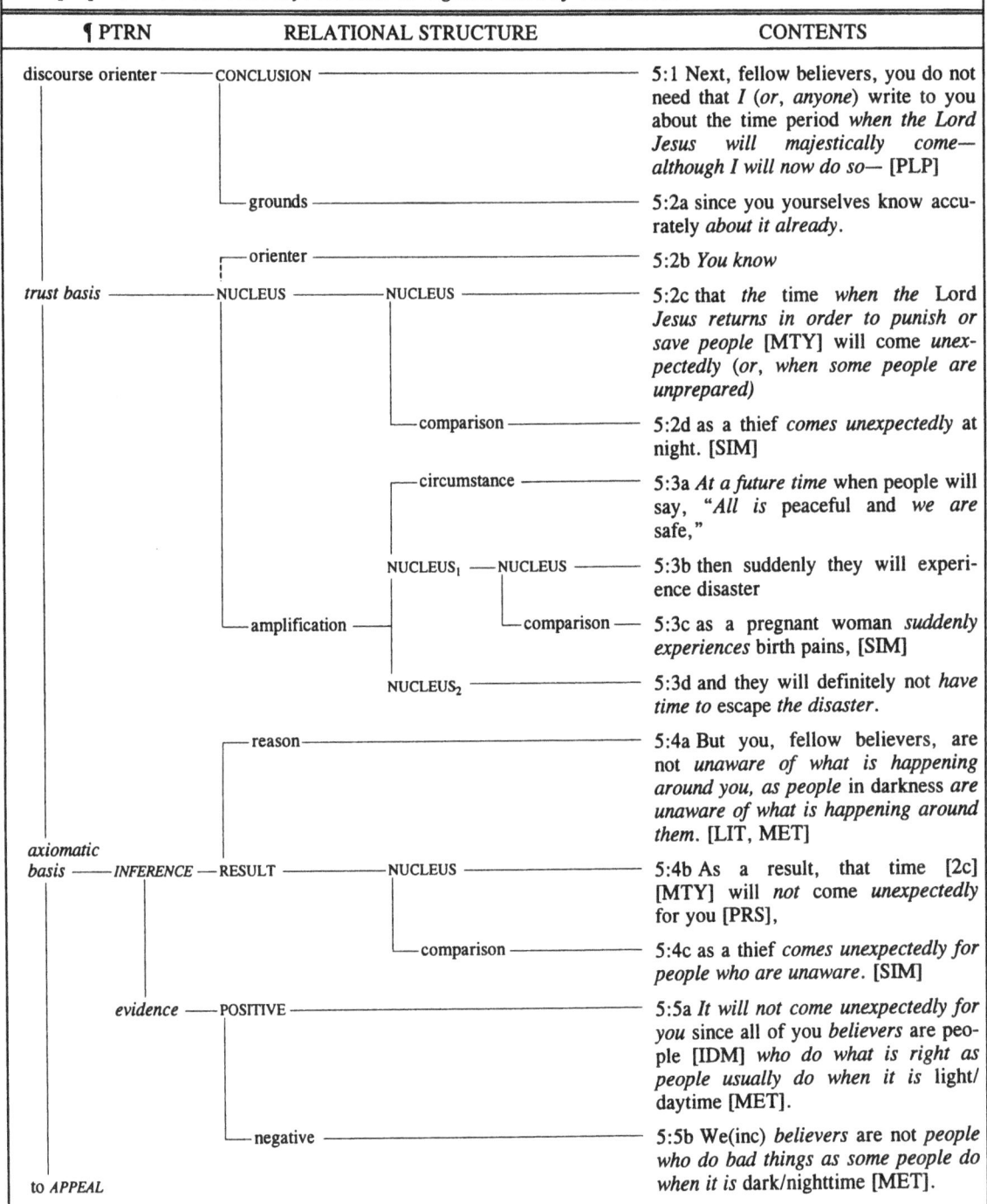

¶ PTRN	RELATIONAL STRUCTURE	CONTENTS
discourse orienter	CONCLUSION	5:1 Next, fellow believers, you do not need that *I* (or, *anyone*) write to you about the time period *when the Lord Jesus will majestically come—although I will now do so—* [PLP]
	grounds	5:2a since you yourselves know accurately *about it already*.
trust basis	orienter	5:2b *You know*
	NUCLEUS—NUCLEUS	5:2c that the time *when the Lord Jesus returns in order to punish or save people* [MTY] will come *unexpectedly* (or, *when some people are unprepared*)
	comparison	5:2d as a thief *comes unexpectedly* at night. [SIM]
	circumstance	5:3a *At a future time* when people will say, "*All is* peaceful and *we are* safe,"
	amplification — NUCLEUS₁ — NUCLEUS	5:3b then suddenly they will experience disaster
	comparison	5:3c as a pregnant woman *suddenly experiences* birth pains, [SIM]
	NUCLEUS₂	5:3d and they will definitely not *have time to* escape *the disaster*.
	reason	5:4a But you, fellow believers, are not *unaware of what is happening around you, as people* in darkness *are unaware of what is happening around them*. [LIT, MET]
axiomatic basis — INFERENCE — RESULT — NUCLEUS		5:4b As a result, that time [2c] [MTY] will *not* come *unexpectedly* for you [PRS],
	comparison	5:4c as a thief *comes unexpectedly for people who are unaware*. [SIM]
evidence — POSITIVE		5:5a *It will not come unexpectedly for you* since all of you *believers* are people [IDM] *who do what is right as people usually do when it is* light/daytime [MET].
	negative	5:5b We(inc) *believers* are not *people who do bad things as some people do when it is* dark/nighttime [MET].
to APPEAL		

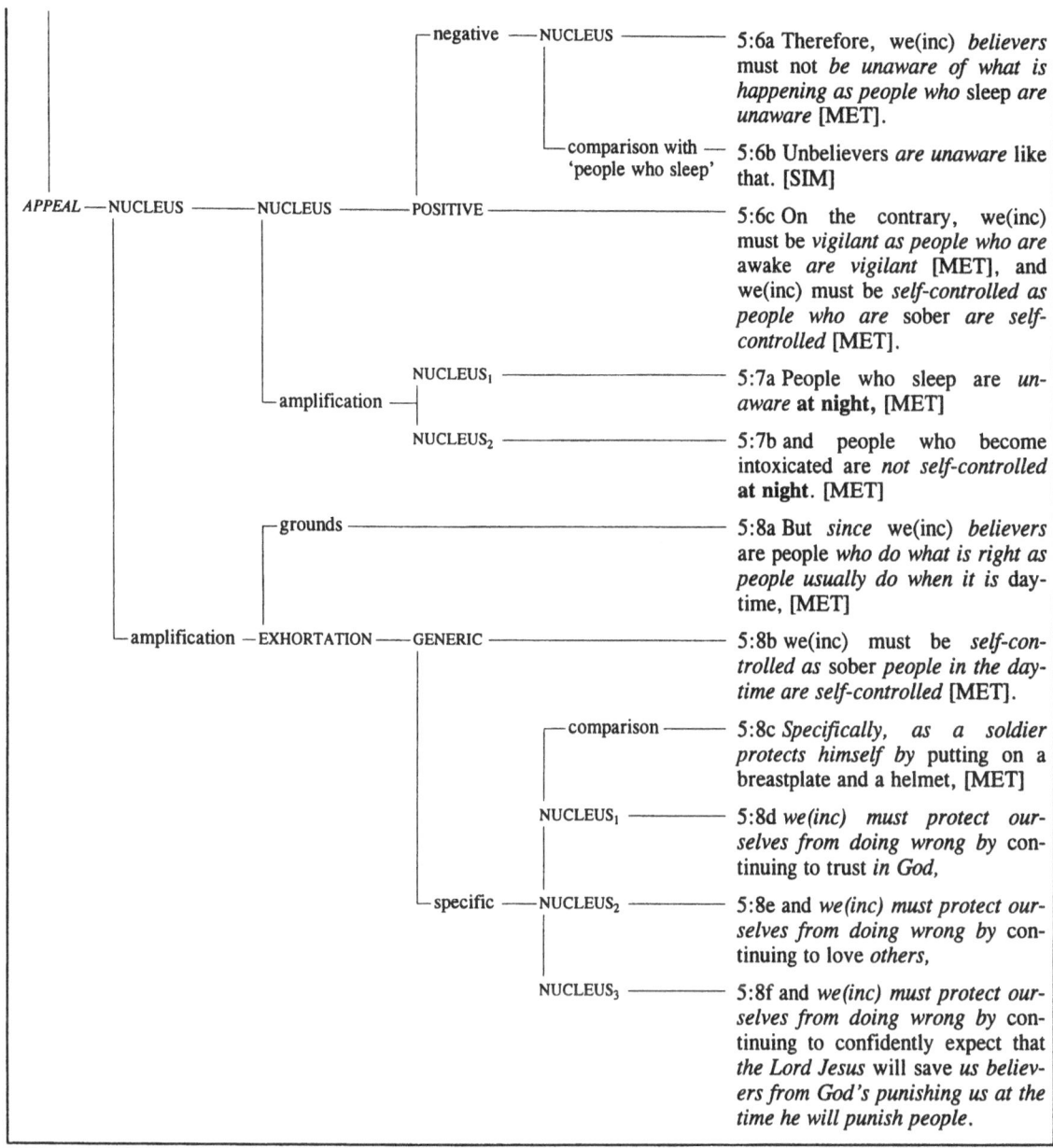

INTENT AND PARAGRAPH PATTERN

Paul's intent in the 5:1-8 paragraph is to affect the behavior of his readers. In 5:6 he exhorts the Thessalonians: ἄρα οὖν μὴ καθεύδωμεν ὡς οἱ λοιποὶ ἀλλὰ γρηγορῶμεν καὶ νήφωμεν 'so therefore let us not sleep as the rest (do) but let us keep awake and let us be sober/self-controlled'. He repeats the verb νήφωμεν 'let us be sober/self-controlled' in v. 8 and adds a participial phrase that has an imperatival function also: ἐνδυσάμενοι θώρακα πίστεως καὶ ἀγάπης καὶ περικεφαλαίαν ἐλπίδα σωτηρίας 'having put on a breastplate of faith and of love and a helmet (which is the) hope of salvation'. Thus the genre is hortatory.

The paragraph consists of four propositional clusters: 1-2a, 2b-3d, 4a-5b, and 6a-8f. The first, 1-2a, is a discourse orienter and contains the rhetorical device known as paralipsis, by which Paul tells the Thessalonians that they already know about the day the Lord Jesus will return. The second cluster, 2b-3d, relates what they know.

In the third cluster, 4a-5b, Paul's intent is to affect the ideas of the Thessalonians. He tells them that as believers they are not in darkness (unaware and unprepared) but that they are 'sons of the light' who do what is right. Thus the third cluster is an embedded expository paragraph. In

4a–5b no stated problem is being refuted (which would be solutionality). And because the grounds propositions in v. 5 are axiomatic and support Paul's conclusion in v. 4, no further proof is offered (which would be the case in a volitionality subtype). Instead, the 4a–5b cluster consists of a conclusion-grounds relation; thus it is a simple causality subtype of expository paragraph pattern, with its constituents labeled *INFERENCE* and *evidence*.

The fourth cluster, 6a–8f, of the 5:1–8 hortatory paragraph is introduced by ἄρα οὖν 'so therefore'. This indicates that it is in a grounds-exhortation relation to the second and third clusters.

There is no problem mentioned in 5:1–8 that would indicate a paragraph pattern of the solutionality subtype, nor does Paul give any means to accomplish the exhortation as would be the case in the volitionality subtype. Instead, Paul's exhortations follow naturally from the axiomatic and trust grounds that he presents, showing that this is the causality subtype of hortatory paragraph pattern, with its constituents labeled *basis* and *APPEAL*.

Paragraph 5:1–8 is the climactic unit both of 4:1–5:24 and the epistle (see "Intent" under 4:3–5:11).

NOTES

5:1 Next, fellow believers, you do not need that I (*or, anyone*) write to you . . . —*although I will now do so*— There is a fronted discourse orienter (περὶ δέ 'now/but concerning') here that is identical to and fulfills the same function as the orienter in 4:9a. Also, Paul again uses paralipsis: the wording is almost identical to the wording of 4:9a. (See the 4:9a note concerning the discourse orienter and the figure.) Paralipsis was a common feature of hortatory style and here implies that Paul will repeat something he has previously taught them (Bruce, Marshall, Morris, Wanamaker). The contraexpectation phrase 'although I will now do so' is supplied in the display since it is what was omitted in the paralipsis.

about the time period *when the Lord Jesus will majestically come* The Greek has two nouns here, χρόνος 'times' and καιρός 'seasons'. These words were used in the singular or plural (they are plural here) with no apparent difference of meaning (Frame). Morris sees a fine distinction in the terms, with the first referring to duration of the times and the second to the quality of the times. Moore calls them a near-synonymous doublet. However, others feel that any distinction between the words in Classical Greek probably disappeared by NT times, so that the terms can be taken as completely synonymous (Best, Bruce, Marshall, Wanamaker). Because the terms were often used together (Dan. 2:21; 7:12 [LXX]; Acts 1:7) Bruce calls them a conventional doublet. Both nouns have the definite article; Best suggests that this indicates a well-known technical collocation related to the coming of Christ. NIV translates the two Hebrew equivalents as "period of time" in Dan. 7:12, based on its being considered a synonymous doublet in the Hebrew as well.

In the NT both terms can refer to a period of time or a point of time (Louw and Nida 67.1, 67.78). Here they could refer to the time when Christ returns (Best, Frame, Marshall) or a period of time associated with that event (Morris, Wanamaker). Paul's aim in 5:1–8 is not to discuss the exact time of Christ's return. Instead he tells the Thessalonians that events of that time period will alert them to its nearness. The 'day of the Lord' in the OT often involved a period of time (see the note on 2a). Therefore it seems preferable to understand the terms 'times' and 'seasons' to refer to a period of time that includes Christ's coming.

5:2a since you yourselves know accurately about it already Here the conjunction γάρ 'for' introduces the reason or grounds for v. 1 (Marshall, Frame, Wanamaker). It is better taken as grounds, since 2a is support for the statement in v. 1. The adverb ἀκριβῶς 'accurately, well' qualifies the verb οἴδατε 'you know'. Morris takes the adverb to mean 'completely'. Best, Bruce, and Marshall give it the meaning 'accurately'. Paul can say the Thessalonians know about this topic because he had already instructed them about the period when Christ would return (see 2 Thess. 2:5). He fronts the intensive pronoun 'yourselves' for emphasis (Morris, Wanamaker). Best and Morris feel it is somewhat ironic for Paul to say in 2a–d 'you yourselves know accurately that some people will not know accurately when the Day of the Lord will come because it will come as a thief at night'.

5:2b *You know* The verb 'you know' in the 2a grounds proposition introduces an orienter-content relation which extends through 3d. That series of propositions has marked prominence because of Paul's use of figurative speech (similes) and amplification. Therefore it seems appropriate to indicate this prominence in the display by beginning a new propositional cluster with the repetition of the cognitive orienter 'you know' at 2b. Otherwise the orienter and content propositions would be diagrammed under the 2a subordinate grounds proposition.

Propositions 2b-3d are the *trust basis* for the APPEAL in 6-8. Paul expresses assurance that his readers know facts about the Lord's return as a basis for his exhortation to act on them.

5:2c-d that *the time when the Lord Jesus returns in order to punish or save people* will come unexpectedly (*or, when some people are unprepared*) as a thief *comes unexpectedly* at night Here the conjunction ὅτι 'that' introduces the content of what the Thessalonians knew. The next phrase is 'day of the Lord'. It expresses an eschatological concept that originated with OT prophets. Being a well-known fixed phrase, it is used without the article (Best, Frame, Wanamaker). It refers to a future period, either near or distant, when the Lord will punish wrongdoers (Joel 1:15-20; Amos 5:18-20; Zeph. 1:14-18) and also deliver his people (Joel 2:31-32; Zech. 14:1-21; Mal. 4:5). (For references in which the terms 'time' and 'season' are used of periods of divine intervention and judgment, see Wanamaker, p. 178.) In 5:1-8 (and the subsequent paragraph, 5:9-11) both of the elements—punishment and deliverance/salvation—are present: punishment in 3b-d and 9a and deliverance in 8f and 9b. It seems that in this passage Paul had the concept of the OT day of the Lord very much in mind. This is a metonymy in which a period of time ('day') represents events done during that period.

In the NT 'Lord' is most often a reference to Jesus, and 'day' is associated with his name as well, for example, 'day of our Lord Jesus Christ' (1 Cor. 1:8) and 'day of the Lord Jesus' (2 Cor. 1:14). Commentators feel that 'Lord' in 2c refers to the Lord Jesus (Bruce, Frame, Marshall, Wanamaker). Righteous behavior is implied in the metaphors of this paragraph (5a, 6c, 8a-f), and other passages in the letter connect Christ's coming with his examining of believers' work (2:19e) and with their being blameless in God's sight (3:13b-c, 5:23c-d). Because these concepts are associated with Christ's return and because of the extended discussion of his return in the preceding passage (4:13-18), it is most probable that 'day of the Lord' here includes not only judgment and salvation, but Christ's return as well.

The verb ἔρχεται 'it comes' is present tense. According to Frame, it is a general or gnomic present, used in a generalization. Morris suggests the present indicates certainty. The context is speaking of a future time period and that meaning is best expressed by 'will come', as in the display.

A comparison (simile) is indicated by the conjunctions ὡς . . . οὕτως 'as . . . thus' in 2c-d. Its topic is the day of the Lord, and the image is a thief at night. The ground of comparison is unexpectedness (Bruce, Marshall, Morris, Wanamaker; JBP, NCV, NLT). The phrase 'at night' reinforces the manner (slyly, unexpectedly) rather than the time of the thief's coming (Hiebert). The simile implies that it is important to be alert and not be taken by surprise (Bruce) and unprepared. Some say that another ground of comparison is suddenness (Best, Frame) or even unwelcomeness (Marshall). However, the fact that a thief comes at night when people are sleeping and not watching for him and the succeeding metaphors about nighttime, darkness, sleep, and drunkenness (times or states when people are not aware) support unexpectedness as the ground of comparison.

When speaking of his coming in Matt. 24:42-44, Jesus compares it to the unexpected coming of a thief and to the need for watchfulness. Rev. 3:3 and 16:15 are similar. These passages support the idea mentioned earlier that 'day of the Lord' in v. 2 includes the event of Jesus' return.

5:3a In UBSGNT there is no conjunction at the beginning of v. 3. Thus propositions 3a-d could be related structurally either to what precedes or to what follows. If the former, they provide an amplification of Paul's statement that the day of the Lord will come unexpectedly (Marshall, Morris, Wanamaker). If the latter, they provide a negative contrast in Paul's *axiomatic basis*: some (unbelieving) people will be suddenly overcome by disaster, but you, fellow believers, are not unaware so that the day of the Lord will not surprise you when it comes. The former interpretation seems preferable for the following reasons: (1) The simile in 3b-c has a ground of comparison closely related to that of the simile in 2c-d. (2) The mention of disaster in 3b fits the 'day of the Lord' concept mentioned earlier in 2c. (3) Asyndeton (i.e., absence of a conjunction) is sometimes found in restatement relations such as amplification (Levinsohn, p. 62), the relation proposed here. (4) Another reason for connecting v. 3 with what precedes is that the vocative 'brothers' occurs near the beginning of v. 4, and Paul often inserts the vocative at a major or minor break in the discourse. Finally, (5) connecting v. 3 with what precedes is supported by the presence of γάρ 'for' in MJTGNT at 3a.

***At a future time* when people will say** Proposition 3a is a circumstance of 3b and 3d. The adverb ὅταν 'at the time that, when' together with a verb in the subjunctive mood (as here) indicates contingency. The time when people will speak thus is in the future, just before the day of the Lord comes.

The verb λέγωσιν 'they say' is impersonal. The people who speak the words to follow will be unbelievers (Frame, Morris), as the contrast of 4a makes clear. (It is uncharacteristic of Paul not to identify referents; and that fact, along with words in 3a-b that he uses nowhere else in his letters, leads commentators such as Best and Wanamaker to suppose that 3a-b is based on a general statement, proverb, or a saying of Jesus.)

"*All is* peaceful and *we are* safe" The compressed exclamation is three words: εἰρήνη καὶ ἀσφάλεια 'peace and security'. Both of these nouns can be used to describe outer conditions. Peace is "a set of favorable circumstances involving peace and tranquility" (Louw and Nida 22.42), and security is "a state of safety and security, implying a complete lack of danger" (ibid., 21.9). These words speak of conditions on local and international levels that cause people to feel secure. This is probably the primary meaning here. Some view the terms as expressing inner reactions to outer circumstances: peace is then the absence of alarms and security, a feeling of sureness and safety not shaken by outward circumstances (Morris). CEV has "People will think they are safe and secure." In either case distinctions between the two words are slight; some view them as synonymous (Frame) or nearly so (Moore). They are two sides of the same coin: peaceful outward circumstances contribute to an inner sense of security. The display rendering incorporates both the external and internal sense. The nouns represent states, and they are so rendered in the display.

This bit of direct speech has its origins in the OT, where false prophets gave similarly reassuring messages (Jer. 6:13-14; Ezek. 13:8-16). Jesus also spoke of the false sense of security people will have and of the suddenness of the coming disaster (Luke 17:26-33).

5:3b then suddenly they will experience disaster The Greek is τότε αἰφνίδιος αὐτοῖς ἐφίσταται ὄλεθρος 'then sudden destruction comes on them'. The adjective 'sudden' represents an adverbial idea and is fronted for emphasis: immediately after these people speak, disaster strikes. Unexpectedness is implied, but this seems to be derived from the context rather than from the meaning of the word (Louw and Nida 67.113).

The word ὄλεθρος means 'destruction, ruin'. 'Destruction comes on them' is rendered in the display as 'they will experience disaster'. It describes God's punishment on unbelievers, the opposite of the 'salvation' of believers in 8f and 9b. It is not destruction in terms of cessation of existence (Frame, Morris). Some take it to mean eternal ruin, separation from Christ's presence (Frame, Morris). Or it can signify sudden, temporal calamities similar to those described by Jesus in Luke 21:20-24 and Matt. 24:15-22 (where pregnant women are also mentioned) and in Luke 21:34-36. The latter view may be preferable because when Paul means spiritual destruction he uses the term 'eternal' (2 Thess. 1:9).

5:3c as a pregnant woman *suddenly experiences* birth pains The conjunction ὥσπερ 'as' here introduces a second comparison (simile). Its topic is the disaster unbelievers are about to experience, and the image is labor pains. The ground of comparison is the suddenness with which both come (Bruce, Frame, Wanamaker). Some say unexpectedness (Marshall) or inevitability (Bruce, Morris, Wanamaker) may also be in view. However, suddenness seems to be the primary ground of comparison in the figure. A woman pregnant for almost nine months expects labor pains; she just doesn't know when they are going to come. This simile is found often in the OT prophets (Isa. 13:6-8; Jer. 22:20-23; Mic. 4:9-10), but with a different connotation than here. There it is "almost always used of the distress experienced in the face of divine judgment" (Wanamaker). What is rendered as 'pregnant woman' here is an idiom in the Greek: 'the one having in womb'.

5:3d and they will definitely not *have time to* escape *the disaster* The conjunction καί 'and' conjoins 3d to 3b-c. This added proposition seems to confirm the idea that the ground of comparison of the preceding simile is suddenness: suddenly they will experience disaster and they will not have time to escape. If the ground of comparison in the previous figure is taken as inevitability rather than suddenness, 3d could be considered result: suddenly they will experience disaster, as inevitably as a pregnant woman experiences birth pains and (as a result) they will not escape. The double negative οὐ μή makes the statement emphatic: 'definitely not escape'.

5:4a But you, fellow believers, are not *unaware of what is happening around you, as people* in darkness *are* The Greek is ὑμεῖς δέ, ἀδελφοί, οὐκ ἐστὲ ἐν σκότει 'but you, brothers, are not in darkness'. This is a form of litotes; the litotes is retained in the display rendering ('not unaware') to preserve the interplay of metaphors that Paul uses throughout this unit.

The fronted pronoun ὑμεῖς 'you' and the developmental marker δέ 'and/but' indicate a change of topic: The people who will be caught unawares was the previous topic; the new topic is the Thessalonian believers who are aware. The δέ also has an adversative function, 'but', because this is a contrast.

The vocative 'brothers' and the various figures of speech that Paul now introduces help to establish a minor break in the discourse, indicating that 4a–5b is a new sub-unit relating to Paul's 6a–8f *APPEAL*. In this sub-unit Paul tells the Thessalonians that they are 'not in darkness'; that they all are 'sons of light', 'sons of day'; and that believers are 'not of night' and 'not of darkness'. Propositions 4a–5b form an *axiomatic basis* for the *APPEAL*: since they are such people, the Thessalonians should be alert and prepared for the time the Lord will return. The fronted pronoun ὑμεῖς 'you' (indicating emphasis and a change of topic), the vocative 'brothers', and the conjunction δέ 'but' together establish a contrast with the 3a–d amplification propositions of the preceding *trust basis*: some people will suddenly experience disaster when the day of the Lord comes, but you fellow believers should not, since you are different.

Both the OT and NT use the metaphor of darkness (as well as light) to describe a spiritual reality. It is used with three different meanings:

(1) Darkness sometimes refers to unrighteous behavior (light, to righteous behavior). Asaph associates the "haunts of violence" with "the dark places of the land" (Ps. 74:20, NIV). Paul tells the Roman believers to "put aside the deeds of darkness and put on the armor of light" and "behave decently, as in the daytime" (Rom. 13:12–13, NIV; see also Eph. 5:8–14). (The figures of Rom. 13:11–14 are strikingly similar to those in 1 Thess. 5:1–8.)

(2) Darkness sometimes refers to spiritual ignorance (light, to knowledge). Asaph writes of rulers who "know nothing, they understand nothing. They walk about in darkness" (Ps. 82:5a, NIV; see also Prov. 4:18–19). Paul uses the metaphor of light to describe the knowledge believers have: "For God . . . made his light shine in our hearts to give us the light of the knowledge of the glory of God in the face of Christ" (2 Cor. 4:6, NIV).

(3) Darkness sometimes refers to Satan and his followers (light, to the Lord and those who give allegiance to him). Isaiah says, "The people walking in darkness have seen a great light" (9:2a, NIV). Paul says, "giving thanks to the Father, who has qualified you to share in the inheritance of the saints in the kingdom of light. For he has rescued us from the dominion of darkness and brought us into the kingdom of the Son he loves" (Col. 1:12–13, NIV; see also 2 Cor. 6:14).

Some interpret the metaphor of darkness in 5:4 and the following verses as having the third meaning, those alienated from God (Frame, Best, Wanamaker); others take it with the first meaning, those in the darkness of sin (Marshall). However, there is a difference of surface form between the prepositional phrase 'in darkness' here and the genitive nouns 'of light', 'of day', 'of night', and 'of darkness' in the next verse, so it is possible that there is a difference of meaning as well. Paul uses the phrase 'in darkness' metaphorically in Rom. 2:19 to speak of those in need of spiritual direction and instruction. The meaning of spiritual ignorance in Rom. 2:19 is appropriate also here in this verse, in which a thief is said to be coming unexpectedly (4c). NAB renders 5:4a with an English idiom which denotes ignorance: "You are not in the dark, brothers" (similarly REB). Even those who understand the metaphor to mean those in the darkness of sin (Marshall) or those alienated from God (Wanamaker), say that those conditions imply or lead to ignorance.

The topic of the 'not in the dark' metaphor is believers. The image is being in a physically dark place. The ground of comparison is unawareness, but note that Paul uses the negative: people in a dark place are unaware of their surroundings but believers are not unaware of what is happening. The ground of comparison is not explicit in the Greek of 4a but is deduced from the simile of the thief in 4b–c. Instead of being ignorant about the Lord's return, as unbelievers are, believers will know the signs of its nearness. The metaphors for unawareness in vv. 4-7 may be based on the words of Jesus in Luke 21:34-36.

5:4b-c As a result, that time [2c] will *not* come *unexpectedly* for you The Greek of 4b-c is ἵνα ἡ ἡμέρα ὑμᾶς ὡς κλέπτης καταλάβῃ 'so that the day should come upon you as a thief'. The conjunction ἵνα 'so that' introduces the RESULT of the preceding proposition (BDF, §391(5); Bruce; Frame; Wanamaker). It is an extension of the metaphor in 4a; the ground of comparison ('unawareness, unexpectedness') is implicit in 4b. Because Paul applies the result to his believing readers, 4b has to be negated as was 4a: you are not in darkness and as a result that time should not come unexpectedly for you.

The time referred to is the day of the Lord (Bruce, Wanamaker), which Paul first mentions in 2c. It is personified as coming upon a person as a thief would. The verb καταλαμβάνομαι can mean simply 'to arrive, come upon', or it can mean "*seize w. hostile intent, overtake*" (BAGD, p. 413.1b). Either is appropriate here; the former is perhaps primary, because the ground of comparison of the thief simile here is most likely unexpectedness (Bruce, Marshall, Morris; NIV, NJB, TEV), as it was in 2d. That this is a threatening and undesirable overtaking is a valid inference (Wanamaker), because a prominent aspect of the day of the Lord is judgment.

as a thief *comes unexpectedly for people who are unaware* The conjunction ὡς 'as' introduces a comparison (simile); see the note on 2c-d regarding 'as a thief'. Some mss. have the plural form of the noun, that is, 'thieves'. However, UBSGNT and MJTGNT both have the singular form, and UBSGNT rates that reading as "certain".

5:5a *It will not come unexpectedly for you* since The conjunction γάρ 'for' is omitted in MJTGNT, but UBSGNT includes it without comment, considering it to have good support. This proposition has been interpreted as expressing grounds (Best), reason (Frame, Wanamaker), or amplification of what precedes (Marshall). Grounds seems most appropriate: Paul bases his statement that the time of the Lord's return will not take the Thessalonians by surprise on the fact that they live righteously and are aware, awake, like people in the daytime.

all of you *believers* **are people** *who do what is right as people usually do when it is* **light/ daytime** The Greek of 5a is πάντες γὰρ ὑμεῖς υἱοὶ φωτός ἐστε καὶ υἱοὶ ἡμέρας 'for you all are sons of light and sons of day'. The fronted 'you all' indicates change of topic as did 'you' in 4a, thus continuing the contrast with unbelievers, who will be unprepared for the day of the Lord (v. 3).

Twice in 5a Paul uses a common Hebrew idiom in which "[t]he word 'son', when qualified by another noun, denotes the *nature* and character of the person or persons so named, and even their source and origin" (Bullinger, p. 503): for example, 'son of wickedness' in Ps. 89:22 and 'sons of valor' in 2 Sam. 2:7. Depending on the referent, 'sons' in this idiom can mean both male and female persons, or 'people', which is the rendering in NCV, TEV, and the display.

In Luke 16:8 Jesus contrasts 'the sons of light' with 'the sons of this age' (see also John 12:36). Paul's usage in 5:5a could be similar. 'Light' may refer here to the Lord and the people who give allegiance to him, the third meaning listed in the note on 4a. Wanamaker says, "It clearly distinguishes those who belong to the community of faith from those outside, who are part of the darkness to be judged and condemned when the Lord Jesus comes. . . ." This is probably the interpretation of versions that have 'belong to (the light/day and night/darkness)' in 5a and 5b (NCV, TEV, TNT). Some versions holding this interpretation have the words 'belong to' in 5b only (NAB, NIV, NJB, NLT, REB).

Bruce and Morris, however understand 'light' (in the phrase 'sons of light') in the ethical sense of righteous behavior, which is the first meaning listed in the note on 4a. In Eph. 5:8 Paul uses 'light' and 'children of light' with this ethical sense. This meaning is particularly appropriate in 1 Thess. 5:1-8, in which Paul exhorts his readers in 6c and 8b to be awake (vigilant) and sober (self-controlled), and in 8d-f to exercise faith, love, and hope. It also fits with the new phrase that Paul appends, 'sons of day'. (It is found only here in the NT.)

Some commentators (including Bruce and Morris) say that this use of 'day' refers to 'the day of the Lord' (v. 2): believers are people who expectantly await deliverance at Christ's return (as in 1:10). However, the noun 'day' here does not have an article, which would make a reference to the day of the Lord more certain. 'Sons of day' is better taken as referring to behavior characteristic of daytime, even though the word 'day' may retain an allusion to 'the day of the Lord' (Best, Frame, Wanamaker). Paul has already spoken of a thief who comes at night (2d). He will shortly speak of those who get drunk at night

(v. 7). Paul tells the Thessalonians that they are not to be characterized by such behavior.

The phrases 'sons of light' and 'sons of day' form a figurative doublet (Moore). The terms 'light' and 'day' are very closely related, and their imagery seems virtually synonymous. Thus the two are represented by one rendering in the display. It is the ethical sense, favored by Best, Frame, and Wanamaker, which seems most appropriate to the context.

The topic of both metaphors is believers; the images, light and day. The ground of comparison is doing what is right: believers are people who do what is right as people usually do when it is daytime.

5:5b We(inc) *believers* **are not** *people who do bad things as some people do when it is* **dark/ nighttime** The Greek is οὐκ ἐσμὲν νυκτὸς οὐδὲ σκότους 'we are not of night nor of darkness'. This clause constitutes an opposing proposition to the POSITIVE proposition in 5a. Paul switches from a second person reference in 5a, 'you', to a first person reference, 'we'. This prepares for his mitigated APPEAL ('Let us') in vv. 6–8 (Frame, Wanamaker). By changing pronouns Paul applies the truth in both halves of v. 5 to all believers (Frame, Marshall), even as he then addresses his APPEAL to all.

The words 'nighttime' and 'darkness', used figuratively, can signify the realm of people who do not acknowledge God (Wanamaker). They may also allude to the day of the Lord, which will be a time of judgment (Wanamaker). Paul does not repeat 'sons' here, but he continues to use the genitive case for the nouns 'night' and 'darkness'. This may be to focus on the idea of behavior rather than the idea of a realm of darkness. Paul arranges the terms of 5a–b in a chiastic pattern with negated antonyms in the third and fourth lines:

    A All of you are sons of light
      B and sons of daytime
      B′ We are not of nighttime
    A′ nor of darkness

The genitive nouns 'of nighttime' and 'of darkness' can be considered a figurative doublet (Moore). The terms 'nighttime' and 'darkness' are very closely related, and the meaning of their imagery seems virtually synonymous. Thus the two are represented by one rendering in the display, as were 'sons of light' and 'sons of daytime'. The topic is believers; the images, darkness and nighttime. The ground of comparison is doing bad things as some people do when it is dark or nighttime. Note the negative: God's people do *not* do bad things.

5:6a Therefore The sequence of words found here, ἄρα οὖν 'so therefore', is rare. (Paul uses οὖν 'therefore' about a hundred times in his letters, but ἄρα οὖν only twelve times.) It brings force to the conclusion (see the discussion on 2 Thess. 2:15 in J. Callow 1982:80–81). It introduces an APPEAL that is an ethical conclusion of Paul's *axiomatic basis* in vv. 4–5 (Wanamaker): we believers are people who do right as people do in the light; therefore, we must not be unaware as people asleep in darkness are, but instead we should be vigilant and self-controlled.

we(inc) *believers* **must not** *be unaware of what is happening as people who* **sleep** *are unaware* Paul softens his exhortation by using the hortatory subjunctive once in 6a (μὴ καθεύδωμεν 'let us not sleep'), twice in 6c, and once in 8b. All four times a metaphor is involved. The topic of the metaphor here is Paul, his readers, and believers in general. The image is people who are asleep. The ground of comparison is being unaware: believers should *not* be unaware of what is happening around them as people who sleep are unaware. Marshall and Morris call such unawareness spiritual insensitivity. In v. 2 Paul says that the day of the Lord will come unexpectedly for some people just as a thief comes at night. Similarly in 4a–5b he says believers are people of light and are not ignorant of spiritual realities. Based on these figures Paul exhorts the Thessalonians to be vigilant so that they can sense when the time of Christ's return is near and so that they can be religiously and morally prepared for it (Wanamaker).

5:6b Unbelievers *are unaware* **like that** There is a comparison (simile) in v. 6. It is introduced by the conjunction ὡς 'as'. The Greek of 6a–b is ἄρα οὖν μὴ καθεύδωμεν ὡς οἱ λοιποί 'so therefore let us not sleep as the rest'. Paul used the phrase 'the rest' previously, in 4:13c (see the note there). Here he says unbelievers are like people who sleep; that is, they are unaware of things that have spiritual significance. In the display the conjunction 'as' is rendered 'like that' to avoid having a second 'as' clause immediately after the one in 6a.

5:6c On the contrary The conjunction ἀλλά 'but' introduces a POSITIVE exhortation here, corresponding to the negative one in 6a.

we(inc) must be *vigilant as people who are awake are vigilant* The verb γρηγορέω 'to be awake' is the antonym of καθεύδω 'to sleep' in 6a. It is used metaphorically as was the previous verb. The topic of the metaphor is believers and the image is being awake. The ground of comparison is that believers are to be alert and vigilant as people who are awake are vigilant (Frame, Marshall, Wanamaker; NIV). This verb 'to be awake' is used three times in Mark 13:34–37 and twice in Matt. 24:42–44 to urge watchfulness for the coming of the Lord. The latter passage speaks of watching for a thief who could come at an unexpected time. The similarity between that passage and this one is noteworthy.

and we(inc) must be *self-controlled as people who are* sober *are self-controlled* The third verb in v. 6 is νήφωμεν 'let us be sober'. Some understand this literally, that is, that believers should not become drunk. Bruce (p. 112) takes this view for 6c and 7b because the parable of Matt. 24:48–51 speaks of a servant who gets drunk and is unprepared for the master, who comes when he doesn't expect him. However, because the preceding two verbs are obviously metaphorical, it seems appropriate to understand this verb in that way also. The topic is again believers. The image is not being drunk. The ground of comparison is being clear-headed (Best, Louw and Nida 30.25; JBP) or being in control of oneself (Louw and Nida 88.86, Morris, Wanamaker; NCV, NIV). The latter seems preferable because Paul uses the term again in v. 8 when he speaks of exercising faith, love, and hope. Wanamaker says, "Watchfulness without such self-control would prove fruitless since readiness for the day of the Lord means moral and religious readiness for the judgment of God."

5:7a–b Proposition 7a begins with γάρ 'for'. Commentators who discuss the relation of v. 7 to the context have various views. It has been called an illustration (Frame), explanation (Williams), basis (Marshall, p. 138), and confirmation (Hiebert) of the previous exhortation. Wanamaker characterizes v. 7 as an interruption to clarify and drive home the point of v. 6 before the exhortation is resumed in v. 8 (so also Marshall). Verse 7 appears to be an amplification of 6a at least. Paul uses καθεύδω 'to sleep' in both 6a and 7a. In v. 7 he adds μεθύσκω 'to become intoxicated' (which corresponds to νήφω 'to be sober' in 6c) and emphasizes the concept of 'night' as the time of improper behavior. Thus v. 7 amplifies and supports Paul's exhortation in 6a–c. It also sets the stage for the contrast with 'day' in 8a. Because 7a and b are amplification propositions the conjunction γάρ 'for' is not rendered explicitly in the display (as in CEV, JBP, NAB, NCV, NJB, NLT, REB, TEV, and TNT).

People who sleep are *unaware* at night, and people who become intoxicated are *not self-controlled* at night Here Paul states what appears to be a truism: οἱ γὰρ καθεύδοντες νυκτὸς καθεύδουσιν καὶ οἱ μεθυσκόμενοι νυκτὸς μεθύουσιν 'for the (ones) sleeping at night sleep and the (ones) being drunk at night are drunk'. It is possible that these two clauses are merely factual statements (Bruce, Frame, Morris). However, Paul emphasizes the adverbial 'at night' by placing it before the finite verb in each clause (Frame, p. 179). (This emphasis is brought out in JBP, NJB, NLT, and TEV.) Thus it seems that he has firmly in mind the metaphors he has already used: night (5b), being asleep or awake (6a–c), and being sober (6c). And he sets up a contrast with the metaphor 'day' in 8a. All of this supports the understanding that v. 7 is "a figurative underscoring of the exhortation in v. 6" (Wanamaker). Best and Marshall agree.

The participles in the Greek clauses are rendered literally in the display ('sleep', 'become intoxicated'), and the finite verbs figuratively ('are unaware', 'not self-controlled'). The words 'at night' are in bold type in the display to indicate the emphasis in the Greek. NJB renders this emphasis effectively and gives a hint that 'sleep' is figurative: "Night is the time for sleepers to sleep and night the time for drunkards to be drunk. . . ."

5:8a But *since* we(inc) *believers* are people *who do what is right as people usually do when it is* daytime The Greek is ἡμεῖς δὲ ἡμέρας ὄντες 'but we being of day'. The conjunction δέ 'but' with the fronted pronoun 'we' and the fronted genitive 'of day' indicates a contrast and change of topic, from unbelievers who sleep and drink 'at night' to believers who are 'of day'. Coming before the finite verb νήφωμεν 'let us be sober', the words establish a minor break in the discourse similar to that at 4a. Verse 8 therefore constitutes a new sub-unit; it is taken as an amplification of Paul's exhortation in vv. 6–7 since the verb νήφω 'be sober' is repeated from 6c and expanded upon.

The participle ὄντες 'being' has been translated as identification (JBP, KJV, NAB, NLT, REB, TNT); REB has "but we, who belong to the daylight, must keep sober." The identification seems to function, however, as grounds for the following exhortation (Best, Frame, Marshall, Morris; CEV, NCV, NIV, NRSV): since we are people of day we must be self-controlled, as sober people are in the daytime.

There is nothing in the context to indicate that the metaphorical phrase 'of day' has a different meaning from 'sons of day' in 5a (see the note there), and thus it is rendered in the same way here.

5:8b we(inc) must be *self-controlled as sober people in the daytime are self-controlled* The verb νήφωμεν 'let us be sober' is most likely used metaphorically as it was in 6c (see the note there). Because of the close proximity of 'day' in 8a, Paul may have had in mind that sobriety is expected behavior during the daytime; those who "carouse in broad daylight" (2 Pet. 2:13, NIV) are notoriously evil.

5:8c–f *Specifically, as a soldier protects himself by* putting on a breastplate and a helmet, *we(inc) must protect ourselves from doing wrong* The finite verb 'let us be sober' in 8b is modified by a participial phrase: ἐνδυσάμενοι θώρακα πίστεως καὶ ἀγάπης καὶ περικεφαλαίαν ἐλπίδα σωτηρίας 'having put on a breastplate of faith and of love and a helmet (which is) hope of salvation'. The reference to putting on a breastplate and helmet is metaphorical, the topic of which is believers who trust, love, and hope. The image is a soldier's armor. The ground of comparison is protection (Bruce, Wanamaker; NCV, NLT): believers need to protect themselves from doing wrong and thus being judged just as a soldier protects himself by equipping himself with armor. Bruce says, "In this hope, with faith and love, the believer is equipped with all necessary protection against the judgment to be unleashed on the Day of the Lord." An alternative view is that the protection is from the forces of evil, as in Eph. 6:11 (Frame, Hiebert). Some understand the image to be a soldier on guard and the ground of comparison as vigilance or watchfulness (Best, Marshall, Morris). However, in that case Paul would need only to have mentioned a soldier, not the protective pieces of armor, which elsewhere are associated with righteous actions. In Rom. 13:12 putting on the armor of light is the counterpart of putting aside the deeds of darkness.

The metaphor probably has its origins in Isa. 59:17: the LORD "put on righteousness as his breastplate, and the helmet of salvation on his head. . . ." (NIV). This speaks of the Lord's arming himself for battle against the ungodly, as he also will on the day mentioned in 1 Thess. 5:2-10. In the Thessalonians passage, however, the metaphor is applied to the actions of believers.

The participle ἐνδυσάμενοι 'having put on' is in the aorist tense, which could indicate action prior to that of the main verb (Wanamaker). This could point to a previous exercising of faith, love, and hope, perhaps at conversion. However, for Isa. 59:17 the LXX uses the aorist tense, as does Paul whenever he metaphorically speaks of putting on armor or clothing. In Rom. 13:12 'to put on' is an aorist subjunctive exhortation, and here as well the aorist participle seems to indicate an exhortation coincident with 'let us be sober' in 8b (Best, Frame, Marshall). Therefore, in the display 'let us be sober' is taken as a GENERIC exhortation, elucidated by the specific 'put on faith, love, and hope' (8c–f). Alternatively, the metaphor of putting on armor, together with the nouns 'faith', 'love', and 'hope', speaks of behavior, so 8c–f could instead be understood as the means by which believers can live self-controlled lives (Best). By continuing to exercise these virtues, believers will be self-controlled (sober).

by* continuing to trust *in God* and . . . *by* continuing to love *others* and . . . *by* continuing to confidently expect that *the Lord Jesus* will save *us believers from God's punishing us at the time he will punish people The nouns 'faith', 'love', and 'hope' represent events and undergoers and are rendered as verbal phrases in the display. In 1:3 Paul expressed his thankfulness to God for these virtues in the lives of the Thessalonians: trust in God, love for other people, and confident expectation that the Lord Jesus would deliver them from God's punishment. It is not that Paul is exhorting the Thessalonians to begin to believe, love, and hope (as at conversion); rather, he is exhorting them to continue to do so (Marshall, Wanamaker). The undergoer of 'faith' could be God, Christ, or both; but in this SSA 'faith' is consistently rendered as 'trust in God' unless 'Christ' is explicit in the context. The undergoer of 'love' could be believers, people in general, God, or a combination of these. There is no contextual reason to consider the implied objects to be any other than those proposed in 1:3 (see the note there).

Best points out that Paul emphasizes hope by setting it apart with its own piece of armor (faith and love together are associated with the breastplate) and by mentioning it last. This is particularly appropriate in 5:1-8 where the day of the Lord in is view: 'hope' has as its object a future 'salvation'. This salvation is freedom from God's wrath and fellowship with Christ (Frame). In the context of 5:1-8 and of the epistle as a whole (see 1:10, 2:16, 5:9-10) salvation from God's wrath is most likely deliverance from the punishment which accompanies the day of the Lord, to be experienced by the people of night and darkness.

BOUNDARIES AND COHERENCE

The initial boundary of 5:1-8 was discussed under 4:13-18 (see "Boundaries"). The terminal boundary is considered to occur between 5:8 and 5:9, since Paul closes v. 8 with the word σωτηρία 'salvation' and uses it again in v. 9. The twofold reference to salvation appears to function as a tail-head linkage, indicating a boundary. Paul thus introduces and then develops a new subject. (These are the only occurrences of σωτηρία 'salvation' in this epistle.) A boundary before vv. 9-11 is also justified by the change of intent and verb mood. In 5:1-8 Paul's intent is to affect behavior, and he uses imperatival subjunctives in vv. 6-8. In 5:9-11 his intent is to affect emotions, and he switches to imperative verbs in v. 11. The grammatical structure and content of 5:10b-11a are very similar to 4:17d-18, where his intent is the same—to affect the emotions of his readers. CEV, EHP, and NBV place a boundary between 5:8 and 5:9. Other versions do not, perhaps because v. 9 begins with the subordinating conjunction ὅτι 'because, for', which rarely initiates a new unit. (But see 1 John 3:11 in UBSGNT, where ὅτι begins a new section.) Discontinuity between 5:8 and 5:9 is recognized by UBSGNT, which ends v. 8 with a colon, and by MJTGNT, which ends it with a period.

CEV, NIV, and NJB place a boundary between 5:3 and 5:4. They do this perhaps because of the new, fronted topic 'you' and the vocative 'brothers' in v. 4. These features do establish a minor break in the discourse (see the note on 4a). However, a paragraph break at this point would separate the *trust basis* from the APPEAL and leave vv. 1-3 with an incomplete paragraph pattern. Thus a break does not seem justified.

The day of the Lord (2c, 4b) is a central concept in 5:1-8. A number of contrasts arising from that concept bring strong referential coherence to the unit: 'day' (5a, 8a) and 'night' (2d, 5b, 7a, 7b); 'light' (5a) and 'dark' (4a, 5b); 'become drunk' and 'be drunk' (both in 7b) and 'be sober' (6c, 8b); 'sleep' (6a, 7a) and 'be awake' (6c); 'disaster' (3b) versus 'peace' (3a), 'safety' (3a), and 'salvation' (8f). There is also the contrast between unbelievers, 'the rest' in 6b, and believers, who are referred to as 'brothers' (1, 4a), 'you' (4a, 4b, 5a), or 'we' (8a).

Relational coherence is established by ἄρα οὖν 'therefore' in 6a, which ties the APPEAL to the preceding *trust basis* and *axiomatic basis*.

PROMINENCE AND THEME

The naturally prominent constituent of 5:1-8 is the APPEAL.

The contrast between unbelievers and believers is given prominence by means of the extended metaphors and numerous contrasting terms. This contrast is developed and is most marked in the *axiomatic basis* (4a-5b).

The theme for the paragraph is derived from the prominent propositions of the *axiomatic basis* (that is, from 4a-c) and from the NUCLEUS (6c) of the APPEAL. The idea of 'unexpectedly' in 4b-c is stated in terms of unpreparedness (the alternative for 'unexpectedly' in 2c), because unpreparedness better captures the implication of the 'thief' simile. Also, 6c is conveyed nonfiguratively. Although Paul changes his referent for believers from 'you' in 5a to 'we' in 5b, this is handled uniformly in the theme as 'we believers' and 'we'.

SUBSECTION CONSTITUENT 5:9-11
(Expressive Paragraph: Nucleus₃ of 4:13–5:11)

THEME: God has destined us believers to be saved from being punished in the future and to be able to live together with our Lord Jesus after he returns. Since this is true, encourage each other.

¶ PTRN	RELATIONAL STRUCTURE			CONTENTS
belief	RESULT	POSITIVE	negative	5:9a God did not destine us(inc) to *be people whom he will* punish [MTY].
				5:9b On the contrary, *he destined us to be saved (or, to obtain his saving) from being punished in the future*
	means	SPECIFIC MEANS	generic	5:9c by means of *what our(inc) Lord Jesus Christ has done for us.*
				5:10a *Specifically, Jesus* died *to benefit* us(inc) (*or, to atone* for our *sins*)
			purpose	5:10b in order that whether we(inc) are alive or whether we(inc) are dead [EUP] *when he returns to earth,* we(inc) might be able to live together with him.
CONTROL	NUCLEUS	NUCLEUS		5:11a Since *this* [9a-10b] *is true*, encourage/comfort each other;
		equivalent		5:11b *that is*, help each other *to remember what I have written* [9a-10b],
	comparison			5:11c as indeed you are doing.

INTENT AND PARAGRAPH PATTERN

Paul's intent in the 5:9-11 paragraph is to affect the emotions of his readers. This is clear from the exhortation in 11a-b: διὸ παρακαλεῖτε ἀλλήλους καὶ οἰκοδομεῖτε εἰς τὸν ἕνα 'therefore encourage/comfort one another and build up one the other'. The grounds for the exhortation are emotionally encouraging and comforting: God did not destine us to suffer wrath but to obtain salvation through our Lord Jesus (9a-b), who died for us (10a); and when he returns, believers who are still alive and those have died will live together with him (10b). The genre of 5:9-11 is emotive, and of the expressive type since Paul develops his thought with a grounds-exhortation relation rather than a sequential relation.

The paragraph consists of two propositional clusters, 9a-10b and 11a-c. The second begins with διό 'therefore', which indicates that it is in a grounds-exhortation relation with the preceding cluster. Since Paul does not present an emotional problem, the paragraph pattern is not the solutionality subtype, as was 4:13-18. Instead, Paul intentionally directs the Thessalonians' attention to truths with which they can encourage and comfort each other; the control of their grief or fear is made possible by the true beliefs he presents in 9a-10b. Therefore this is the volitionality subtype. The constituents of a volitionality subtype of expressive paragraph pattern are labeled *belief* and *CONTROL*.

NOTES

5:9a Verse 9 begins with the subordinating conjunction ὅτι 'for'. Some understand it to introduce grounds for 8f (Best, Frame, Marshall): we are to continue to confidently expect that the Lord Jesus will save us since God did not destine us to be people whom he will punish but people whom he will save. Alternatively, Wanamaker takes the conjunction as introducing the grounds for Paul's exhortations in vv. 6-8: we must be alert and self-controlled since God did not destine us to be people he will punish. The MJTGNT places a period before the conjunction, and the UBSGNT, a colon. This seems to indicate very loose subordination (see BAGD, p. 589.3b). In 9b Paul repeats the word σωτηρία 'salvation', with which he closed 8f. The twofold reference to salvation appears to function as a tail-head linkage. This linkage, together with Paul's development of the 'hope of salvation' theme in 9-10 (which is different from the exhortation to vigilant and sober behavior in 6-8), indicates discontinuity in the discourse. It indicates that 9-10 functions as more than grounds for what precedes. In fact, vv. 9-11 are best considered a separate unit (see "Boundaries" under 5:1-8). The ὅτι 'for' is not rendered in the display, nor in CEV, NAB, NCV, NJB, REB, TEV.

God did not destine us(inc) to *be people whom he will* punish The Greek is οὐκ ἔθετο ὑμᾶς ὁ θεὸς εἰς ὀργήν 'God did not destine us for wrath'. Though the verb τίθημι, which means "*destine* or *appoint someone to* or *for something*" (BAGD, p. 816.I2b), occurs only here in this letter, it is consistent with other words that speak of God's divinely choosing (1:4), calling (2:12; 4:7; 5:24), and destining (3:3) believers. The word ὀργή 'wrath' occurs here (also in 1:10 and 2:16). As in its two earlier occurrences it is a metonymy standing for punishment (see the note on 1:10c). In the OT the day of the Lord (mentioned in 5:2, 4) is a time when God punishes disobedience and brings destruction (Zeph. 1:14-15; Joel 1:15).

This verse continues the negative-positive alternation of 5:1-8 between people of night/darkness and people of day/light. Here the focus is on the contrasting destinies of both groups (Frame, Wanamaker): God has not destined the Thessalonians to be in the group of people living in darkness whom he will punish, but in the group of people he will save. The punishment Paul has in mind could be eternal; it contrasts with living together with Jesus after his return (10b), which in turn brings to mind the statement in 4:17d that believers shall be with the Lord *forever*.

5:9b-c On the contrary, *he destined us* to be saved (*or, to obtain his saving*) *from being punished in the future* by means of *what* our(inc) Lord Jesus Christ *has done for us* The Greek is ἀλλὰ εἰς περιποίησιν σωτηρίας διὰ τοῦ κυρίου ἡμῶν Ἰησοῦ Χριστοῦ 'but for obtaining of salvation through our Lord Jesus Christ'. The conjunction ἀλλά 'but' introduces the POSITIVE counterpart to 9a. There is an ellipsis in the Greek; the words 'he destined us(inc)' from 9a are implied.

The two nouns in the phrase 'obtaining of salvation' both represent events and are rendered as such in the display. The first, περιποίησις, means "*gaining, obtaining*" (BAGD, p. 650.2). The second, σωτηρία 'salvation', can mean the future state of salvation (Marshall) or both present life in Christ and future life with Christ (Bruce). Marshall's view seems preferable because the reference to 'salvation' here was occasioned by 'hope of salvation' in 8f, and 'hope' indicates something as yet unrealized. In 5:1-11 salvation is viewed as a process, something yet to be obtained because it is an object of hope (Wanamaker). Although believers do not earn salvation, since it is graciously provided by means of Jesus' atoning death (9b-10b), they do, according to Paul, work together with God toward *obtaining* that salvation (Frame), for example, by being alert and self-controlled (6c) and continuing in faith and love and hope (8d-f). They live lives worthy of God's calling (2:12; 4:7) through his enabling (5:23-24). "Paul does not simply say 'God has destined us for salvation', because he wants to bring out the need for Christians to play their part in receiving salvation" (Marshall). The same idea of believers, together with God, working their salvation out through obedience is in Phil. 2:12-13: "Therefore, my dear friends, as you have always obeyed . . . continue to work out your salvation with fear and trembling, for it is God who works in you to will and to act according to his good purpose" (NIV). Here in 9b the primary aspect of salvation is the avoidance of God's wrath (Wanamaker); this is rendered 'from being punished in the future'.

The phrase 'through our Lord Jesus Christ' states the means by which believers obtain the salvation mentioned in 9b (Bruce, Frame, Wanamaker). One implicit aspect of this means is obviously the death of Christ for them, which Paul makes specific in 10a. Another could be Christ's indwelling activity (Frame): they obtain that salvation by means of (διά) Christ's acting in them to do now what pleases him and later to guarantee their resurrection from the dead. Hendriksen says it is both by the death of Christ for believers and his power operating in them that they are able to obtain this salvation. This interpretation is appropriate in that it relates the means phrase to both nouns in the phrase περιποίησιν σωτηρίας 'obtaining of salvation'.

5:10a *Specifically, Jesus* died *to benefit* us(inc) (*or, to atone* for our *sins*) Verse 10 begins with a relative clause that may have come from an early Christian formula about Christ (Bruce, Wanamaker). It gives one specific explanation of 'by means of our Lord Jesus Christ' in 9b (Marshall, Wanamaker). The Greek is τοῦ ἀποθανόντος ὑπὲρ ἡμῶν 'the (one) having died for us'. Some mss. have the preposition περί 'for, concerning' instead of ὑπέρ 'for'. This variant περί is not mentioned in MJTGNT or UBSGNT. But even if it had sufficient support to make it an option, the variation is probably inconsequential as there is no significant difference of meaning (Best,

Frame, Marshall). The preposition ὑπέρ indicates that Jesus died for the benefit of, or on behalf of, believers (Bruce, Marshall, Wanamaker). It could mean he died as an atonement for their sins (Frame) or that he died as a substitute in their place (Hiebert). But the usage here probably does not specifically refer to the full-fledged doctrine of substitutionary atonement (Wanamaker).

5:10b in order that whether we(inc) are alive or whether we(inc) are dead *when he returns to earth*, we(inc) might be able to live together with him The statement here on the purpose of Christ's death is introduced by ἵνα 'in order that' (Bruce, Frame, Marshall, Wanamaker). This is followed by two conditional clauses, each beginning with the particle εἴτε 'if, whether'.

The verbs in the 'if' clauses are γρηγορέω 'to be awake' and καθεύδω 'to sleep'. Earlier in this chapter Paul used these verbs metaphorically to mean 'be vigilant' (6c) and 'be unaware' (6a). Thomas takes them to mean the same here as well: whether we believers are watching for the Lord's coming or are unprepared. However, it seems strange that in a passage in which Paul exhorts believers to be vigilant and prepared for the Lord's coming he would allow for the possibility that they needn't be. Bruce says, "It is ludicrous to suppose that the writers mean, 'Whether you live like sons of light or like sons of darkness, it will make little difference: you will be all right in the end.'" Thus it is more likely that καθεύδω 'to sleep' here is a euphemism for death, as its synonym κοιμάω is in 4:14b, and that γρηγορέω 'to be awake' is being used in the unusual sense of being physically alive (Best, Bruce, Frame, Marshall, Morris, Wanamaker; NCV, TEV). This interpretation is confirmed by the close correspondence of the last phrase in v. 10, ἅμα σὺν αὐτῷ ζήσωμεν 'together with him we will live', with 4:17d, πάντοτε σὺν κυρίῳ ἐσόμεθα 'always with (the) Lord we shall be'. The words 'together with him' are fronted in v. 10 as are the words 'always with (the) Lord' in 4:17d, making the correspondence more striking. The context of 4:17d makes clear that the dead in Christ who will be raised and the believers who are still alive at his return will come together to be with the Lord Jesus for eternity. The verbs here in v. 10, καθεύδω 'to sleep' and γρηγορέω 'to be awake', are to be taken in the same sense as κοιμάω 'to sleep' and ζάω 'to live' in the corresponding passage: they mean 'physical death' and 'physical life' respectively.

The auxiliary of the subjunctive verb ζήσωμεν 'we may live' is variously rendered as 'may' (NIV, NRSV), 'can' (NCV, NLT), 'could' (CEV), 'might' (NAB, REB, TEV, TNT), and 'should' (KJV, NJB). In the display it is 'might be able to'. The bound pronoun 'we' of the Greek verb could be taken to mean 'we, both living and dead believers together' (Frame; NAB), this being implicit in 4:17. However, that idea is much more obvious from the context of 4:15-18 than here. The phrase here (σὺν αὐτῷ ζήσωμεν 'we may live together with him') primarily makes clear that the salvation Paul speaks of in 8f and 9b involves living together with Christ after his return (Bruce, Frame, Marshall, Wanamaker). Some take 'live together' as referring to the believer's fellowship with Christ in this life as well as the future (Morris; JBP), but this seems unlikely considering the similarity of this clause with the one in 4:17 (which is in the context of a discussion of the Lord's return) and in view of the references to 'the day of the Lord' in 5:2 and 5:4. In the display (as in CEV, NCV, TEV) a phrase about the time when the Lord Jesus returns to earth is supplied.

5:11a-b Since *this* [9a-10b] *is true*, encourage/ comfort each other; *that is*, help each other *to remember what I have written* [9a-10b] Verse 11 is an exhortation that begins with the inferential conjunction διό 'therefore', which functions to join 11a-c to 9a-10b in a grounds-exhortation relation. The *CONTROL* of the Thessalonians' grief is grounded in the *belief* Paul expresses in 9a-10b.

The first verb of the exhortation, παρακαλέω, probably means 'to encourage, cheer up' as it does in 4:18 (see the note on this verb there). The words in 4:17d (immediately preceding 4:18) are πάντοτε σὺν κυρίῳ ἐσόμεθα 'always with the Lord we shall be'; the words that immediately precede 5:11 are similar: ἅμα σὺν αὐτῷ ζήσωμεν 'together with him (our Lord Jesus Christ) we may live'. This idea of believers—those living as well as those who have died before Christ's return—being together with the Lord is encouragement and comfort that the Thessalonians can give to each other.

In 11b Paul adds a second verb, οἰκοδομέω 'to strengthen, to edify'. This seems to be a verb that requires context to provide the element that is in process of being strengthened or built up, as suggested by Louw and Nida's definition, "to in- crease the potential of someone or something, with focus upon the process involved" (74.15). In this context in which Paul's intent is to affect the emotions of his readers, the element to be strengthened is most likely the Thessalonians' assurance of the hope presented in vv. 9–10 (see CEV). Frame, Morris, and Wanamaker understand the exhortation of v. 11 to relate to much if not all of what precedes in 5:1–10, and that is possible as well. This second verb of the exhortation clarifies or amplifies the first verb (παρακαλέω 'to encourage, cheer up'), according to Wanamaker. Thus the relation of equivalence is indicated in the display, and it is rendered 'help each other to remember what I have written'.

Marshall, Best, and Morris understand οἰκοδομέω 'to strengthen, to edify' to be a live metaphor in v. 11. Its basic meaning is 'to build, erect'. In this case the topic is believers; the image, erecting a building. The ground of comparison is growth and stability of the sort that is common to a building under construction and a community of believers who are edifying each other. However, there is no indication in the context that this is a live metaphor (as for example in 1 Pet. 2:5). Paul is probably using it "without any consciousness of its basic [meaning]" (BAGD, p. 558.3); in other words, it is a dead metaphor here.

With each of the verbs of 11a and b Paul uses an expression meaning 'each other': ἀλλήλους 'one another' with the first and εἷς τὸν ἕνα 'one the one' with the second. The latter expression is very unusual, but it does not seem to differ greatly in meaning from the former (Best, Morris).

5:11c as indeed you are doing The conjunction καθώς introduces a comparison proposition, by which Paul affirms the Thessalonians for the encouragement they are already giving each other.

BOUNDARIES AND COHERENCE

The initial boundary of 5:9–11 was discussed under 5:1–8, and the terminal boundary under 4:3–5:11. (See "Boundaries.")

The concept of σωτηρία 'salvation' is central and brings referential coherence to 5:9–11. It is what God plans for believers, not his contrasting ὀργή 'wrath' (9a–b). Salvation was accomplished through the death of Christ (9c–10a) in order that believers may live together with him after he returns to earth (10b). Believers are referred to by pronouns in each of the verses; Christ is referred to in vv. 9 and 10. These references also lend coherence.

Relational coherence is established by διό 'therefore', which ties the exhortative CONTROL in v. 11 to the *belief* that Paul expresses in vv. 9–10.

PROMINENCE AND THEME

The naturally prominent constituent of 5:9–11 is the CONTROL (11a–c). Its NUCLEUS (11a) and the purpose proposition (10b) of the *belief* are also prominent on a higher discourse level because 10b–11a is parallel to and almost identical with Paul's statements in 4:17d–18. The repetition emphasizes the key truth with which the Thessalonians are to encourage and comfort each other.

The paragraph's theme is derived from the prominent proposition (9b) of the *belief* and the NUCLEUS (11a) of the CONTROL. Also included is the 10b purpose proposition because of its key function in the total discourse.

DIVISION CONSTITUENT 5:12–22
(Hortatory Section: General Appeal of 4:1–5:24)

THEME: Highly esteem and love the leaders who care for and instruct you. Warn believers who will not work, and encourage and help those who need it. Be patient with all people and do good deeds to them all. Always rejoice, pray, and thank God. Evaluate all messages that people claim the Holy Spirit gave them. Accept authentic messages and obey them.

MACROSTRUCTURE	CONTENTS
GENERAL APPEAL₁	5:12–15 Highly esteem and love the leaders who care for and instruct you. Warn believers who will not work, and encourage and help those who need it. Be patient with all people and do good deeds to them all.
GENERAL APPEAL₂	5:16–22 Always rejoice, pray, and thank God. Evaluate all messages that people claim the Holy Spirit gave them. Accept authentic messages and obey them.

INTENT AND MACROSTRUCTURE

In the 5:12–22 section Paul appeals to the Thessalonians to do a number of things which will help them live together as fellow believers and grow strong in their individual Christian lives. Therefore the genre is hortatory.

The section consists of two conjoined subsections, 5:12–15 and 5:16–22. Each subsection deals with different issues, all of which seem equally important or prominent. Thus both labels are in uppercase letters in the display.

BOUNDARIES AND COHERENCE

The initial boundary of 5:12–22 was discussed under 4:3–5:11 (see "Boundaries"). The terminal boundary is between 5:22 and 5:23, and this is a well-established boundary. Paul switches from numerous infinitives and imperatives expressing appeals in vv. 12–22 to the optative mood in v. 23, where he expresses a wish-prayer for the Thessalonians. At the beginning of v. 23 is the phrase αὐτὸς δὲ ὁ θεὸς τῆς εἰρήνης 'now the God of peace himself' as a point of departure for the new unit, 5:23–24.

The two orienters, two infinitives, and seven imperatives of 5:12–15 and the eight imperatives of 5:16–22 create strong relational coherence between the section's two subsections.

PROMINENCE AND THEME

The two subsections of 5:12–22 deal with different subjects, Christian community relationships and personal piety, but they appear to be of equal prominence. Thus the theme of 5:12–22 is a combination of the themes of both its constituents.

SECTION CONSTITUENT 5:12–15
(Hortatory Subsection: General Appeal₁ of 5:12–22)

THEME: Highly esteem and love the leaders who care for and instruct you. Warn believers who will not work, and encourage and help those who need it. Be patient with all people and do good deeds to them all.

MACROSTRUCTURE	CONTENTS
APPEAL₁	5:12–13 Recognize as leaders those people who care for and instruct you; highly esteem and love them. Live peacefully with each other.
APPEAL₂	5:14–15 Warn believers who will not work, and encourage and help those who need it. Be patient with all people. Do good deeds to them all, including those who do evil deeds to you.

INTENT AND MACROSTRUCTURE

Paul's intent in the 5:12–15 subsection is to affect behavior. He urges proper social relationships and ministry within the fellowship of Thessalonian believers in order that the body grow and mature. The believers are to esteem and love those who perform ministry functions. They are to admonish believers who are not behaving properly. They are to encourage and help those who need it. They are to be patient with each other and not retaliate when wronged, not even when wronged by unbelievers. Thus the genre is hortatory.

The subsection consists of two conjoined paragraphs, 5:12–13 and 5:14–15.

BOUNDARIES AND COHERENCE

The initial boundary of 5:12–15 was discussed under 4:3–5:11 (see "Boundaries"). Its terminal boundary is between 5:15 and 5:16. This is marked by a change of grammatical style in the next unit (5:16–22), even though the general exhortations continue. In 12–15 the commands are related to two orienters (at 12a and 14a) and the orienters and the majority of exhortation verbs are clause initial. But in 16–22 there are no orienters and the verbs are all clause final. There is also a difference in referential content between the two units. In 12–15 Paul commands the believers in regard to their relationships with their leaders, with each other, and with outsiders. In 16–22 he exhorts them with respect to personal worship, such things as prayer, giving thanks, and allowing the Spirit to minister in and to them. Because of these differences of grammar and content, a boundary between 5:15 and 5:16 is justified. CEV, GHL, NAB, NCV, NIV, REB, TEV, UBSGNT, and WFB all place a boundary at this point.

Parallel propositions begin each of the two paragraphs of the 5:12–15 subsection, which brings strong referential and relational coherence:

ἐρωτῶμεν δὲ ὑμᾶς, ἀδελφοί
'now we ask you, brothers' (in 12a)

παρακαλοῦμεν δὲ ὑμᾶς, ἀδελφοί
'now we urge you, brothers' (in 14a)

The parallelism is noteworthy because the verbal orienters are synonyms and were used together in 4:1c.

The concept of ministry to others brings referential coherence as well. Believers are to live peacefully 'with each other' (13c), to be patient 'with all' (14e), and to do good 'to each other' and 'to all (others)' (15b). Referential coherence is also fostered by the following related ideas: those who work hard (12b–c, 13b) and those who will not work (14b); those who care for others (12d) and those who need to be cared for (14c, 14d); being at peace with each other (13c), being patient with all (14e), and doing good to each other and to all (15b).

PROMINENCE AND THEME

The two constituent units of 5:12–15 are equally prominent due to their parallel structure: the initial propositions (12a, 14a) of each of them have identical vocatives and synonymous orienters.

The theme of 5:12–15 is derived from the themes of the constituent paragraphs.

SUBSECTION CONSTITUENT 5:12–13
(Hortatory Paragraph: Appeal₁ of 5:12–15)

THEME: Recognize as leaders those people who care for and instruct you; highly esteem and love them. Live peacefully with each other.

¶ PTRN	RELATIONAL STRUCTURE	CONTENTS
APPEAL₁	NUCLEUS₁ — orienter	5:12a Fellow believers, I(&S&T) ask
	NUCLEUS₁ — 'those'	5:12b that you recognize *as leaders/valuable* those *people*
	identification — generic	5:12c who work hard for you,
	identification — SPECIFIC — NUCLEUS₁	5:12d *specifically*, who care for (*or*, lead) you *as fellow believers united* to *the* Lord *Jesus*
	identification — SPECIFIC — NUCLEUS₂	5:12e and who warn you *to stop doing wrong* (*or*, who instruct you *to do what is right*).
	NUCLEUS₂ — EXHORTATION	5:13a And (*or*, That is,) I(&S&T) ask that you consider those people great and love them
	grounds	5:13b since they work *hard to help you*.
APPEAL₂		5:13c Live peacefully with each other.

INTENT AND PARAGRAPH PATTERN

In the 5:12–13 paragraph Paul's intent is to affect behavior. He wants to strengthen relationships among the believers in Thessalonica. Therefore he exhorts them to recognize and highly esteem those who care for and instruct them, and he exhorts them to live in harmony with each other. Thus the genre is hortatory.

The paragraph consists of a propositional cluster (12a–13b) and a conjoined proposition (13c). Because the relation between 13a and 13b is a simple exhortation-grounds relation this is a causality subtype of paragraph pattern. The constituents of the causality subtype of hortatory paragraph pattern are labeled *basis* and APPEAL. Here no *basis* label appears in the display. However, a secondary function of the 12c–e identification propositions is as axiomatic basis for the 12a–b APPEAL. Likewise, the 13b grounds proposition functions as an axiomatic basis for the 13a exhortation. The implicit basis for the second APPEAL (13c) is the relationship that Paul had with the Thessalonians as the one who brought the gospel to them.

NOTES

5:12a Fellow believers, I(&S&T) ask A new series of APPEALS is introduced with the vocative 'brothers' and the conjunction δέ 'now'. The δέ indicates Paul's intent to develop the discourse by building on what has preceded (Frame). There is no obvious contrast in the context which would justify translating δέ as 'but' as in NASB, RSV, and NRSV. The δέ is not translated in the display, as is the case in previous units where it functions as a high-level marker (see the note on 2:17a). The orienter verb ἐρωτῶμεν 'we ask' here in 12a is the same as the one used in 4:1b, where it occurred together with παρακαλοῦμεν 'we urge' (see the note there). The latter verb occurs in the initial proposition of the paragraph that follows this one.

5:12b that you recognize *as leaders/valuable* those *people* The first content cluster (12b–e) of the orienter 'we ask' (in 12a) begins with ὑμᾶς εἰδέναι 'you to know'. Some understand the verb οἶδα here to mean 'to respect, appreciate the worth of' (Best, Bruce, Frame, Louw and Nida 87.12, Marshall, Morris; NAB, NCV, NIV, NRSV, TEV, TNT). A modification of this meaning is "to be considerate to" (NJB) or "to be thoughtful of" (CEV). But since Paul uses a construction in the next verse (13a) that most likely means 'to respect' or 'esteem', it would be a tautology if 'respect' were the meaning here also. The verb οἶδα was used in 4:4a with the meaning 'to know how'. Here it is possible that Paul tells the Thessalonians 'to know' in the sense of 'recognize as their leaders' those people who work hard among them (Bruce, p. 120; Wanamaker; possibly JBP, REB); later in 13a he will tell them to think highly of such people. Wanamaker proposes that certain people who had means and ability stepped forward to work for, protect, and care for the group of believers, and also to admonish them. Paul is telling the Thessalonians to recognize the part such people play in their group. Wanamaker feels that such recognition probably implies obedience to them as well, and this view has merit. Because the first view, that οἶδα means 'to respect, to appreciate', is more widely accepted, both are represented in the display.

5:12c who work hard for you Paul identifies the people the Thessalonians should recognize by a series of three participial phrases, all linked to a single article. Thus it is one group of individuals that do the three things (Bruce, Wanamaker, Frame), not three separate groups. The first of these phrases is τοὺς κοπιῶντας ἐν ὑμῖν 'those who work hard among you'. The verb κοπιάω 'to work hard' can refer to physical labor (see the cognate noun in 2:9a); here, however, it probably is speaking of hard work in ministry. (The cognate noun may have this meaning in the phrase 'labor of love' in 1:3. Paul often applied the concept to his own spiritual ministry as in 1 Cor. 15:10 and Phil. 2:16.) This view is supported by the prepositional phrase 'in/among you', which indicates the sphere of the labor (Frame). These people performed this work within the fellowship and to meet the needs of believers in Thessalonica (Wanamaker). That it is spiritual work is also made clear in the subsequent propositions. The display follows EHP, which has "who work so hard for you."

5:12d *specifically*, who care for (*or*, lead) you *as fellow believers united* to the Lord *Jesus* The phrase προϊσταμένους ὑμῶν ἐν κυρίῳ 'caring for, or directing, you in (the) Lord' is preceded by the conjunction καί 'and', just as in the following phrase in 12e. The series of phrases can be viewed as conjoined (Bruce, Wanamaker; NIV, REB, TNT), with each describing a different activity. This relation would be especially appropriate if the focus of κοπιάω in 12c is on working *hard*, the noteworthy *effort* of their labor. On the other hand, 'work' has a more general meaning than 'lead', 'care for', and 'admonish' (Best, Frame, Morris; NAB, NJB). Therefore, 12d and 12e are labeled SPECIFICS of 12c: who work hard, specifically, who care for and admonish you.

Some say the verb προΐστημι primarily means 'to lead, direct' (Frame, Louw and Nida 36.1, Marshall, Morris; KJV, NAB, NCV, NIV, NJB, NRSV, REB, TEV, TNT). Others say it means 'to care for' (Best, Bruce, Wanamaker). BAGD (p. 707.1 and 2) list both meanings as possible. The verb, which is not an official designation of a leader, combines the ideas of leading and protecting and caring for (Bruce, Frame, Marshall, Wanamaker). In the pastoral Epistles it is used of managing or caring for one's household (1 Tim. 3:4, 5, 12), of devoting oneself to doing good (Titus 3:8, 14), and of elders performing their duties well (1 Tim. 5:17). The meaning 'to provide for, especially in a material way,' has merit. In a list of spiritual gifts in Rom. 12:8, this verb comes next to last, between contributing to the needs of others and showing mercy, not at the beginning of the list where leadership gifts of prophesying, serving, and teaching are mentioned. Paul uses the cognate noun προστάτις to describe Phoebe as one who "has been a great help to many people, including me" (Rom. 16:2, NIV). Stephanas (1 Cor. 16:15–18) may have been such a patron for the church at Corinth (Wanamaker). People with means helped to care for the needs of poorer believers in a congregation. This would have given them status and authority. The second meaning, 'to care for', has excellent support from passages outside 1 Thessalonians, but all versions render it here with the first meaning, 'to lead'. Therefore, both are given as alternatives in the display.

The phrase 'in the Lord' could indicate authority if the preceding verb primarily means 'lead' (Frame; Hale, p. 47; Marshall; Morris). NAB has "whose task is to exercise authority in the Lord." However, because the verb seems to connote the kind of leadership that cares for or provides for others, a different understanding of this phrase is preferable. It could mean spiritual ministry focusing on lifestyle (Louw and Nida 36.1). TEV has "who guide and instruct you in the Christian life." Or it could mean ministry focusing on the people themselves (Best), as REB has it: "leaders and counselors in the Lord's fellowship." Basic to the idea of the Christian life or the Lord's fellowship is the concept that these are people who are united to the Lord.

5:12e and who warn you *to stop doing wrong* (*or*, who instruct you *to do what is right*) The meaning of the verb νουθετέω can be 'to admonish, warn' (Frame, Wanamaker; KJV, NAB, NIV, NJB, NRSV) or 'to instruct' (Bruce, Louw and Nida 33.231; NCV, TEV), depending on the implied content. J. Callow (1982:106) says the verb "carries the components of (a) a warm relationship between the parties concerned (such as parents and children, friends, brothers) and (b) that the one who is the object of the verb is in error of some sort, doctrinal or behavioral, or in danger of falling into error." In 14b Paul uses this verb when he urges the Thessalonians to warn the idle of the consequences of not working (see also 2 Thess. 3:15). Here in 12e the content is not mentioned. The meaning 'admonish, warn' may be slightly preferable to 'instruct' because in 14b the verb means 'admonish' and because the negative idea of 'admonish' balances the positive idea of 'care for' in 12d (Best).

5:13a And (*or,* That is) In v. 13 is an infinitive phrase conjoined to the infinitive phrase in 12b–e by καί 'and'. It is a second content of the verb 'we ask' in the 12a orienter. If 12b–e means '(we ask you) to respect people who . . .', then 13a is a restatement (Ellingworth and Nida) or, better still, an amplification of 12b, because the basic meaning is the same. If, however, 12b–e means '(we ask you) to consider as leaders people who . . .', then 13a is a conjoined proposition adding a second part of the APPEAL (Wanamaker): 'and esteem them in love'. The latter is chosen for the display because it fits with the interpretation of 12b taken earlier.

I(&S&T) ask that you **consider those people great and love them** Commentators and versions basically arrive at the same meaning for ἡγεῖσθαι αὐτοὺς ὑπερεκπερισσοῦ ἐν ἀγάπῃ 'to consider them exceedingly in love' but by different routes because of the unusual grammar.

The verb ἡγέομαι means "*think, consider, regard*" (BAGD, p. 343.2). Although it does not mean 'esteem, respect' anywhere else (Frame, Wanamaker), it is taken in that way here by BAGD, Frame, Marshall, Morris; KJV, NAB, NCV, NASB, and NRSV.

The adverb ὑπερεκπερισσοῦ is a strong comparative (BAGD, p. 840; see its use in 3:10a). Those who understand ἡγέομαι to mean 'to esteem' render the verb and adverb something like "esteem them very highly" (NRSV; also Morris). If ἡγέομαι is taken to mean 'to think, consider', the combination can be rendered 'to consider them exceedingly highly', in other words 'to esteem them' (Wanamaker; NIV, NJB, NLT, REB, TNT). The rendering in the display is based on the latter interpretation.

Following the infinitive and adverb is the phrase 'in love'. Paul wants those who are being led or cared for to love those who lead or care for them. But the problem is how this prepositional phrase should be rendered. It can be understood as action parallel to the preceding verb, with both actions modified by the adverb: "have the greatest respect and affection for them" (NJB; also CEV, JBP, REB, TEV, TNT) or with only the second action modified by the adverb: "give them your whole-hearted love" (NLT; also NAB). Alternatively, it can be understood as manner: "esteem them with the greatest love" (NAB; also NCV). Or it can be motive or grounds: esteem them very highly, "not from fear or distrust but from love" (Frame; also Best, Marshall).

The concepts 'esteem' and 'love' are not usually associated with each other, so the understanding that they are parallel actions seems best for the display rendering. The noun 'love' represents an event; hence 'in love' is rendered as a verb.

5:13b since they work *hard to help you* The phrase διὰ τὸ ἔργον αὐτῶν 'because of their work' gives the reason (grounds) for the believers to esteem these leader-protectors (Bruce, Marshall, Wanamaker). It is for their hard work of caring for and warning the believers that they are to be esteemed (Best, Wanamaker). Bruce and Frame say they deserve high esteem because they do the Lord's work. The noun phrase 'their work' represents an agent and event and is rendered as a clause in the display.

5:13c Live peacefully with each other Paul now switches from the infinitives in his first APPEAL to the imperative mood for a second APPEAL. Some mss. have the pronoun αὐτοῖς 'them' ('live peacefully with them') instead of ἑαυτοῖς 'yourselves' ('live peacefully among yourselves'). The MJTGNT mentions the variant, but both it and UBSGNT have ἑαυτοῖς 'yourselves'. Commentators consider ἑαυτοῖς as the preferred form (Frame, Marshall, Wanamaker). The command is addressed to the leaders as well as those they care for. All believers are to avoid quarrels, which lead to division and strife (Marshall, Morris).

The reason for this added injunction, a common one found in other such lists of general commands (Rom. 12:18; 2 Cor. 13:11; Heb. 12:14), is not made explicit. Best calls it merely a general command here. Other commentators have proposed that there may have been tensions in Thessalonica between the wealthy believers who were leaders-providers and the others (Morris, Wanamaker) or between those who admonished and administered funds and those who weren't receiving funds because they were idle (Frame).

BOUNDARIES AND COHERENCE

The initial boundary of 5:12-13 was discussed under 4:3-5:11 (see "Boundaries"). The closing boundary is between 5:13 and 5:14 and is supported by the presence of the developmental marker δέ and the vocative 'brothers' in v. 14. (Both of these features also appear at the beginning of 5:12-13). In addition, v. 14 begins with the orienter verb παρακαλοῦμεν 'we exhort'; this parallels the orienter verb ἐρωτῶμεν 'we ask' at the beginning of 5:12-13. Verses 5:12-13 are recognized as a distinct unit by Bruce, Frame, NLT, TEV, TNT, and WFB.

Some place a boundary between 5:13b and 5:13c (NCV, NJB, REB), perhaps because 13c has no conjunction to connect it with what precedes and the imperative 'be at peace' in 13c is different from the infinitives in 12b and 13a. (In fact, it is almost identical in form to the six imperatives in vv. 14-15, which follow an initial indicative verb.) Moreover, the basis for the injunction to live peacefully in 13c is implicit.

On the other hand, the surface structure of 14a indicates the start of a new unit in that it is so clearly parallel with 12a. This would leave 13c as an isolated unit, which no one suggests. Also, commentators have given plausible suggestions as to why Paul follows his appeal in 12a-13b with the injunction to live peacefully with each other. Thus it seems that 13c belongs with what precedes rather than its being the initial proposition of a new unit.

Referential coherence in 5:12-13 is established by the references to two groups of believers, those who have leadership ministry functions and those who are led and cared for. The second group is exhorted in 12a-13b; both groups are exhorted in 13c. The verbs εἰδέναι 'to recognize' (12b) and ἡγεῖσθαι 'to consider' (13a) are in the same semantic domain, as are the verb κοπιάω 'work hard' (12c) and the noun ἔργον 'work' (13b); these pairs lend further coherence.

In the Greek the conjoined infinitives of 12b and 13a are the content of the orienter 'we ask' in 12a. This structure brings relational coherence.

PROMINENCE AND THEME

The naturally prominent constituents of 5:12-13 are the two *APPEALS*. The theme of the paragraph, therefore, is derived from their principle propositions (12b, 13a, 13c). Propositions 12d-e also are included, as they identify the people referred to in the first exhortation (12b): "people who care for and instruct you."

SUBSECTION CONSTITUENT 5:14–15
(Hortatory Paragraph: Appeal₂ of 5:12–15)

THEME: Warn believers who will not work, and encourage and help those who need it. Be patient with all people. Do good deeds to them all, including those who do evil deeds to you.

¶ PTRN	RELATIONAL STRUCTURE	CONTENTS
APPEAL₁	orienter	5:14a Fellow believers, I(&S&T) urge
	NUCLEUS₁	5:14b that you warn *believers* who *will* not work *in order to obtain the things they need to live/survive that they are behaving wrongly,*
	NUCLEUS₂	5:14c that you encourage *believers* who are fearful/discouraged,
	NUCLEUS₃	5:14d that you help people who are weak *in any way,*
	NUCLEUS₄	5:14e *and* that you be patient with all *your fellow believers and other people.*
APPEAL₂	NEGATIVE	5:15a Make sure that no one *of you* does/repays evil *deeds* to anyone *who has done* evil *to you.*
	POSITIVE	5:15b On the contrary, always aim to do good *deeds* to each other (*or,* to fellow believers) and to all *other people* (*or,* to everyone else).

INTENT AND PARAGRAPH PATTERN

In the 5:14–15 paragraph Paul's intent continues to be to affect the behavior of the believers at Thessalonica. He exhorts them to minister to each other in areas of specific need. He also exhorts them to resist the natural inclination to retaliate when wronged and instead do good to all men. Such behavior will knit the church together and witness to outsiders.

The genre of the paragraph is hortatory, and the paragraph pattern subtype is causality. It consists of two groupings of exhortations (14a-e and 15a-b). Paul is exhorting fellow believers as the apostle who originally brought the gospel message to them. That relationship serves as the implicit basis for the *APPEALS* here.

NOTES

5:14a Fellow believers, I(&S&T) urge The Greek is the same as in 12a, except that in place of the orienter ἐρωτάω 'we ask', Paul uses a synonym, παρακαλοῦμεν 'we urge' (see the note on 12a). Some church fathers felt that Paul here addresses the leaders mentioned in vv. 12–13, because warning believers is one of their functions (cf. 12e and 14b). However, the context in no way indicates a narrowing of the focus from what it was in the general appeal to the congregation in vv. 12–13. Moreover, the same vocative, 'brothers', is used to introduce vv. 12–13 and vv. 14–15. Therefore, it seems best to understand this to refer to the Christian community as a whole (Best, Bruce, Frame, Marshall, Morris, Wanamaker). Certain of the commands here might be more applicable to certain individuals in the community than to others, but not exclusively so (Bruce).

5:14b that you warn *believers* who *will* not work *in order to obtain the things they need to live/survive that they are behaving wrongly* This is the first of four content exhortations that appear without connecting conjunctions. The Greek of this first one is νουθετεῖτε τοὺς ἀτάκτους 'warn the idle/unruly'. The verb νουθετέω 'to warn, to instruct' was used in 12e. The context here requires the meaning 'to warn'. Implicit in warning is the idea of the addressee behaving wrongly and the need to change; the former is supplied in the display.

The adjective ἄτακτος has been taken to mean 'disorderly, insubordinate' by CEV, JBP, KJV, NAB, and NJB (NJB has "undisciplined") but 'idle, lazy' by others (Best, Bruce, Frame, Louw and Nida 88.247, Marshall, Wanamaker; JB, TEV, NCV, NIV, NLT, NRSV, REB, and TNT). Either meaning is appropriate here, but the latter seems preferable considering the broader context of the Thessalonian letters. Paul had heard that there were believers in Thessalonica who were not earning a living and commanded that they do so (2 Thess. 3:11–12). He uses himself and his companions as examples of proper behavior in this matter (2 Thess. 3:7–10). The 2 Thessalonians passage has cognates to the adjective here, that is, the verb ἠτακτήσαμεν 'we were not idle' (3:7) and the adverb ἀτάκτως 'idly' (3:6, 11). Previously in 1 Thessalonians Paul told his readers "to work with your hands . . . so that you will not be dependent on anybody" (4:11-12, NIV). This is additional support for understanding 5:14b as having the more specific second meaning, 'idle, lazy'. Wanamaker points out, however, that the more general meaning 'unruly' applies as well to the Thessalonian situation; it may be that unruly behavior is what causes Paul to tell his readers to "lead a quiet life, to mind your own business" (4:11, NIV; also see 2 Thess. 3:11-12).

It is made clear in the display that the people who are to be admonished are idle not because they can't find work, but because they *will* not work (Frame; NLT has "lazy"). The larger issue is also made clear: that they are not providing for their own needs (Bruce).

5:14c that you encourage *believers* who are fearful/discouraged The Greek is παραμυθεῖσθε τοὺς ὀλιγοψύχους 'encourage the fainthearted'. The verb παραμυθέομαι 'to encourage, to console' was used previously (see the note on 2:12a). The adjective, ὀλιγόψυχος 'faint-hearted', is used only here in the NT. It means 'worried', fearful', or 'discouraged' (Best). Commentators suggest that there may have been believers in Thessalonica who felt inadequate (Bruce, Morris), who were shaken by the persecutions they were experiencing (Marshall, Wanamaker), who were saddened by the death of loved ones (Marshall), who were anxious about aspects of the Lord's return (Frame, Wanamaker), or who doubted things regarding their new faith (Frame, Wanamaker).

5:14d that you help people who are weak *in any way* The Greek is ἀντέχεσθε τῶν ἀσθενῶν 'help the weak'. One of the meanings of the verb ἀντέχω is "*take an interest in, pay attention to*," which leads to the meaning "*help* τινός *someone*" (BAGD, p. 73.2). The people who are to be helped are 'the weak'. In its literal sense the adjective ἀσθενής refers to physical weakness, such as sickness. But commentators understand it in a broader sense here (the sense in Romans 14 and 1 Corinthians 8, for example), though the meaning of physical weakness may be included as well (Wanamaker). There is insufficient context to indicate what Paul specifically means. It could mean economic need (Wanamaker) or moral weakness (Frame, Marshall) or spiritual weakness (Best, Bruce, Morris). The display has 'weak in any way', which is an attempt to indicate latitude of meaning. In translation a term should be used that does not limit meaning to physical weakness.

5:14e *and* that you be patient with all *your fellow believers and other people* The Greek is μακροθυμεῖτε πρὸς πάντας 'be patient with all'. The verb μακροθυμέω means 'to be patient, forbearing'. Frame defines it as "'long-tempered,' slow to anger and retaliation. . . ." The words 'all' and 'be patient' make this proposition a bridge from the preceding commands in 14a-d to the admonition of 15a-b: patience is an attribute needed to follow the injunctions not to repay evil but to do good to all. Some interpret 'all' as referring to those believers mentioned in 14b-d (Marshall, Wanamaker). Thus NRSV has "all of them." Others understand it to refer to all believers in the community (Best) or to believers and nonbelievers alike (Bruce, Frame, Morris). This latter interpretation is supported by 15b, where Paul uses the same word to indicate people other than believers, 'everyone (else)'. (Taking 14b-d as concerned with ministry to believers and 14e, with patience toward all people, Frame ties 14e more closely to 15a-b than to what precedes; however, because 14a-e and 15a-b are separate APPEALS with distinct orienters, this is hard to justify.) When Paul says 'all', he most likely refers to the fellow believers he has spoken of in immediately preceding propositions, but with outsiders included as well. This meaning is supplied in the display.

5:15a Make sure that no one *of you* does/repays evil *deeds* to anyone *who has done* evil *to you* The Greek is ὁρᾶτε μή τις κακὸν ἀντὶ κακοῦ τινι ἀποδῷ 'See (that) not anyone recompenses evil for evil to anyone'. The orienter 'see (that)' establishes v. 15 as a new set of appeals parallel to those in v. 14. There seems to be a referential relationship between 'all' in 14e and 'all' in 15b and also between the idea of being patient in 14e and not recompensing evil in 15a (Best, Frame. Morris). Wanamaker, however, discounts this relationship, saying that this is a series of loosely connected exhortations.

The negative exhortation in 15a has a corresponding positive (an amplification) in 15b introduced by ἀλλά 'but'. A positive is naturally prominent, but here the negative seems to have marked prominence because it mentions the specific concept of retaliation, which is necessary in order to understand an aspect of the more generic positive exhortation (i.e., forgiveness demonstrated by good deeds). Moreover, 15b amplifies

15a by saying that believers are to aim to do good 'to all (people)'. Hence, both 15a and 15b are prominent and are labeled with uppercase letters in the display.

The Greek 'see' together with the negative 'not' constitutes a warning to be on guard in order that something not happen. It is rendered in the display 'Make sure that no one . . .'. Another way of saying this is "Each of you must see to it that he does not . . ." (Marshall).

Wanamaker thinks that Paul bases 15a on an aphorism, because the orienter '(you) see' is directed to believers (second person plural), but the content verb 'repay' switches to third person singular and has the indefinite pronoun 'anyone' as subject. On the other hand, it may be that Paul uses τις 'anyone' (μή τις 'no one') and τινι 'to anyone' (which each require the third person singular) to express an all-inclusive appeal. The display thus has 'no one of you does/repays evil deeds to anyone'.

Hiebert says, "*Evil* here has the meaning of that which is injurious or harmful, harm caused by evil intent. It is a categorical prohibition against retaliation." In the expression 'recompensing evil for evil' the verb representing the action of the first party is omitted, but it is supplied in the display: 'who has done evil to you'. Many languages have a word or expression for 'payback, retaliation', and that may be appropriate here.

5:15b On the contrary, always aim to do good *deeds* to each other (*or*, to fellow believers) and to all *other* people (*or*, to everyone *else*) The POSITIVE exhortation (amplification) here is introduced with ἀλλά 'but'. The Greek is ἀλλὰ πάντοτε τὸ ἀγαθὸν διώκετε [καὶ] εἰς ἀλλήλους καὶ εἰς πάντας 'but always seek the good both for one another and for all'. The verb διώκω means 'to run after, pursue'. However, it is probably a dead figure here, meaning 'to strive for, aspire to'. Immediately after the verb MJTGNT has καί 'and', which UBSGNT has bracketed to indicate uncertainty in including it. The addition is accepted by Bruce, KJV, and NKJV; they render it 'both': "both for yourselves and for all" (NKJV). But whether accepted or not, the meaning is unaffected.

The substantive 'good' refers to "acts that are beneficial and helpful, rather than harmful" (Hiebert). It is rendered 'good deeds' in the display. Such behavior is to be 'toward each other' (fellow believers) and 'all' (those outside the Christian community).

Paul's teaching in v. 15 is not merely that a believer should not retaliate for evil done to him. Rather, the believer must respond by doing good in return (Marshall). This injunction is based on Jesus' teaching in Matt. 5:38–48 that his followers should love their enemies. The 'always' and 'all' in 15b indicate that the command is considerable, extending to all occasions and all people (Marshall).

BOUNDARIES AND COHERENCE

The initial boundary of 5:14–15 was discussed under 5:12–13; the closing boundary, under 5:12–15. (See "Boundaries.")

The paragraph consists of two *APPEALS* (14a–e and 15a–b), which lends a bit of relational coherence to it. Commentators see referential coherence in the repetition of πάντας 'all' (14e, 15b) and the fact that the command to be patient in 14e is assumed in the 15a–b commands not to retaliate for evil but to do good instead.

NLT and REB have a boundary between 5:14 and 5:15, perhaps because of the difference of structure between the two verses: v. 14 has an orienter that is an indicative verb and a series of four parallel injunctions, each beginning with a verb in the imperative mood, while v. 15 has an orienter that is an imperative, followed by subjunctive and imperative verbs, neither of which is at the beginning of the clause as the verbs in v. 14 are. Besides this structural difference, there is a negative-positive relation in v. 15 that is quite different from the relations in v. 14. These differences are acknowledged. However, v. 15 is more similar to vv. 12–14, which precede it, than to the verses that follow in 16–22. None of the verses that follow have an orienter, and all of them have clause-final imperative verbs, which is not true of v. 15. One option is to isolate v. 15 as a separate unit, which NLT and REB have done. But because of the referential coherence, it seems better to consider 5:14–15 a unit as in GHL, GW, NBV, TEV, and WFB.

PROMINENCE AND THEME

Both *APPEALS* in 5:14–15 seem to be equally prominent, as are the constituent parts of each *APPEAL*. As these are general appeals to a congregation, there is no close semantic relation between them. Thus the theme of 5:14–15 is an attempt at succinctly stating the *APPEALS*.

SECTION CONSTITUENT 5:16-22
(Hortatory Subsection: General Appeal₂ of 5:12-22)

THEME: Always rejoice, pray, and thank God. Evaluate all messages that people claim the Holy Spirit gave them. Accept authentic messages and obey them.

MACROSTRUCTURE	CONTENTS
APPEAL₁	5:16-18 Always rejoice, pray, and thank God.
APPEAL₂	5:19-22 Evaluate all messages that people claim the Holy Spirit gave them. Accept authentic messages and obey them.

INTENT AND MACROSTRUCTURE

Paul's intent in the 5:16-22 subsection is to affect behavior, and thus the genre is hortatory. He exhorts the Thessalonians to be faithful with regard to their personal religious practices and attitudes and to be discerning with regard to the Holy Spirit's ministry to them individually and as a community.

The subsection consists of two conjoined *APPEAL* paragraphs, 5:16-18 and 5:19-22.

BOUNDARIES AND COHERENCE

The initial boundary of 5:16-22 was discussed under 5:12-15, and the terminal boundary under 5:12-22. (See "Boundaries.")

The unit consists of eight short, imperatival clauses, each of which has an adverbial expression or direct object preceding the verb. (Only the grounds propositions in 18b-c are not imperatival.) This structure creates relational coherence. Referential coherence is seen in the mention of 'God' (18b), 'Christ Jesus' (18c), and the 'Spirit' (v. 19). It is further strengthened by πάντοτε 'always' (v. 16), ἀδιαλείπτως 'unceasingly' (v. 17), ἐν παντί 'in all (circumstances)' (18a), πάντα 'all (messages)' (21a), and παντός 'all (kinds)' (v. 22).

PROMINENCE AND THEME

The two constituent paragraphs of the 5:16-22 subsection are equally prominent. The first (16-18) ends with an *authoritative basis*, which perhaps marks it as prominent. The second (19-20) consists of contrasting negative and positive propositions, which perhaps marks it as prominent also.

The themes of these two paragraphs are combined to form the theme of 5:16-22.

SUBSECTION CONSTITUENT 5:16-18
(Hortatory Paragraph: Appeal₁ of 5:16-22)

THEME: Always rejoice, pray, and thank God.

¶ PTRN	RELATIONAL STRUCTURE	CONTENTS
APPEAL	NUCLEUS₁	5:16 Be joyful **at all times**,
	NUCLEUS₂	5:17 pray **continually**,
	NUCLEUS₃	5:18a *and* thank God **in all** *circumstances*,
authoritative basis	RESULT	5:18b *since God wants you to behave this way* [16-18a]
	reason	5:18c *because of what* Christ Jesus *has done (or, because you are united to Christ Jesus)*.

INTENT AND PARAGRAPH PATTERN

In the 5:16-18 paragraph Paul's intent is to affect behavior, and thus its genre is hortatory. He urges the Thessalonians to practice the spiritual attitudes and disciplines of rejoicing, prayer, and thanksgiving. He emphasizes their importance with three nearly synonymous adverbials meaning 'always' or 'in all situations' and by appending a strong grounds statement that this is what God desires.

The paragraph consists of two propositional clusters (16-18a and 18b-c). The second cluster is introduced with γάρ 'for' and gives authoritative support for the first. This indicates that 18b-c is grounds for 16-18a. The relation is exhortation-grounds of the simple causality type and functions as *APPEAL-basis* in the causality subtype of hortatory paragraph pattern.

NOTES

5:16 Be joyful at all times This is the first of a series of three parallel and conjoined exhortations. The adverb here, πάντοτε 'always', and the adverbial expressions in 17 and 18a are fronted. The fronting and the similar meaning of the three adverbials emphasize that these disciplines of the Christian life are essential and never to be neglected. (The emphasis is indicated in the display by bold type.) Even in adverse situations and persecutions the Thessalonians were joyful, as Paul says in 1:6c, using the cognate noun; they were joyful because the Holy Spirit caused them to be. Paul wants such joy to be perpetual.

5:17 pray continually The adverb here, ἀδιαλείπτως 'unceasingly', is parallel in placement and meaning to πάντοτε 'always' in v. 16. These same adverbs occur in parallel propositions also at 1:2a and 1:3. Bruce says the idea here is probably the same as in Rom. 12:12, "persist in prayer" (NEB). The verb προσεύχομαι 'to pray' is a general term. However, Paul perhaps intends to denote the aspect of intercession here (Frame, Marshall, Wanamaker), because the aspect of thanksgiving is mentioned in the next proposition.

5:18a *and* thank *God* in all *circumstances* The undergoer of the verb 'to give thanks' is understood to be 'God' (Best, Frame). The adverbial phrase ἐν παντί 'in all' has been taken by some to mean 'at all times' (Wanamaker; NAB), the same meaning as the adverbs in v. 16 and v. 17. However, Paul does not use the phrase elsewhere with this meaning and neither does the LXX (Frame); in 2 Cor. 9:8 he distinguishes it from πάντοτε 'always'. Therefore it seems best to understand the phrase as referring to 'all circumstances' (Best, Bruce, Frame, Marshall, Morris; NCV, NIV, NRSV, REB, TEV, TNT). There is virtually no difference of meaning, however, between 'at all times' and 'in all circumstances' (Marshall).

5:18b since God wants you *to behave* this way [16-18a] The Greek is τοῦτο γὰρ θέλημα θεοῦ . . . εἰς ὑμᾶς 'for this (is the) will of God . . . for/concerning you'. The demonstrative pronoun 'this' is singular; some commentators have therefore understood 18b to refer only to the one exhortation which immediately precedes it in 18a. (The punctuation of vv. 16-18 in CEV, NIV, and NLT perhaps indicates that they follow this interpretation.) However, propositions 16, 17, and 18a are closely tied together by identical structure and almost synonymous adverbial expressions, showing that Paul most likely viewed them as a unit, with 'this' referring to all three (Bruce, Frame, Wanamaker). This is the interpretation chosen for the display, hence 'this way'.

Thus the conjunction γάρ 'for' is taken as introducing grounds for the preceding three exhortations (Best, Bruce, Frame, Marshall, Wanamaker). This 18b grounds proposition is the *authoritative basis* for Paul's *APPEAL*. It is very similar to the orienter in 4:3a. Here, as there, it places a strong warrant on Paul's commands (Morris, Wanamaker). The phrase 'will of God' represents an agent and state and is rendered in the display 'God wants'.

5:18c *because of what* Christ Jesus *has done* (*or, because you are united* to Christ Jesus) In the Greek the phrase 'will of God' is followed immediately by ἐν Χριστῷ Ἰησοῦ 'in Christ Jesus', which can be taken as adverbial, modifying 'will' (Best, Frame, Marshall; GHL and probably NKJV, NRSV): because of Christ Jesus God wants you to do these things. Alternatively, it can be understood as adjectival, modifying the pronoun 'you' at the end of the verse (Bruce; EHP, NLT, TEV, TNT): God wants you who are united to Christ Jesus to do these things. Because of the Greek word order the adverbial interpretation seems preferable, but commentators have difficulty expressing what it means. Best says God wants the believer to do these things because he has redeemed him and is ministering to him 'in Christ'. Frame says that it is through Christ Jesus, who is accessible to believers and recognized as an authority by them, that God commands these things. Hale (p. 47) proposes four possible renderings for the adverbial option, but basically they involve only two alternatives: 'for this is God's will for you *because of the work done* by Christ Jesus' and '. . . *because you are united* with Christ Jesus.' These options, with slight modification, are in the display. The first rendering is intended to fit what Best and Frame say this phrase means.

BOUNDARIES AND COHERENCE

The initial boundary of 5:16-18 was discussed under 5:12-15 (see "Boundaries"). A closing boundary is postulated between 5:18 and 5:19. It seems justified for the following reasons: The 5:18b-c *authoritative basis* creates a natural break between the exhortations in 5:16-18 and those in 5:19-22. In 5:16-18 Paul exhorts his readers regarding spiritual attitudes and disciplines; then in 5:19-22 he moves on to exhortations concerning the Holy Spirit and his gifts of prophecy and discernment. The commands in 16-18 begin with adverbials; those in 19-22 begin with nouns or substantives. The first two exhortations of 19-22 are negative and contrast with the positive exhortations of 16-18. Frame, Wanamaker, CEV, EHP, JBP, NAB, NCV, NJB, NIV, NLT, REB, TEV, and WFB place a boundary between 5:18 and 5:19.

Referential coherence in 16-18 is established by the fronted, and very similar, adverbials: πάντοτε 'always', ἀδιαλείπτως 'unceasingly', and ἐν παντί 'in all (circumstances)'. The exhortations to rejoice, pray, and give thanks are all in the domain of spiritual attitudes or disciplines.

The exhortations in 16-18 are related by asyndeton (lack of conjunctions). The 18b-c *authoritative basis* is related to the 16-18a APPEAL by the conjunction γάρ 'for'. These factors create relational coherence in the unit.

PROMINENCE AND THEME

In the 5:16-18 paragraph the APPEAL is naturally prominent. In the APPEAL the forefronted adverbials 'always', 'unceasingly', and 'in all (circumstances)' have marked prominence.

The theme of 5:16-18 consists of the three imperatives of the APPEAL preceded by the adverb 'always'.

SUBSECTION CONSTITUENT 5:19-22
(Hortatory Paragraph: Appeal₂ of 5:16-22)

THEME: Evaluate all messages that people claim the Holy Spirit gave them. Accept authentic messages and obey them.

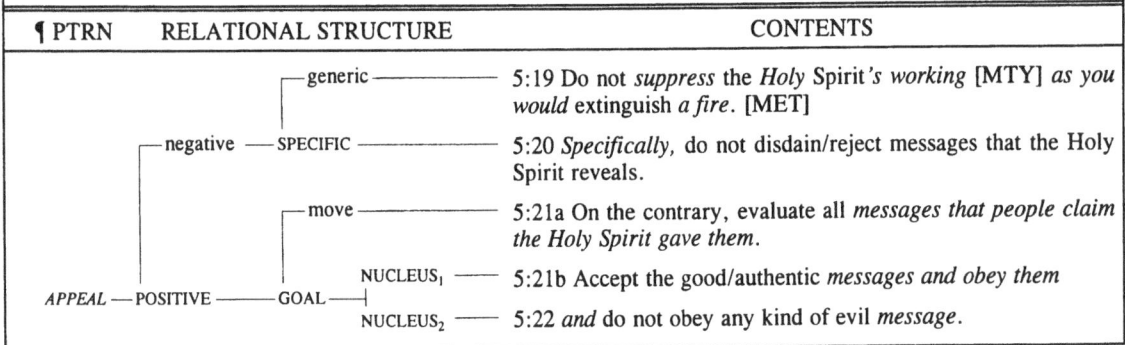

INTENT AND PARAGRAPH PATTERN

Paul's purpose in the 5:19-22 paragraph is to affect behavior; thus its discourse genre is hortatory. He exhorts the Thessalonians to do what will facilitate the Holy Spirit's ministry in their individual lives and to do what will prevent misuse of spiritual gifts in the fellowship.

It is a hortatory paragraph of the causality subtype. It consists of two negative exhortations in vv. 19-20 and two positive exhortations in v. 21, the second of which is accentuated by another negative in v. 22. The first negative and positive groupings are joined by δέ in its adversative function ('but, on the contrary'). Paul bases his APPEAL on the ministry relationship that he has with the Thessalonians.

NOTES

5:19 Do not *suppress* the *Holy* Spirit's *working* as you would extinguish *a fire* The Greek is τὸ πνεῦμα μὴ σβέννυτε 'the spirit do not quench'. In v. 18 Paul spoke of the 'will of God in Christ

Jesus'. This perhaps leads him to speak of 'the spirit', which is the divine Spirit (Frame, Wanamaker). The verb σβέννυμι literally means 'to extinguish, put out a fire'. Here it is used in a live figure. The reference to the Spirit is a metonymy: it signifies the special gifts and abilities that the Spirit works in and through individuals. The reference to quenching is a metaphor, the topic of which is the work of the Holy Spirit and the image, a fire. The ground of comparison is causing to stop: the work the Spirit produces can be stifled or stopped just as a fire is quenched. Paul tells the Thessalonians not to do this. (The Spirit's work is also associated with the image of fire in other passages of Scripture, e.g., in Matt. 3:11, Acts 2:3-4, and 2 Tim. 1:6-7).

The present tense of the imperatives here and in the following verses may indicate that Paul was attempting to deal with a problem that had already arisen in Thessalonica (Best, Wanamaker). However, Bruce doubts the present tense can be pressed to mean 'stop doing . . . '; rather he feels these commands are things believers should habitually do or refrain from doing, as the case may be.

Standing by itself, v. 19 is unclear. Morris understands it as a very general admonition, prohibiting anything that would quench the Spirit, and he names several sins. However, the following negative exhortation in v. 20 can be understood to clarify the first. Since one way of suppressing the Spirit is by rejecting prophetic messages inspired by him (Bruce, Marshall), it seems appropriate to understand v. 19 as a generic and v. 20 as a specific (Frame, Marshall, Wanamaker).

5:20 *Specifically*, **do not disdain/reject messages that the Holy Spirit reveals** Regarding the relation of this proposition to the previous one, see the note on 5:19. The Greek is προφητείας μὴ ἐξουθενεῖτε 'prophecies do not despise'. BAGD (p. 277.2) define the verb ἐξουθενέω here as "*reject w. contempt*." The ability to prophesy is given by the Holy Spirit to some believers (1 Cor. 12:10-11). Here Paul could be telling his readers not to reject the gift of prophecy or not to reject particular utterances. Because Paul uses the plural form of the noun without the definite article, the latter understanding may be preferable (Wanamaker). Prophetic messages can be rejected either by refusing to utter such messages oneself or by disdaining, or preventing from being delivered, messages that the Spirit gives to others (Best, Bruce).

Popular understanding often associates prophecies with messages of future events. However, they can be any 'messages that the Holy Spirit reveals' (display rendering) in order to edify a fellowship of believers. Paul values such messages highly (1 Cor. 14:1-25). It was the Spirit who enabled Paul, Silas, and Timothy to speak effectively on their first visit to Thessalonica (1:5c), and Paul doesn't want such messages to be rejected.

Some think that prophecy is merely an example and that Paul's exhortation in v. 19 refers as well to the Spirit's other gifts, for example, those mentioned in 1 Cor. 12:7-11 (Best, Frame, Wanamaker). This is possible, but there is not enough information in the context to decide for certain.

5:21a On the contrary, evaluate all *messages that people claim the Holy Spirit gave them* UBSGNT and MJTGNT both have the conjunction δέ 'but/now', but some important mss. omit it. Some such conjunction seems necessary to make the transition from negative to positive exhortations. So δέ probably should be read (Best, Bruce, Frame, Morris, Wanamaker). It has its adversative function here (Frame, Morris, Wanamaker; NCV, NLT, NRSV, REB) and introduces the POSITIVE exhortations of v. 21 that correspond to the preceding negative exhortations in vv. 19-20. Some versions (NAB, NIV, NJB, TEV) omit the conjunction, probably because of questionable manuscript support or because they view 21a-22 as relating only loosely to what precedes.

The Greek here is πάντα δὲ δοκιμάζετε 'but all (things) test'. Louw and Nida (27.45) define the verb δοκιμάζω as "to try to learn the genuineness of something by examination and testing. . . ." This meaning is confirmed by the next two propositions, in which Paul tells his readers that after examination and evaluation they are to hold on to what is good and avoid what is evil. Thus the relation between 21a and 21b-22 seems best taken as move-goal. In the context of vv. 19-20, 'all things' most likely includes messages that people claim the Holy Spirit enables them to speak (Bruce, Marshall; NLT, REB). It may include other gifts of the Spirit as well (Best, Frame, Wanamaker). The ability to discern is itself a gift of the Spirit (1 Cor. 12:10-11). Morris feels that 21a is a general command that extends beyond prophecy to everything that affects a believer. However, the commands of vv. 21-22 go specifically with the statements regarding the Spirit and his work in vv. 19-20, even though they certainly can have wider application (Wanamaker, p. 204). In this context they at least refer to Spirit-inspired messages.

5:21b Accept the good/authentic *messages and obey them* The testing of messages results in a determination of which are Spirit-inspired and acceptable and which are not (Best, Frame, Wanamaker). The Greek is τὸ καλὸν κατέχετε 'the good hold fast'. The verb κατέχω here means to "*hold fast, retain* faithfully" (BAGD, p. 423.1bβ). Included in holding fast is action, because Paul tells his readers to abstain from evil in v. 22. If Paul's readers determine that a message is good he wants them to "take the message to heart, believe it and act upon it" (Marshall).

5:22 *and* **do not obey any kind of evil** *message* The exhortation ἀπὸ παντὸς εἴδους πονηροῦ ἀπέχεσθε 'from every kind/appearance of evil abstain' corresponds to 21b. Propositions 21b and 22 are probably equal in prominence because they speak of two types of messages and a person has to decide which of the two to accept. Semantically, they are not in a basic positive-negative relation as are 19-20 and 21a-22, thus the label NUCLEUS for each.

The noun εἴδος can mean either 'appearance' or 'kind'. The latter meaning is more appropriate here (Best, Bruce, Frame, Marshall; NIV, TEV), as the strong verb 'to abstain' might indicate. (Paul also uses this verb in 4:3c.) Nothing in the context suggests that Paul has 'appearance' in mind, that is, avoiding what is not evil but simply appears to be, or avoiding evil that can be seen.

The three imperatives of vv. 21-22 could have general application, namely, to test all things, hold fast to whatever is good, and abstain from whatever is evil (Hiebert, Morris). However, the major negative-positive alternation in 19-22 probably indicates that 21-22 specifically relates to 19-20, the statements regarding the Spirit and the messages he inspires (Best, Frame, Marshall, Wanamaker). Propositions 21b and 22 speak of accepting messages of the Spirit that promote edification and love and rejecting those that do not (Frame). In the display 'message' is therefore supplied in both commands.

BOUNDARIES AND COHERENCE

The initial boundary of 5:19-22 was discussed under 5:16-18, and the terminal boundary under 5:12-22. (See "Boundaries.")

Relational coherence is established by the identical structure of the five clauses, that is, a direct object followed by a present-tense imperative. The conjunction δέ 'but' relates the negative commands in vv. 19-20 to the following group of positive and negative commands in vv. 21-22. Referential coherence is established by the mention of 'the Spirit' (v. 19), Spirit-inspired 'prophecies' (v. 20), and 'testing' (21a), which may refer to the Spirit's gift of discernment. That 5:19-22 is a unit is the view of Best, Frame, Hendriksen, Hiebert, Marshall, Morris, Wanamaker, CEV, EHP, JBP, NAB, NCV, NIV, NJB, REB, and TEV.

PROMINENCE AND THEME

Since the 21a and 21b positive exhortations of the APPEAL are naturally more prominent than the negative exhortations (19, 20, 22), the theme of 5:19-22 is based on the 21a and 21b exhortations.

DIVISION CONSTITUENT 5:23-24
(Expressive Paragraph: Closing of 4:1-5:24)

THEME: I pray that God will cause you to be distinct people who behave right in every way, and I am sure that he will do this.

¶ PTRN	RELATIONAL STRUCTURE			CONTENTS
REACTION	NUCLEUS	orienter		5:23a *I(&S&T) pray to* God, who causes *his people* to live well/peacefully,
				5:23b that he will cause you to be distinct people in every way.
		amplification	NUCLEUS	5:23c *That is, I(&S&T) pray* that *he* will cause all that you think, desire, and do to be right/blameless
			circumstance	5:23d *until* our(inc) Lord Jesus Christ majestically comes *to earth*.
	grounds₁			5:24a *God* summons you *to be distinct people*,
	grounds₂			5:24b *and* he *is* **trustworthy**.
BELIEF	CONCLUSION			5:24c *Therefore, I am sure that* he will do *this* [23b-d].

INTENT AND PARAGRAPH PATTERN

In the 5:23-24 paragraph Paul expresses his desires in a second wish-prayer, parallel to the one in 3:11-13 (see "Intent" under 3:11-13). Its genre is not hortatory: Paul is not appealing to his readers to do something. Neither is he directly appealing to God to act; the main relationship is still between author and readers as shown by Paul's use of second person plural pronouns three times in the two verses. Rather, the genre is emotive: Paul's primary intent is to affect the emotions of his readers. He expresses to them his sincere desire that God will enable them to be distinct people who behave right in every way until the Lord Jesus returns to earth. It is the expressive type of emotive paragraph in that Paul develops his thoughts in a grounds-conclusion relation rather than a sequential one. Regarding the subtype of paragraph pattern, no emotive problem is stated that would make this solutionality, nor is there focus on control of emotions as in the expressive volitionality subtype. Thus it seems best to take this as the causality subtype of paragraph pattern, the constituents of which (in expressive genre) are labeled *situation*, REACTION, and *belief*.

The paragraph consists of two propositional clusters, 23a-d and 24a-c. There is no connecting word between them, but the second cluster functions to verify that Paul's wish in the first will be carried out. The verification seems to be both to the readers and to the author himself; thus the second cluster is labeled BELIEF, and the first cluster REACTION. The situation is implicit; it is Paul's relation to the Thessalonians as the one who brought them the gospel and who desires that they live blamelessly in God's eyes. In the display both labels are in uppercase letters; the REACTION has natural prominence and the BELIEF, marked prominence.

From the content of the wish-prayer it is obvious that Paul also has a strong secondary intent. He says he desires that the Thessalonians be a people distinct from others, that is, righteous in everything they think, desire, and do. Such a communication should affect their behavior, a secondary hortatory intent.

The 5:23-24 paragraph is a fitting closing of the 4:1-5:24 division in that the division's prominent concepts are restated here. The wish that God will enable the Thessalonians to be a distinct people who behave right in every way reminds the readers of Paul's various appeals and references to holiness in this part of the epistle. The mention of the Lord Jesus' return to earth reminds them of Paul's earlier exposition and appeals regarding that event.

NOTES

5:23a *I(&S&T) pray to* God The first four words of this orienter are identical to the ones in the 3:11-13 wish-prayer: αὐτὸς δὲ ὁ θεός 'now/but he/himself the God'. See the note on 3:11a for a discussion of these terms and their rendering, which is the same here.

who causes *his people* to live well/peacefully The phrase τῆς εἰρήνης 'of peace' identifies God as the source of his people's peace (Bruce, Marshall, Wanamaker; CEV, TEV, TNT). Here 'peace' has the same meaning as in 1:1b (see the note there); it is the state of those who are experiencing God's blessing. Paul probably also had in mind harmony between fellow believers as in 5:13c where 'peace' is also used, but here the term has a broader significance, namely spiritual prosperity (Bruce, Frame, Wanamaker). This is appropriate here where Paul speaks of God keeping his people pure so that they will be blameless when the Lord Jesus returns.

5:23b that he will cause you to be distinct people in every way The 23b NUCLEUS and 23c–d amplification are expressed by clauses with verbs in the optative mood and aorist tense, as is characteristic of wish-prayers.

The Greek is ἁγιάσαι ὑμᾶς ὁλοτελεῖς 'may he sanctify you completely'. The meaning of the verb ἁγιάζω 'to sanctify' here is the same as that of the cognate noun ἁγιασμός 'sanctification' in 4:3b (see the note there) and of its synonym ἁγιωσύνη 'holiness' in 3:13b. Paul has exhorted his readers to be distinct people by behaving in a morally pure way (4:3–8) and in other righteous ways as well (4:9–12, 5:1–22). He sums up these commands in this wish-prayer. The sanctification Paul speaks of in this letter is devotion to God and right conduct, "ethical soundness" (Frame).

The predicate adjective ὁλοτελής qualifies the verb 'to sanctify'. The adjective can signify degree: 'completely, wholly' distinct (Bruce, Louw and Nida 78.47, Morris; CEV, NRSV, TNT). Or it can signify the extent of the distinctness, that is, 'through and through, in every respect' (Frame, Wanamaker; NIV, REB, TEV). There seems to be no semantic difference between the two. The display follows the TEV, "in every way."

5:23c *That is, I(&S&T) pray* that *he* will cause all that you think, desire, and do to be right/blameless The Greek for 23c–d is καὶ ὁλόκληρον ὑμῶν τὸ πνεῦμα καὶ ἡ ψυχὴ καὶ τὸ σῶμα ἀμέμπτως ἐν τῇ παρουσίᾳ τοῦ κυρίου ἡμῶν Ἰησοῦ Χριστοῦ τηρηθείη, literally 'and entire your spirit and soul and body blamelessly in the coming of our Lord Jesus Christ may be kept'. The conjunction καί 'and' conjoins 23c–d to what precedes. Proposition 23c–d may be considered specific (Frame), equivalent (Hiebert, Morris) or amplification (Wanamaker). The last seems preferable since 23d adds new information, the circumstance of the Lord's return.

The verb τηρέω can mean "*keep,* etc. unharmed or undisturbed" (BAGD, p. 815.2b). Here it is in the passive and modified by ἀμέμπτως 'blamelessly'. The meaning of 'kept blamelessly' is probably 'preserved/caused to do right so there is no blame for sinning'. A person's whole being is "kept blamelessly (that is, so as to be blameless) at the coming of our Lord Jesus Christ" (Frame). This is the same meaning Paul expresses earlier in 3:13a–c.

The Greek passive verb is rendered as active in the display, and the agent is supplied: 'he will cause . . . to be right/blameless'. The pronoun refers to God, who is the agent in 23b as well. The Greek adverb 'blamelessly' is rendered as a predicate adjective, 'right/blameless', because 'right/blameless' modifies the substantive 'all that you think, desire, and do'.

The grammar of 23c–d is complicated. The term ὁλόκληρος 'whole, entire' can be taken either as modifying the verb, that is, 'to be kept complete' (Wanamaker; CEV, NAB, NRSV, REB, TNT) or as modifying the series of nouns that follow it (Bruce, Frame, Morris; NCV, NIV, TEV), your 'whole spirit, soul, and body'. The latter is probably the preferable of these options because then the term is close to the words it modifies and the verb is modified only by the adverb ἀμέμπτως 'blamelessly', not by both 'blamelessly' and 'whole'. The meaning in either case seems to be that no part of the Christian's being should lack this sanctification.

There are three terms here (rather than two, which is more common in the OT and NT): 'spirit', 'soul', and 'body'. They are probably used to emphasize the completeness of the sanctification; Paul wants every part of the Thessalonians to be kept entirely without fault (Bruce, Morris). These terms are not used in their primary sense, that is, as references to physical or immaterial parts of being. In conjunction with the verbal phrase 'be kept blamelessly' they express that all that emanates from the various parts of an individual (desires, thoughts, and actions) are to be righteous and not sinful. Paul has already used 'soul' in 2:8c to mean all that he and his companions did for the Thessalonians. In 2:4f and 3:13a he used 'heart' to mean inner thoughts, will, and feeling. He used 'vessel', a euphemism for the genitalia, in 4:4a to speak not of the physical body parts but of sexual passion, which needs to be controlled. So it seems inner thoughts and emotions and outward behavior are Paul's intention here as well. In 5:23 'spirit', 'soul', and 'body' can be considered terms from popular anthropology for man's constituent parts (Schweizer, p. 435). From them emanate all thoughts, emotions, desires, and actions. The Thessalonians "are involved in the process of sanctification by virtue of what they do or do not do" (Wanamaker). Paul wants them to be without fault in every aspect of their lives when Christ returns (3:13c, 5:23d) and they appear before God their Father (3:13b). The TEV renders 5:23c-d more clearly than most versions: "and keep your whole being—spirit, soul, and body—free from every fault at the coming of our Lord Jesus Christ."

The term 'entire' and the nouns it modifies are rendered in the display 'all that you think, desire, and do'.

5:23d *until* our(inc) Lord Jesus Christ majestically comes *to earth* This phrase is similar to the one in 3:13c and has the same role of circumstance. The context determines the meaning of the first word of this phrase, ἐν; for example, it means 'when' in 3:13c but 'until' here. Verse 3:13 speaks of the Thessalonians' being declared blameless in the presence of God *when* the Lord returns. Verse 5:23, on the other hand, implies that the Thessalonians are to do what is right and blameless *until* the Lord returns and they are declared blameless. "[T]he writers' prayer is that their converts may be preserved entirely without fault *until* the Parousia and be so found *at* the Parousia, when they will be perfected in holiness" (Bruce). TNT renders this idea clearly: "May he keep you undamaged, spirit, soul and body, so that when our Lord Jesus Christ comes you will be blameless" (5:23c-d).

5:24a-c The Greek of 24a-c is πιστὸς ὁ καλῶν ὑμᾶς, ὃς καὶ ποιήσει 'trustworthy (is) the (one) calling you, who also/indeed will do (it)'. Paul uses deductive reasoning. The two propositions concerning God in the first half of the verse (24a and 24b) are true; therefore the third (24c) is necessarily true. In the display 24a and 24b are labeled grounds, and 24c is labeled CONCLUSION. On the paragraph level v. 24 is a strong statement of *BELIEF*, which verifies that Paul's wish in v. 23 will be fulfilled.

God* summons you *to be distinct people The subject of the first clause in v. 24 is a participial phrase, 'the (one) calling you'. Paul used the verb καλέω 'to call' previously, in 2:12c and 4:7a, where it is rendered 'to summon', as here. (See the note on 2:12c for views on the present tense of the verb 'to call' and for the rationale for the rendering.) In the earlier occurrences it is explicit that the one who calls or summons the Thessalonians is God, and both 2:12 and 4:7 mention God's call in connection with righteous behavior. Marshall feels that the call here is to enter God's kingdom and glory, which can be justified from 2:12. Others, however, feel that the call in 5:24 is to sanctification (Frame, Bruce). The latter view seems preferable because of the context of 5:23 and especially when it is compared with 4:7. There Paul uses the noun ἁγιασμός 'sanctification', which is cognate with the verb ἁγιάζω 'to sanctify', the form here in 5:23b. In the 4:3-8 display, 'called to sanctification' is rendered, 'he summoned us to be distinct people who behave in a morally pure way' (4:7c). The phrase supplied in the display for 5:24a, 'to be distinct people', is intended to express the same meaning as in 4:7.

***and* he *is* trustworthy** God is characterized in 24b by the predicate adjective πιστός, meaning "*trustworthy, faithful, dependable*" (BAGD, p. 664.1). It is fronted for emphasis in the Greek, and this emphasis is shown in the display by bold type. Paul's main point is that God is faithful as caller and doer (Frame).

***Therefore, I am sure that* he will do *this* [23b-d]** Verse 24 ends with a relative clause, 'who also/indeed will do (it)', that functions as a CONCLUSION to the preceding grounds propositions (Frame, Marshall; NAB, TEV). This relation is rendered by 'therefore'. The conjunction καί 'also/indeed' gives certainty. TNT renders this certainty "and he will indeed do this" (Bruce is similar). This certainty is expressed in the display by 'I am sure that'.

Paul leaves unwritten the object of the verb 'will do'. However, from the context it is obvious that his confidence is that God will cause the Thessalonians to be distinct people who behave blamelessly in every way until the coming of the Lord Jesus (Best, Frame, Wanamaker; CEV, NCV, NLT, NRSV). This is a fulfillment of the 23b-d content of Paul's prayer.

BOUNDARIES AND COHERENCE

The initial boundary of 5:23-24 was discussed under 5:12-22, and the terminal boundary under 1:2-5:24. (See "Boundaries.")

Coherence, both referential and relational, is created by the fact that 'God' is the agent in both verses and the only nonsubordinate verbs are the aorist optative verbs in 23b and 23c, establishing this as a wish-prayer. Verses 23 and 24 are taken as a unit by Bruce, Frame, CEV, EHP, JBP, NAB, NCV, NIV, NJB, NRSV, REB, TEV, and TNT.

PROMINENCE AND THEME

In 5:23-24 the naturally prominent constituent is the REACTION. The forefronted πιστός 'faithful, trustworthy' marks the BELIEF as prominent also. There is no subordinating conjunction between the two constituents, which supports the idea that they are of equal prominence.

The theme of 5:23-24 is derived from the REACTION's orienter (23a) and NUCLEUS (23b) and from the BELIEF's conclusion (24c).

EPISTLE CONSTITUENT 5:25-28
(Complex Paragraph: Closing of the Epistle)

THEME: Pray for us. Affectionately greet all the fellow believers for us, and make certain that someone reads this letter aloud to all of them. May the Lord bless you.

STRUCTURE	CONTENTS
REQUEST	5:25 Fellow believers, pray for me(&S&T).
GREETING	5:26 Affectionately greet all the fellow believers *for us(exc) when you gather together*.
APPEAL	5:27 Promise me (*or*, Make certain) before the Lord *Jesus, who sees what you do*, that you *will* (*or*, will order someone to) read this letter *aloud* to all the believers.
BLESSING	5:28 I(&S&T) desire that our(inc) Lord Jesus Christ *will continue to act* graciously toward you.

INTENT AND MACROSTRUCTURE

Paul has a dual intent in the 5:25-28 closing paragraph of the epistle. The first is the emotive purpose of maintaining rapport with his readers; he does this by requesting them to pray for him, by sending greetings to all, and by wishing God's blessing for them. The second intent is the hortatory purpose of affecting their behavior: he appeals for his letter to be read to the believers. The vocative ἀδελφοί 'brothers' indicates the close relationship basis on which Paul makes his requests and appeal.

The unit consists of four propositions that do not relate to one another in a typical paragraph pattern (thus the heading 'structure' in the display rather than 'paragraph pattern'). Theoretically, the analysis of 5:25-28 could show two, three, or four paragraphs, depending on whether one chooses to group some propositions or make each a separate paragraph. But it seems that little would be gained by dividing 5:25-28. The Greek gives no clue as to how to make such division. (See "Boundaries" for the diverse ways versions have handled vv. 25-28.) Experience teaches us that language is very complex on all levels, and we can't expect a discourse to conform exactly to a particular theoretical system. At the beginning and ending of letters it often happens that constituents having different intents and functions are compressed together. That is the case here. Thus, in the heading of the display, 5:25-28 is labeled a complex paragraph.

NOTES

5:25 Fellow believers, pray for me(&S&T) The Greek is ἀδελφοί, προσεύχεσθε [καὶ] περὶ ἡμῶν 'brothers, pray also for us'. Paul used the same verb, προσεύχομαι 'to pray', in 5:17 (see the note there); he used the cognate noun προσευχή 'prayer' in 1:2b. The present tense here indicates that he desires the Thessalonians to continually pray for him and his companions (Hiebert, Morris; EHP).

The textual evidence for including or omitting καί 'and/also' is almost evenly divided. MJTGNT omits it, and UBSGNT has it in brackets, indicating difficulty in deciding whether or not to include it. It is accepted by Best, Bruce, Frame, Marshall, NAB, REB, TEV, and TNT. If it is part of the original text, it indicates the relation of congruence: pray for us 'in accordance with our custom of praying for you' (Best, Bruce, Marshall, Morris, Wanamaker) or 'in accordance with your custom of praying for yourselves and other people' (Frame). Support for the first of these views comes from Paul's mentioning previously in the letter his thanksgiving and prayers for the Thessalonians, the last such being in the immediately preceding verses, 23-24. Support for the second view comes from Paul's general injunction in 5:17 for intercessory prayer.

5:26 Affectionately greet all the fellow believers *for us(exc)* The Greek is ἀσπάσασθε τοὺς ἀδελφοὺς πάντας ἐν φιλήματι ἁγίῳ 'greet all the brothers with a holy kiss'. Similar instructions are given in Rom. 16:16, 1 Cor. 16:20, 2 Cor. 13:12, and 1 Pet. 5:14. In each of those references the injunction to greet with a holy kiss is coupled with greetings to the readers from churches, brothers, saints, or named individuals who are with Paul or Peter. This may indicate that the request to greet with a holy kiss is also a personal greeting, but from the author himself to the recipients of the letter; it is to be expressed by the recipients to each other in his absence. Thus, in 5:26 Paul most likely is conveying personal greetings by asking the Thessalonians to greet each other 'for me/us' (Frame, Marshall, Morris).

There is no indication that Paul is addressing just the leaders or just the laity with this command, so most likely the entire group of believers are to express the greeting (Best, Bruce, Frame, Marshall). Instructions from the early fourth century for the Lord's Supper say that men are to kiss men in the Lord and women, women (Bruce); we do not know that this was the case when Paul wrote. The fourth-century injunction may have been written to curb excesses that arose in previous years.

In the four other epistles that have this greeting, the letters' recipients are to greet 'one another'. Here Paul says greet 'all the brothers', and his use of the word 'all' is probably significant (Bruce, Marshall). Paul, having spoken of people who need to be cared for patiently, who refuse to work, and who weren't living at peace with others, now makes it clear that none were to be excluded from the greeting.

The method of greeting was to be a holy kiss. The adjective 'holy' may function to differentiate this greeting from ordinary salutations or romantic kisses. In one respect it was an expression of Christian love (Frame) or of the family bond between believers (Best, Bruce, Marshall, Wanamaker). TEV has "with a brotherly kiss." In another, more important respect it was a greeting which had religious significance and which perhaps was a part of a worship service (Best, Bruce, Morris, Wanamaker). Justin Martyr, a church father of the mid-second century, wrote of the exchange of a kiss after the regular prayers and before the prayers for the bread and wine of the Lord's Supper (Bruce, Frame). Though we do not know for sure that this was practiced in Thessalonica when Paul wrote, such an understanding of the holy kiss seems appropriate in this context.

Different cultures have different ways of expressing an affectionate greeting. "The kiss is common in eastern lands in salutation, etc, on the cheek, the forehead, the beard, the hands, the feet, but not (in Pal[estine]) the lips" (Walker, p. 1813D). However, "Paul clearly intended the function to be understood and carried out more than the form" (Deibler, in his note on Rom. 16:16). Thus the rendering in the display for 'greet with a holy kiss' is generic and does not specify the form of the action. This is similar to the rendering in the CEV, "Give all the Lord's followers a warm greeting." Such a translation is probably better than trying to convey the form 'kiss' or providing a substitute such as "with a holy embrace" (NAB, EHP) or "give a handshake all around" (JBP).

when you gather together In the next verse Paul charges the Thessalonians to be sure that all hear this letter. It would most likely be read aloud when the believers met together to worship. Moreover, 'holy kisses' or 'kisses of peace' were a part of worship services (at least in the second century). Therefore, the phrase 'when you gather together' is supplied in the display as the circumstance of this affectionate greeting. NCV has "Give each other a holy kiss when you meet."

5:27 Promise me (*or*, Make certain) before the Lord *Jesus, who sees what you do* In v. 27 Paul switches to 'I'. This may correspond to 2 Thess. 3:17, where Paul apparently takes the pen from his secretary to write the final greeting (Bruce, Wanamaker). He writes here ἐνορκίζω ὑμᾶς τὸν κύριον 'I adjure you (before) the Lord'. Ἐνορκίζω is a strong verb which means that Paul wants to extract an oath from the addressees (BAGD, p. 267; Bruce; Louw and Nida 33.467; Morris; Wanamaker). Louw and Nida render 1 Thess. 5:27 as "I ask you to swear by the name of the Lord to read this letter to all the Christian brothers." The phrase 'the Lord' is in the accusative case and indicates the person by whom the Thessalonians were to swear (Bruce, Wanamaker). When a person swears in the name of God it is usually with the idea that God will watch what he does and will punish him if he fails to fulfill the oath. Bruce says those addressed were responsible to the Lord himself, hence 'who sees what you do' in the display. It may be that Paul gave such a stern command because he felt the contents were important for everyone to hear (Bruce, Wanamaker) or because he knew that there were those who did not want to follow his instructions as in 2 Thess. 3:14 (Frame).

The name 'Lord' could refer to either the Lord God or the Lord Jesus. It is probably best to understand the latter (with Frame, Hiebert), considering Paul's usual referent for the term and the particular usage of 'Lord' to refer to Jesus in this letter. The addressees 'you' could be the leaders of the Christian community (Best, Bruce) or the believers in general (Frame).

that you *will* (*or, will order someone to*) read this letter aloud The second meaning of the verb ἀναγινώσκω listed in BAGD (p. 51.2) is "*read aloud in public.*" This is most likely the meaning here (BAGD, Bruce, Frame, Wanamaker). The verb is passive in the Greek but is rendered as active in the display. Paul does not necessarily mean that the person or persons who receive the letter should themselves read it to the congregation but that they should see that it is read. Thus in the display the words 'will order someone to' are given as an alternative.

to all the believers MJTGNT has 'to all the holy brothers' rather than 'to all the brothers' as in UBSGNT. The UBS committee thought that textual support for the latter is slightly superior (Metzger, pp. 565–66). Of the versions consulted only the KJV and NKJV accept the former reading.

5:28 *I(&S&T) desire that* our(inc) Lord Jesus Christ *will continue to act* graciously toward you As is his custom, Paul closes the letter with a blessing (in place of the farewell found in secular letters). It is similar to the blessing in the letter opening (see the note on 1:1b) and the blessings that close his other letters. It expresses Paul's desire or prayer. The noun χάρις 'grace' represents an event and is rendered as such in the display.

In MJTGNT this blessing closes with ἀμήν 'amen'. This may have been added through liturgical usage (Best; Metzger, p. 566). UBSGNT rejects this reading with certainty. Of the versions consulted only the KJV and NKJV accept it.

BOUNDARIES AND COHERENCE

The initial boundary of 5:25–28 was discussed under 1:2–5:24 (see "Boundaries"). The terminal boundary is the end of the letter.

Referential coherence is established by the use of the term ἀδελφοί 'brothers' in vv. 25, 26, and 27 (in 26 and 27 it is 'all the brothers').

Relational coherence is established by Paul's adherence to the form of Greco-Roman letter closings. He includes personal greetings (26), requests (25, 27), and a blessing (28) in place of the usual farewell.

The unique grammatical structure and function of the closing of a Greek letter set it apart from other paragraphs in the epistle. Thus versions variously punctuate vv. 25–28: EHP and NIV unite vv. 25–27; NAB, NASB, NCV, NJB, NRSV, TNT, MJTGNT, and UBSGNT unite vv. 26–27; CEV, GW, REB, RSV, and TEV make each of the verses a separate unit or paragraph. All make the blessing (v. 28) a separate unit.

PROMINENCE AND THEME

In 5:25–28 the imperatives, 'pray' (25) and 'greet' (26), are naturally prominent. The orienter 'I adjure you' (27) is prominent because of its strong wording, and it in turn marks the content of the 5:27 proposition as prominent.

The theme of 5:25–28 is derived from the *REQUEST* (25), *GREETING* (26) *APPEAL* (27) and *BLESSING* (28).

BIBLIOGRAPHY

SELECTED COMMENTARIES, LEXICONS, AND OTHER GENERAL REFERENCES

Banker, John. 1996. *A semantic and structural analysis of Philippians*. Dallas: SIL.

Bauer, Walter; William F. Arndt; and F. Wilbur Gingrich. 1979. *A Greek-English lexicon of the New Testament and other early Christian literature*. 2d ed. Revised and augmented by F. Wilbur Gingrich and Frederick W. Danker from Walter Bauer's 5th German ed. of 1958. Chicago: University of Chicago Press.

Beekman, John; John Callow; and Michael Kopesec. 1981. *The semantic structure of written communication*. Prepublication draft, 5th revision. Dallas: SIL.

Best, Ernest. 1972. *A commentary on the First and Second Epistles to the Thessalonians*. Black's New Testament Commentaries. London: Adam & Charles Black.

Blass, F., and A. Debrunner. 1961. *A Greek grammar of the New Testament and other early Christian literature*. A translation and revision of the ninth–tenth German edition by Robert W. Funk. Chicago: University of Chicago Press.

Blight, Richard C. 1989. *An exegetical summary of 1 & 2 Thessalonians*. Dallas: SIL.

Bruce, F. F. 1982. *1 and 2 Thessalonians*. Word Biblical Commentary, vol. 45. Waco, Tex.: Word.

Bullinger, E. W. [1898] 1968. *Figures of speech used in the Bible*. Grand Rapids: Baker.

Callow, John. 1982. *A semantic structure analysis of Second Thessalonians*. Dallas: SIL.

———. 1983. *A semantic structure analysis of Colossians*. Dallas: SIL.

Callow, Kathleen. Forthcoming. *Man and message*. Lanham, Md.: University Press of America.

Callow, Kathleen, and John C. Callow. 1992. Text as purposive communication: A meaning-based analysis. In *Discourse description: Diverse linguistic analyses of a fund-raising text*, eds. William C. Mann and Sandra A. Thompson, pp. 5–37. Amsterdam/Philadelphia: John Benjamins.

Cervin, Richard S. 1993. A critique of Timothy Friberg's dissertation: New Testament Greek word-order in light of discourse considerations. In *Journal of Translation and Textlinguistics* 6:1:56–85. (Dallas: SIL.)

Crofts, Marjorie. n.d. Metaphors of the New Testament: Their interpretation and translation. Prepublication draft. Dallas: SIL.

Deibler, Ellis W., Jr. Forthcoming. *A semantic and structural analysis of Romans*. Dallas: SIL.

Eadie, John. [1877] 1979. *Commentary on the Greek text of the Epistles of Paul to the Thessalonians*. John Eadie Greek Text Commentaries, vol. 5. Reprint. Grand Rapids: Baker.

Ellingworth, Paul, and Eugene A. Nida. 1976. *A translator's handbook on Paul's letters to the Thessalonians*. Helps for Translators. New York: UBS.

Findlay, G. G. [1904] 1982. *The Epistles of Paul the Apostle to the Thessalonians*. Grand Rapids: Baker.

Frame, James Everett. 1912. *A critical and exegetical commentary on the Epistles of St. Paul to the Thessalonians*. International Critical Commentary. Edinburgh: T. & T. Clark.

Greenlee, J. Harold. 1986. *A concise exegetical grammar of New Testament Greek*. 5th ed., revised. Grand Rapids: Eerdmans.

Hale, Clarence B. 1991. *The meaning of "in Christ" in the Greek New Testament*. Dallas: SIL.

Hendriksen, William. 1955. *Exposition of 1 and 2 Thessalonians*. New Testament Commentary. Grand Rapids: Baker.

Hiebert, D. Edmond. 1971. *The Thessalonian Epistles: A call to readiness*. Chicago: Moody.

Larson, Mildred L. 1984. *Meaning-based translation: A guide to cross-language equivalence*. Lanham, Md.: University Press of America.

Lee, Robert, and Carolyn Lee. 1975. An analysis of the larger semantic units of 1 Thessalonians. In *Notes on Translation* 56:28–42. (Dallas: SIL.)

Lenski, R. C. H. 1946. *The interpretation of St. Paul's Epistles to the Colossians, to the Thessalonians, to Timothy, to Titus and to Philemon*. Minneapolis: Augsburg.

Levinsohn, Stephen H. 1992. *Discourse features of New Testament Greek: A coursebook*. Dallas: SIL.

Longacre, Robert. 1996. *The grammar of discourse*. 2d ed. New York: Plenum.

Louw, Johannes P., and Eugene A. Nida, eds. 1988. *Greek-English lexicon of the New Testament based on semantic domains*. 2 vols. New York: UBS.

Marshall, I. Howard. 1983. *1 and 2 Thessalonians*. New Century Bible Commentary. Grand Rapids: Eerdmans.

Metzger, Bruce M. 1994. *A textual commentary on the Greek New Testament*. 2d ed. Stuttgart: UBS.

Miller, Neva, and Catherine Rountree. n.d. 1 and 2 Thessalonians: Analyzed translation with exegetical notes by Neva Miller. Prepublication draft. Dallas: SIL.

Moffatt, James. [n.d.] 1980. *The First and Second Epistles to the Thessalonians*. Expositor's Greek Testament. Reprint. Grand Rapids: Eerdmans.

Moore, Bruce R. 1993. *Doublets in the New Testament*. Dallas: SIL.

Morris, Leon. 1991. *The First and Second Epistles to the Thessalonians*. Rev. ed. New International Commentary on the New Testament. Grand Rapids: Eerdmans.

Moule, C. F. D. 1959. *An idiom book of New Testament Greek*. 2d ed. Cambridge: Cambridge Univ. Press.

Park, James. 1975. Discourse analysis of 1 Thessalonians. Typescript. Dallas: SIL.

Schrenk, Gottlob. 1964. βάρος. In *Theological dictionary of the New Testament*, ed. Gerhard Kittel, tr. Geoffrey W. Bromiley, vol. 1, pp. 553–56. Grand Rapids: Eerdmans.

Schweizer, Eduard. 1968. πνεῦμα, πνευματικός. In *Theological dictionary of the New Testament*, ed. Gerhard Friedrich, tr. Geoffrey W. Bromiley, vol. 6, pp. 332–451. Grand Rapids: Eerdmans.

Sherman, Grace E., and John C. Tuggy. 1994. *A semantic and structural analysis of the Johannine Epistles*. Dallas: SIL.

Smith, Robert E., and John Beekman. 1981. *A literary-semantic analysis of Second Timothy*. Dallas: SIL.

Stott, John R. W. 1991. *The gospel and the end of time: The message of 1 & 2 Thessalonians*. Downers Grove, Ill.: InterVarsity.

Thomas, Robert L. 1978. 1, 2 Thessalonians. In *The expositor's Bible commentary*, vol. 11, pp. 227–337. Grand Rapids: Zondervan.

Tuggy, John C. 1992. Semantic paragraph patterns: A fundamental communication concept and interpretive tool. In *Linguistics and New Testament interpretation: Essays on discourse analysis*, ed. D. A. Black, pp. 45–67. Nashville: Broadman.

Turner, Nigel. 1963. *Syntax*. Vol. 3, *A grammar of New Testament Greek*. Edinburgh: T. & T. Clark.

Walker, W. L. 1960. Kiss. In *The international standard Bible encyclopedia*, vol. 3, pp. 1813D–1814. Grand Rapids: Eerdmans.

Wanamaker, Charles A. 1990. *The Epistles to the Thessalonians: A commentary on the Greek text*. New International Greek Testament Commentary. Grand Rapids: Eerdmans.

Wiles, Gordon P. 1974. *The significance of the intercessory prayer passages in the letters of St. Paul*. Society for New Testament Studies, 24. Cambridge: Cambridge Univ. Press.

Williams, David J. 1992. *1 and 2 Thessalonians*. New International Biblical Commentary, vol. 12. Peabody, Mass.: Hendrickson.

GREEK TEXTS AND TRANSLATIONS

Aland, Barbara, Kurt Aland, Johannes Karavidopoulos, Carlo M. Martini, and Bruce M. Metzger, eds. 1993. *The Greek New Testament*. 4th rev. ed. Stuttgart: UBS.

Aland, Kurt, Matthew Black, Carlo M. Martini, Bruce M. Metzger, and Allen Wikgren, eds. 1975. *The Greek New Testament*. 3d ed. Stuttgart: UBS.

Beck, William F., tr. 1964. *The New Testament in the language of today*. St. Louis: Concordia.

Friberg, Barbara, and Timothy Friberg, eds. 1981. *Analytical Greek New Testament*. Grand Rapids: Baker.

God's Word. 1995. Grand Rapids: World.

Good news Bible: The Bible in today's English version. 1976. New York: American Bible Society.

Goodspeed, Edgar J., tr. 1923. *The New Testament: An American translation*. Chicago: Univ. of Chicago Press.

Die Gute Nachricht. 1982. Goettingen: Vandenhoeck & Ruprecht.

Hodges, Zane C., and Arthur L. Farstad, eds. 1985. *The Greek New Testament according to the majority text*. 2d ed. Nashville: Thomas Nelson.

The Holy Bible. Authorized (or King James) version. 1611.

The Holy Bible, contemporary English version. 1995. New York: American Bible Society.

The Holy Bible, new century version. 1991. Dallas: Word.
The Holy Bible, new international version. 1985. Grand Rapids: Zondervan.
The Holy Bible, new King James version. 1990. New York: American Bible Society.
Holy Bible, new living translation. 1996. Wheaton, Ill.: Tyndale.
The Holy Bible, new revised standard version. 1989. New York: Oxford Univ. Press.
The Holy Bible, revised standard version. 1971. New York: Thomas Nelson.
The Jerusalem Bible. 1968. Garden City: Doubleday.
Ledyard, Gleason H., tr. 1976. *The new life testament.* Canby, Ore.: Christian Literature International.
The living Bible. 1971. Wheaton, Ill.: Tyndale.
The new American Bible. 1971. Camden, N.J.: Thomas Nelson.
The new American standard Bible. 1963. La Habra, Calif.: Foundation Press.
The new English Bible: New Testament. 1970. New York: Oxford Univ. Press and Cambridge Univ. Press.
The new Jerusalem Bible. 1985. Garden City, N.Y.: Doubleday.
The NIV study Bible. 1985. Grand Rapids: Zondervan.
Peterson, Eugene H., tr. 1993. *The message: The New Testament in contemporary English.* Colorado Springs: NavPress.
Phillips, J. B., tr. 1972. *The New Testament in modern English.* New York: Macmillan.
The revised English Bible. 1989. New York: Oxford Univ. Press and Cambridge Univ. Press.
The Septuagint version, Greek and English. 1970. Grand Rapids: Zondervan.
The translator's New Testament. 1973. London: British and Foreign Bible Society.
Verkuyl, Gerrit, ed. *The Holy Bible, the new Berkeley version in modern English.* 1969. Grand Rapids: Zondervan.
Williams, Charles B., tr. 1963. *The New Testament in the language of the people.* Chicago: Moody.

www.ingramcontent.com/pod-product-compliance
Lightning Source LLC
Chambersburg PA
CBHW081421230426
43668CB00016B/2310